Neoliberalism
and
Education Reform

edited by

E. Wayne Ross
University of British Columbia

Rich Gibson
San Diego State University

HAMPTON PRESS, INC.
CRESSKILL, NEW JERSEY

Printed in the United States of America

Library of Congress Cataloging-in-Publication Data

Neoliberalism and education reform / edited by E. Wayne Ross, Rich Gibson.
    p. cm. -- (Critical education and ethics)
    Includes bibliographical references and index.
    ISBN 1-57273-676-3 -- ISBN 1-57273-677-1
    1. Education--Economic aspects. 2. Education and globalization. 3. Critical pedagogy. 4. Educational change. 5. Neoliberalism. I. Ross, E. Wayne II. Gibson, Rich (Rich J.) III. Series.

LC65.N46 2006
338.4'337--dc22   2006043570

Hampton Press, Inc.
23 Broadway
Cresskill, NJ 07626

Neoliberalism
and
Education Reform

Critical Education and Ethics
Editors
Barry Kanpol, Indiana University—Purdue University Fort Wayne
Fred Yeo, University of Wisconsin-Oshkosh

Mediating the Culture Wars
Eric Bain Selbo

The Academy and the Possibility of Belief: Essays on Intellectual
and Spiritual Life
*Mary Louise Buley-Meissner, Mary McCaslin Thompson, and
Elizabeth Bachrach Tan* (eds.)

Critical Multicultural Conversations
Greg S. Goodman and Karen Carey (eds.)

Issues and Trends in Critical Pedagogy
Barry Kanpol

Teachers Talking Back and Breaking Bread
Barry Kanpol

JOY as a Metaphor of Convergence: A Phenomenological and Aesthetic
Investigation of Social and Educational Change
Delores D. Liston

Red Seminars: Radical Excursions in Educational Theory, Cultural
Politics, and Pedagogy
Peter McLaren

Neoliberalism and Education Reform
E. Wayne Ross and Rich Gibson (eds.)

Body Movements: Pedagogy, Politics and Social Change
Sherry Shapiro and Svi Shapiro (eds.)

To
George Schmidt

And all those who fiercely resist capitalist schooling

Contents

Foreword

Richard A. Brosio

The authors of *Neoliberalism and Educational Reform* have produced important analyses and explanations with regard to what is occurring in public education during this historical period, which is characterized by the agents and allies of capitalism seeking to solve the "accumulation crisis"— namely the alleged need for more profit.

The contributors could be equated to members of a swing era band in which the various musicians often play in harmony and agreement; although there are times when one or another is featured as a soloist. The underlying jazz and even blues orientation of the swing musicians' work provide an earthy, even visceral, dimension that audiences would find difficult to miss. As has been said: "It don't mean a thing if it ain't got that swing!" The necessary component in this book is the authors' agreement that the crises affecting teaching and learning processes around the world must be grounded in the history of capitalism and its constant crises. The current "gales of creative destruction" are aimed at garnering greater profits; moreover, this necessitates exercising greater control over every person, organization, institution, process, and activity that threaten neoliberal goals.

The individual and comradely contributors make clear that although conditions and realities are not similar to what Marx faced and analyzed during his work life, the fact remains that his brilliant unraveling of how the capitalist system really works allows them, and us, to stand on his sturdy forbear shoulders. The overall message of the book indicates that capitalism is structurally the same as in Marx's time, but that it has become more total-istic—logically and necessarily pushing far beyond controlling the work-places of the past. In fact, our schools have become the compulsory work-places for students from pre-kindergarten through college and university. Readers can benefit from the analyses that explain how the capitalist imper-ative upon public education has all but defeated the incompatible democrat-ic imperative. The No Child Left Behind legislation in the United States is explained and situated in the larger neoliberal project that has been defined accurately as, in part, a version of class war from above.

This is not to say that all is lost! The authors make clear that contested terrains still exist and that many millions of people are beginning to realize what is at stake in the face of this coordinated attack on all that has been accomplished in the past by those of us who sought to force the various class-states to provide the means for everyone to live well, while being inde-pendent of market outcomes alone. The current drive to privatize every inch of every place on earth is being recognized as an important component of the attempts to overcome the accumulation crisis by capitalists and their agents.

In this volume, readers are treated to rich philosophical, economic, political, social, historical, and educational arguments and analyses. For those who are continuously faced with the onslaught caused by attempts to make all of civil society even more useful to capitalism—attacks that make it very difficult to think through some of the most important causes for their necessarily defensive posture—this book provides a packed tool bag with which to inquire around and beneath what seems "natural" and immutable at first glance. We know that democratic Marxism is a tradition whose adherents claim that we can and must make our own histories; however, nei-ther just as we choose nor just as we might like. It is not inevitable that cap-italism can be overcome. However, if we can understand better that the key to dismantling this undemocratic system is to smash the appropriation of surplus value by the capitalists and their governmental allies, then we will be aiming at the most determinative target.

The kind of education that most teachers, students, and the public want is not possible unless the political forms of democracy are able to intrude into the economy itself as well as throughout the entire social system. Education for democratic empowerment, socioeconomic justice, respect for diversity, and making it more possible to act altruistically—if not "caring-ly"—must be in *correspondence* with societies that are characterized by these ideals, goals, actions, and realities. Alert readers can come away from read-ing—and studying—this fine work with a realization that democracy and schooling for bona fide democracy depend in the end on radical conceptions and implementations of rough equality throughout the polity and political economy.

Acknowledgments

We would like to thank the contributors to this volume for their extraordinary contributions as well as their commitment to critical scholarship and practice in education.

The idea for this book began as we worked on a special issue of the journal *Cultural Logic* and early versions of a several chapters appeared there. We extend special thanks to *Cultural Logic* and, in particular, editors David Siar and Gregory Meyerson for their support.

Over the past 7 years, we have had the opportunity to work with a group of deeply committed teachers, students, parents, and scholars as part of The Rouge Forum (www.RougeForum.org). Literally thousands of people have attended Rouge Forum events across North America as part of the larger struggle to create a democratic society and schools that operate in the public interest. Space doesn't allow us to thank everyone who has contributed to the work of The Rouge Forum, however, Amber Goslee and Greg Queen deserve special mention for their outstanding leadership and service to the group.

There are also numerous comrades and friends whose scholarship, activism, and advice we have benefited from including Stephen C. Fleury, Perry Marker, Kevin D. Vinson, David Gabbard, Marc Pruyn, Patrick Shannon, Valerie Pang, Michael Peterson, Kathleen Kesson, Rudolfo Chávez Chávez, Richard Brosio, Dave Hill, Pauline Lipman, Marc Bousquet, Heather Julien, Chris Carter, Larry Stedman, Kenneth

Teitelbaum, John Welsh, Cesar Rossatto, João Paraskeva, Joe Bishop, and Curry Malott.

The people associated with Hampton Press have been wonderful to work with and have been supportive and patient with us as the project was pulled together. Special thanks to Barry Kanpol, Fred Yeo, and Barbara Bernstein for all they have done to make this book a reality.

For key insights into schools, skateboarding, art, video games, and life as a sixth grader we thank Colin Ross.

Finally, we receive daily care and love from our partners—Sandra Mathison and Amber Goslee. There is no way to repay all they have given us, but we're going to try, each in our own way.

E. W. R.

R. G.

Introduction

E. Wayne Ross
Rich Gibson

WHAT IS NEOLIBERALISM?

Although often used interchangeably with the term *globalization* and regarded as an economic theory, neoliberalism is a complex of values, ideologies, and practices that affect the economic, political, and cultural aspects of society. Martinez and Garcia (2000) define neoliberalism as:

> a set of economic policies that have become widespread during the last 25 years or so. Although the word is rarely heard in the United States, you can clearly see the effects of neo liberalism here as the rich grow richer and the poor grow poorer. . . . Around the world, neo-liberalism has been imposed by powerful financial institutions like the International Monetary Fund (IMF), the World Bank and the Inter-

1

> American Development Bank . . . the capitalist crisis over the last 25 years, with its shrinking profit rates, inspired the corporate elite to revive economic liberalism. That's what makes it "neo" or new.

Thus, *neoliberalism* is another term for global market liberalism and for free-trade policies.

Liberalism can refer to a range of ideas (e.g., political, economic, religious). In the United States, political liberalism is generally presented as a "progressive" (left-wing) ideology marked by broadmindedness or tolerance for diverse social practices, concern for civic liberties and social welfare and it is contrasted with "conservative" (right-wing) politics. It is important to understand that political conservatives and liberals (in mainstream U.S. politics) both support economic (neo)liberalism.

Neoliberalism is the prevailing political economic paradigm in the world today and has been described as an ideological "monoculture," in that when neoliberal policies are criticized a common response is that "there is no alternative" (aka TINA). Although the term *neoliberalism* is largely unused by the public in the United States, it references something everyone is familiar with—policies and processes "whereby a relative handful of private interests are permitted to control as much as possible of social life in order to maximize their personal profit" (McChesney, 1998, p. 7). Neoliberalism is embraced by parties across the political spectrum, from right to left, in that the interests of wealthy investors and large corporations define social and economic policy. The free market, private enterprise, consumer choice, entrepreneurial initiative, deleterious effects of government regulation, and so on, are the tenets of a neoliberalism. Indeed, the corporate-controlled media spin would have the public believe that the economic consequences of neoliberal economic policy, which serves the interests of the wealthy elite, is good for everyone.

In fact, neoliberal economic policies have created massive social and economic inequalities among individuals and nations. For example, the same combination of growing personal debt and widening wealth gap that preceded the Great Depression underlies today's economy and is fueled by declines in wages, savings rates, and the number of workers covered by private pension plans. Presently, the top 1% of households in the United States own 40% of the nation's wealth (Collins, 1999). The wealth gap is particularly large for African Americans and Latinos. Despite a "strong economy" the number of Americans who do not have health insurance increased from 1998 to 1999 by nearly 1 million to 44.3 million (Pear, 1999). The United States has the highest level of child poverty in the industrial world (Chomsky, 1999).

On the global scene, neoliberal economic policies have reproduced these inequalities among nations. These policies, created by the U.S. government and international financial institutions, have decimated the economies of countries like Brazil and Mexico, whereas local elites and transnational corporations reap huge profits (Petras & Veltmeyer, 1999).

Neoliberalism also works as a political system, one in which there is formal democracy, but the citizens remain spectators, diverted from any meaningful participation in decision making. McChesney (1998) describes neoliberal democracy in a nutshell: "trivial debate over minor issues by parties that basically pursue the same pro-business policies regardless of formal differences and campaign debate. Democracy is permissible as long as the control of business is off-limits to popular deliberation or change, i.e., so long as it isn't democracy" (p. 9). A depoliticized and apathetic citizenry, such as in the United States, today, is a key outcome of neoliberalism; one that is arguably abetted by new education "reforms."

Martinez and Garcia (2000) describe the main points of neoliberalism as follows:

1. *The rule of the market.* Liberating free/private enterprise from any restrictions imposed by the state (government) no matter the social damage that results. The aim is total freedom of movement for capital, goods, and services, which is facilitated by trade agreements such as North American Free Trade Agreement (NAFTA) and General Agreement on Trade in Services (GSTS).
2. *Cutting public expenditures for social services* (such as education and health care).
3. *Deregulation.* Reduction of government regulation that might diminish profits, including regulations that are intended to enhance on-the-job safety or protect the environment.
4. *Privatization.* Selling state-owned enterprises, goods, and services to private investors (including public education services). Although usually done in the name of increased efficiency, privatization has mainly had the effect of concentrating wealth in fewer hands and making the public pay more for its needs.
5. *Elimination of the concept of "the public good" or "community"* and replacing it with "individual responsibility" and pressuring the poorest people to find solutions to their lack of education, health care, etc.

Neoliberalism is not new. It is merely the current version of the wealthy few's attempt to restrict the rights and powers of the many. Although democracy and capitalism are popularly understood (and often taught) as birds of a feather, the conflict between protecting private wealth and creating a democratic society is conspicuous throughout U.S. history (see Ross, 2006).

NEOLIBERALISM AND EDUCATIONAL REFORM

Public education is under attack in North America and across the globe as a result of neoliberal government policies.[1] Education is a key target of the neoliberal project because of market size (e.g., global spending on education is more than $1 trillion[2]), education's centrality to the economy, and its "potential to challenge corporate globalization if education succeeds in producing critical citizens for a democratic society" (Kuehn, 1999).

Governments have introduced curricular reforms, via legislation such as the No Child Left Behind (NCLB) Act in the United States (which is extensively discussed in this volume), which commodify public education by reducing learning to bits of information and skill to be taught and tested and marketize education through programs that promote privatization and user fees in place of free, public education.

Neoliberal educational reforms (aimed at K–12 schools and universities) emphasize opening up the educational services market to for-profit educational management organizations (such as Edison Schools) and via international trade and investment agreements such as GATS (see Rikowski, Chapter 6, this volume), which in turn affects the scope of collect agreements (e.g., establishing working conditions, rates of pay, teacher autonomy, etc.).

Relatedly, efforts are made to reduce educational costs, often through economies of scale. Closing school libraries, reducing the number of special needs teachers, increasing class size, expanding online learning programs are examples. These actions intensify the work of teachers and isolate them from decision making and from one another.

Third, neoliberal educational reform policies focus on creation of curriculum standards (where the state defines the knowledge to be taught) and "accountability." The specification of curriculum standards is nearly always accompanied by accountability strategies. As Mathison (2004) pointed out, it does no good to establish expectations if one does not ensure they are met and, if they are not met that there is a planned remedy. The dominant approach to educational accountability is an "outcomes-based bureaucratic" one (i.e., most often mandated testing).

> Whether the stakes are high or low and whether the locus of control is local, state, or national, this strategy is one where a distant authority sets

---

[1]For an extensive examination of this attack on public schools in the United States as well as discussion of responses to defend public education in the public interests see Ross, Gabbard, Kesson, Mathison, and Vinson (2004).
[2]Kuehn (1999) points out that this figure represents costs of more than 50 million teachers, 1 billion students, and hundreds of thousands of educational establishments across the globe.

performance goals for students, schools, or school systems; holds individuals and units directly accountable for meeting the goals; and consequences are applied, including rewards for meeting performance goals and sanctions for not meeting them. (Mathison, 2004, pp. 13–14)

Neoliberalism and Education Reform in British Columbia: A Brief Example

The economy in British Columbia (B.C.) is booming and the provincial government enjoys a surplus. The benefits of this strong economy, however, are not finding their way into public schools. In fact, private interests, as a result of the provincial government policies, are trumping public interests.

The Liberal Party of B.C. has sold off public assets such as the provincial railroad and ferry networks and drastically cut funding for public education. What follows is a brief look at the economic situation in the B.C. and the incongruous treatment of public school financing.

- In December 2004 there were 17,000 new jobs and overall employment for the year rose by 2%. As a result, the jobless rate in the province hit 6.1%, its lowest level in 24 years.
- B.C. leads all of Canada in the increase of housing starts for 2004, up 32%. In Vancouver, the housing market saw double-digit appreciation across the board in the fourth quarter of 2004. Home sales in B.C. generated $9.4 billion in economic activity since 2001 (all figures are in Canadian dollars).
- The Canadian Federation of Independent Business recently released a survey that shows B.C. business owners are among the most optimistic in Canada. Nearly one third of businesses expected to add jobs in 2005 and only 9% expected reductions.
- The provincial government has forecast a $1.2 billion surplus due to higher natural resources royalties and income from Crown corporations. Provincial debt is expected to decline by more than $600 million.
- The Liberal government in Victoria, the provincial capital, touts the fact that no corner of the province has been immune from this economic boom.

One would think that under these economic conditions public schools would be expanding services and resources to all students. Instead, this same government—led by Premier Gordon Campbell—has produced a series of budgets that are devastating schools and making education less accessible. Canada's spending on public education lags behind the average developing nation's spending ($7,480 per student) according to the Organization for

Economic Co-operation and Development and B.C. spends 13% less than that ($6,529 per student).

Under the current government, real per student education funding has plunged since 2000. Cuts in the provincial education budget have produce 92 school closings since 2002, displacing more than 14,000 students. And 2,881 teaching positions have been cut, even though enrollment is 12% higher now than it was in the mid-1990s.

The number of school librarians in the province fell from 939 to 706 since 2000. A study by the B.C. Teacher Librarians shows money available for library materials declined by 12% over the same period.

According to Statistics Canada, the student–educator ratio for B.C. rose nearly 5% from 2001 to 2003. Although most other provinces were experiencing a decrease in student–educator ratios, B.C. saw the largest increase in the nation. Tom Christensen, B.C.'s Liberal minister of education, argued for the importance of flexibility in labor contracts over the impact of large class size on student learning and safety in B.C. schools. Christensen claimed that "students in B.C. are better off since class limits were removed from teacher union contracts" (Ross, 2005, ¶12).

The B.C. government has refused to fund treatment for children with autism. In July 2000, the B.C. Supreme Court ruled that the treatment intervention known as Lovaas (or applied behavioral analysis) was a medically necessary service and must be funded by the government. That court concluded that the failure to fund this treatment constitutes direct government discrimination against children with autism spectrum disorder and is a breach of the Canadian Charter of Rights and Freedoms. The provincial government appealed to the Supreme Court of Canada and in November 2004 the lower court rulings were overturned. CBC News reported that B.C. Attorney General Geoff Plante "hailed the judgment, while extending his sympathy to parents with autistic children."

In his election, campaign Campbell promised a 5% reduction in higher education tuition, but instead delivered steep increases. Since 2002, tuition fees have increased by more than 80% at B.C. universities and by 100% at B.C. colleges. If tuition had risen by the rate of inflation since 1995, the average university student would be paying $2,907, rather than the current $4,735. (It is even worse for international students, who are paying up to five times as much as Canadian students. One recent report described international students at the University of British Columbia who were having to work illegal jobs and sift garbage for food to make ends meet.)

At the same time, provincial government funding per full-time postsecondary student fell by 9%. Government support for postsecondary education in the province is at its lowest level in B.C. since the 1950s.

The cuts to public education funding in a time of plenty are much more than an absurdity. As in the United States and United Kingdom, which are examined in depth in the chapters that follow, the current situation in B.C. is a reflection of neoliberalism—the policies and processes that permit a handful of private interests to control as much as possible of social life in order to maximize their personal profit. The Vancouver based Fraser Institute is leading the charge in the war on public schools in Canada and has close ties to the U.S. Business Roundtable, Manhattan Institute, Olin and Thomas B. Fordham Foundations, all of which are players in the assaults on public schools in the United States. The free market, private enterprise, consumer choice, entrepreneurial initiative, and government deregulation are fundamental principles driving the attack on public education across North America.

Neoliberal educational reform policies, such as the ones enacted in B.C., reflect a number of the key features of capitalism in its stage of "globalization," which Bertell Ollman (2001) described as "capitalism with the gloves off and on a world scale" (p. 9).

> Taken together, these developments, which are all internally related constitute a new stage in capitalism. It is a serious error to think that they have brought us beyond capitalism. If anything, with these changes, our society is more thoroughly capitalist than ever before. After all, more and more of the world is privately owned, more and more wealth is devoted to maximizing profits rather than serving needs (and only serving needs in so far as they maximize profits), more and more people sell their labor power in order to live, more and more objects (ideational as well as material) carry price tags and can be bought in the market, and money and those who have a lot of it have more power and status then ever before. This is capitalism, capitalism with a vengeance, and that's globalization. Which means, too, that the problems associated with globalization cannot be solved—as so many liberals would like to do—without dealing with their roots in the capitalist system. (pp. 93–94)

Ollman set the stage for the chapters that follow, which aim to both analyze the current state of education, but also begin developing solutions to the problems faced by public education that have their roots in the capitalist system.

OVERVIEW OF THE BOOK

In recent years, critical educational theory has been largely ignored in North America as postmodernism dominated high-theory discussions among academics and market-based approaches to education ruled educational practices. However, as the *Times Literary Supplement* recently opined "classical

Marxist critique of capitalism remains as valid as ever . . . a fact . . . evident for those willing to look. . . . [T]he *Communist Manifesto* now reads as if it was written just a few weeks ago." Contributors to this book argue that Marx's dialectical and materialist analyses remain the sharpest tool for critical educators seeking to teach and organize for social justice.

Many scholars believe the pinnacle of marxian educational theory in the West was reached in the mid-1970s, with the publication of Bowles and Gintis' (1976) *Schooling in Capitalist America* and Paul Willis' (1977) *Learning to Labour.* Despite utilizing Marx's concepts, it has been argued that both books have tenuous links to Marx and Marxism (e.g., Sarup, 1978). For example, Sarup criticized Bowles and Gintis for their crude application of the base/superstructure model and argued that the study's methodology had more in common with functionalism and positivism than with Marxism. Rikowski (1997) argued that marxian educational theory in the late-1970s took a reactive trajectory that included futile attempts to either synthesize or salvage something from the marxian educational theory of the mid-1970s or, ignoring the problems these studies posed, merely applied Bowles and Gintis' "correspondence principle" to developing educational issues.

This book undertakes two primary projects: (a) a critique of educational reforms that result from the rise of neoliberalism; and (b) providing marxian alternatives to neoliberal conceptions of education problems and solutions and thus advancing marxian educational theory (and practice) by utilizing Marx's own works in the examination of education as it is theorized and practiced today. This is not an altogether new approach (e.g., Sharp, 1986), however, it has great significance for the field of education in the contradictory contexts of, on one hand, the contemporary belief in the "triumph" of capitalism and the market and, on the other hand, the escalating social divisions and extreme economic and social injustices of global capitalist society. Education is an integral aspect of social (and individual) transformation (processes that are themselves inseparable). As Allman (1999) argues, an understanding of how human consciousness is constituted and how it can be made critical of existing social arrangements as well as the role that education can play in these processes are crucial because "these understandings are the necessary bases for transforming the educational relations and developing forms of engagement that can lead to and eventually bring about justice for all humankind" (p. 2).

Marx's vision of socialism emerges from his study of capitalism—socialism is the unrealized potential inherent in capitalism itself (Ollman, 1971). Chapter authors draw on the main theories of Marx's work—his theory of alienation, the labor theory of value and the materialist conception of history—in examination of contemporary educational thought and practice. Particular attention is given to the following: (a) the commodification of literacy; (b) alienation and the demands of high-stakes standardized tests, (c) the relationship of school work and the creation of value (and surplus value), (d) schooling and the partisan state; (d) segregation as seen through the windows of race and class; (e) the reciprocal relationship of curriculum and instruction in insurgent pedagogy; and (f) the centrality of schools for social change.

Our aim is to rethink the theoretical grounds of radical educational practice aimed at social transformation while at the same time building a vision of social transformation that is firmly grounded in the material life of capitalist society. Forging a clear understanding of what is wrong with capitalist society (and schools) and what needs to be changed is not enough, because this understanding alone does not lead to social transformation. Therefore, a key issue addressed by contributors is how forms of critical consciousness adequate to the task of terminating the destructive social relations of capitalist society can be engendered throughout society via schools. This means paying attention to the practical aspects of pedagogy for social transformation and organizing to achieve a more just society. Each contributor offers critical examinations of the pragmatics of pedagogy and organizing for social transformation.

The Chapters

Neoliberalism and Educational Reform opens with three chapters that provide broad overviews of the how neoliberal educational policies work in the United States and the United Kingdom.

Chapter 1, by David Hursh, describes how, over the last two decades, neoliberal policies have transformed educational systems around the globe, with public schools being replaced with private, for-profit, competitive, market-based schools that increase inequality and undermine democracy. He describes how in the United States, state and federal governments now require that students and schools be evaluated through statewide standardized exams. In some states, students must pass the exams in order to be promoted from one grade to another or from high school. Under the federal NCLB Act, schools failing to make adequate progress must fund tutoring for their students, often through private for-profit organizations. Furthermore, failing schools face the prospect of being administered by or turned over as a charter school to a private corporation. The Bush administration strongly supports the privatization of education through voucher programs and charter schools. Hursh also describes how in England, schools are competing with one another for students, test scores, and funding. There is compelling evidence regarding the harmful affect competition has on the culture of the school, including teacher professionalism and student success. Hursh argues that these reforms are not, contrary to their proponents' claims, improving education for all. Rather, the gap between schools is widening. He describes how comprehensive schools in England and the United States are in decline, creating a hierarchy of schools in both countries. Because of the requirement of raising test scores, teachers have less flexibility in creating curriculum that responds to the need of the students in their class.

The NCLB Act is the focus of the Pauline Lipman's chapter. She argues that NCLB further integrates education into a global and national neoliberal agenda and intensifies the war on youth of color. NCLB is rooted in global competition over markets and investments and by cultural struggles over race, ethnicity, language, and national identity. By framing education in the language of accountability and choice, NCLB further consolidates—materially and ideologically—corporate control of education for profit. NCLB policies and the discourse surrounding them become a "discourse policy" directed to society as a whole, defining educational problems and their solutions so as to limit the possibilities we have of thinking and acting otherwise. Lipman calls for an alternative discourse rooted in social justice to speak to the real urgency to address the profound inequalities and miseducation that define public schools. She concludes that despite their profound failures, free public schools need to be fought for as a democratic public space *and* fought over ideologically.

In Chapter 3, Kevin D. Vinson and E. Wayne Ross argue that education today must be understood according to a setting in which spectacle and surveillance come together, a state of affairs in which discipline is established and maintained as individuals and groups are monitored simultaneously by both larger and smaller entities. They make use of standards-based educational reform (SBER) within the NCLB Act of 2001 as an indicative "case" (especially vis-à-vis the conditions of curriculum standards and mandated high-stakes testing), one in which this form of disciplinary power relates dynamically with and to what we (can) know and how we (can) know it. Their chapter demonstrates that with respect to contemporary education, disciplinary power (i.e., "disciplinarity") must be understood within a context defined in part according to the *convergence* of surveillance and spectacle (as opposed, that is, to either one or the other separately). Vinson and Ross use NCLB to illustrate (a) the mechanisms by which such a confluence of power elements occurs; (b) the contexts within which such a state of affairs is made possible; (c) the extent to which this conceptualization might provide insights into accepted and prevailing pedagogical practices, viewpoints, and policies; (d) the potential practical consequences (i.e., those of surveillance, spectacle, *and* "surveillance-spectacle") of this disciplinary setting; and (e) the increased complexity and turbulence made necessary by this convergence of surveillance and spectacle in terms of the production, establishment, evolution, and maintenance of any effective mode (or modes) of critique and/or resistance.

In Chapter 4, Gilbert G. Gonzalez examines the history of U. S. imperialism and the education of Mexican immigrants in the 20th century. This chapter argues that the United States is an imperialist power and that U.S.–Mexico relations since the late 19th century falls squarely into the definition of imperialism. Furthermore, this relationship has significantly impacted the history of the Mexican immigrant community. Gonzalez's analysis differs fundamentally from the general approach to Chicano history. In the main, Chicano historiography exhibits an overwhelming tendency to limit analyses to themes and topics originating north of the border. Such an approach confines the analysis by failing to take into account those transnational factors, that is, U.S. imperialism, impacting on the Chicano experience. But, as Gonzalez points out, Chicano historiography is not alone; the imperialist dimensions of 20th-century U.S. history are also generally ignored in academia. Nevertheless, historians have made a strong case for arguing that an economic hegemony distinguished U.S.-Mexico relations beginning in the late 19th-century. It is this domination that differentiates the Mexican immigrant experience in the United States from the experiences of other immigrant communities. Immigration studies tend to follow well-worn sociological paths that lumps all immigrants into a "one-size-fits-all" theoretical scheme. Consequently, when explicating the history of the Mexican immigrant community, in particular their educational experiences, the analysis falls wide of the mark. Gonzalez presents the case that the political and economic conditions imposed on the Mexican immigrant community have led to a century of struggle for democratic schooling. However, the struggle for democratic schooling is, ultimately, a struggle against imperialism.

In Educational Perversion and Global Neoliberalism, Dave Hill situates the increasing inequality in and between education, economic, and social systems within the policy context of neoliberal capitalism. Neoliberal capitalism is a global phenomenon—restructuring of schooling and education has taken place internationally under pressure from international capitalist organizations and compliant governments. The effects of neoliberal policies in increasing inequalities globally and nationally, in diminishing democratic accountability and in stifling critical thought is presented along with a critique of the theory of neoliberalism in education policy—in particular how the marketization of education has perverted the goals, motivations, methods, standards of excellence and standards of freedom in education. Although the intrusion of capital into education threatens to undermine one of the best sites for its contestation, there are various other arenas of resistance for cultural works to engage and these are briefly described.

According to Glenn Rikowski, "One day, a company in Detroit or Vancouver that focuses primarily on the bottom-line could control a local secondary school in England." The general explanation for why the business takeover of schools is occurring is based on the fact that we live in capital's social universe. However, in his chapter, Schools and the GATS Enigma, Rikowski provides multiple interlinked explanations as to how the business takeover of schools is happening, particularly in the United Kingdom, and the role that the World Trade Organization's (WTO) GATS is nurturing the corporate takeover of schools and other public services. Rikowski examines the historical contexts of the WTO and the GATs, to provide a "clearer view of the monster casting a shadow over state schools in England."

Chapters 7 and 8 examine neoliberalism and education reform through the lens of literacy policy and practices. In Reading Marxism, Patrick Shannon uses Marxism to provide a historical and theoretical explanation for the alarming increase in the regulation of teachers' and students' actions as part of elementary school reading programs, to explain the commodification of literacy, and to offer explicit suggestions on what teachers and others might do. Shannon emphasizes the importance of small- and large-scale resistance movements and concludes that to really address the essence of the issues faced in reading education, we must stop the unmediated expansion of capitalism into social institutions. "This means teachers should join the movements toward livable minimum wages, national health insurance, affordable housing, and repeal of NAFTA and GATT. They should make their presence know at the protests of the World Trade Organization and the International Monetary Fund. These are large projects of possibility that show promise on a large scale."

In Chapter 8, Rich Gibson presents a critical analysis of the life and practices of Paulo Freire as a pathway for the development of a revolutionary pedagogy for social justice. Gibson's critique of Freire in theory and practice uses the central role Freire played in the development of education systems in the Grenadian revolution of 1979–1983 as a lens into the implications of his work. He critiques Freire as both the "objective idealist" and the "mechanical materialist." Freire's journey is presented as a model for how radical educators (and others) can search for answers to the questions "where do we want to go and how we hope to get there?"

Chapters 9 and 10 focus specifically on higher education issues. Meta-analyses of research in higher education typically contrast "positivist" and "cultural" conceptions of research orientations in higher education and offer varied laments about the disciplinary status of research on colleges and universities. In The Unchained Dialectic: Critique and Renewal of Higher Education Research, John F. Welsh provides an alternative typification of higher education research using Habermas' categories of scientific interest as a way of understanding important distinctions among methodological approaches. The chapter also examines "immanent critique" in the work of Marx, Gramsci, and Lukacs as the core of critical, dialectical, and emancipatory approaches to social research. Hegel's concept of the "Absolute Idea" is also discussed as a basis for understanding the epistemological, and ontological foundations of a dialectical methodology in higher education research.

"Higher education has special stakes for capitalist rule. Universities define the skills of professional workers for labor markets, reinforce ruling ideologies, and represent the needs of the state and industry as those of society. Despite that prevalent role, students and staff often succeed in creating spaces for critical citizenship, even for overt challenges to capitalist agendas." So opens Lev Levidow's chapter Marketizing Higher Education. Levidow examines the neoliberal strategies used to transform higher education, specifically focusing on the information and communication technology (ICT). In the ruling ideology, marketization is attributed to the socioeconomic imperatives of ICT. In general, the neoliberal project seeks to undo past collective gains that limited labor exploitation and maintained public goods, instead fragmenting people into vendors and consumers. The chapter examines circumstances in Africa, Europe, and North America and in the process Levidow's analyzes the marketizing strategies that are being applied to higher education on global scale serve as the development of effective counterstrategies and alternatives.

The book concludes with Peter McLaren's analysis the roles of critical pedagogy and class struggles in the age of neoliberal globalization. McLaren describes how, within the North American progressive education tradition, critical pedagogy has been a widely discussed project of educational reform that challenges students to become politically literate so that they might better understand and transform how power and privilege works on a daily basis in contemporary social contexts. As a project of social transformation, critical pedagogy is touted as an important protagonist in the struggle for social and economic justice, yet it has rarely ever challenged the fundamental basis of capitalist social relations. Among the many and varied proponents of critical pedagogy in the United States, Marxist analysis has been virtually absent; in fact, over the last decade, its conceptual orientation has been more closely aligned with postmodernism and poststructuralism. This chapter argues that unless class analysis and class struggle play a central role in critical pedagogy, it is fated to go the way of most liberal reform movements of the past, melding into calls for fairer resource distribution and allocation, and support for racial diversity, without challenging the social universe of capital in which such calls are made.

It is our hope that the analysis of neoliberal educational reform provided in these chapters (as well as the suggested counterstrategies) will contribute in multiple ways to the programs of critical scholars, educators, and activists working for education and schools that serve the broad interests of the public and against capitalist educational practices.

REFERENCES

Allman, P. (1999). *Revolutionary social transformation: Democratic hopes, political possibilities, and critical education.* Westport, CT: Bergin & Garvey.

Bowles, H., & Gintis, S. (1976). *Schooling in capitalist America.* New York: Basic.

Chomsky, N. (1999). *Profits over people: Neoliberalism and global order.* New York: Seven Stories Press.

Collins, C. (1999). The wealth gap widens. *Dollars & Sense, 225,* 12–13.

Kuehn, L. (1999, October). *Responding to globalization of education in the Americas: Strategies to support public education.* Paper presented at the IDEA conference in Quito, Ecuador. Retrieved from: http://www.vcn.bc.ca/idea/kuehn.htm

Martinez, E., & Garcia, A. (2000, February 26). *What is "neo-liberalism?" A brief definition.* Retrieved from: http://www.globalexchange.org/campaigns/econ101 /neoliberalDefined.html

Mathison, S. (2004). Educational assessment and standards-based educational reform. In S. Mathison & E. W. Ross (Eds.), *Defending public schools: The nature and limits of standards-based reform and assessment* (Vol. 4, pp. 3–14). Westport, CT: Praeger.

McChesney, R. W. (1998). Introduction. In N. Chomsky, *Profit over people: Neoliberalism and the global order* (pp. 7–16). New York: Seven Stories Press.

Ollman, B. (1971). *Alienation: Marx's conception of man in capitalist society.* Cambridge: Cambridge University Press.

Ollman, B. (2001). *How 2 take an exam ... and remake the world.* Montreal: Black Rose Books.

Pear, R. (1999, October, 4). More Americans were uninsured in 1998, U.S. says. *The New York Times,* p. 1.

Petras, J., & Veltmeyer, H. (1999). Latin America at the end of the millennium. *Monthly Review, 51*(3), 31–52.

Rikowski, G. (1997). Scorched Earth: Prelude to rebuilding Marxist educational theory. *British Journal of Sociology of Education, 19*(4), 551–574.

Ross, E. W., (2005). Public schools and neoliberal madness in Canada. *Substance, 30*(6), 5-6. Retrieved February 23, 2006, from http://www.substancenews.com /content/view/174/81.

Ross, E. W. (2006). Remaking the social studies curriculum. In E. W. Ross (Ed.), *The social studies curriculum: Purposes, problems, and possibilities* (3rd ed., pp. 319–332). Albany: State University of New York Press.

Ross, E. W., Gabbard, D., Kesson, K., Mathison, S., & Vinson, K. D. (Eds.). (2004). *Defending public schools* (Vols. 1–4). Westport, CT: Praeger.

Sarup, M. (1978). *Marxism and education.* London: Routledge & Kegan Paul.

Sharp, R. (Ed.). (1986). *Capitalist crisis and schooling.* South Melbourne: Macmillan.

Willis, P. (1977). *Learning to labour.* New York: Columbia University Press.

1

Marketing Education

The Rise of Standardized Testing, Accountability, Competition, and Markets in Public Education

David W. Hursh

Over the last several decades, education in the United States and elsewhere has undergone a profound transformation. In the not so distant past, students attended the school to which they were assigned, learned from teachers who used and adapted the school's and district's curriculum, and were evaluated based on teacher-prepared assignments. Now, students often ostensibly choose which school to attend (although some students have significantly more choices than others), and learn from teachers who teach what is needed to do well on the state's standardized tests. These changes reflect policymakers' greater faith in markets and competition than in teachers and students. Furthermore, data from the United States and the United Kingdom show that rather than the reforms improving education for all, they result in increasing educational inequality.

In this chapter, I focus on the policies implemented in United States, England, and Wales. Recent state and federal policies in the United States have emphasized using standardized tests to evaluate students and schools and have introduced market competition between schools. Some states, such as New York and Texas, require students, in order to graduate from high school, to pass one or more standardized exams. In Florida, schools with high test scores (most often those with White middle- to upper class students) receive a financial reward and those with low test scores lose funding and their students are provided vouchers to help pay private school tuition.[1] At the federal level, the No Child Left Behind (NCLB) Act uses student scores on standardized exams to determine whether schools are succeeding or failing to make "adequate yearly progress." Schools that fail to make adequate yearly progress (in New York almost always underfinanced urban schools) face losing students to competing schools, having students tutored by for-profit and faith-based corporations, and ultimately reopening as a charter school or turning over "operations either to the state or to a private company with a demonstrated record of effectiveness" (U.S. Department of Education, 2002, September, p. 7). The costs for the student transportation to another school and for tutoring are borne by the "failing school," therefore reducing funding to the already inadequately funded schools.[2]

While in England and Wales[3] students applying to university have, in the past, experienced the pressure of high-stakes standardized tests, the tests are now high stakes for every student, teacher, and school. The market-oriented policies of England and Wales (and from now on I only refer to England as if it includes Wales) have introduced competition between schools and between students both within and across schools. English schools, which essentially have open enrollment, receive funding based on

---

[1]The Florida voucher program currently sends 26,000 students to private schools at public expense. The program is rife with abuse, ranging from private schools doubling their tuition rate to take advantage of the voucher money, to schools lacking accreditation. For excellent coverage of the issue see the *Palm Beach Post* at www.palmbeachpost.com.

[2]Whether a school is or is not making "adequate yearly progress" tells us very little about the quality of the school. Contrary to what might be a commonsense interpretation of progress, "adequate yearly progress" often requires not that a school makes progress but that it reach a minimal but increasing benchmark. In New York, urban poor schools in which scores are rising are often designated as failing whereas wealthier suburban schools in which scores remain stable or fall can be succeeding. I have described this in more depth in Hursh and Martina (2003) and Hursh (2004).

[3]England and Wales have adopted similar education policies, whereas Scotland and Northern Ireland have retained their previous less market-oriented policies (see Nixon, Walker, & Baron, 2002).

the number of students in the school, with no increased funding for students with disabilities, students from low-income families, or students who are English-language learners. Consequently, schools compete for the White middle-class students because students who have fewer needs arising from poverty, disabilities, or as English-language learners require fewer financial resources and are more likely to raise the school's aggregated test scores published in the annual school "league tables." Those schools with high test scores are likely to admit high-scoring students to their few openings, whereas those schools with low scores are desperate to retain their "more able" middle-class students (Gillborn & Youdell, 2000). Schools serving diverse students and needs struggle to retain their students and funding. Already advantaged schools gain, whereas disadvantaged schools lose.

Moreover, Gillborn and Youdell (2000) noted that not only does the market system exacerbate the inequalities *between* schools, the competitive examination system exacerbates inequalities *within* schools. Because secondary schools are judged based on what percentage of students attain on their exams five or more grades of A to C, schools focus on those students who are seen as likely to achieve a grade of C or better and pay less attention to those who are likely to be failures, again typically students of color, students with disabilities, and students who are English-language learners. Students who are disadvantaged are neither sought after by schools, nor, if admitted, likely to receive much attention.

In summary, since 1980s, we have witnessed in the United States, England, and elsewhere (most notably New Zealand and Australia) the increasing transformation of schools into institutions governed by market principles of accountability, choice, and efficiency (Robertson, 2000; Whitty, Power & Halpin, 1998). The questions then become: What has been the rationale for these policy changes? Why have they met so little resistance? What have been their consequences? Therefore, I first turn to placing the educational changes within the context of the global rise of neoliberal economic policies, policies that promote private interests over the public good. For example, neoliberal policies promote corporate growth through increased trade and decreased taxation and regulation, and decreased public support for or even the privatization of public services such as health, transportation, and education. Furthermore, the shift toward promoting corporate over social welfare redefines the relationship between the individual and society. Because governments are less responsible for the welfare of the individual, the individual becomes responsible for him or herself. As Peters (1994) described, within neoliberal societies the goal becomes creating the competitive, instrumentally rational individual who can compete in the marketplace. Not only does society become less responsible for individual welfare but also, as Marx observed, under market systems workers, which includes all those who must sell their labor to survive, are reduced to commodities. Under market-oriented education systems, students and teachers also become commodities.

To understand why these reforms are occurring, we need to understand how recent educational reforms fulfill the state's (national and provincial governments) legitimation and accumulation functions (Dale, 1989). The state seeks to retain its legitimacy in the public's eyes by blaming schools for increasing economic inequality and reforming schools in order to appear to be doing something about it. In undertaking the reforms, the state can also fulfill its accumulation function of contributing to economic, particularly corporate, growth by cutting corporate taxes and preparing students to be more productive workers.

Hursh and Apple (1983) revealed how *A Nation at Risk* (National Commission, 1983) explicitly blamed schools for the Reagan-induced economic recession of the early 1980s (Parenti, 1999) and the perceived failure of the United States to compete internationally. *A Nation at Risk* and subsequent policies reflect the effort by capital, through the state, to blame schools for the essential injustices and contradictions of capitalism. In this way, the state can appear to be legitimately concerned about the general welfare, even as social and economic inequalities increase. Educational reforms provide the appearance that the state has taken responsibility for improving society and, therefore, increase the state's legitimacy. Apple (1996) wrote, "governments must be seen to be doing something. . . . Reforming education is not only widely acceptable and relatively unthreatening, but just as crucially, its success or failure will not be obvious in the short term" (p. 88). However, as the United States regained its economic dominance, those who criticized public schools have not now praised them for creating economic growth.

Moreover, recent reform proposals provide several means for the state to fulfill its accumulation function. First, proponents of market reforms assert that schools do not need more money but only need to become more efficient by competing with other public and private schools. By contending that schools do not need more funding and promoting privatization through voucher or charter school programs, the state can serve capital's needs to reduce corporate taxes and make public schooling a potential source of corporate profits.

Furthermore, a competitive market requires indicators of each school's effectiveness, therefore justifying states' implementing systems of standardized testing and accountability. Because the conservative governments implementing the reforms have historically claimed to be loathe to intervene in individual's lives, the state and corporations have devised accountability systems in which they do not directly intervene into everyday school practices but steer from a distance (Ball, 1994). Schools and teachers are provided with the goals they are to achieve but not explicitly directed in how they are to be achieved.

Second, by transforming the relationship between the individual and society, the recent policies work to diminish expectations for the provision of education and community involvement in setting educational goals. Without wanting to romanticize the benefits of local schooling, in the past, when students attended the schools in their own neighborhood, they and their parents shared responsibility with others for the quality of the school. Schools in the United States and England have had a long history of local control, with families committed to making schools work because the school was the community school. Parents were likely to come to know other parents in their neighborhood and discuss curriculum and pedagogical issues. However, under school choice, parents are encouraged to transfer their children from school to school, undermining their allegiance to the local school and their incentive to engage in public discourse regarding the nature and purpose of schooling.

Third, recent education reforms emphasize those subjects and dispositions that increase citizens' economic productivity. Robertson (2000) described the changing mandate as requiring "educational systems, through creating appropriately skilled and entrepreneurial citizens and workers able to generate new and added economic values, will enable nations to be responsive to changing conditions within the international marketplace" (p. 187).

The rise of standardized testing, markets, and competition fit within the larger shift over the last several decades from a government that provides for the general welfare to one that leaves that provision to private corporations. That shift occurred as the preceding Keynesian economic policies came under attack for not providing an adequate rate of profit to corporations and for providing too many personal rights to individuals.

THE RISE OF NEOLIBERAL POLICIES FOCUSING ON CORPORATE GROWTH THROUGH THE EXPANSION OF INTERNAL AND INTERNATIONAL MARKETS

Neoliberal economic policies arose as a corporate and political response to the previous Keynesian economic accommodation that existed to different degrees in Europe and North America after World War II. In contrast to the years preceding and immediately after the war, an unusual level of agreement between corporations and workers marked the first two decades after the war. During this period, in exchange for improving wages, workers consented to capital's right not only to control the workplace but also to allow capitalist control of investment and growth, primarily through the growth of multinational corporations. At the same time, workers, women, and people of color struggled for and were able to extend their personal and political rights for education, housing, health, workplace safety, and the vote (Bowles & Gintis, 1986). In part fuelled by workers' growing wages, the post-war period was marked by unusually rapid and stable economic growth. However, as workers earned and spent more, businesses' net rate of profit fell by more than 50% between 1965 and 1974 (Parenti, 1999). Profits fell primarily because cost pressures from labor could not be passed on to consumers in the increasingly competitive and open world economy (Bowles & Gintis, 1986).

In order to restore higher rates of profit, the United States and other developed countries implemented monetarist and neoliberal policies (Gill, 2003) that would support corporations over workers. In the United States, Reagan's monetarist policies restored the power of capital by inducing a recession to deflate wage demands, escalate the scarcity of jobs and reverse the growth of social spending. Such policies were instituted with the intent of reducing the living standards of all but wealthy Americans. In 1979, Paul Volcker, Federal Reserve Board chairman, provided the following rationale for the recession: "The standard of living of the average American has to decline. I don't think you can escape that" (Parenti, 1999, p. 119).

Such monetarist policies were soon linked with neoliberal policies that emphasize "the deregulation of the economy, trade liberalization, the dismantling of the public sector [such as education, health, and social welfare], and the predominance of the financial sector of the economy over production and commerce" (Vilas, 1996, p. 17). Tabb (2002) wrote that neoliberalism stresses

> the privatization of the public provision of goods and services—moving their provision from the public sector to the private—along with deregulating how private producers can behave, giving greater scope to the single-minded pursuit of profit and showing significantly less regard for the need to limit social costs or for redistribution based on nonmarket criteria. The aim of neoliberalism is to put into question all collective structures capable of obstructing the logic of the pure market. (p. 7)

Two forces contribute to the global dispersal of neoliberal policies. First, as the leading economic countries adopt neoliberal policies, other countries are forced to reduce social costs, and thus taxes, in order to compete for capital investment. Second, the U.S.-dominated World Bank and International Monetary Fund increasingly required that national governments develop economic policies that emphasize economic growth and property rights over social welfare and personal rights. In some countries, such a Chile, social security, health care, postsecondary education and, to some extent, elementary and secondary education have been highly privatized (Collins & Lear, 1995). Such global changes led Gill (2003) to conclude, "[t]he social settlements and forms of state created after World War II have been transformed and in some respects destroyed" (p. 9).

Although the discourse of globalization and neoliberal economic policy is new, the expansion of the economy around the globe and the emphasis on increasing worker productivity is not. More than 150 years ago, Marx and Engels commented on just such developments in *The Manifesto of the Communist Party*. As Harvey (2000) stated:

> [w]hat we now call "globalization" has been around in some form or another for a very long time — at least as far back as 1492 if not before. The phenomenon and its political-economic consequences have likewise been the subject of commentary, not least by Marx and Engels who, in *The Manifesto of the Communist Party*, published an impassioned as well as thorough analysis of it. (p. 21)

Although some of the *Manifesto* has become outdated or reflects an inadequate understanding of the world beyond Europe and the United States, much remains relevant. For example, Marx and Engels accurately described current globalization thusly:

> The need for a constantly expanding market chases the bourgeoisie over the whole surface of the globe. It must settle everywhere, establish connexions everywhere. The bourgeoisie has through its exploitation of the world market given a cosmopolitan character to production and consumption in every country. All old established industries have been destroyed or are daily being destroyed. They are dislodged by new industries, whose introduction becomes a life or death question for all civilized nations, by industries that no longer work up indigenous raw material, but raw material drawn from the remotest zones; industries whose products are consumed, not only at home, but in every quarter of the globe. In place of the old wants, satisfied by the production of the country, we find new wants, requiring for their satisfaction the products of distant lands and climes. In place of the old local and national seclusion and self-sufficiency, we have intercourse in every direction, universal interdependence of nations. (Marx & Engels, 1952, pp. 46–47)

Furthermore, under capitalism, workers are required to create value through their work that can be taken by the corporate owners (whether an individual or stockholders) as profit. Because competition requires that corporations focus on their bottom-line — produce a profit or go bankrupt — workers become valued solely for their economic productivity. Under capitalism, people must create a product or service that can be sold or exchanged for more than the cost of their own labor or, in other words, they must create surplus value. If they create products, they must, if capital is to make a profit, produce products that sell for more than it cost to produce the product. If they provide a service, they must provide a service that sells for more than they are paid. As Marx stated, personal worth is reduced to exchange value. People become valued for what they can produce; the more one can produce, the greater one's worth. People become commodities to be exchanged. Again, Marx and Engels (1952):

> [Capital] has left remaining no other nexus between man and man than naked self-interest, than callus "cash payment." It has drowned the most heavenly ecstasies of religious fervor, of chivalrous enthusiasm, of philistine sentimentalism, in the icy water of egotistical calculation. It has resolved personal worth into exchange value, and in the place of the numberless indefensible chartered freedoms, has set up that single unconscionable freedom—Free Trade. . . . The bourgeoisie has stripped of its halo every occupation hitherto honored and looked up to with reverent awe. It has converted the physician, the lawyer, the priest, the poet, the man of science [and the educator], into its paid wage laborers. (p. 44)

It is clear that for Marx and Engels, "workers" refer to everyone other than corporate owners or capitalists, and all workers are degraded. Furthermore, this is exactly as Peters (1994) described the plight of the individual under neoliberalism: the individual is free, free to compete in the marketplace to exchange one's own value.

Not only are workers reduced to commodities to be exchanged, but such processes create laborers alienated from their own creative capacities, according to Marx and Engels. "Laborers," wrote Harvey, "are necessarily alienated because their creative capacities are appropriated as the commodity labor power by capitalists," Laborers continually face "skilling, deskilling, and reskilling of the powers of labor in accord with technological requirements"; and the "acculturation to routinization of tasks" (Harvey, 2000, p. 103).

We can see the results of this process in education. Although a central purpose of education has always been to produce economically productive workers (Kliebard, 1995), this is even more so today as schools are pushed to produce efficient workers who can compete within the global workforce by adapting and developing new skills, but who do not question the hierarchical work structure. As Harvey, (2000) noted: "[o]n the one hand capital requires educated and flexible laborers, but on the other hand it refuses the idea that laborers should think for themselves. While education of the laborer appears important it cannot be the kind of education that permits free thinking" (p. 103).

Second, as education is transformed into a market in which schools compete with one another not only for test grades, but also for the students and teachers to fill the school, students and teachers become commodities, with some students and teachers valued over others. Moreover, because the control over schooling has shifted from the local school and district to the state directed by capital, teachers have less control of their own work and become, like other workers, alienated from their own creative capacities.

PROMOTING ACCOUNTABILITY, MARKETS, AND CHOICE IN EDUCATION

Educational reforms of the last two decades, then, have been central of neo-liberal policies in which social spending is to be reduced, whereas schools are to better serve the needs of capital for productive workers. These policies have transformed education throughout the world (Apple, 2003). Whitty et al. (1998), Robertson (2000), and others (Hatcher, 2003) described how the United States, the United Kingdom and its former colonies have embraced markets and choice as a means of improving education. Whitty et al. analyzed the changing educational system in five countries—New Zealand, Australia, Sweden, United States, and England/Wales—and concluded, that "within the range of political rationales, it is the neo-liberal alternative which dominates, as does a particular emphasis on market mechanisms" (p. 35). In this system, government "steers at a distance, while the notion of the free economy is extended to a marketized civil society in which education and welfare services are offered to individual consumers by competing providers than provided collectively by the state to all citizens" (Whitty et al., 1998, p. 35).

Whitty et al. described how proponents of market reforms argue that they will result in more efficient and more effective schools. Similarly, Robertson (2002) noted, "Much of the choice/markets agenda has been shaped by the criticism of schools as inefficient bureaucracies that are unresponsive either to community or individual interests" (p. 174). Schools, and particularly teachers, are unresponsive, write the critics, because they know parents cannot take their children elsewhere. Therefore, proponents of choice and markets argue, "efficiency and equity in education could only be addressed through 'choice' and where family or individuals were constructed as the customers of educational services" (Robertson, 2000, p. 174). Increasing the range of parents' choice over their children's schools and funding schools based on the number of students that they attract introduces a competitive market approach to the allocation of resources.

According to those promoting markets, Robertson wrote that, markets are

> more efficient modes for the allocation of goods and services (cf. Chubb & Moe, 1990; Coleman, 1990); (2) more equitable, in that they are responsive to the needs and desires of their clients (as opposed to pub-

lic sector bureaucracies characterized by quasi-monopoly status and therefore provider capture); (3) and more democratic in that they maximize the freedom of individuals to choose intervention in their own lifestyles, unhindered by the state. (p. 174)

Chubb and Moe, in particular, "argue that turning to the *market* as an instrument to arbitrate choice will lead to autonomy. Markets promote autonomy by enabling all participants to make decisions for themselves" (Robertson, 2000, p. 138, italics in original).

In the United States, the views of Chubb and Moe are seconded by socially conservative and neoliberal foundations and think tanks. Laitsch, Shaker, and Heilman (2002) summarized the optimistic views of several influential conservative think-tanks regarding the power of market competition and choice to radically transform education for the better. Organizations such as the Heritage Foundation, the Fordham Foundation, The Hoover Institution, and the Education Leaders Council emphasize the "principles of individual, economic, and political freedom; [and] private enterprise" (Hoover Institution's Center for Research on Educational Outcomes [CREDO] and "diversity, competition and choice" (Fordham Foundation).

Leaders from these organizations advise and move in and out of leadership positions in the current Bush Administration, forming the "brain [*sic*] trust" behind the administration's support for educational markets and the privatization of public education. The U.S. Department of Education, to an unprecedented degree, has thrown its support behind privatization by allocating funds to organizations that promote vouchers and for a $50 million experimental voucher program in Washington, DC (Miner, 2004). In *Rethinking Schools*, Miner described how the Bush Administration siphons funds from public schools to pay private corporations. For example, under NCLB, students in schools failing to make adequate yearly progress are offered supplemental tutoring primarily through for-profit and faith-based corporations. Consequently, "so-called failing schools," most often financially distressed urban schools, have funds taken from their budget and given to private corporations (Miner, 2004).

Furthermore, from 2001 to 2003 the Bush Administration granted $77.6 million to groups dedicated to privatization through voucher programs. These groups aim to replace public schools with private schools. Miner showed how the NCLB legislation supports the administration's goal of privatizing education. The leaders of the organizations receiving funding to promote or put in place voucher programs desire that NCLB increase parents' and students' frustration with the public schools, leading to more support for privatization. For example, Howard Fuller, founder of the pro-voucher organization Black Alliance for Educational Options (BAEO), in a 2002 interview with the National Governor's Association, said: "Hopefully, in years to come the [NCLB] law will be amended to allow families to choose private schools as well as public schools" (cited in Miner, 2004, p. 11).

In the previous section I described how the Bush Administration has promoted the corporate takeover of public education through voucher programs and charter schools, especially as the testing requirements under NCLB labels most schools as failing. Florida's testing requirements have already resulting in labeling 90% of the schools and all of the districts as failing (Pinzur, 2003). Most knowledgeable observers have stated that almost every school in every state will, in the end, be found to be failing (Bracey, 2003). Such results, conservative and neoliberal proponents hope, will increase public support for school privatization.

In England, privatization efforts have preceded more quickly than in the United States. Increasingly, education is perceived as an opportunity for corporations to "produce human capital for competitiveness in the global economy" and "to open up state education systems to private education-for-profit companies" (Hatcher, 2003, p. 1).

Hatcher showed how England is incorporating the business agenda promulgated by the Organization for Economic Cooperation and Development (OECD). He described how the OECD's Public Management Service

> claims "a new paradigm for public management has emerged, aimed at fostering a performance-oriented-culture in a less centralized public sector" (OECD, 1995, p. 8). The key elements of the "new public management" are "corporatization and commercialization, privatization, competition and contracting, deregulation and liberalization, performance management and restructuring the financing of services" (Whitfield, 2001, p, 114). (Hatcher, 2003, p. 1)

The above characteristics of the new public management are reflected in the profound transformation of public schooling in England. These include but are not limited to the following:

- School inspections and professional development, previously carried out by state, are now conducted by private corporations (Hatcher, 2003). Corporations can sponsor "specialist schools," and through their sponsorship gain the ability to appoint the majority of the school board and control the direction and curriculum of the school. Although corporations cannot now make a profit from their sponsorships, conservatives are hoping to eliminate that restriction (Peterson, 2004).
- Schools are encouraged to market their curriculum; one school has made $10 million profit over 2 years selling its courses that prepare students for the exams (Peterson, 2004).

England serves as an example of the kinds of changes that might occur next in the United States if neo-liberal advocates have their way. While Hatcher notes that there is increasing resistance to privatization in England, it has not been effective (Hatcher, 2003, p. 14). The question that I turn to next, therefore, is how is it that such radical transformations in public schooling have been successfully implemented?

THE CORPORATE STATE: SERVING CORPORATE INTERESTS WHILE RETAINING LEGITIMACY

It clearly serves corporate financial interests if education is partially privatized, if corporate taxes for social services are reduced, and if school curricula focus on producing efficient employees. In the United States and England, governments are making all these changes possible. How is it then that changes that benefit corporations but may harm the larger social welfare, as Hatcher in England and Wells (2002) and others in the United States have demonstrated, are being implemented? Obviously, I cannot fully answer that question in a few pages. However, such reforms, I argue, are being successfully implemented, in part, because of the strategies and discourses used by the proponents.

First, in order to reduce resistance to cuts in social services, neoliberal governments have attempted to retain legitimacy by shifting social responsibility from the community to the individual. They have reduced resistance by joining business leaders to embark on an ideological crusade to shift social responsibility from the community to the individual, thereby transforming the relationship between the individual and society. Margaret Thatcher portrayed this ideology most succinctly when she stated: "there is no such thing as society. . . . There are individual men and women, and there are families. And no government can do anything except through people, and people must look to themselves first" (Thatcher 1993; cited in Gillborn & Youdell, 2000, p. 39). Thatcher's statement shifts responsibility for success or failure entirely onto the individual and family. Gillborn and Youdell (2000) noted that, Thatcher "perfectly encapsulated an ideological drive that reduced everything to individualized relationships between providers and consumers, and understood inequality variously as a sign of personal/community deficit or part of the necessary spur to achievement in a meritocracy" (p. 39). By reducing success to individual merit, schooling becomes one more consumer choice where one benefits by choosing wisely. Those who work hard are admitted to good schools and do well; those who do not work hard have only themselves to blame. Inequality is explained as differences in personal effort.

Second, Berliner and Biddle (1995) showed how *A Nation at Risk* (National Commission, 1983) was just the beginning of the conservative "manufactured crisis" in education. They described how the critics of public schooling ignored the improvements of the previous three decades (in fact, until recently, the racial achievement gap was declining) and blamed education for the U.S. economic and social problems. A parallel process occurred in England (Furlong & Phillips, 2001). Such fallacious criticisms increased public receptivity to promises to improve education through raising standards, testing, and competition. The state managed to shift the blame away from its own policies and to retain legitimacy by appearing to improve schooling and, therefore, society.

Third, the state has collaborated with corporations to shift power away from the local schools and districts toward the larger entities of corporations and state and federal governments. In New York, for example, the powerful Business Council recently sent a letter to all the state representatives urging them not to back off from the greatly flawed and criticized state Regents testing and graduation requirements. A letter from the president/CEO of the Business Council stated the following:

> Without reliable measures, high standards are vulnerable to being compromised for the neediest children in our State. Though tests cannot assess all that is valuable to know, they represent a strong indicator of achievement in the five key subject areas. New York State's economic strength is intertwined with an education system that gives all children an opportunity to learn to the highest levels.
>
> I urge you to oppose any legislation weakening the Regents' graduation requirements. (Walsh, 2004, p. 1)

Although conservative political parties in the United States and the United Kingdom have long argued for less rather than more intervention by the state into people's lives, as the letter above indicates, they defend the state education departments' intervention into local schools through standards and standardized testing.

The reliance first on standards and testing and more recently on markets and competition also demonstrates that the neoliberal strategy in the United States has not been to directly intervene into the classroom but affect the educational system by focusing on output, leaving the means to achieving those goals to the schools. Ball (1990) described this strategy as " steering from a distance," whereas others have described it as the rise of the "audit" (Clarke & Newman, 1997; Gewirtz, 2002) or "evaluative" state (Whitty et al., 1998).

Whitty et al. described the policy shift as one in which "[w]hat matters is not the process by which goals might be achieved, but the output . . . by focusing on output, it redefines the purpose of education in terms of the economy rather than individual demand . . . it provides a powerful instrument for steering individual institutions" (p. 37).

This new evaluative state operates differently than the former bureaucratic state. Rather than operating as a bureaucracy in which long-term goals are determined, resources allocated, and assessments made, the new evaluative state "maintains overall strategic control through fewer, but more precise, policy levers" (Neave, 1988; cited in Whitty et al., 1998, p. 37). They described how this shift is also likely to lead to the leaders of governmental agencies, such as in state education departments and the federal Department of Education, "hav[ing] a higher public profile than conventional state bureaucrats and hav[ing] a significant role in setting new political agendas through close contact with the media" (p. 37). In New York, Commissioner Mills is frequently seen meeting with teachers and students in which through a tightly controlled agenda he portrays himself as supporting learning for all children while his critics are portrayed as giving up on children. Similarly, Rod Paige, U.S. secretary of education, regularly describes himself as continuing the fight for students' civil rights while those that disagree with him are settling for inequality. In a recent defense of the NCLB Act he stated, "I find it staggering that the very critics and organizations that fought so hard for civil rights could leave our African-American, Hispanic-American and special needs children behind. Some critics are just on the wrong side of history" (Schemo, 2004, p. 14).

Finally, as hinted at by the New York Business Council's self-reference to its concern for the state's "neediest children" and "economic strength" and Paige's self-description as fighting for students' civil rights, proponents use discourses of fairness, equity, and economic growth in arguing for the reforms. Repeatedly, corporate and educational leaders describe their efforts as improving the welfare of both the individual and the economy. Furthermore, standardized test scores will provide parents and teachers with a valid and reliable means of assessing student learning. Such objective methods are required, government and corporate officials state, because teachers cannot be trusted to assess student learning objectively and accurately. The Parents' Guide to NCLB states that the act "will give them [parents and communities] objective data" through standardized testing (U.S. Department of Education, 2002, September, p. 12).

In summary, the educational reforms have been a means for the state and corporations (who also often fund commissions and organizations that support such reforms) to take an active role in reforming society by introducing a competitive market system in which some students and schools succeed and some fail. The reforms are couched within a discourse in which the previously neglected will now be helped through a system of high standards, objective testing, and equal opportunity. The system of testing and accountability permits the state to determine the goals and output without directly intervening in the process itself, thereby reducing resistance.

CREATING EQUITY OR EXACERBATING INEQUALITY?

Over the last several years, my own political efforts have focused on combating, primarily as a member of the Coalition for Common Sense in Education, the effects of high-stakes testing in New York. In those efforts, we have compiled significant quantitative and qualitative data on the effects of testing on educational equality. Contrary to state and corporate claims that high-stakes testing has improved educational opportunity, the data speak otherwise; high-stakes standardized testing in New York has harmed educational achievement. The data include an increased dropout rate, especially for students of color and students with disabilities. For example, from 1998 to 2000, the number of students dropping out increased by 17%. In fact, a recent report from The Civil Rights Project at Harvard University concluded that New York has the lowest graduation rate of any state for African-American (35%) and Latino (31%) students (Orfield, Losen, Wald, & Swanson, 2004). In New York City, only 38% of *all* students graduate on time, fifth worst of the 100 largest cities in the nation (Winter, 2004). Another recent study lists New York state's graduation rate as 45th in the nation (Haney, 2003). The tests have also negatively affected English language learners, who have gone from the highest diploma-earning minority in 1996 to the highest dropout minority in 2002 (Monk, Sipple, & Killeen, 2001). Furthermore, dropouts among students with disabilities have increased from 7,200 in 1996 to 9,200 in 2001. Many of those that do not drop out receive an individual education plan (IEP) diploma. An IEP diploma is not a high school diploma but a certificate of completion of a special education student's educational plan.

In our own study (Martina, Hursh, Markowitz, Hart, & Debes, 2003) of the exams' effects on teachers, teachers described how the tests restrict their autonomy and professional decision making. We recently interviewed six Rochester area teachers who participated in a curriculum reform project that aimed to integrate curricula on the relationship between the environment and health into various subject areas. The teachers expressed significant frustration with implementing innovative curricula within the context of high-stakes standardized exams. Although our study size was small, all the teachers described ways in which the standardized exams determined into which course and what extent the curricula would be implemented. All the teachers articulated how they felt pressure not to diverge from the curriculum content that was likely to be included on the final state exam (Martina et al., 2003).

Although there is less quantitative data regarding the effects on teachers, the anecdotal information is compelling. Elementary teachers report that they are pressured to spend more time preparing students for the tests given at their own or subsequent grade levels and less time teaching those subject areas not tested. For example, fourth-grade teachers are pressured to prepare students not only to do well on the English language arts exam, the first standardized exam given to elementary students, but also to prepare fourth-graders for the social studies exam given in the fall of fifth grade. The pressure placed on fourth-grade teachers is causing many of them to request transfers to other grades or to resign from teaching (Goodnough, 2000; Monk et al., 2001). Secondary teachers report that they devote increased time to teaching toward the test.

In England, where not only high-stakes standardized tests have been implemented but also education choice, the data are just as compelling. Gillborn and Youdell (2000) described how the market system works against students who are neither middle-class nor White or have learning disabilities or are English-language learners. In England, schools' aggregate test scores are published annually in the "league tables." These tables list, among other things, the percentage of students scoring at least five grades of A through C on the culminating exams. Because students may apply for admission to other schools, the league table serves as a public ranking of the supposed (a school's aggregate grades strongly correlate to their students' class background) quality of each school. Those schools with a high percentage of A through C grades are able to recruit to their school students who are likely high scorers, leaving behind likely low scorers. Advantaged schools cream off the better students from other schools. Consequently, as Gillborn and Youdell described in great detail, the schools are becoming more unequal and those schools largely filled with students who are not middle class and white lose their stronger students to the already advantaged schools.

Moreover, because a school's reputation is so strongly tied to the percentage of students achieving at least five grades of A–C on their tests, the schools institute strategies that they feel will most effectively yield the highest percentage of A–C passes. Gillborn and Youdell described a process of triage in which the schools focus on the most "profitable" borderline students who with adequate attention are likely to pass to exams. The schools consciously decide to give less effort to those students who are most unlikely to pass the exams. The academically weakest students fall further behind, therefore, increasing the gap between the advantaged and disadvantaged students. Gillborn and Youdell described what they called the "A–C economy" or the process in which not only do the already advantaged schools increase their advantages by recruiting and admitting only the better and least problematic students but the process through which schools make decisions that result in not less but more inequality between students. Students are treated literally as commodities; the greater a student's potential, the more likely schools are to recruit and focus on them. Although I know of no similar study conducted in the United States, anecdotal data from teachers indicate that schools also are like to focus on those students who with help might achieve passing grade on the standardized exam and neglect those students unlikely to pass.

High-stakes standardized testing, school choice, and educational markets, then, are not resulting in increased educational equality. Rather, schools are becoming more separate and unequal and even the student composition within a school is becoming more unequal.

Over the last two decades, neoliberal policies have transformed educational systems around the globe. In this chapter I focused on the United States and England. In the United States, state and the federal governments now require that students and schools be evaluated through statewide standardized exams. In some states, students must pass the exams in order to be promoted from one grade to another or from high school. Under NCLB, schools failing to make adequate progress must fund tutoring for their students, often through private for-profit organizations. Furthermore, failing schools face the prospect of being administered by or turned over as a charter school to a private corporation. The Bush Administration strongly supports the privatization of education through voucher programs and charter schools.

In England, schools are competing with one another for students, for test grades, and, for funding. Gewirtz (2002), Gewirtz, Ball and Bowe (1995), and Gillborn and Youdell (2000) have provided compelling evidence regarding the harmful affect competition has on the culture of the school, including teacher professionalism and student success.

Contrary to their proponents' claims these reforms are not improving education for all. Rather, the gap between schools is widening. The comprehensive school in England and the United States are in decline, creating a hierarchy of schools in both countries. Because of the requirement of raising test scores, teachers have less flexibility in creating curriculum that responds to the need of the students in their class.

As I have shown, these reforms should not be surprising given that capitalism requires that capitalists seek to expand their markets and to squeeze surplus value from workers. Teachers and students, like all workers, are valued for their contribution to the economy: Teachers are expected to create "appropriately skilled and entrepreneurial citizens and workers able to generate new and added economic values" (Robertson, 2000, p. 187).

It is crucial that we understand that the global educational system is undergoing a profound change. Politicians and corporate leaders are replacing our public school system with a private, for-profit, competitive, market-based system that increases inequality and undermines democracy. To continue to ignore and not resist the changes may result in the demise of public schooling.

REFERENCES

Apple, M. W. (1996). *Cultural politics and education.* New York: Teachers College Press.

Apple, M. W. (2003). *The state and the politics of knowledge.* New York: Routledge Falmer.

Ball, S. (1990). *Politics and policymaking in education: Explorations in policy sociology.* London: Routledge.

Ball, S. (1994). *Education reform: A critical and post-structural approach.* Buckingham, England: Open University Press.

Berliner, D., & Biddle, B. (1995). *The manufactured crisis: Myths, fraud and the attack on America's public schools.* Reading MA: Addison-Wesley.

Bowles, S., & Gintis, H. (1986). *Democracy and capitalism: Property, community, and the contradictions of modern thought.* New York: Basic Books.

Bracey, G. (2003, February). NCLB—A plan for the destruction of public education: Just say "NO!" *No Child Left, 1*(2). Retrieved August 28, 2003, from http://www.nochildleft.org/2003/feb03no.html.

Chubb, J., & Moe, T. (1990) *Politics, markets and America's schools.* Washington, DC: Brookings Institute.

Clarke, J., & Newman, J. E. (1997). *The managerial state.* Thousand Oaks, CA: Sage.

Coleman, J. (1990), Choice, community, and future schools. In W. Clune & J. Witte (Eds.), *Choice and control in American education* (pp. ix-xxii). London: Falmer.

Collins, J., & Lear, J. (1995). *Chile's free-market miracle: A second look.* Oakland, CA: The Institute for Food and Development Policy.

Dale, R. (1989). *The state and education policy.* Milton Keynes: Open University Press.

Furlong, J., & Phillips, R. (Eds.). (2001). Introduction and rationale. In R. Phillips & J. Furlong (Eds.), *Education, reform and the state: Twenty-five years of politics, policy and practice* (pp. 3-11). New York: Routledge.

Gewirtz, S. (2002). *The managerial school: Post-welfarism and social justice in education.* New York: Routledge.

Gewirtz, S., Ball, S., & Bowe, R. (1995). *Markets, choice and equity in education.* Buckingham: Open University Press.

Gill, S. (2003). *Power and resistance in the new world order.* New York: Palgrave Macmillan.

Gillborn, D., & Youdell, D. (2000). *Rationing education: Policy, practice, reform and equity.* Philadelphia, PA: Open University Press.

Goodnough, A. (2000, June 14). Strain of fourth-grade tests drives off veteran teachers. *The New York Times,* p. A–1.

Haney, W. (2003, September 23). *Attrition of students from New York schools.* Invited testimony at public hearing "Regents learning standards and high school graduation requirements." New York State Senate Standing Committee on Education, New York.

Haney, W. (2000, August 19). The myth of the Texas miracle in education. *Education Policy Analysis Archives.* Retrieved from: http://epaa.asu.edu/v8n1.

Harvey, D. (2000). *Spaces of hope.* Berkeley: University of California Press.

Hatcher, R. (2003, December 12). *Business agendas and school education in England.* Retrieved from: http.www.socialist-teacher.org/dossiers-asp?d=y&id-75.

Hursh, D. (2004). No child left behind: The rise of educational markets and the decline of social justice. In J. O'Donnell & R. Chavez Chavez (Eds.), *Social justice in these times* (pp. 173-190). Greenwich, CT: Information Age Publishing.

Hursh, D., & Apple, M. W. (1983, June). *The fiscal crisis, politics and education: A critical analysis of the report of the National Commission on Excellence in Education.* Unpublished manuscript.

Hursh, D., & Martina, C.A. (2003, October). Neoliberalism and schooling in the U.S.: How state and federal government education policies perpetuate inequality. *Journal for Critical Education Policy Studies, 1*(2). Retrieved from: http://www.jceps.com

Kliebard, H. (1995). *The struggle for the American curriculum 1893-1958.* New York: Routledge.

Laitsch, D., Shaker, P., & Heilman, E. (2002). Teacher education, pro-market policy and advocacy research. *Teaching Education, 13*(1), 252–272.

Martina, C. A., Hursh, D., Markowitz, D., Hart, K., & Debes, P. (2003, October). *Contradictions in educational policy: Developing integrated problem-based curriculum in a high-stakes environment.* Paper presented at the annual American Educational Studies Association Conference, Mexico City, Mexico.

Marx, K., & Engels, F. (1952) *Manifesto of the Communist Party.* Moscow: Foreign Language Publishing House.

Miner, B. (2004). Seed money for conservatives. *Rethinking Schools, 18*(4) 9–11.

Monk, D., Sipple, J., & Killeen, K. (2001, September 10). *Adoption and adaptation, New York States school districts' responses to state imposed high school graduation requirements: An eight-year retrospective.* New York: Education Finance Research Consortium. Retrieved from www.albany.edu/edfin/CR01_Msk Report.pdf

National Commission on Excellence in Education. (1983). *A nation at risk: A report to the nation and the Secretary of Education.* Washington, DC: U.S. Department of Education.

Neave, G. (1988). On the cultivation of quality, efficiency and enterprise: An overview of recent trends in higher education in Western Europe, 1968-1988. *European Journal of Education, 23*(1/2), 7–23.

Nixon, J., Walker, M., & Baron, S. (2002) The cultural mediation of state policy: The democratic potential of New Community Schooling in Scotland. *Journal of Education Policy, 17*(4), 407–421.

OECD. (1995). *Governance in transition: Public management reform in OECD countries.* Paris: Author.

Orfield, G., Losen, D., Wald, J., & Swanson, C. (2004). *Losing our future: How minority youth are being left behind by the graduation rate crisis.* Cambridge, MA: The Civil Rights Project at Harvard University.

Parenti, C. (1999). Atlas finally shrugged: Us against them in the me decade. *The Baffler, 13,* 108–120.

Peters, M. (1994). Individualism and community: Education and the politics of difference. *Discourse, 14*(2), 65–78.

Peterson, B. (2004). Privatization, English style. *Rethinking Schools, 18*(4), 31–34.

Pinzur, M. (2003, August 8). State schools fail to meet new federal test standards: Federal, state results differ. *Miami Herald.* Retrieved from: http://www.miami.com/mld/miamiherald/6484226.htm.

Robertson, S. (2000). *A class act: Changing teachers' work, the state, and globalization.* New York: Falmer Press.

Schemo, D. J. (2004, January 28). Bush education chief defends policy and past. *The New York Times,* p. A–14.

Tabb, W. (2002). *Unequal partners: A primer on globalization.* New York: The New Press.

Thatcher, M. (1993). *The Downing Street years.* London: HarperCollins.

U.S. Department of Education, Office of Elementary and Secondary Education. (2002, September). *No child left behind: A desk reference.* Washington, DC: Author.

U.S. Department of Education, Office of the Secretary. (2002, April). *What to know and where to go: A parents' guide to no child left behind.* Washington, DC: Author.

Vilas, C. (1996). Neoliberal social policy: Managing poverty (somehow). *NACLA Report on the America, 29*(2), 16–21.

Walsh, D. (2004, May 12). *Letter to New York state legislators.* Albany: The Business Council of New York State, Inc.

Wells, A. (2002). *Where charter school policy fails: The problems of accountability and equity.* New York: Teachers College Press.

Whitfield, D. (2001). *Public services or corporate welfare.* London: Pluto Press.

Whitty, G., Power, S., & Halpin, D. (1998). *Devolution and choice in education: The school, the state and the market.* Philadelphia: Open University Press.

Winter, G. (2004, February 26). Worst rates of graduation are in New York. *The New York Times,* p. B-3.

2

"No Child Left Behind"

Globalization, Privatization, and the Politics of Inequality

Pauline Lipman

George W. Bush's blueprint to reform education, known as the *No Child Left Behind (NCLB) Act* of 2002, crystallizes key neoliberal and neoconservative business-oriented education policies. Two main components of this reauthorization of the federal Elementary and Secondary Education Act—mandatory high stakes testing and education privatization—have a long history, going back to the free-market proposals of Milton Friedman (1962), Chubb and Moe's (1990) argument for introduction of market forces and school choice, and the education reforms advocated under Reagan. Beginning with *A Nation at Risk* (National Commission, 1983) and other education reform manifestoes of the 1980s, there has been a steady push for standards, accountability, and regulation of schools, teachers, and students and an explicit linkage of corporate interests with educational practices and goals. The business rhetoric of efficiency and performance standards and the redefinition of education to serve the labor market has become the common vocabulary of education policy. Indeed, apart from Bush's failed proposal to use public funds for vouchers for private school tuition, NCLB is not unlike Clinton and Gore's emphasis on standards and tests. It was, after all, Clinton who declared Chicago, with its high-stakes testing and sanctions for failure, a model for the nation.

Scholars have examined ways in which accountability, centralized regulation, and standardization undermine democratic purposes of public education, intensify inequality, and bring schools increasingly under the economic and cultural domination of corporations (see e.g., Apple, 2001; Aronowitz & Giroux, 1993; Ascher, Fruchter & Berne, 1996; Lipman, 2004; McNeil, 2000; Molnar, 1996; Saltman, 2000). NCLB solidifies and streamlines these trends, while also promoting favorite neoconservative causes, including dismantling bilingual education, military recruitment in schools, school prayer, sexual abstinence, and attacks on gays and lesbians. In this chapter, I focus on implications of NCLB for intensified race and class inequality in the context of neoliberal globalization, the stratified labor force, and the cultural politics of racism. This analysis draws on data from the Texas state education accountability system and from Chicago's accountability-based school reform begun in 1995. Both were models for key elements of NCLB and both provide data on the effects of these policies over time.

NCLB has succeeded in redefining education reform in the United States. This is not only because it has been widely supported by politicians, neoliberal and neoconservative intellectuals, and business, but also because it speaks to real problems. Proponents justify tough accountability measures by pointing to the profound failure of public schools, particularly their failure to educate children of color (see "Don't Turn Back the Clock," 2003). Tough accountability measures suggest that something is finally being done to make sure that all children can read and do math, with schools, educators, and students held accountable for results. Tying educational programs to accountability for results (test scores) resonates with the often repeated idea that schools have not improved despite a proliferation of reforms—in Bush's words "Congress has created hundreds of programs . . . without asking whether or not the programs produce results." NCLB also follows the pervasive neoliberal logic that the market can do all things better than public institutions, from managing retirement funds, to providing health care, to running prisons. Test scores serve as a surrogate for productivity, and business is called on to supplement the work of educators, who by definition have failed.

Although these trends may dominate the agendas of school boards and education policymakers and win the battle of common sense (Gramsci, 1971), they do not go uncontested in classrooms and schools, in school districts, and in the national conversation about education. Dominant policies are never imposed or adopted unilaterally but exist in tension with both residual and emergent ideologies and policy histories and the cultures of individual schools and school districts (see Ball, 1994). I do not have space here to discuss resistance that is reflected in growing opposition to high-stakes testing coming from professional organizations (e.g., the National Council on the Social Studies and the National Council of Teachers of English), education reform groups (e.g., Fair Test and Parents United for Responsible Education in Chicago), and parents, students, and teachers (e.g., the movement against high stakes graduation tests in Massachusetts). There are also competing educational agendas in specific schools and districts. The complexity of this contention deserves an extensive analysis (see Lipman & Haines, in press, for a discussion of resistance in Chicago). My focus here is the hegemonic policies of NCLB in their 2005 iteration.

NO CHILD LEFT BEHIND

The centerpiece of NCLB is mandatory testing and a system of sanctions tied to the tests. The law requires states to test all students in Grades 3–8 and once in Grades 10–12 in reading and math. By 2006, they must also test in science. Scores must be disaggregated by subcategories that include race, special education, and English-language learners. By 2014, all students in all subcategories are to be proficient in all subjects tested. Schools in which any subgroup does not make adequate yearly progress (AYP) toward this goal are subject to a set of progressively more stringent sanctions including permitting students to transfer to another school, corrective action and pro-vision of supplemental education services, reconstitution (including replacement of school staff), and restructuring (including state take-over, reconstitution as a charter school, or private management). Although theo-retically states can design their own assessments, in practice, limited fund-ing ensures the selection of standardized tests in most cases.[1] Other key provisions are (a) all limited English-proficient students are to be tested in English after 3 years in U.S. schools, (b) students with learning difficulties (special education students) are not exempt from mandated assessments, (c) all teachers are to be "highly qualified" (certified) in their subject areas.

The conservative social agenda behind the equity rhetoric of leaving no child behind is less well known. An analysis of NCLB by Chicago Teachers for Social Justice (TSJ, 2004) reveals an ideologically driven and highly

---

[1]An exception is Nebraska which uses multiple assessments, including teacher analy-sis of student work, but Nebraska has a very small student population.

racialized "hidden" agenda.[2] This includes intensified surveillance and policing of students, militarization of schools, abstinence-based sex education, school prayer, and support for organizations with gay-exclusionary policies. Using the rationale of drug and violence prevention—real concerns of many students and parents—NCLB promotes more policing of youth rather than addressing underlying causes of violence in schools. NCLB "empowers" teachers to remove "violent or persistently disruptive students from the classroom," makes it easier for school districts and law enforcement "to share information regarding disciplinary actions and misconduct by students," establishes "Project Sentry" to "identify, prosecute, punish, and supervise juveniles who violate state and firearms laws," increases funds for "character" education, establishes the School Security Technology and Resource Center in partnership with the Sandia National Laboratory and the National Law Enforcement and Corrections Technology Center to employ new surveillance and policing technology in schools, and "shields" teachers, principals, and school board members from federal liability arising from classroom discipline practices. These measures, which primarily affect schools serving low-income students of color, the schools designated as "dangerous," are an institutionalized escalation of the surveillance of youth and the criminalization of African-American and Latino youth in particular.

At the same time, the bill requires schools to pass on to the military the student records of all high school juniors, and to give military recruiters the same access to schools and student information as colleges have. (Students can individually request to "opt out" of this requirement.) This is turning some high schools into military recruitment centers at a time when joining the military may lead to real combat. Other provisions authorize "constitutionally protected" school prayer and require schools to allow the Boy Scouts of America to use school facilities although the organization explicitly excludes gays and lesbians. The requirement that English-language learners "achieve English fluency in 3 years" runs counter to bilingual education programs that promote proficiency in the student's native language as well as English because it sanctions schools whose English-language learners do not pass mandated tests in English.

As a whole, NCLB is a mix of weak and strong state interference. It is probably best understood as what Roger Dale calls (1989–1990) "conservative modernization"—"the attempt to simultaneously 'free' individuals for economic purposes but to control them for social purposes" (p. 4). Taken together, the policies promote an unfettered market and a strong state in areas of values, standards, conduct, culture, and the body (Apple, 2001).

---

[2]The TSJ Study Group on NCLB includes: Maria Ruiz Blanco, Allison Epstein, Eric Gutstein, Pauline Lipman, Margaret Nugent, Vanessa Rangel, Greg Simmons, Kendall Taylor.

NCLB brings under one umbrella social conservatives, proponents of the market, and business interests concerned with preparation of a literate and disciplined workforce through education standards and measurement.

THE CONTEXT: GLOBALIZATION, THE RESTRUCTURED ECONOMY, AND DEEPENING INEQUALITY

The implications of NCLB can only be fully understood in relation to neoliberal globalization, the restructuring of the economy, and the changing role of the state. As a worldwide economic process, globalization is characterized by the primacy of financial and speculative capital, highly integrated and flexible systems of production of goods and services, the reorganization of the labor process, and increased mobility of transnational circuits of labor. These new dimensions of capital's historical drive to dominate national economies and world markets are a response to the structural crisis of capitalism in the early 1970s. They were facilitated by the revolution in information processing, transformations in the speed and efficiency of global transport of goods, and the dissolution of the Socialist Bloc. The goal of these processes is to open up new arenas for capital accumulation. This includes new territories (e.g., the Amazon rain forest), new spheres of social life (including education), whole economies (e.g., the former Soviet Bloc), and nature itself (i.e., seeds, native plants, the genome) while degrading labor on a global scale. This is a process David Harvey (2004) calls "accumulation by dispossession." This process is at the heart of global neoliberal economic and social policies, including education.

As a result, the politics of neoliberalism is pushing the logic of the market into every facet of social life. The neoliberal state response to the failures of Keynesian state policies and pressures of global competition for markets and investment is drastic reductions in spending for social services, government deregulation of corporations, privatization of the public sphere, environmental degradation, regressive tax policies, and attacks on organized labor. The gutting of social welfare programs and privatization of public institutions and services in the name of individual responsibility, efficiency, and freedom has opened up new investment opportunities and sources of profit on a global scale. The growth of the for-profit health care industry and the prison–industrial complex are but two examples. Education is becoming a third. These economic and social changes are degrading living standards and working conditions of millions of people, dislocating populations, and increasing social polarization along lines of race, ethnicity, gender, class, and nationality on a global scale (Gill, 2003; Harvey, 2004).

In the United States, the result of economic restructuring is simultaneous upgrading, downgrading, and exclusion of labor (Castells, 1989). A dramatic increase in service jobs, which are highly segmented by wages/salaries, education, and benefits, and a dramatic decrease in manufacturing have led to a fast rate of growth at both ends of the occupational structure. High-paid technical, professional, and managerial jobs at the upper end are tethered to an abundance of low-wage service jobs at the lower end. "Just-in-time" production, so essential to global competition, requires a flexible workforce (Ray & Mickelson, 1993) for multitask, part-time, and temporary jobs with few to no benefits. This new low-wage contingent workforce is primarily women, people of color, and immigrants, many of whom work two, three, even four part-time or temporary jobs to make ends meet. Meanwhile, the upscale lifestyles of high-income professional, managerial, and technical workers are made possible by the personal services of a bevy of these low-wage service workers (e.g., dog walkers, nannies, producers of gourmet take-out foods and custom-made clothes; Sassen, 1994).

As a whole, these trends mean that the bulk of new jobs have lower wages and less social protection than in the recent past (Castells, 1989, 1996). In the new, "dual America," economic growth is enriching the very wealthy while further driving down the wages and working conditions of the poor and working class as well as pushing down a section of the middle class. The ratio of chief executive officer pay to worker pay grew from 44.8 times in 1973 to 172.5 times in 1995 whereas real average weekly earnings for production and nonsupervisory workers went from $479.44 to $395.37 (Castells, 1998). By 1995, almost 30% of U.S. workers earned poverty-level wages (Castells, 1998), and poverty is increasingly reflected in homelessness and social exclusion. In Chicago, estimates for the late 1990s suggest that there were more than 200 workers available for every job opening that paid a living wage (Ranny, 2003). At the same time, large sections of the potential new labor force, particularly African Americans and some Latinos, are superfluous from the standpoint of capital. Many can find no work at all in the formal economy (Castells, 1989; Sassen, 1994). They have become a surplus population to be regulated, policed, and expelled from the city. I turn now to NCLB and its implications in relation to these trends.

LESSONS FROM TEXAS AND CHICAGO

George W. Bush built his reputation as an education reformer on the "Texas accountability system" (McNeil, 2000) based on the Texas Assessment of Academic Skills (TAAS) test. Actually the TAAS, preceded Bush but became the centerpiece of Texas education reform under his administration.

TAAS is a multiple-choice standardized test in reading and math. Beginning in 1994, it was given to all Texas public school students every year in Grades 3–8, and 10. Other subjects were tested in specific grades. Students had to pass the Grade 10 TAAS to graduate, and evaluation of teachers and principals and principal salaries were tied to TAAS scores. In 2003, Texas replaced the TAAS with another high-stakes test and changed the intervals at which it was given. Holding everyone's feet to the TAAS fire has been credited with the "Texas miracle"—large gains in TAAS scores and reduced gaps between the average scores of White students and students of color. NCLB is modeled on Texas.

A Closer Look at the Texas Miracle

It is important to look closely at the Texas accountability system in order to determine what it has actually accomplished and to infer what may be the implications of such a system on a national scale. If we assess the Texas miracle empirically and within its own framework, robust gains on the TAAS should show up on other achievement tests such as the National Assessment of Education Progress (NAEP), advanced placement exams, and college admission tests. There should also be reductions in grade retention, more students completing high school, and growing participation in higher education. However, recent studies suggest just the opposite. A Rand Corporation study (Klein, Hamilton, McCaffrey, & Stecher, 2000) compared the achievement gains and reductions in racial gaps on the TAAS with scores on the NAEP, which compares a representative sample of students across the nation. Although the TAAS presents a picture of very large gains for all groups of students, the Rand study found that between 1994 and 1998, the average test score gains on the NAEP in Texas exceeded the rest of the country in only one comparison, grade 4 math. Although Texas credited its reforms with reducing racial gaps on the TAAS, the Rand study found that the Texas Black–White test score gap on the NAEP in fourth-grade reading and fourth and eighth-grade math actually increased from 1994 to 1998. The Rand study found the same trend for Latinos (Hispanics), a slight increase in the gap with Whites on the NAEP. Similarly, Haney (2000) found that from 1990 to 2000 Texas students' math scores on the SAT deteriorated compared with students nationally. The authors of the Rand study concluded the following:

> Our findings from this research raise serious questions about the validity of the gains in TAAS scores. More generally, our results illustrate the danger of relying on statewide test scores as the sole measure of student achievement when these scores are used to make high-stakes decisions about teachers and schools as well as students.

Haney (2001) also found extremely high grade retention in Texas in ninth grade, the year before students took the 10th-grade TAAS which determined if they would graduate from high school. By 2000, 25–30% of African-American and Hispanic students compared with 10% of Whites were failed in Grade 9. Haney concludes, "These results clearly suggest the possibility that after 1990 schools in Texas have increasingly been failing students, disproportionately Black and Hispanic students, in grade nine in order to make their grade 10 TAAS scores look better" (p. 11). It is likely that high failure rates and grade retention would also increase the drop-out rate. There is a pattern of falling graduation rates in high-stakes states (Neil, Guisbond, & Schaeffer, 2004). According to Haney, during the 1990s (since the TAAS was phased in), slightly less than 70% of students actually graduated from high school (one in three dropped out), and the racial gap in progression from Grade 9 to graduation increased. By the time the Grade 9 cohort got to grade 12, only about 50% of African-American and Hispanic students graduated. There was also an increasing number of general education degree (GED) test-takers under age 20 (who are not counted as dropouts in Texas). Haney also found that Texas dramatically increased the number of students classified as special education between 1998 and 1999, thus eliminating these students' scores. Haney contends these data suggest that improved pass rates on the 10th-grade TAAS and reductions in racial gaps in the pass rate may be the result of classifying students as special education and retaining high percentages of Black and Latino students.

Thus, rather than increasing the graduation rate, the TAAS may have worsened it, especially for African-American and Hispanic students.[3] In 2003, this outcome became public when Robert Kimball, an assistant principal in Sharpstown High School in Houston, Texas, revealed that the school's freshman class of 1,000 had decreased to 300 by senior year, yet the school reported zero dropouts, as did other high schools in the city. Based on Dr. Kimball's revelations the local media broke the story that Sharpstown had falsified its data and a state audit revealed that of 5,500 students who left school, 3,000 should have been classified as dropouts but were not (Winerp, 2003). Moreover, Haney noted that three separate studies (Haney, 2001; National Center for Public Policy, 2000; University of Texas, 1999) showed that the Texas educational system under TAAS had not been very successful for those who did graduate. It made little progress relative to the rest of the United States on preparation for and participation in higher education. In

---

[3]Haney argues the same pattern occurs with the new Regents high school exit exam in New York. He finds the exam is a likely cause of graduation rates plummeting from more than 60% in 1987-1988 to less than 50% in 2001-2002, with the worst consequences for African Americans and Latinos who have a graduation rate of less than 40% (Haney, 2003).

short, recent studies indicate that Texas' system of high-stakes testing, the prototype for NCLB, has not increased academic achievement as measured on standardized tests. The studies also point to increasing racial inequality, high dropout rates, and poor preparation for college, yet Texas is the prototype for NCLB.

"YOU CAN'T FATTEN A PIG BY PUTTING IT ON A SCALE": HIGH-STAKES TESTS AND EDUCATIONAL STRATIFICATION

When the fate of individual students, teachers, principals, and schools hinges on the results of a single, high-stakes test, that test becomes the center of teaching and learning. McNeil's (2000) ethnographic account of Houston high schools and my study of Chicago elementary schools (Lipman, 2004) provide a picture of teachers and administrators pressured to gear teaching and curriculum to passing high-stakes tests. This is especially so in low-scoring schools serving low-income students of color. For example, McNeil reports that a low-scoring school serving primarily Mexican-American students had no library, a shortage of texts and little laboratory equipment, yet administrators spent $20,000 for commercial test-preparation books. McNeil (2000) describes the educational consequences in Texas:

> The clear picture that emerges is that the standardized reforms drastically hurt the best teachers, forcing them to teach watered down content because it was computer gradable. The standardization brought about by the state policies forced them to teach artificially simplified curricula that had been designed by bureaucrats seeking expedient (easily implemented, noncontroversial) curricular formats. The quality of their teaching, their course content and their students' learning all suffered. In addition, those relations within the school essential to fostering a culture of both equity and authentic academics were undermined. (p. 192)

Similarly, Robert Hauser (1999), chair of the Committee on Appropriate Test Use of the Board of Testing and Assessment at the National Research Council (NRC), reported that "The NRC Committee concluded that Chicago's regular year and summer school curricula were so closely geared to the ITBS [Iowa Test of Basic Skills—Chicago's high-stakes test] that it was impossible to distinguish real subject mastery from mastery of skills and knowledge useful for passing this particular test."

While education geared to standardized tests degrades the work of the best teachers, it is little help to the weakest teachers, because it does not increase their knowledge, skill, or commitment to richer teaching and learning. Nor do high-stakes tests address the huge inequalities between affluent schools and low-income and urban schools. In Chicago, my data suggested that the domination of high-stakes tests exacerbated inequalities in curriculum and instruction between affluent, selective schools and low-income schools and masked unequal opportunities to learn (see also Neil et al., 2004). As one Chicago teacher said, "You can't fatten a pig by putting it on a scale."

Although high-stakes testing potentially degrades education for all students, it is having the most drastic consequences in low-achieving schools that are compelled to use test-preparation materials as texts, narrowly focus on the tasks that are tested, concentrate much class time on test-taking skills, and reduce learning to passing the tests (see Lipman, 2004; McNeil, 2000). The students in these schools are generally low-income African Americans and Latinos who are now being held responsible for the systemic racism, class oppression, second-class schooling, deindustrialization, and disinvestment in their communities. Meanwhile, high-scoring schools (generally also more affluent and more White) are relatively more free to maintain a richer, more holistic, and less test-driven curriculum. This is demonstrated by New York's Board of Education 2003 mandate that all its 1,291 schools follow a standard curriculum—except for 208 exempt schools, five-sixths of which are in middle or upper income neighborhoods (Hoff, 2003). In Chicago in 2003, local control over curriculum and budgets in low-scoring schools (the majority of schools) was given to central office-appointed area instructional officers. At the same time, high-scoring schools (which generally have more affluent students and/or selective enrollments) got more flexibility. These are examples of how an accountability system, as mandated by NCLB, further institutionalizes educational inequality and may widen disparities in students' educational experiences.

Nor does disaggregation of test data by race, as required by NCLB, necessarily lead to improving the education of children of color. In fact, in Chicago there is evidence that it may contribute to the intensification of racism and racialized blame. Teachers report that in some schools the disaggregation of data has resulted in some teachers and parents blaming African-American and Latino students for bringing down the school's scores.[4] Just exposing racial disparities may lead to little change unless educators and parents examine together the underlying ideologies, structures, school norms, and practices, and dominant assumptions responsible for the marginalization and low-achievement of students of color, immigrants, and language minority students. In fact, in the context of systemic racism and NCLB's focus on individual students, I found that disaggregated test scores in a

---

[4]Report of teachers at a forum on No Child Left Behind sponsored by Chicago Teachers for Social Justice, November 2003.

Chicago school that supposedly "worked" for white and middle-class students reinforced the belief that those for whom the school was not "working" had something wrong with them. It led to a focus on improving these "deficient" individuals rather than looking at what was going on in the school (Lipman, 2004). If the record of centralized accountability in Chicago and Texas is to intensify educational inequality, push out students of color, and reduce education to test preparation, particularly in low-income schools, the results of NCLB may be to increase the stratification of educational experiences nationally. This has significant implications in a highly stratified labor market.

ACCOUNTABILITY AND THE LABOR MARKET

Economic restructuring has created a highly segmented workforce and polarized social structure along lines of class, race, national origin, and gender. Although a majority of growing occupations are projected to require education or training beyond high school, there is expected to be only a modest change in educational levels for all new jobs. Contrary to claims about the need to prepare all students to be postindustrial knowledge workers (National Center on Education and the Economy, 1990), the bulk of jobs do not require sophisticated new knowledge but basic literacies, ability to follow directions, and certain (accommodating) dispositions toward work. A national system of standardized tests with strict penalties for failure helps to ensure a workforce that has the basic literacies and compliant dispositions needed by the low-wage labor force (Ray & Mickelson, 1993).

NCLB's focus on competency in reading and math is aligned with skills needed for many low-wage service and manufacturing jobs. For example, the majority of 51 urban and suburban Chicago employers interviewed in 1997 said they needed employees with "eighth-grade math skills and better than eighth-grade reading and writing skills" (Rosenbaum & Binder, 1997, p. 73). In the Fordist, industrial era, workers primarily needed specific, job-related skills (such as welding), but rapid technological advances in informational technology require service and production workers who can adapt to changing job demands and changing jobs. Good reading skills (and sometimes math skills) are necessary for many of these jobs and for adapting to the constantly changing nature of work. Dale (1989/1990) argues that the shift to neoliberal accountability and testing reforms in Britain was intended to serve capital accumulation by ensuring " basic literacy, numeracy and a sufficient acquaintance with information technology to enable adequate performance of consumption as well as production and service roles in those parts of the economy that become 'post-industrialized'" (p. 8). The same could be said for NCLB.

NCLB is explicitly designed to meet the needs and technical rationality of business. Secretary of Education, Rod Paige (2004), speaking to business leaders, put it succinctly: "Like a successful business, the No child Left Behind Act introduced measurement of progress, made the system transparent and accountable, and introduced consumer choice." Discursively, the policies define education as a commodity whose production can be quantified, standardized, and prescribed. Symbolically, as well as practically, national testing constitutes a system of quality control, verifying that those who survive the gauntlet of tests and graduate have the literacies and dispositions business requires. A system of individual accountability and test-driven curricula also works as a program of social discipline for an obedient labor force.

In the face of growing economic polarization, if NCLB results in more dropping out, test-driven teaching, and curriculum dualization, it will widen the gap between White and middle-class students and low-income students of color. This is at a time when one's intellectual resources are a key determinant of whether one will be a high-paid knowledge worker or part of the downgraded sector of labor, and education is central to who has which job. The boredom and regimentation of schooling geared to standardized tests also serves to weed out youth who are already largely dispensable in the restructured economy and are socially marginalized. These are primarily African Americans and Latinos. If Bush's policies succeed in driving more of these students out of school, as evidence from Texas suggests, they will push them into the surplus labor force and the informal economy and make more youth of color targets of police enforcement, criminalization, and prison (Parenti, 1999).

Gearing schools to labor force preparation also undermines democratic and social purposes of education. Linda McNeil (2000) reminds us that a whole generation of students now graduating in Texas has known no other kind of education than that dominated by policies that structure out "the possibility for discussing student learning in terms of cognitive and intellectual development, in terms of growth, in terms of social awareness and social conscience, in terms of social and emotional development" (p. 262). As Henry Giroux (2003) points out, we are witnessing the end of any notion of education as a public space to critically engage ideas and prepare students for thoughtful democratic participation. In a case study Eric Gutstein and I did of a Chicago elementary school serving Mexican immigrants (Lipman, 2004), we found that high-stakes tests further constrained teachers' opportunities to develop critical approaches to knowledge. Teaching directed to standardized test preparation promoted an emphasis on one right answer, speed over thoughtfulness, and a standardized definition of what constituted legitimate knowledge. Test preparation countered knowledge as socially constructed, education as dialogue and debate among multiple perspectives, and curriculum that was socially/culturally situated. Yet, these are precisely the kinds of educational experiences students need to help them think critically and ethically about the inequalities that structure their life chances.

Gutstein and I also found that standards and accountability undermined curricula and pedagogies rooted in the language, culture, lived experiences, and identities of Mexican/Mexican-American students. Our data suggest that policies that mandate acquisition of academic English in 3 years (i.e., NCLB requires testing in English after 3 years in U.S. schools) not only fly in the face of research on effective bilingual education (Cummins, 2000), they concretely and symbolically devalued students' home languages. In the school we studied, the pressure to pass standardized tests in English was so intense that even bilingual Mexican teachers sacrificed the Spanish fluency of their own children. Although the policy is part of a conservative attack on bilingualism and multiculturalism, it also serves business' demand for an assimilated and easily managed (i.e., English-speaking) workforce.

NCLB AND THE MARKETIZATION OF EDUCATION

The end of Keynsian economic policies and welfare state provisions has had significant implications for the privatization of education. Morrow and Torres (2000) remind us that "Thatcherism and Reaganism became the ideological reference points for a vast process of restructuring that reduced demands on the welfare states and provided more flexible regulatory environment within which globalizing economic process could proceed with fewer obstacles" (p. 37). Education privatization is one result of the hollowed-out neoliberal state and the marketization of the public sphere, and NCLB is a significant step toward this agenda.

In Bush's original proposal for NCLB, federal Title I funds were to be used for vouchers that students in failing schools would be able to use to attend private schools or to receive educational services from private providers. The proposed bill also included funding for charter school startups, a fund to promote "school choice," and increase in the ceiling on tax-free education savings accounts that could be used for K–12 private school as well as college tuition. In the final version, the most blatant privatization measures, particularly vouchers, were eliminated. Instead, as others have argued (Karp, 2002; Saltman, 2005), NCLB introduces privatization through the back door. First, sanctions for failing to meet AYP open up schools to corporate penetration through contracts for a variety of educational services. In addition to the enormous profits for testing and textbook companies, setting up and monitoring accountability systems is big business. For example, Standard and Poors, a division of McGraw-Hill Corp., won a U.S.

Department of Education $55.6 million contract to help states and districts analyze student performance data for NCLB. NCLB has also created a flourishing market in tutoring and remediation services because schools that don't make AYP for 3 years must use part of their Title I funds to purchase these services from an outside provider such as Kaplan or Sylvan Learning Corp.

Second, the requirement that students in schools that do not meet AYP requirements be allowed to transfer to nonfailing schools is likely to provide a powerful rationale for the direct corporate take over of public education. In Chicago in 2003, 270,757 student were eligible to transfer but there were just 1,097 slots in nonfailing schools. Only 300 students actually transferred. The inevitable failure of schools to meet impossible AYP targets, particularly without significant new resources, and the lack of nonfailing schools to accept transferring students provides "proof" that public education does not work. In this context, turning schools over to the market, which supposedly can do a better job, will be a commonsense solution. This is the same chain of events that justified dismantling public housing and ending public assistance to the poor. Also, schools that fail for 5 years are "restructured," which can mean everything from state takeover to being put under private management or turned into privately run charter operations.

This scenario is already playing out in Chicago. The persistent failure of schools to meet test score benchmarks has become a rationale to dismantle them and replace them with privatized versions. In July 2003, the Civic Committee of the Commercial Club of Chicago, an organization of the most powerful financial and corporate interests and elite civic leaders in Chicago, called for the creation of at least 100 public charter schools to "increase parental choice and put meaningful competitive pressure on chronically failing neighborhood schools" (Civic Committee, 2003). In June 2004 Mayor Daley announced at an event hosted by the Commercial Club, that Chicago would indeed turn 100 schools, mostly in low-income African-American communities in the process of gentrification, into "new" schools. Under the plan, called Renaissance 2010, two thirds would be charter or contract schools that would be run by independent operators of Chicago Public Schools (CPS) (i.e., by nonprofit or for-private organizations). Daley hailed the plan as a bold move that would "bring in outside partners who want to get into the business of education." These schools would not be required to have local school councils, the grassroots governance bodies composed of majority parents and community residents that were instituted by the Chicago School Reform law of 1988, nor would they be bound by union contracts or other district regulations. In short, the plan, called Renaissance 2010, will reduce labor costs at school employees' expense, weaken unions, and undermine local control of schools and the potential of real accountability through local school councils. It will open up a new public arena to the market.

Third, NCLB lays the ideological groundwork for marketization. The option to transfer out of a "failing" or "dangerous school and to "choose" another school "facilitate(s) a shift from collectivism to individualism, from a view that a common school is desirable to one that encourages parent/consumers to shop around and maximize their children's opportunities of enjoying an "uncommon" education" (Dale, 1989/1990, pp. 12–13). NCLB establishes a framework to officially rank schools that allows parents to identify and jockey for choices. As Dale notes in relation to Thatcher's project in education in England, "Before education can be brought into the market place and made subject to consumer choice, a range of possible alternatives has to be created" (p. 9). Choice is the central feature of Chicago's Renaissance 2010. And if choices aren't sufficient, parents and teachers are offered the option to get into the school business themselves and open a charter school. At a town hall meeting on Chicago's south side at which African-American parents protested the plan, school officials encouraged concerned principals to be entrepreneurs and submit a proposal to run one of the new schools.

In summary, NCLB is the essence of a neoliberal policy process. It uses the past failure of the public sector to meet social needs to justify harsh measures. It mandates accountability as a radical corrective, then uses the inevitable failure to meet accountability standards to justify privatization.[5] Schools that are not run by businesses may become public shells—public schools with many educational services privatized (e.g., teaching, curriculum, special services), union contracts nullified, and all of it paid for by public tax dollars.

The Record on Vouchers

Although Bush failed to make vouchers a centerpiece of NCLB, it is worth examining vouchers because they may be the endpoint of NCLB after all. Even within narrow notions of academic achievement, there is no compelling evidence to support the claim that voucher programs are effective. Witte's annual evaluations of the highly publicized Milwaukee voucher plan from 1991 to 1995 found no gains in achievement for students who used vouchers to attend private schools as compared with Milwaukee public school students as a whole (Olson, 1996).[6] Studies on privately funded

---

[5]Secretary of Education, Rod Paige, explicitly made this argument in a June 2004 speech to business leaders (Paige, 2004).

[6]A counter evaluation by Paul Peterson and others who advocate vouchers reported students gained in achievement in their third and fourth years in the voucher plan; however Peterson's study is of a very small sample of students in only three private schools who were not compared with MPS students as a whole but with students who had failed to get into private schools with vouchers (Olson, 1996).

voucher plans in New York, Washington, Cleveland, and Dayton, Ohio are also inconclusive. A study of the Cleveland voucher plan by researchers from the University of Indiana found that the academic performance of kids in corporate-run schools in the voucher plan was dramatically lower in math, reading, science, social studies, and language skills than Cleveland public school students (Walsh, 1998). And in Baltimore where Education Alternatives Inc. (EAI) took over or was consultant to 12 public schools, researchers found EAI was more expensive with no better results. To cut costs, EAI eliminated teaching and counseling positions and replaced experienced paraprofessionals who lived in the neighborhood with interns. Levin also found that for-profit education companies cut costs by hiring less experienced teachers, standardizing curriculum and recruiting less demanding students (e.g., students with learning needs and disabilities) (Saltman, 2005).

International evidence on voucher and private school choice indicates that they also make access to quality education more unequal by race and class. Whitty, Power, and Halpin (1999) conclude that in Sweden and England voucher plans increase social segregation by race and class as private schools choose public school students who are middle class and White. Blackmore draws the same conclusion in Australia: "paradoxically, the market exacerbates differences between schools on the basis of class, race, and ethnicity, but does not encourage diversity in image, clientele, organization, curriculum or pedagogy" (cited in Whitty et al., 1999, p. 120). Those with various forms of socially valued capital (material resources, time, knowledge, "whiteness," fluency in English, strong academic and discipline records, lack of "disability," etc.) benefit. Indeed, throwing more students into the private school market with public funds allows these schools to be even more selective. Even if getting a voucher to attend a private school may be a solution for a few students, it cannot solve the problem of quality education for all students. Vouchers will withdraw money from already drastically underfunded public schools leaving the remaining students with even fewer resources while transferring public funds to corporations. This is already happening in Chicago in schools that are forced to use Title I funds for contracted-out supplemental education services. Nor will competition for students necessarily spur public schools to improve, as has been demonstrated by the failure of competition in the health care industry, for example.

Real choice through vouchers or charters is also an illusion. Few public school students, particularly urban students of color, will be trading in their vouchers for admission to an elite private school whose tuition is far more than the per pupil expenditure in urban school districts. Nor are they likely to get into good parochial schools that already have long waiting lists and are likely to become more selective with the windfall of voucher applicants. Unlike public schools, private schools have the option to choose their students, and they are not obligated to provided services for students who speak languages other than English or for students with disabilities. Some kind of selection process is also necessary for charter and contract schools. There is already a waiting list for Chicago's existing charters. Finally, although vouchers and charters are promoted as a solution for low-income students, these students are being used to pry open the door to privatizing public education in general and creating greater educational inequalities as a result. In some cases, community organizations and teachers have opened culturally relevant, social-justice oriented charter schools, but these schools face a fierce counter stream of overarching neoliberal policy (Wells, Scott, Lopez, & Holme, 2005).

In summary, NCLB's privatization measures promise to intensify racial, ethnic, and class inequalities and create a dual system, as has happened with the corporatization of health care through health maintenance organization's and for-profit hospitals. Apple (1996) argues there will be relatively elite, unregulated private schools for the wealthy and increasingly regulated minimalist public schools and new corporate-run schools for low-income children of color in urban areas. "[These] schools will be tightly controlled and policed, and will continue to be under funded and unlinked to decent paid employment" (p. 29). A dual system is ideally suited to an economically and socially polarized society. As Whitty et al. argue "the main purpose of the recent moves toward greater choice is not to build a more fair and generous educational system but to put an end to egalitarianism, and rebuild a differentiated educational system that will more closely aid social reproduction" (Wolford, cited in Whitty et al., 1999, p. 124). They go on to point out that "the ideology of choice, which implies that anyone can benefit, acts partially to mask and thus legitimate this process."

NCLB AND THE GLOBAL NEOLIBERAL AGENDA

Neoliberalism reframes all social relations, all forms of knowledge and culture in the terms of the market. All services established for the common good are potential targets of investment and profit-making. In the discourse of neoliberalism, the society becomes synonymous with the market, democracy is equated with consumer choice, and the common good is replaced by individual advantage. This is the essence of NCLB provisions that open up public education to a massive transfer of public funds to corporations. Education has been growing as a major new investment sector, and NCLB is a boon to the corporate education industry. The U.S. investment in learning (everything from corporate training to teaching kids) is more than is spent on defense. A 1998 *Fortune* magazine article reported: "Many analysts believe that education, broadly defined, will emerge as one of the leading investment sectors over the next 20 years . . . comparable to, say, the health-care industry over the past 20" (Justin, 1998, p. 198). Secretary of Education, Rod Paige, (2004) speaking about NCLB, made the point: "It's time we recognize a central, cardinal fact: education is a big business."

The full import of this comment should be interpreted in relation to global neoliberal trade policies, particularly the General Agreement on Trade in Services (GATS)—a 1994 World Trade Organization (WTO) multilateral agreement on liberalizing trade in services—and the Free Trade Act of the Americas (FTAA). Under GATS, for the first time, services, including education, are regarded as commodities (Robertson, Bonal, & Dale, 2002). Any institution that involves payment of fees, even in a public system, is considered a commercial activity and must be open to the market without state interference. Initially, GATS may mainly expedite the penetration of developing countries' education systems by U.S. and European capital. However, as sectors of U.S. education become privatized (e.g., supplemental educational services), GATS can be used to open up the whole system to the market. Similarly, the FTAA requires participating nations to allow private competition with government services if those services have any private component. Saltman (2004) argues that this would include all public schools because they have some private contracts. NCLB's privatization measures would facilitate this.

GATS and FTAA are also about the control of knowledge production through global sales of textbooks, educational media such as Channel One, and commercially produced curricula. Again, the mandate under NCLB that failing schools purchase supplemental education services, including remediation and tutoring, and the pressure to gear teaching to high-stakes tests, opens up the U.S. education system to even greater corporate control of knowledge. It authorizes corporations to define the purposes of education, determine what knowledge is legitimate,, and set the parameters of social relations and discourse in schools (see Saltman, 2000).

DISCIPLINING AND CRIMINALIZING YOUTH: THE POLITICS OF RACE

Globalization is producing impoverishment, social dislocation, destruction of traditional ways of life, devastation of whole countries, possibly irreversible environmental degradation, intensified exploitation, and unfathomable disparities of wealth and poverty within and among nations. These conditions have spawned growing resistance both globally and locally. The brutal suppression of demonstrators at WTO conferences in Seattle, Genoa, and Davros and at meetings of other supranational finance and trade organizations leaves no doubt that those who organize and benefit from globalization intend to use force as well as false promises to control those for whom the new global order produces devastation and impoverishment. The intensification of policing and imprisonment of African-American males, in particular, is also an effort to control the crisis in Black communities created by disinvestment and deindustrialization over the past 25 years. As Gill (2003), Harvey (2004), McLaren (1999), and others point out, because of its inherent contradictions, globalization is accompanied by efforts to strengthen the state against civil society by increasing the power of the police, building more prisons, and increasing surveillance. NCLB's tough discipline policies and further integration of schools with police and the juvenile court system are part of a discourse of regulation and enforcement that permeates the entire education blueprint. Everyone from students and teachers to schools and states will be subject to punishments and rewards meted out by the federal government. The authoritarian character of the plan as a whole (despite the rhetoric of choice) reflects the intersection of the conservative impulse to re-establish order and hierarchies (Apple, 1996) and the needs of the neoliberal state to address problems of control, authority, and legitimacy in a nation ripe with potentially explosive contradictions.

This is racialized social control. With whole sectors of African-American and some immigrant communities relegated to the informal economy or marginal positions in the formal economy and confined to disinvested urban areas or decaying ring suburbs, the state needs strict enforcement policies as well as forms of legitimation. NCLB employs these dual tactics, merging discourses of equity and stepped-up policing of youth of color. The focus on youth is important. Just as globally "it has become possible for vast tracts of humanity to be dismissed now as simply having nothing of relevance to contribute to the new world economy" (Gee, Hull, & Lankshear, 1996, p. 149), many African American and Latino youth are, from the perspective of capital, largely irrelevant (in fact, problematic) in the new economy and the social landscape of major U.S. cities.

In "global cities" (Sassen, 1994), command centers of the global economy, attracting high-paid technical, professional, and managerial workers is dependent on securing gentrified enclaves against those to whom the global economy offers little but dreams of consumption. At the same time, as Saskia Sassen (1998) argues, the global city is a strategic site for those who are disempowered because "it enables them to gain presence, to emerge as subjects, even when they do not gain direct power. Immigrants, women, African Americans in U.S. cities, people of color, oppressed minorities emerge as significant subjects in a way they are unlikely to do in a suburban context or small town" (p. xxi). The claims on the economy and urban areas increasingly dominated by high-paid knowledge workers, international business people, and tourists pose a potential challenge to capital and to the state. This challenge has been explicit in sporadic urban rebellions over the past 15 years (e.g., Los Angeles and Cincinnati). In this context, NCLB further criminalizes "disruptive" students in order to weed out those that capital writes off as extraneous yet "dangerous." At the same time charter schools and choice plans legitimate the educational disenfranchisement of low-income students of color while enticing the new urban gentry to gentrify the city (Lipman, 2002).

These policies are not simply motivated by economic interest. They represent cultural struggles over race, ethnicity, and power that are intensified by the contradictions of neoliberal globalization. The subtext of gentrification, militarization of urban high schools, regimented curriculum, zero-tolerance discipline policies, and the criminalization of youth is the white supremacist desire to police and contain those who threaten "white places" of order and civility (Haymes, 1995). African-American youth (and some Latinos) are pathologized and constructed as needing special forms of regulation and control. The African-American, Latino, and other youth of color who make up the majority of the 20 largest school districts, are disproportionately suspended and expelled from school, and often attend schools that are more like jails than educational institutions, are certainly the target of "safe schools" policies. With more African-American youth headed for prisons than college, African Americans and some Latinos are the youth from whom "our" schools are to be made safe, whose school records become police records and whose police records become school records. These are youth whom teachers and schools can punish without liability. In a hyperracialized context, NCLB provides a common sense solution to "discipline problems," diverting attention from underlying social, economic, and ideological roots of oppression and resistance.

CONCLUSION

I have argued that NCLB further integrates education into a global and national neoliberal agenda. It also intensifies the war on youth of color. NCLB is rooted in global competition over markets and investments (the Bush Administration is quite explicit about this; see Paige, 2004) and in cultural struggles over race, ethnicity, language, and national identity. By framing education in the language of accountability and choice, NCLB further consolidates—materially and ideologically—corporate control of education for profit. NCLB policies and the discourse surrounding them become a "discourse policy" directed to society as a whole, defining educational problems and their solutions so as to limit the possibilities we have of thinking and acting otherwise (Ball, 1994). When we step outside this hegemonic discourse, we can only be outraged at the inevitable suffering and loss, the shameful waste of a generation sacrificed at the altar of greed and racism that is cynically promoted under the slogan "Leave No Child Behind."

An alternative discourse rooted in social justice would speak to the real urgency to address the profound inequalities and miseducation that define public schools. It would propose massive new funds and programs to rebuild crumbling urban schools, to drastically reduce classes sizes of 35 to 40 students, to vastly improve the quality of science and technology in the poorest schools where there are often no science labs or lab equipment and little technology, to fund the further education and increase the salaries and professional working conditions of teachers; to build school libraries, arts and athletics programs and facilities in underfunded urban and rural schools. An alternative discourse would focus on fostering rich scientific and mathematical literacies; knowledge of history and society, of arts and literature, and the ability to examine knowledge critically from multiple perspectives. It would call for schools that encourage students to ask questions as well as answer them; that require students to use knowledge to work on real-world problems of personal, social, and ethical significance; that respect and build on students' cultures, languages, experiences — schools that give them the tools to survive and struggle against race and class inequalities and injustices.

Critical scholarship over the past 30 years has illuminated the ways in which public schools reproduce race, gender, and class inequality. It is important to criticize public schools while defending the institution of universal public education and its democratic potential. With all their profound failures, public schools can be forums for democratic public debate about what kind of society we want. Public education policy has historically been an important arena of struggle over issues of difference, the rights of oppressed groups, what constitutes culture and history, how identities are to be represented publicly, and how the common good is defined. Although contentious, debates about language, race, gender, sexual orientation, "disability," immigration, cultural diversity, school knowledge, sexuality, civic responsibility, connections between schools and communities, and so on, are critical to strengthening democratic civic life. Unlike the private sector, public schools can't avoid these debates. As Henig notes, the real danger of policies that privatize education and throw it into the corporate market is that they "will erode the public forums in which decisions with social consequence can be democratically resolved" (cited in Asher et al., 1996, p. 9). In a world circled ever more tightly by the forces of global capital and facing the catastrophe of unlimited imperial wars, the institution of universal, free public schools needs to be fought *for* as a democratic public space and fought *over* ideologically. The popular appeal of the Bush agenda is that it makes sense in the absence of a sharply defined alternative discourse that not only reframes education in the language of democracy and social justice, but rethinks schooling in relation to the racial, ethnic, gender, and class oppression and conflict of the present (global) moment.

REFERENCES

Apple, M. (1996). *Cultural politics and education.* New York: Teachers College Press.

Apple, M. W. (2001). *Educating the "right" way.* New York: Routledge.

Aronowitz, S., & Giroux, H. A. (1993). *Education still under siege* (2nd ed.). Westport, CT: Bergin & Garvey.

Ascher, C., Fruchter, N., & Berne, R. (1996). *Hard lessons: Public schools and privatization.* New York: Twentieth Century Fund.

Ball, S. J. (1994). *Education reform: A critical and post-structural approach.* Buckingham, England: Open University Press.

No Child Left Behind. U.S. Department of Education. [On-line]. Available: http://www.ed.gov/inits/nclb

Castells, M. (1989). *The informational city.* London: Blackwell.

Castells, M. (1998). *End of the millennium.* London: Blackwell.

Chubb, J., & Moe, T. (1990). *Politics, markets, and America's schools.* Washington, DC: Brookings Institute.

Civic Committee of the Commercial Club of Chicago. (2003, July). *Left behind* (A report of the Education Committee). Chicago: Author. Retrieved from http://www.commercialclubchicago.org/civiccommittee/initiatives/education/studentachievement.html

Cummins, J. (2000). *Language, power and pedagogy.* Clevedon, UK: Multilingual Matters Ltd.

Dale, R. (1989/1990). The Thatcherite project in education: The case of the City Technology Colleges. *Critical Social Policy, 9*(3), 4–19.

Don't turn back the clock. (2003). Education Trust. Available: http//www.edtrust.org

Friedman, M. (1962). *Capitalism and freedom.* Chicago: University of Chicago Press.

Gee, J. P., Hull, G., & Lankshear, C. (1996). *The new work order: Behind the language of the new capitalism.* Boulder, CO: Westview Press.

Gill, S. (2003). *Power and resistance in the new world order.* New York: Palgrave Macmillan.

Giroux, H. (2003). *Public spaces, private lives: Democracy beyond 9.11.* Lanham, MD: Rowman & Littlefield.

Gramsci, A. (1971). *Selections from the Prison Notebooks.* New York: International Publishers.

Haney, W. (2000). The myth of the Texas miracle in education. *Educational Policy Archives, 8*(41). Retrieved from: http://epaa.asu.edu/epaa/v8n41

Haney, W. (2001). *Revisiting the myth of the Texas miracle in education: Lessons about dropout research and dropout prevention.* Paper prepared for the "Dropout Research: Accurate Counts and Positive Interventions" Conference sponsored by Achieve and the Harvard Civil Rights Project, Cambridge.

Haney, W. (2003). Attrition of students from New York schools. Invited testimony before New York Senate Standing Committee on Education, September 23, 2003. On-line. Available: http://www.timeoutfromtesting.org/testimonies/923_ Testimony_Haney.pdf

Harvey, D. (2004). *The new imperialism.* Oxford. Oxford University Press.

Haymes, S. N. (1995). *Race, culture and the city.* Albany: State University of New York Press.

Hoff, D. J. (2003, March 9). Complaints pour in over NYC curriculum exemptions. *Education Week.* Retrieved March 14, 2003, from http://www.edweek.org.

Justin, M. (1998, July 6). Lifelong learning spells earnings. *Fortune, 138*(1), 197– 200.

Karp, S. (2002). Let them eat tests. *Rethinking Schools.* [On-line]. Available: http://www.rethinkingschools.org/special reports/bushplan/Eat164/shtml

Klein, S.P., Hamilton, L.S., McCaffrey, D.F., & Stecher, B.M. (2000). What do test scores in Texas tell us? Issue Paper, Rand Corporation. Retrieved from http://www.readn.org/publications.IP/IP202/

Lipman, P. (2002). Making the global city, making inequality: The political economy and cultural politics of Chicago school policy. *American Educational Research Journal, 39*(2), 379–419.

Lipman, P. (2004). *High stakes education: Inequality, globalization, and urban school reform.* New York: Routledge.

Lipman, P., & Haines, N. (in press). From accountability to privatization and African American education—Chicago Public Schools' Renaissance 2010. *Educational Policy.*

McLaren, P. (1999). Traumatizing capital: Oppositional pedagogies in the age of consent. In M. Castells et al. (Eds.), *Critical education in the new information age,* (pp. 1–36). Lanham, MD: Rowman & Littlefield.

McNeil, L. M. (2000). *Contradictions of school reform: Educational costs of standardized testing.* New York: Routledge.

Molnar, A. (1996). *Giving kids the business: The commercialization of America's schools.* Boulder, CO: Westview Press:

Morrow, R. A., & Torres, C. A. (2000). The state, globalization, and educational policy. In N.C. Burbules & C. A. Torres (Eds.), *Globalization and education: Critical perspectives* (pp. 27–56). New York: Routledge.

National Center for Public Policy and Higher Education. (2000). *Measuring up: the state-by-state report card for higher education.* Washington, DC: Author.

National Center on Education and the Economy. (1990). *America's choice: High skills or low wages.* Rochester, NY: Author.

National Commission on Excellence in Education. (1983). *A nation at risk: The imperative for educational reform.* Washington, DC: U.S. Government Printing Office.

Neil, M., Guisbond, L., & Schaeffer, B. (2004). *Failing our children: How "No Child Left Behind" undermines quality and equity in education.* Cambridge, MA: Fair Test, National Center for Fair and Open Testing.

Olson, L. (1996, September 4). New studies on private choice contradict each other. *Education Week.* [On-line]. Available: http://www.edweek.org/ew/1996/ 01choice.h16

Paige, R. (2004, June 26). Remarks by Secretary Paige at the Executive Leaders Forum, Committee of 100, San Francisco Chamber of Commerce. Available: http://www.ed.gov/news/speeches/2004/06/06282004.html

Parenti, C. (1999). *Lockdown America: Police and prisons in the age of crisis*. London: Verso.

Ranny, D. (2003). *Global decisions, local collisions: Urban life in the New World Order*. Philadelphia: Temple University Press.

Robertson, S. L., Bonal, X., & Dale, R. (2002). GATS and the education service industry: The politics of scale and global reterritorialization. *Comparative Education Review, 46*(4), 472–496.

Ray, C. A., & Mickelson, R. A. (1993). Restructuring students for restructured work: The economy, school reform, and non-college-bound youths. *Sociology of Education, 66*, 1–20.

Rosenbaum, J. E., & Binder, A. (1997). Do employers really need more educated youth? *Sociology of Education, 70*, 68–75.

Saltman, K. J. (2000). *Collateral damage: Corporatizing public schools—a threat to democracy*. Lanham, MD: Rowman & Littlefield.

Saltman, K. (2005). *The Edison Schools: Corporate schools and the assault on public education*. New York: Routledge Falmer.

Sassen, S. (1994). *Cities in a world economy*. Thousand Oaks, CA: Pine Forge Press.

Sassen, S. (1998). *Globalization and its discontents*. New York: The New Press.

Teachers for Social Justice (TSJ). (2004). No Child Left Behind talking points. Chicago: Author. Online. Available: www.teachersforjustice.org

University of Texas System. (1999, February 10). Presentation to the Education Subcommittee of the House Appropriations Committee. Austin, TX: Author.

Walsh, M. (1998, December). Vouchers yield mixed results. *Education Week*. [Online]. Retrieved from http://www.edweek.org/ew/Vol-18/14vouch.h18

Whitty, G., Power, S., & Halpin, D. (1999). *Devolution and choice in education: The school, the state, and the market*. Buckingham, England: Open University Press.

Winerp, M. (2003). Houston's "zero dropout." *Rethinking Schools, 18*(1), 8.

3

Education and the New Disciplinarity

Surveillance, Spectacle, and the Case of SBER

Kevin D. Vinson

E. Wayne Ross

Antiquity had been a civilization of spectacle. *"To render accessible to a multitude of men [sic] the inspection of a small number of objects"* (italics added): this was the problem to which the architecture of temples, theaters, and circuses responded. With spectacle, there was a predominance of public life, the intensity of festivals, sensual proximity. In these rituals in which blood flowed, society found new vigour and formed for a moment a single great body. The modern age poses the opposite problem: *"To procure for a small number, or even for a single individual, the instantaneous view of a great multitude"* (italics added). In a society in which the principal elements are no longer the community and public life, but, on the one hand, private individuals and, on the other, the state, relations can be regulated only in a form that is the exact reverse of the spectacle: It was to the modern age, to the ever-growing influence of the state, that was reserved the task of increasing and perfecting its guarantees, by using and directing, towards that great aim the building and distribution of buildings intended to observe a great multitude of men at the same time. (Foucault, 1975/1979, pp. 216-217)

As Foucault suggested, both spectacle and surveillance can be and have been used in the establishment and maintenance of regulatory power. But whereas he characterized "ancient" civilization as a civilization of "spectacle" (control grounded in the observation of the few by the many) and "modern" civilization as a civilization of panoptic "surveillance" (control grounded in the observation of the many by the few), in this chapter we contend that the two in fact have merged (or that they at least coexist), creating, in effect, an even more problematic and insidious mode of gaze-based disciplinarity.

Examples of both working contemporaneously (if not conjointly) include the present popularity (and power) of "tabloid" and "reality" television (e.g., *Survivor* and *American Idol*), examples of "spectacle," and the parallel functioning of e-mail (and other communications) monitoring (e.g., the recently publicized efforts of the Department of Homeland Security [DHS] and the FBI) and "nanny cams" (i.e., Webcams that make it possible for working parents to observe the actions of their children's day-care providers) examples of "surveillance." Interestingly, the news media provide examples of both—spectacle, for instance, in their increasingly intrusive investigation of individuals' private lives (e.g., various politicians, Monica Lewinsky, Scott Peterson, Kobe Bryant, Martha Stewart, etc.) and their evermore continuous coverage of such "media events" as the high-profile criminal cases of football stars O.J. Simpson and Ray Lewis (what Rich, 2000, 2003, called the "mediathon")—as well as surveillance, for instance in their "investigative reports" or "hidden camera" documentaries of large (and often corrupt) organizations (e.g., Enron; see also Haliburton). Frequently, these spiral into a surveillance–spectacle–surveillance-spectacle chain. In some ways, those with formal and official positions of power see them as mutually corrective, such that "fixing" the effects of spectacle requires increased surveillance (and so on, as the U.S. government's reactions to the events of September 11 suggest).

In this chapter, we argue that education today must be understood according to a setting in which spectacle and surveillance come together, a state of affairs in which discipline is established and maintained as individuals and groups are monitored simultaneously by both larger and smaller entities. We make use of standards-based educational reform (SBER) within the No Child Left Behind (NCLB) Act of 2001 as an indicative "case" (especially vis-à-vis the conditions of curriculum standards and mandated high-stakes testing), one in which this form of disciplinary power relates dynamically with and to what we (can) know and how we (can) know it. In this instance, for example, state bureaucrats "monitor" school performance within a "micro"-setting (surveillance) while at the same time the "public" considers school performance (or "accountability") via media-reported (frequently as headlines) standardized test scores (spectacle). In the extreme, given the potential of new virtual and online, audio and visual computer capabilities, these (educational and social) circumstances make available a new disciplinarity, one in which regulation can occur via the absurd possibility of "everybody watching everybody all the time," one that signals a qualitative shift in the mechanisms of the gaze, one conceivable only in light of technological advances (e.g., the Internet, hyperreality, YouTube; Steinberg & Kincheloe, 1997) and changing political/cultural/social/economic relationships between the "public" and "private" spheres and between "corporate" and "individual" identities.

We intend first to demonstrate that with respect to contemporary education, disciplinary power (i.e., "disciplinarity") must be understood within a context defined in part according to the *convergence* of surveillance and spectacle (as opposed, that is, to either one or the other separately). We utilize the case of SBER/NCLB to illustrate the following: (a) the mechanisms by which such a confluence of power elements occurs; (b) the contexts within which such a state of affairs is made possible; (c) the extent to which this conceptualization might provide insights into accepted and prevailing pedagogical practices, viewpoints, and policies; (d) the potential practical consequences (i.e., those of surveillance, spectacle, *and* "surveillance–spectacle") of this disciplinary setting; and (e) the increased complexity and turbulence made necessary by this convergence of surveillance and spectacle in terms of the production, establishment, evolution, and maintenance of any effective mode (or modes) of critique and/or resistance. More precisely, we address the following questions:

- To what extent might contemporary K–12 education be understood in terms of a "blending" of surveillance and spectacle?
- To what benefits?
- Within what contexts and via what mechanisms does this merging occur?
- What are the potential practical consequences of this arrangement?
- How might SBER (as a case study) illuminate the fusion of surveillance and spectacle in terms of cause(s), effect(s), context(s), mechanism(s), consequence(s), critique(s), and resistance(s)?

IMAGE AND EDUCATION

Increasingly, conceptualizations of public schooling rest on the influence of dominant and dominating *images* rather than on any more authentic understanding of the complex realities of classroom life. Based on what we see in the movies and on television and what is presented within the mainstream "news" media, we create our interpretations of what is, what was, and what should (or will) be. This especially holds true in the ever more powerful sociocultural-political-economic-pedagogical settings of SBER/NCLB (e.g., Vinson, Gibson, & Ross, 2001; Vinson & Ross, 2001, 2003), most clearly, perhaps, within the current commitment to high-stakes standardized testing, a collective regime in which both the cultural knowledge and the behavior of students, teachers, administrators, classrooms, schools, and districts are not only (in)validated but also disciplined. In summary, the convergence of a number of phenomena related to image and high-stakes testing, including various means by which scholars might seek critical and practical insight, the mechanisms by which image and high-stakes testing both reflect and are reflected by contemporary societal circumstances, the enforcing consequences of such actualities, and the techniques by which such statuses might be resisted define the scope of this chapter's efforts.

We recognize first a certain "hegemony of the image" that mirrors and is mirrored by—made possible by, is reinforcing of and reinforced by—several developments in contemporary U.S. society, specifically within the realms of technology, standardization, and globalization. It is, for instance, consistent with the advent of the possibility of "24–7" access to cameras, in terms both of *seeing* and of *being seen*. This emerges, for example, in the proliferation of Webcams, around-the-clock broadcast and cable (and satellite and Internet) TV, state-sponsored privacy monitoring (e.g., the FBI's "Carnivore"), the multiplication of media outlets, and "reality" television. Moreover, it is constructed within an economic environment of conglomeration and oligopolification, a setting in which media giants merge their abilities to even more strongly control access to both technology and the (re)production of, contact with, and manipulation of public images (e.g., the evolving and generally weird relationship between AOL and Time Warner, etc.).

Contemporary regimes of high-stakes testing must be understood within such contexts, as mutually (re)inforcing and as specific instances of the hegemonic dominance of media images. For example, how many times do individuals and groups determine the "effectiveness" of particular schools by relying on reported test scores—*images*—whether or not they have any first-hand information on what actually occurs in any unique and concrete school environment? Moreover, as public education increasingly comes to dominate U.S. political discourse (e.g., Jones, 2001), to what extent do such standardization policies normalize the cultural and behavioral interests of the economically and culturally powerful, especially as "liberals" and "conservatives" continue to merge around a singular idealized view of schooling (e.g., President Bush's "NCLB Act"; see Vinson, 1999; Vinson & Ross, 2001; Vinson & Ross, 2001 (March); Vinson & Ross, 2003)?

As society's rulers coalesce and more generally use both surveillance (the disciplinary observation of the many by the few) and spectacle (the disciplinary observation of the few by the many) as conjoint means of controlling individuals and groups, high-stakes testing represents not only the plane on which the school–society link is played out, but also a reinforcing context within which the interests of the wealthy and powerful work to legitimize what counts as both knowledge and appropriate behavior, especially as national education policy continues to be determined by the representatives of elite cultural and economic ideologies (e.g., in post-*A Nation at Risk* commissions comprised of key corporate leaders [e.g., IBM's Lou Gerstner], union officials [e.g., National Education Association's former president Bob Chase and American Federation of Teacher's President Sandra Feldman], and politicians [e.g., the National Governors' Association, former Secretary of Education Rod Paige] convened for the purposes of determining the *nature and meanings* of U.S. public schooling). In effect, such powerful elites control not only public/media images of contemporary education, but also how they are (re)produced vis-à-vis the contents of "official knowledge" and "proper" pedagogical behavior (e.g., Ross, 2000; see also Business Roundtable, 2001; Department of Education, 1990, 1991; Dianda, McKeon, & Kapinus, n.d.).

What are the mutual relationships between images of public schooling and the operations of high-stakes testing, particularly regarding the degree to which both work to enforce, control, and discipline both cultural knowledge and behavior? To what extent do these images seek to "normalize" the interests of the economically and politically powerful as "natural," "neutral," or "correct"? Drawing on the vast literatures surrounding, for example, the notion of *image* (e.g., Barthes, 1977 [on the "rhetoric of the image"]; Bakhtin, 1981, 1990 [on "chronotope"]; Boorstin, 1961/1992 [on the "pseudo-event"]; Baudrillard, 1995 [on "simulacra"]; and McLuhan, 1964/1994 [on the idea that "the medium is the message"]), *surveillance* (e.g., Foucault, 1975/1979), *spectacle* (e.g., Debord, 1967/1995), and high-stakes standardized testing (e.g., Kohn, 2000; McNeil, 2000; Ohanian, 1999), we pursue the following:

1. The relationships between images of schooling and the contemporary societal merging of surveillance and spectacle.
2. The means and mechanisms by which such relationships work to enforce certain dominant and dominating norms.
3. The school–society relationship(s) vis-à-vis high-stakes standardized testing.

4. The consequences of such conditions (e.g., regarding architecture [schools as casinos?] and pedagogy ["impersonal" "distance education"]).

5. Various mechanisms by which such circumstances might be resisted and/or transcended (e.g., Guy Debord's conceptualizations of dérive and detournement), including in terms of how they indicate the various problematics of everyday life (e.g., de Certeau, 1984; Lefebvre, 1947/1992; 1968/1971, Perlman, 1969; Vaneigem, 1967/1972; see also Vinson & Ross, 2003).

UNDERSTANDING THE CONTEMPORARY SCENE: STANDARDIZATION AND IMAGE[1]

The contemporary state of the school curriculum—its appearance-of-uniformity–appearance-of-diversity paradox (e.g., Vinson & Ross, 2001)—reflects in part two recent and evolving sociopedagogical trends: (a) the contradictory commitment to both "standardization" *and* "diversity" and (b) the increasingly important convergence (or at least co-existence) of "spectacle" and "surveillance." On some level, both work to create the conditions by and within which schooling broadly reflects and is reflected by the characteristics (political, economic, social, cultural) of the larger (global) society.

That those who run public schooling continue their call for "higher standards," "high-stakes testing," "accountability," and "competition" while simultaneously praising the merits of individual and cultural differences should surprise no one, and in fact mirrors and is mirrored by not only the current empirical pedagogical debates surrounding uniformity and diversity but also prevailing U.S. societal conditions—especially those reflected *economically* vis-à-vis global, state-sponsored, corporate, "infotech" capitalism and *politically* in terms of an apparent fusion or de-evolution of political independence toward a bland, insincere, uniform, and stultifying "centrism" (see, e.g., the "New Democrat," the "Compassionate Conservative," the Blair–Clinton project of the "Third Way," etc.). Taken together, these contexts produce an uneasy and ultimately false coalition of *sameness*, with the politically powerful claiming to promote the common ("mainstream") good while at the same time their corporate/financial allies and supporters pursue profit-seeking policies at the expense of authentic economic opportunity, social justice, meaningful democracy, the environ-

---

[1]In this section we draw heavily from our previous work, especially Vinson and Ross (2001).

ment, human rights, and so on. No wonder the cynicism, "voter apathy," and electoral mistrust. With little real difference between the dominant Democratic and Republican parties (see, e.g., the "lesser of two evils" mentality among many members of the citizenry and the tag-team effort to marginalize third parties), and with their joint endorsement by and of the elite corporate hierarchy, there ultimately is little or no room indeed for the less wealthy, the less powerful, and the less well-connected (note, for instance, Ralph Nader's difficulties getting his name on presidential electoral ballots).

Clearly, *educational* leaders, including those responsible for establishing, maintaining, and reforming(?) curriculum and instruction are to some extent beholden to the demands of multiple political interests (including those of *government* leaders who, in turn, depend on and benefit from the interests of the economically and culturally powerful, for example, in terms of campaign contributions). Yet, these same educational leaders are influenced by (and thus beholden to) a range of additional constituencies. These include, among others, parents and students, teachers, scholars, community leaders, activists, and residents of local neighborhoods, many of whom hold little positive concern for the politically and economically privileged. That these various groups and individuals present and experience a vastly more diverse reality than that of those who represent the U.S./global corporate-state is an understatement. Yet it explains, in part, the odd and conflicting dual commitments of today's public school managers, existing as they do between the two worlds of elitist-socioeconomic-competitive-standardization and the everyday experiences of grassroots community activism and pluralistic cultural diversity. But perhaps more importantly it hints at the necessary extent to which this paradoxical state of affairs can only be understood contextually.

The move toward curriculum standardization can be seen, of course, in the myriad official policy statements and content documents created and put forth by an array of professional academic organizations, for example, those that seek control over the meaning or "nature" of social studies education— that domain of curriculum work historically charged with "democratic" and "citizenship" education (e.g., Center for Civic Education, 1991, 1994; Geography Education Standards Project, 1994; National Center for History in the Schools, 1994a, 1994b; National Council for the Social Studies [NCSS], 1981; NCSS Curriculum Standards Task Force, 1994; National Council on Economic Education, 1997). Although it signifies an attempt to mask any real paradigmatic conflict or struggle, ironically SBER (here, especially, curriculum standards and high-stakes standardized testing) may instead reflect a multiplicity of tensions and confusions over the relative place and meaning of not only the range of constituent school disciplines but also fundamental questions relative to purpose, content, instructional methodologies, and assessment (i.e., What is it that citizens "need" to know?

How do/can they come to know it? and How can we be sure they have learned it?). As such, this issue—standardization versus diversity—may in fact be related to and encompass an assortment of other continuous yet equally contentious and relevant issues in terms of curriculum design and development, including the degree to which curricula should be constructed at the "grassroots" level or "hierarchically," the extent to which *purpose* or *testing* should "drive" curriculum and instruction, the relative merits of "progressive" and "traditional" orientations, and the overall pedagogical balance between "discipline-centeredness" (or "disciplinarity") and "a/anti/interdisciplinarity."

At present, this move toward curriculum standardization represents the dominant, status quo viewpoint and its underlying and foundational aims (e.g., Levin, 1998; Tucker & Codding, 1998; for a general overview of national standards as an issue, see, e.g., Wolf, 1998). Its fundamental features include formal and official curriculum standards frameworks, of course, but also a hypercommitment in favor of high-stakes standardized testing and a one-size-fits-all view of classroom/school conformity. As previously indicated, this perspective is manifested vis-à-vis a host of policy statements developed at multiple levels, including the national (e.g., Department of Education, 1991; National Commission on Excellence in Education, 1983), the state (Finn & Petrilli, 2000), and the professional academic organizational (e.g., NCSS Curriculum Standards Task Force, 1994). It grows out of the current "liberal–conservative consensus" among politicians, corporate leaders, the news media, and educational policy makers (e.g., apparent *liberals* such as Nash, Crabtree, & Dunn, 1997; and *conservatives* such as Ravitch, 2000) that both "higher standards" (read SBER-curriculum standardization and high-stakes standardized testing) and greater "accountability" are *essential* to the well-being and strengthening of U.S. public schools (note that both major party candidates supported "stronger accountability" and more standardized testing during the 2000 and 2004 presidential campaigns). It is grounded in formal reports such as *A Nation at Risk* and reflected, endorsed, and expanded in works of typically conservative (culturally and economically) scholarship (e.g., Hirsch, 1987, 1996; Ravitch, 2000; Ravitch & Finn, 1987; see also Mathison, Ross, & Vinson, 2001; Vinson & Ross, 2001; Vinson & Ross, 2001 (March), of course, also see NCLB, 2001).

Although dominant and indicative of a powerfully elitist consensus, the recent move toward SBER must and can only be understood contextually and against certain overlapping and contiguous sociocultural, economic, and political currents, including changes in technology, the advent of state-sponsored global-corporate capitalism, and the "triumph" of the U.S. "one-party system" (e.g., Business Roundtable, 2001; Magdoff, Wood, & McNally, 1999). More precisely (and significantly) we must understand that SBER reflects and is reflected by such contexts as they produce/construct/create and are produced/constructed/created by a characteristic feature of 21st-century life in the United States.: namely, the imperatives (in terms both of *desire* and *opportunity*) of *seeing and being seen* (i.e., both *how* we see and are being seen and *that* we see and are being seen; one might consider related notions of the "cult of celebrity," Warhol's "15 minutes of fame," and Orwell's "Big Brother"). These imperatives induce a clear disciplinarity, a conformity, and a perceived necessity to standardize/become standardized (e.g., Fukuyama, 2002). It remains to be seen whether the 2006 Congressional and 2008 Presidential elections to be played out in the aftermath of Senator Joseph I. Liberman's loss in the Connecticut Democratic primary, in the wake of the enduring effects of Hurricane Katrina, against the backdrop of the unending debacle in Iraq, and within the context increasingly influenced by YouTube and the blogosphere, will encourage us to rethink our present positions.

So, specifically, what are these various contexts and changes? In terms of technology (*here* a sociocultural change) one might consider, again, several fairly recent developments, including the advent of 24/7 television "broadcast" via hundreds of cable/satellite channels, the Internet, and the proliferation of such innovations as Webcams, MySpace, and YouTube, making it possible, of course, both to see and be seen simultaneously and continuously. Economically, within the environment of globalized capitalism, see for instance how daily, around-the-clock updates reveal the scope to which stock prices increase or decrease for financial powerhouses regardless of profit (or crime, e.g., post-Martha Steward, Enron, etc.)—image here apparently matters more than "real" performance. Similarly, note how the current race to the "middle" waged between the major political parties (e.g., year 2000 Democratic and Republican presidential candidates Bush and Gore) depends less on any authentic issue advocacy and more on how they are *seen* (and how they themselves see things). In effect, this leads to the establishment of a one-party system in which powerful Republicans seek to appease their right wing (e.g., Patrick J. Buchanan, the Christian Coalition) while simultaneously staking a claim in the "center" (aka "compassionate conservatism"), and powerful Democrats do the same with respect to their left wing (e.g., Ralph Nader, environmentalists; see the "New Democrat"). As a result, meaningful difference is marginalized and traditional allies (e.g., Nader via the Democrats and Buchanan via the Republicans) are forced out and compelled to accept an existence *viewed* as extremist, contrarian, and nonmainstream. This would be, perhaps, not so problematic were it based less on *mere* image (i.e., polling data, focus group results, Public Relations, advertising) and more on a heartfelt dedication to significant issues and differences. For both sides, however, the goal seems to be less one of defending and promoting the collective social good and instead one of ensuring first *that* the major players are in fact seen, and second that *how*, essentially, they are seen (Democrats *and* Republicans) is as "conservative" but not "too" conservative and "liberal" but not "too" liberal.

At heart, these contexts—sociocultural, economic, political—(re)establish the priority of sight—the "gaze"—as a mechanism of discipline and social control. More specifically, they create and are created by the conditions within which the convergence of surveillance and spectacle occurs; they establish in part the setting for what might be called the *new disciplinarity*, a mode of often subtle coercion grounded in the extreme potentials of continual seeing and being seen, of both surveillance *and* spectacle.

For Foucault, surveillance represented a disciplinary power built out of the (eventually automatic and invisible) possibilities of the many being visible to the few (á la the architecture of the modern prison created according to the design of Bentham's Panopticon). At present, elements of surveillance exist in such features of society as "Carnivore" (the FBI's e-mail-tapping framework), and "Echelon" (the government's [National Security Agency's] program for monitoring virtually all worldwide telecommunications), and the USA Patriot Act (see Keefe, 2006).

As a case in point, *The Wall Street Journal* recently reported on how the FBI, INS, IRS, and other federal agencies circumvent the Privacy Act of 1974 and various agency policies to collect information on millions of Americans (Simpson, 2001). Note that following the surveillance scandals of the 1960s and 1970s, in which the FBI compiled files on thousands of Vietnam War protesters, civil rights activists, and others on an apparently random (yet political-ideological) basis, Congress adopted laws that discouraged the collection of data on presumably law-abiding citizens. Moreover, the FBI's own *Manual of Investigations, Operations, and Guidelines* states that "only that information about an individual which is relevant and necessary to accomplish a purpose authorized by statute, executive order of the president, or by the Constitution is to be recorded in FBI files." *The Wall Street Journal* describes the agency's "end run" around these guidelines in which it outsources its "Big Brother" activities to private companies like ChoicePoint—the same corporation that supplied faulty data to the state of Florida that led to thousands of Floridians, primarily African Americans, being purged from the voter rolls for the November 2000 election. According to the *Journal's* report, 20,000 IRS agents have access to outside data on taxpayer assets, driving histories, phone numbers, and other personal statistics compiled by ChoicePoint, which claims to have information on nearly every American with a credit card. FBI agents use a password to log on to a customized Web site (www.cpfbi.com, "ChoicePoint Online for the FBI") that links them with privately owned data about millions of U.S. citizens (Simpson, 2001). (See all recent domestic spying controversies.)

Spectacle, conversely, presupposes a mode of disciplinarity based on the processes of the few being visible to the many (á la the ancient architectures of theaters, circuses, and temples). Yet according to philosopher Guy Debord (1967/1995) in *The Society of the Spectacle*, it describes contemporary society as well, especially in that "The whole of life of those societies in which modern conditions of production prevail presents itself as an immense accumulation of *spectacles*. All that once was directly lived has become mere representation" (p. 12).

Furthermore:

> The spectacle is not [merely] a collection of images; rather, it is a social relationship between people that is mediated by images. In form as in content the spectacle serves as total justification for the conditions and aims of the existing system. It further ensures the *permanent presence* of that justification, for it governs almost all time spent outside the production process itself. [Moreover, the] language of the spectacle is composed of signs of the dominant organization of production—signs which are at the same time the ultimate end-products of that organization. (pp. 12-13; see also Bracken, 1997; Debord, 1988/1990; Jappe, 1993/1999)

Although perhaps not as familiar as Foucault's (1975/1979) interpretation of "surveillance" and "discipline," the concept of spectacle has gained increased acceptance, notably with respect to aesthetics and "film studies" (e.g., Eilenberg, 1975; Matthews, 1975; Polan, 1986), although it has acquired some level of attention in educational theory as well (e.g., Coleman, 1987; Roman, 1996; Senese & Page, 1995; Vinson & Ross, 2003).

What makes today unique, however, is the merging or at least co-existence of the two, making it *possible* and among some people (even) *desirable* to see and be seen continuously and simultaneously (i.e., because of the Internet and cable/satellite/wireless technologies). In the extreme, the potential becomes more real that society will (or at least *can*) be understood as nothing but a medium through which everybody *can* watch everybody all the time and across and throughout all space—nothing more than a totality of images and spectacular relationships. Standardization/SBER/NCLB in fact represents the extent to which this setting occurs, and presents a case not only by which the surveillance–spectacle merger can be understood but also one that can itself be understood against and according to surveillance and spectacle.

Although curriculum standardization represents the dominant, consensus view, and granting its status as a major public policy issue (e.g., Johnson & [with] Duffett, 1999), it has not remained without its share of critics (e.g., Kohn, 2000; Mathison et al., 2001; Ohanian, 1999; Ross, 2000; Vinson, 1999; Vinson et al., 2001), most of whom have sought other avenues, including those comprising the notion of *diversity*. In many cases, these critiques have emphasized the nature of SBER/NCLB as *oppressive* (e.g., drawing on, e.g.,

Freire, 1970; Young, 1992), *anti-democratic* (e.g., drawing on Dewey, 1916/1966; Herman & Chomsky, 1988), and in contradiction with the demands of the *collective* good (for a discussion of curriculum standards as oppressive, antidemocratic, and anti-collective good, see, e.g., Vinson, 2001).

SBER/NCLB, SURVEILLANCE, AND SPECTACLE

SBER/NCLB—especially its high-stakes standardized testing compo-nents—exists within the complex intersection of surveillance and spectacle. The result is a situation, or set of situations, consistent with those charac-teristic of the larger society. Although the consequences of such a frame-work are critical, we consider in this section simply the extent to which, and the means by which, the SBER-surveillance–spectacle association occurs.

High-stakes testing represents a multifaceted setting of surveillance, in terms both of behavior and formal school knowledge. As both "gatekeep-er" and (perhaps) "door closer," it works to ensure first that certain con-tent is being "covered" (and thus *theoretically* "learned"). The "or–else" effect establishes the priority of that particular content (information, facts, skills, values, etc.) as well as the inferiority, unworthiness, and marginaliza-tion of other contents (and knowledges). It operates as a "checks and bal-ances" system of observation that seeks to privilege the dominant and for-mally created curriculum and related modes of instruction. It enables, in other words, curriculum managers to "see" whether and "how well" a pre-scribed program is being followed. Moreover, it works within a panoptic order such that teachers "survey" students, administrators survey teachers and students, and school boards (and other public officials) survey all of them, each in successive and more indirect rounds of disciplinarity. Á la Foucault, the model attains a certain automaticity such that regardless of whether one knows that an administrator is actually in a given hallway peering through a classroom window, the possibility always exists that he or she might be—thus, the system practically, and substantively, runs itself. Behavior is regulated similarly in that test questions demand specific instructional orientations (teacher-centered, behavioral, etc.). As applied at the level of the body (individual as well as group), testing represents the managerial effort to mandate a precisely organized regime of pedagogical activity, a narrowing link between what can be known and, ultimately, what can be done.

This regime becomes spectacular as the relative position of the observer changes, such that it is not a single principal surveying a school or a superin-tendent a district, but a larger viewing public using its broader and collective gaze as a disciplinary mechanism. At the heart of this process rests various news and information media outlets that publish and publicize images of schooling such as test scores. Newspaper readers and TV news viewers represent a public observing schools, one that is intent on influencing schools to perform—or *con*form—in a particular way or toward a particular power-influenced ideal. The repercussions, of course, are great, affecting such factors as property values, reputation, the expansion of employment opportunities, and educational resources. This spectacularization of teaching and learning, SBER/NCLB, has the circular effect of strengthening the conditions of surveillance: As the public views test scores as either too low or contributing to some "achievement gap," they pressure school leaders and other public officials to do something. These officials, in turn, intensify their (and certain allies', including the business community and teachers' unions) control over curriculum, instruction, and assessment vis-à-vis greater and expanded degrees of surveillance (all of which the public "watches" to see whether or not it is effective, that is, whether politicians and administrators deserve continued support). This leaves schools, classrooms, teachers, and students in the middle, within a spiraling surveillance–spectacle cycle. Discipline, deterrence, and conformity increase, or else no promotion, graduation, or funding. The connection between school knowledge and economics intensifies, a condition made more dangerous in view of the expanding gap between the wealthy and the middle and lower classes. Standardization strengthens, presenting a paradox given the ostensible commitment of official U.S. schooling to democracy and diversity.

TEST SCORES AND THE ILLUSION
OF REFORM: TWO EXAMPLES

A further irony stems from the fact that the entire structure of SBER develops purely on the basis of image. Both media and public, via test scores, create understandings grounded not in what actually occurs in schools and classrooms—nor on what teachers and students actually do—but on how this all is *represented*. Furthermore, those responsible for surveillance—often located outside of schools—draw their conclusions about performance or achievement or effectiveness not on what takes place per se, but on whether standardized test scores rise or fall. Higher scores, all is well; lower scores, all is not well—regardless of the authentic actualities and experiences of school and classroom life. Two examples, Texas and Chicago, illustrate the role of image (i.e., the [re]production of test scores) in the convergence and effects of surveillance and spectacle within the contexts of SBER/NCLB.

Texas

The representation of education reform efforts in Texas provides the first example. George W. Bush and other SBER advocates (both Democrat and Republican) have claimed that the introduction of the Texas Assessment of Academic Skills (TAAS) test in 1990–1991 produced a miraculous turn-around in educational achievement in the Lone Star State, reducing dropouts, increasing student achievement, and reducing the test-score gaps among White, African-American, and Latino/a students. Recent studies have raised serious questions about the validity of the reported test score gains in Texas.

A study by Haney (2000) found that the TAAS actually contributes both to retention in grade and dropping out. He reports that only 50% of minority students in Texas have been progressing from Grade 9 to high school graduation since the initiation of the TAAS program (and evidence suggests that slightly fewer than 70% of all students in Texas actually graduated from high school in the 1990s). Over the past two decades there has also been a steady rise in the rates at which African-American and Latino/a students in Texas have been required to repeat Grade 9; by the late 1990s, nearly 30% were "failing" Grade 9. Grade retention rates for African Americans and Latinos/as in Texas are nearly twice as high as for White students.

As test scores on the TAAS soared, however, researchers failed to find similar improvements in other, more reliable measures of Texas students' achievement (e.g., SAT scores and the National Assessment of Educational Progress [NAEP]). Indeed, as measured by performance on the SAT, the achievement of Texas high school students has not improved much since the early 1990s; in fact, SAT-Math scores have *deteriorated* relative to those of students nationally, reports Haney (2000). A study by the Rand Corporation (Klein, Hamilton, McCaffrey, & Stecher, 2000) found that the dramatic reading and math gains indicated by TAAS results were not reflect-ed in the NAEP. Instead, NAEP results indicate only small increases, simi-lar to those observed nationwide. Moreover, according to the NAEP, the test score gap between Whites and students of color in Texas is not only very large but also growing.

There is an expanding consensus among researchers that the "miracle" test-score increases on the TAAS are the result of both intensive test-prep activities that undermine substantive teaching and learning (McNeil, 2000) and the increasing number of students excluded from taking the test (Haney, 2000). McNeil reported that many schools in Texas are devoting tremendous amounts of time to highly specific "skills" intended to improve students' scores on the TAAS. After several years in classes where "reading" assign-ments were increasingly TAAS practice materials, children were unable to read a novel intended for students 2 years younger. Haney (2000) reported that in 1999 Texas tested 48% of its special education students, down from 62% in 1998—that is an additional 37,751 students not taking the test. Those exemptions include 13% of Latino/a, 12% of African American, and only 5% of White students. Haney found that a substantial portion of increases in TAAS pass rates in the 1990s was due to such exclusions, prompting him to conclude that "the gains on TAAS and the unbelievable decreases in dropouts during the 1990s are [were] more illusory than real. The Texas 'miracle' is more hat than cattle" (sec. 8.2).

Chicago

Chicago Public Schools (CPS), touted by SBER advocates as a reform model, provides a second example of how the structure of SBER is largely based on a mere, distorted image, a lie, in effect, rooted in the very power of the surveillance–spectacle gaze. Schmidt (2000), for example, found that CPS's "standards and accountability" campaign, which relies principally on the use of high-stakes testing, functions ultimately to decrease the number of students of color ever even making it into high school. For although CPS reported that student enrollments increased by 20,000 between the 1995–1996 and 1999–2000 school years, the number of students making it to the high school level actually *decreased*, at least in part as a result of SBER/high-stakes testing policies. Additionally, although the number of African American students increased in Chicago elementary schools the number attending high school decreased by nearly 10,000 (a 16% drop). And although the overall number of Hispanic students in CPS dramatically increased in this period (up 18,000), the number of Hispanic students in high school increased by only 700.

What does it mean to be the "best school in Chicago?" *The New York Times* reported that Northside Preparatory was "Chicago's best high school," ignoring the fact that it is also Chicago's whitest high school and that the school admits students only if their standardized test scores are above 80% of their student peers. But as Schmidt (2000) also reported, shifting populations and then taking credit for test score gains is "an urban [schools'] trick of long standing." Jean Baptiste Beaubien Elementary School, for instance, has been identified as well as one of Chicago's "success stories" as the percentage of its students scoring at or above national norms increased from 39.6% in 1995 to 77% in 2000. But as Schmidt (2000) subsequently demonstrated, a closer look at these gains indicates their correspondence to a similar *decrease* in scores at Luther Burbank Elementary School. In reality, both the increase and decrease resulted from a single, commensurate action—the transplanting of 300 students in the "regional gifted student program" from Burbank to Beaubien schools. The bottom line, as Schmidt argued, is that SBER is "a smokescreen behind which growing inequities are being hidden" even as CPS paradoxically is represented as *the* model of contemporary urban school reform.

This all—both Texas and Chicago—signifies the degree to which recent reform attempts often collapse into mere image, the processes by which test scores (and so on) disintegrate from some hypothetical "reality" into some troubling status of illusion. And yet, unfortunately, this state of affairs maintains a certain, unsettling, arguably inherent importance. For, ultimately, such images and illusions represent the means and mechanisms by which both the media and the public at large—or, the public at large through the media—obtain, sustain, reproduce, and/or reconstruct their understandings of the successes or failures of American (if not global) public schooling /education.

SOME CONSEQUENCES: ALIENATION AND ARCHITECTURE

Many of the potential consequences of the SBER–surveillance–spectacle conglomerate are already well known, especially those related to mandated high-stakes standardized testing. As critics such as Haney (2000), Kohn (2000), McNeil (2000), and Ohanian (1999), among others, have pointed out, under such a regime both curriculum and instruction narrow, innovation declines, "achievement gaps" expand, and (perhaps most ironically these days) more children are in fact "left behind." And, as we have already pointed out, connections between formal school knowledge and the economy generally solidify (often via the involvement of and with politicians and educational managers of and with corporate and financial leaders; see, e.g., Ollman, 2001). As we also noted, there are, of course, further risks to the extent that SBER (at least in terms of curriculum standards) may be oppressive, anti-democratic, inauthentic, and against the collective good.

Alienation

Perhaps most clearly, SBER, and schools and education under capitalism more generally, must be understood fully as products and practices of alienation.

What occurs in schools can only be understood by examining the conditions by which certain practices are legitimated or delegitimated (excluded). SBER, as we have shown, is both a product and practice rooted in real social relations that are mediated, in part, by image (i.e., test scores). As Marx (1988) argued in *The German Ideology*:

The ideas of the ruling class are in every epoch the ruling ideas; i.e., the class which is the ruling material force of society, is at the same time its ruling intellectual force. The class which has the means of material production at its disposal, has control at the same time over the means of mental production, so that thereby, generally speaking, the ideas of those who lack the means of mental production are subject to it. The ruling ideas are nothing more than the ideal expression of the dominant material relationships, the dominant material relationships grasped as idea; hence the relationships which make the one class the ruling class, therefore, the ideas of its dominance. (p. 64)

SBER is the primary contemporary means by which schools remain agents of domination—the means by which, as Althusser (1971) suggested, "the school teaches 'know-how,' but in [a] form which ensures the subjection to the ruling ideology or the mastery of its 'practice'" (p. 133). As with other aspects of commodity-capitalism, with regard to schools the social relations among people are not regulated *directly*, but *indirectly* through things, objects, including here such entities as mandated curricula and, most particularly and significantly, test scores.

As Marx (1986) explained, we experience alienation when we are separated from our own activity, the products of our work, and fellow human beings:

Alienation is apparent not only in the fact that my means of life belong to someone else, that my desires are the unattainable possession of someone else, but that everything is something different from itself, that my activity is something else and finally (and this is the case for the capitalist) that an inhuman power rules over everything. (p. 151)

Marx repeatedly insisted that alienation appears not only in the result, but also in the process of production, within the productive activity itself. In his description of what constitutes the alienation of labor, Marx could just as easily been describing the work of students and teachers under the SBER regime dominating schools today.

First, that the work is *external* to the worker, that is not part of his [*sic*] nature, and that, consequently, he does not fulfill himself in his work but denies himself, has a feeling of misery rather that well-being, does not develop freely his mental and physical energies but is physically exhausted and mentally debased. The worker, therefore, feels himself at home only during his leisure time, whereas at work he feels homeless. His work is not voluntary but imposed, *forced labour*. It is not the satisfaction of a need, but only a *means* for satisfying other needs. Its alien

character is clearly shown by the fact that as soon as there is no physical or other compulsion it is avoided like the plague. (Marx, 1964, pp.
122, 124-125)

This powerlessness, lack of agency, and absence of subjectivity can
plainly be found in schools. Block (2000) argued that despite the rhetoric
that schools are community based, capitalist schools

must be viewed as always and already products of alienation. Hence
may arise the possibility of national curriculum and standards despite
the notion that schools function in and for the communities in which
they are situated and in which and by which they are formed. Schools as
institutions do not then belong to either these communities, to the populace which they mean to serve, or to the population which functions
within them. (p. 74)

There is increasing evidence, for example, that the pressure and anxiety
associated with high-stakes testing is unhealthy for children, literally making
them sick. A report by the Alliance for Childhood (2001) includes a description of state test day for third graders by a Massachusetts school nurse: "My
office is filled with children with headaches and stomachaches . . .
one [student] was beside himself on the morning of the test—he could not
stop sobbing." Roy Applegate, president of the California Association of
School Psychologists described "nerve-racked" students, parents, and principals suffering from excessive anxiety related to high-stakes tests. "I
observed a group of low-performing students being given a pep talk by the
principal," Applegate is quoted as saying. "As I looked at the faces of the
seventh- and eighth-grade students, most appeared terrified, depressed, or
disinterested in the principal's words. I think the principal was terrified as
well." Increasingly school counselors are reporting anxiety-related symp-
toms as a result of high-stakes tests, including sleep disorders, drug use,
avoidance behaviors, attendance problems, and "acting out," all of which
degrades test performance and inhibits authentic learning.
    In 1999, Boston College researchers asked students in Grades 4, 8, and
10 to draw pictures detailing their thoughts about Massachusetts' standardized exam (Wheelock, Bebell, & Haney, 2000). About 20% of the students
expressed positive feelings about the test, but 40% had negative reactions,
ranging from anxiety to despair. One student sketched himself sitting in a
growing pool of his own sweat, while another offered this assessment:
"After the first 2 days of tests, your fingers and your mind hurt." The
researchers found that students are further panicked by the intense hype
and scrutiny surrounding high-stakes tests. Children are stressed out not
just by the tests, but by all the public discussion of their consequences. The

fear and anxiety have been exacerbated by the test-mania accompanying SBER.

In his analysis of everyday life in capitalist society, Perlman (1972) said that "the task of capitalist ideology is to maintain the veil which keeps people from seeing that their own activities reproduce the form of their daily life" (p. 3). He argued that the transformation of living activity into capital (alienation) takes place *through* things, but it is not carried out *by* things. Therefore, things that are products of human activities (such as test scores and curriculum standards) *seem* to be active agents because "activities and contacts are established for through" them, and because people's activities are not transparent to them, they confuse the mediating object with the cause.

Perlman presented the story of a "fetish worshipper" to illustrate this point.

> When a hunter wearing an amulet downs a deer with a stone, he may consider the amulet an essential "factor" in downing the deer and even in providing the deer as an object to be downed. If he is a responsible and well-educated fetish worshipper, he will devote his attention to his amulet, nourishing it with care and admiration; in order to improve the material conditions of his life, he will improve the way he wears his fetish, not the way he throws the stone; in a bind, he may even send his amulet to "hunt" for him. His own daily activities are not transparent to him; when he eats well, he fails to see that it is his own action of throwing the stone, and not the action of the amulet, that provided his food; when he starves, he fails to see that it is his own action of worshipping the amulet instead of hunting, and not the wrath of his fetish, that causes his starvation. (p. 8)

The fetishism of commodities, money, and, in the case of SBER, test scores as well as the mystification of one's daily activities and the "religion of everyday life" that attributes living activity to inanimate things has its origin in the character of social relations under capitalism. As Perlman noted, we do in fact relate to each other through things—the fetish is the occasion for which people act collectively and through which they reproduce their activity. But the fetish itself does not perform the activity.

Architecture

There are, of course, consequences more specifically connected to the association of and between surveillance and spectacle. The spiral or circular (if not convergent) and mutually (re)productive character of the relationship, for instance, helps ensure (a) that both in fact are strengthened and (b) that (therefore) school discipline and enforcement (in terms both of content and behavior) are tightened and subsequently made more effective. This is fundamental to our case.

Yet with respect to the quote by Foucault (1975/1979) with which we began this chapter, a framing perspective, a somewhat different and unique potentiality becomes all the more apparent. It involves the necessities, forms, functions, evolutions, impacts, and meanings of *architecture*. Although the scope of this work extends principally only to schooling, certainly some of our conclusions apply as well to the broader society, especially to the extent that the broader society contextualizes and reflects, and is reflected and contextualized by, contemporary public education.

In some ways, the present spectacle–surveillance complex, with its associated contextual components of technological change and so on, makes traditional modes of architecture irrelevant. As Foucault discovered, specific modes of disciplinarity require(d) or encourage(d) specific modes of architecture (e.g., spectacle—temples, theatres, coliseums; surveillance—the panopticonic prison, etc.). But the modern evolution of observational technology changes all this. In fact, it creates and in part is created by at least two new modes of "architecture"—what might be called *teletecture* and *cosmotecture*. The archetypes here are not the theater or the prison, but are instead, respectively although often mutually, the *Internet* and the *casino*. Teletecture represents the demolition of architecture per se. It is a disciplinary mechanism that requires no walls—or in today's slang, no bricks and mortar—because the possibilities of its gaze-based regulation are complete and absolute—without boundaries. With the advent of the Internet (and high-speed digital and wireless connections), Webcams, 24/7 access to the media, again the potential exists for a disciplinary means of control in that everyone *can* watch everyone all the time. Wireless technologies make particular and fixed space unnecessary, so that *any* available space will do. The implications here for education suggest an expanded role for "distance" learning and a reduced role for the historical setting of the school, no longer required, of course, by the disciplinary demands of education (including those relative to SBER).

Cosmotecture presents a distinct yet related state of affairs in which gigantic buildings are created in order to regulate the behaviors of many individuals engaged in multiple activities—all under the gaze of cameras. Although, perhaps, today the casino best represents this spectacle–surveillance hybrid mode of gaze-based discipline, other examples might include the modern international airport and the "mega" shopping mall. In effect, each represents a miniature and self-enclosed world—a cosmos—where the activities of the many can be seen by the few, *and* where the activities of a few can be seen by the many. (Interestingly, we understand that a Website exists where "surfers" can view the operations of casino surveillance.)

Granting that both teletecture and cosmotecture present the merging or co-existence of spectacle and surveillance, they do raise a number of interesting questions relative to the relationships between schools and larger societies. Most clearly related to schooling, they suggest the possibility (which may or may not be feasible or likely) that powerful individuals and groups could standardize both knowledge and behavior without the need for any direct (unmediated by technology), person-to-person, human interaction (for good or for bad).

Additionally, and maybe more problematic to some people, this spectacle–surveillance alliance signals a new relationship between *voyeurism* and *exhibitionism* (e.g., reality TV, internet porn, sensationalistic news stories, YouTube, etc.). In such instances, groups and individuals expose themselves (frequently as images, nonrealities, or digitally altered I-beings), blurring the public and private, while simultaneously (although even this immediacy is no longer imperative given various recording and downloading technologies) other groups and individuals observe them principally for the purposes of entertainment. As to what this might mean for schooling, we can only speculate. What is clear, however, is the potential pedagogical power, whether positive or negative, of the ever-evolving visual make-up of contemporary social and individual life.

Resistance

The merging of surveillance and spectacle presents clear and unique obstacles for any sort of critical and pedagogical resistance, particularly as each (alone and in combination) has infiltrated everyday life. It (obviously) requires in part both a resistance to surveillance and a resistance to spectacle, and implies that we take seriously more traditional forms such as those available via the political process and those accessible via local grassroots organization. Modern discipline, following Foucault, suggests, for example, a continuing struggle against any and all concentrations of power. In practice, this can be observed on the part of teachers and students who have boycotted standardized testing and/or have refused to participate in its encompassing mechanisms (e.g., some students have worked to "sabotage" the system by "faking" scores or by declining to "play" the tests by "opting out"). Such actions, of course, bring with them their own certain and unique risks (see Rossi, 2000).

Debord and his *Situationist International* (e.g., Knabb, 1981) colleagues created specific revolutionary techniques grounded in a variety of theoretical–practical understandings of spectacle and its effects. One, the *dérive*, literally "drifting," involves "a technique of transient passage through various ambiances [and] entails playful-constructive behavior and awareness of psychogeographical effects; which completely distinguishes it from the classical notions of the journey and the stroll" (Debord, 1981, p. 50). It is "A mode of experimental behavior linked to the conditions of urban society" (p. 45).

> In a *dérive* one or more persons during a certain period drop their usual motives for movement and action, their relations, their work and leisure activities, and let themselves be drawn by the attractions of the terrain and the encounters they find there. The element of chance is less determinant than one might think: from the *dérive* point of view cities have a psychogeographical relief, with constant currents, fixed points and vortexes which strongly discourage entry into or exit from certain zones. (Debord, 1981, p. 50)[2]

The extent to which "drifting," the *dérive*, offers practical resistance techniques pertinent to schooling and SBER is an open question. It may offer some insight into *how* to opt out, boycott, and refuse, however. Psychogeography, as it were, may offer a rather novel means for understanding the effects of SBER, particularly high-stakes testing, as it exists and is practiced in its present form.

The second of Debord's techniques is *detournement*, defined as "the reuse of preexisting artistic elements in a new ensemble. The two fundamental laws of detournement are the loss of importance of each detourned autonomous element—which may go so far as to lose its original sense completely—and at the same time the organization of another meaningful ensemble that confers on each element its new scope and effect" (1981, p. 55). It is

> Short for: detournement of preexisting aesthetic elements. The integration of present or past artistic production into a superior construction of a milieu. In this sense there can be no situationist painting or music, but only a situationist use of these means. In a more primitive sense, detournement within the old cultural spheres is a method of propaganda, a method which testifies to the wearing out and loss of importance of those spheres. (1981, pp. 45-46)

---

[2]The members of the *Situationist International* offered the following definitions related to "psychogeography":

Psychogeography: The study of the specific effects of the geographical environment, consciously organized or not, on the emotions and behavior of individuals.

Psychogeographical: Relating to psychogeography. That which manifests the geographical environment's direct emotional effects.

Psychogeographer: One who explores and reports on psychogeographical phenomena. (1981, p. 45)

Readers should also refer to various entries in Knabb (1981).

What might be the meaning or the effect of "detourning" test scores or newspaper headlines about them? Of destroying—negating—their "old" meanings and creating a new one? Or, similarly, of taking images ostensibly about something other than test scores and "reworking" them, perhaps by changing captions, slogans, and so on? *Detournement* presents, perhaps, one of the more direct and possible challenges to the hegemony of the image, including that presented within the framework of SBER. Both *dérive* and *detournement* imply the dangers and possibilities of challenging standardization, testing, image, surveillance, and spectacle as each intrudes on the human-ness of everyday and experiential life.

SUMMARY AND CONCLUSIONS

Such issues as surveillance, spectacle, and the related notion of "privacy" recently have gained an increased degree of notoriety (e.g., Calvert, 2000; Rosen, 2000), although in education Foucauldian perspectives have dominated (e.g., Popkewitz & Brennan, 1998). Still, there has been at least some discussion related to the idea of spectacle (e.g., Coleman, 1987; Roman, 1996; Senese & Page, 1995). With the continued evolution of audio, visual, and virtual technologies, however, we expect an even greater emphasis not only upon spectacle, but on surveillance and their interconnections as well.

Further, especially given President Bush's commitment to testing and the ongoing liberal-conservative consensus around "higher standards" (e.g., NCLB), the issue of SBER seems not to be going away. Hopefully in this chapter we have at least highlighted some of the characteristics of disciplinarity within the current setting of surveillance, spectacle, and surveillance–spectacle. Moreover, we hope to have suggested a few of the contexts and mechanisms by which this setting has emerged and by which it is maintained, its consequences effected, and its powers reinforced. Finally, we hope that we have in some way illuminated SBER as an exemplar case of the merging of surveillance and spectacle and as an image-bound inducement for new modalities of resistance.

Of course, we encourage further investigation, especially theoretical extensions of our work—optimally, forms of inquiry drawn from a range of education-related disciplines—but also empirical studies into the causes, effects, contexts, mechanisms, and consequences of SBER, surveillance, and spectacle, including those aimed at creating a meaningful and sophisticated set of critiques and those dedicated to effective and human(e) methodologies of pedagogical resistance.

REFERENCES

Alliance for Childhood. (2001). *High-stakes testing: A statement of concern and call to action*. College Park, MD: Author. Retrieved from http://www.alliance-forchildhood.net/news/histakes_test_position_statement.htm

Althusser, L. (1971). *Lenin and philosophy* (B. Brewster, Trans.). New York: Monthly Review Press.

Bakhtin, M. M. (1981). *The dialogic imagination: Four essays by M. M. Bakhtin* (M. Holquist, Ed.; C. Emerson & M. Holquist, Trans.). Austin: University of Texas Press.

Bakhtin, M. M. (1990). *Mikhail Bakhtin: Creation of a prosaics* (G. S. Morson & C. Emerson, Eds.). Stanford, CA: Stanford University Press.

Barthes, R. (1977). *Image-music-text* (S. Heath, Trans.). New York: Hill & Wang.

Baudrillard, J. (1995). *Simulacra and simulation* (S. F. Glaser, Trans.). Ann Arbor: University of Michigan Press.

Block, A. A. (2000). *Marxism and education*. Retrieved from http://www.uwstout.edu/chd/edscsp/blocka/750/WEBREADINGS/marxismandeducation.htm

Boorstin, D. J. (1992). *The image: A guide to pseudo-events in America*. New York: Vintage Books. (Original work published 1961)

Bracken, L. (1997). *Guy Debord: Revolutionary*. Venice, CA: Feral House.

The Business Roundtable. (2001). *Assessing and addressing the "testing backlash": Practical advice and current public opinion research for business coalitions and standards advocates*. Washington, DC: Author.

Calvert, C. (2000). *Voyeur nation: Media, privacy, and peering in modern culture*. Boulder, CO: Westview Press.

Center for Civic Education. (1991). *CIVITAS: A framework for civic education* (National Council for the Social Studies Bulletin 86). Calabasas, CA: Author.

Center for Civic Education. (1994). *National standards for civics and government*. Calabasas, CA: Author.

Coleman, H. (1987). Teaching spectacles and learning festivals. *ELT Journal, 41,* 97–103.

Debord, G. (1981). Theory of the *dérive*. In K. Knabb (Ed.), *Situationist international anthology* (pp. 50-54). Berkeley, CA: Bureau of Public Secrets. (Original work published 1958)

Debord, G. (1990). *Comments on the society of the spectacle* (M. Imrie, Trans.). London & New York: Verso. (Original work published 1988)

Debord, G. (1995). *The society of the spectacle* (D. Nicholson-Smith, Trans.). New York: Zone Books. (Original work published 1967)

De Certeau, M. (1984). *The practice of everyday life* (S. Rendall, Trans.). Berkeley: University of California Press.

Definitions. (1981). In K. Knabb (Ed.), *Situationist international anthology* (pp. 45–46). Berkeley, CA: Bureau of Public Secrets.

Department of Education. (1990). *National goals for education*. Washington, DC: USDOE/USGPO.

Department of Education. (1991). *America 2000: An education strategy sourcebook*. Washington, DC: USDOE/USGPO.

Detournement as Negation and Prelude. (1981). In K. Knabb (Ed.), *Situationist international anthology* (pp. 55–56). Berkeley, CA: Bureau of Public Secrets. (Original work published 1959)

Dewey, J. (1966). *Democracy and education.* New York: Macmillan. (Original work published 1916).

Dianda, M., McKeon, D., & Kapinus, B. (n.d.). *A tool for auditing standards-based education.* Washington, DC: National Education Association. Retrieved from http://www.nea.org

Eilenberg, L. I. (1975). Dramaturgy and spectacle: A proportion. *Journal of Aesthetic Education, 9*(4), 43–53.

Finn, C. E., Jr., & Petrilli, M. J. (Eds.). (2000). *The state of state standards 2000.* The Thomas B. Fordham Foundation. Retrieved from http://www.edexcellence. net/library/soss2000/2000soss.html

Foucault, M. (1979). *Discipline and punish: The birth of the prison* (A. Sheridan, Trans.). New York: Vintage. (Original work published 1975)

Freire, P. (1970). *Pedagogy of the oppressed.* New York: Continuum.

Fukuyama, F. (2002). *Our posthuman future: Consequences of the biotechnology revolution.* New York: Farrar, Straus, & Giroux.

Geography Education Standards Project. (1994). *Geography for life: National geography standards: What every young American should know and be able to do in geography.* Washington, DC: National Geographic Research and Exploration.

Haney, W. (2000). The myth of the Texas miracle in education. *Education Policy Analysis Archives, 8*(41). Retrieved from http://epaa.asu.edu/epaa/v8n41

Herman, E. S., & Chomsky, N. (1988). *Manufacturing consent: The political economy of the mass media.* New York: Pantheon.

Hirsch, E. D. (1987). *Cultural literacy: What every American needs to know.* Boston: Houghton Mifflin.

Hirsch, E. D. (1996). *The schools we need and why we don't have them.* New York: Doubleday.

Jappe, A. (1999). *Guy Debord* (D. Nicholson-Smith, Trans.). Berkeley: University of California Press. (Original work published 1993)

Johnson, J., & [with] Duffett, A. (1999, September 30). *Standards and accountability: Where the public stands: A report from Public Agenda for the 1999 National Education Summit.* New York: Public Agenda.

Jones, J. M. (2001, January 10). *Americans rank education as top priority for the Bush Administration.* Princeton, NJ: The Gallup Organization. Retrieved from http://www.Gallup.com/poll/releases/pr010110.asp

Keefe, P. K. (2006). *Chatter: Uncovering the echelon surveillance network and the secret world of global eavesdropping.* New York: Random House.

Klein, S. P., Hamilton, L. S., McCaffrey, D. F., & Stecher, B. M. (2000). *What do test scores in Texas tell us?* (Issue paper 202). Santa Monica, CA: Rand. Retrieved from http://www.rand.org/publications/IP/IP202

Knabb, K. (Ed. & Trans.). (1981). *Situationist international anthology.* Berkeley, CA: Bureau of Public Secrets.

Kohn, A. (2000). *The case against standardized testing: Raising the scores, ruining the schools.* New York: Heinemann.

Lefebvre, H. (1971). *Everyday life in the modern world* (S. Rabinovitch, Trans.). London: Allen Lane/The Penguin Press. (Original work published 1968)

Lefebvre, H. (1992). *Critique of everyday life, volume I* (J. Moore, Trans.). London & New York: Verso. (Original work published 1947)

Levin, H. M. (1998). Educational performance standards and the economy. *Educational Researcher, 27*(4), 4–10.

Magdoff, H., Wood, E. M., & McNally, D. (1999). Capitalism at the end of the millennium: A global survey [Special issue]. *Monthly Review, 51*(3).

Marx, K. (1964). *Karl Marx: Early writings* (T. B. Bottomore, Ed. & Trans.). New York: McGraw Hill.

Marx, K. (1988). *The German ideology.* New York: International Publishers.

Mathison, S., Ross, E. W., & Vinson, K. D. (2001). Defining the social studies curriculum: Influence of and resistance to curriculum standards and testing in social studies. In E. W. Ross (Ed.), *The social studies curriculum: Purposes, problems, and possibilities* (rev. ed., pp. 87-102). Albany: State University of New York Press.

Matthews, J. H. (1975). Spectacle and poetry: Surrealism in theatre and cinema. *Journal of General Education, 27,* 55–68.

McLuhan, M. (1994). *Understanding media: The extensions of man.* Cambridge, MA and London, UK: MIT Press. (Original work published 1964)

McNeil, L. M. (2000). *Contradictions of school reform: Educational costs of standardized testing.* New York and London: Routledge.

Nash, G. B., Crabtree, C., & Dunn, R. E. (1997). *History on trial: Culture wars and the teaching of the past.* New York: Knopf.

National Center for History in the Schools. (1994a). *National standards for United States history.* Los Angeles: Author.

National Center for History in the Schools. (1994b). *National standards for world history.* Los Angeles: Author.

National Commission on Excellence in Education. (1983). *A nation at risk: The imperative for educational reform.* Washington, DC: USGPO.

National Council for the Social Studies. (1981). Statement on the essentials of the social studies. *Social Education, 45,* 162–164.

National Council for the Social Studies Curriculum Standards Task Force. (1994). *Expectations of excellence: Curriculum standards for social studies* (Bulletin 89). Washington, DC: National Council for the Social Studies.

National Council on Economic Education. (1997). *Voluntary national content standards in economics.* New York: Author.

Ohanian, S. (1999). *One size fits few: The folly of educational standards.* New York: Heinemann.

Ollman, B. (2001). *How to take an exam . . . and remake the world.* Montreal/New York/London: Black Rose Books.

Perlman, F. (1969). *The reproduction of everyday life.* Available online: http://www.pipwline.com/~rgibson/repro-daily-life.html

Perlman, F. (1972). *The reproduction of daily life.* Detroit: Black & Red. (Original work published 1969). Retrieved from http://spunk.org/texts/writers/perlman/sp001702/repro.html

Polan, D. B. (1986). "Above all else to make you see": Cinema and the ideology of spectacle. In J. Arac (Ed.), *Postmodernism and politics* (pp. 55–69). Minneapolis: University of Minnesota Press.

Popkewitz, T., & Brennan, M. (Eds.). (1998). *Foucault's challenge: Discourse, knowledge, and power in education.* New York: Teachers College Press.

Ravitch, D. (2000). *Left back: A century of failed school reforms.* New York: Simon & Schuster.

Ravitch, D., & Finn, C. E., Jr. (1987). *What do our 17-year-olds know? A report of the first national assessment of history and literature.* New York: Harper & Row.

Rich, F. (2000, October 29). The age of the mediathon. *The New York Times Magazine,* pp. 58–65, 84.

Rich, F. (2003, June 15). How 15 minutes became 5 weeks. *The New York Times,* section 2, pp.–1 & 8.

Roman, L. (1996). Spectacle in the dark: Youth as transgression, display, and repression. *Educational Theory, 38,* 95–109.

Rosen, J. (2000). *The unwanted gaze: The destruction of privacy in America.* New York: Random House.

Ross, E. W. (2000). The spectacle of standards and summits. *Z Magazine, 12*(3), 45–48.

Rossi, B. (2000, February 18). Students flunking but for a cause. *Chicago Sun-Times,* pp. 1–2.

Schmidt, G. (2000, June). *Looking behind the data.* Paper presented at the International Education Summit for a Democratic Society, Detroit, MI.

Senese, G., & Page, R. (1995). *Simulation, spectacle, and the ironies of education reform.* Westport, CT & London: Bergin & Garvey.

Simpson, G. R. (2001, April 13). Big brother-in-law: If the FBI hopes to get the goods on you, it may ask ChoicePoint. *The Wall Street Journal,* pp. A1, A6.

Steinberg, S. R., & Kincheloe, J. L. (Eds.). (1997). *Kinderculture: The corporate construction of childhood.* Boulder, CO: Westview Press.

Tucker, M. S., & Codding, J. B. (1998). *Standards for our schools: How to set them, measure them, and reach them.* San Francisco: Jossey-Bass.

Vaneigem, R. (1972). *The revolution of everyday life* (J. Fullerton & P. Sieveking, Trans.). (Original work published 1967). Available on-line: <http://www.subsitu.com/kr/ROEL.htm>

Vinson, K. D. (1999). National curriculum standards and social studies education: Dewey, Freire, Foucault, and the creation of a radical critique. *Theory and Research in Social Education, 23,* 50–82.

Vinson, K. D. (2001). Image, authenticity, and the collective good: The problematics of standards-based reform. *Theory and Research in Social Education, 29,* 363–374.

Vinson, K. D., Gibson, R., & Ross, E. W. (2001). *High-stakes testing and standardization: The threat to authenticity.* Burlington, VT: John Dewey Project on Progressive Education/University of Vermont. Retrieved from http://www.uvm.edu/~dewey/monographs/ProPer3n2.html

Vinson, K. D., & Ross, E. W. (2001). In search of the social studies curriculum: Standardization, diversity, and a conflict of appearances. In W. B. Stanley (Ed.), *Critical issues in social studies research for the 21st century* (pp. 39–71). Greenwich, CT: Information Age.

Vinson, K. D., & Ross, E. W. (2001, March). What we can know and when we can know it: Education reform, testing, and the standardization craze. *Z Magazine,* pp. 34–38.

Vinson, K. D., & Ross, E. W. (2003). *Image and education: Teaching in the face of the new disciplinarity.* New York: Peter Lang.

Wheelock, A., Bebell, D. J., & Haney, W. (2000). What can student drawings tell us about high-stakes testing in Massachusetts? *Teachers College Record.* Retrieved from http://www.tcrecord.org/Content.asp?ContentID=10634

Wolf, R. M. (1998). National standards: Do we need them? *Educational Researcher, 27*(4), 22–25.

Young, I. M. (1992). Five faces of oppression. In T. E. Wartenberg (Ed.), *Rethinking power* (pp. 174-195). Albany: State University of New York Press.

4

U.S. Imperialism, Mexico, and the Education of Mexican Immigrants, 1900–1960

Gilbert G. Gonzalez

This chapter argues that the United States is an imperialist power and that U.S.–Mexico relations since the late 19th century falls squarely into the definition of imperialism. Furthermore, this relation has significantly impacted the history of the Mexican immigrant community. This frame of analysis differs fundamentally from the general approach to Chicano history. In the main, Chicano historiography exhibits an overwhelming tendency to limit analyses to themes and topics originating north of the border. Such an approach confines the analysis by failing to take into account those transnational factors, that is, U.S. imperialism, impacting on the Chicano experience. But, Chicano historiography is not alone; the imperialist dimensions of 20th–century U.S. history are also generally ignored in academia. Nevertheless, historians have made a strong case for arguing that an economic hegemony distinguished U.S.–Mexico relations beginning in the late 19th century (Hart, 2002; A. Kaplan & Pease, 1993). It is this domination that differentiates the Mexican immigrant experience in the United States from the experiences of other immigrant communities. Immigration studies tend to follow well-worn sociological paths that lumps all immigrants into a "one-size-fits-all" theoretical scheme. Consequently, when explicating the history of the Mexican immigrant community, in particular the educational experiences, the analysis falls wide of the mark.

The argument here is that the United States expanded economically into Mexico on a large scale in the late 19th century, coming to dominate the nation's economy. In step with the emergence of U.S. economic domination (or economic colonization), a widely promulgated imperial ideology appeared highlighting a "Mexican problem," that is, a catalogue of Mexican cultural and/or genetic pathologies that posed an obstacle to self-attained modernization. The resolution to the Mexican problem concluded that only foreigners, mainly Americans, were capable of meeting the challenge and lead Mexico across the threshold of economic and cultural development. Produced by travelers, journalists, government officials, academics, corporate administrators, Protestant missionaries, retired engineers, and business people, their published accounts written for an American audience ultimately found their way into the popular culture and government bureaucracies of the United States.

That body of literature highlighted a Mexican problem, which not only legitimized and justified an ongoing economic domination by the United States over Mexico, but also rationalized the segregation of Mexican children in public schools. As such, more U.S. capital in Mexico would solve the Mexican problem in Mexico. Upon the massive migration to the United States in the early 20th century, the identification of the immigrant community as the Mexican problem within the United States became widespread conventional wisdom. As migrants traveled northward, the transnational version of the Mexican problem applied in schools legitimized a unique curriculum adapted to the supposed attributes of the Mexican immigrant community in segregated schools.

A CENTURY OF U.S. IMPERIALISM

Except for some frank admissions by imperial minded Americans, throughout most of the 20th century most Americans have tended to recoil at the thought that the United States is an imperialist power. However, in the late 19th and early 20th centuries imperialist boosterism appeared frequently. Not a few urged British-style colonialism like that which the author

Trumbull White (1898) advocated in his work on the defeat of the Spanish armed forces and the taking over of their former colonies at the end of the 19th century. "For good or for ill," wrote White, shortly after the Supreme Court rendered decision avowing the Constitutionality of "Separate But Equal,"

> the United States has entered upon a colonial policy, a policy of expansion, a policy which forces us into a position of world power, deep in the complications of international politics. . . . Without experience or precedents of our own colonial policy, we are forced into the position of creating one. (White, 1898, p. 17)

White was certainly not alone in celebrating the U.S. imperial expansion. However, a few decades after White and others of similar thinking penned such ideas, the admission by America's political leaders that the United States was an imperial power was emphatically denied. News media and academics followed suit. Empire and imperialism became the "E" and "I" words, seldom invoked in analysis of U.S. foreign policy. Americans believed it just to refer to the United Kingdom as the British Empire and to the Soviet Union as the "evil empire." But, Americans have a history of refusing any description of the United States as imperialist, partly because most believe that empires are the epitome of that which has come to be known as "un-American." Furthermore, conventional wisdom contends that imperialists govern defined territorial regions and their inhabitants beyond the nation's borders, that is, colonies ruled by the distant foreign power. However, that reluctance to label the United States as an imperialist power has recently receded and rather quickly, and unfortunately for the wrong reasons.

Of late, a groundswell of articles have "come out," so to speak, on the question of U.S. imperialism, claiming the United States as a benign, humanitarian albeit imperialist power spreading democracy and the "American Dream" around the globe. Nationally recognized political analysts from the neoconservative flank like William Kristol, Max Boot, William Rusher and Ben Wattenberg, among others, have openly declared the United States not only the supreme power but also an imperialist power. In the pages of the *Atlantic Monthly* Robert D. Kaplan (2003), for example, contended "It is a cliché these days to observe that the United States now possesses a global empire—different from Britain's and Rome's but an empire nonetheless. It is time to move beyond a statement of the obvious" (p. 66) Charles Krauthammer added in *The Washington Post*, "We dominate every field of human endeavor from fashion to film to finance. We rule the world culturally, economically, diplomatically and militarily as no one since the Roman Empire" (p. 15) Not to be outdone, Rusher (2001) echoed the comparison, juxtaposing the United States to the empires of the past in his nationally syndicated column: "In two great instances, however—the Roman Empire and the British Empire—one nation did acquire the overwhelming power that is now vested in the United States" (p. A7) Henry Kissinger, secretary of state under Nixon and Ford, expressed nearly identical perspectives on the United States as imperialist power in a televised interview with Ben Wattenberg. Wattenberg, the host of *ThinkTank*, a PBS program, asked Kissinger toward the end of the broadcast:

> Wattenberg: Let me ask you a couple of final questions. Is America an empire? Kissinger: America is the strongest nation in the world. So, in this sense, that it is an empire in the sense that whenever it wants to use its force it can impose its will. On the other hand, the problem of foreign policy is not just to impose your will once, but to make it last. In order to make it last you have to build consensus. Just as the Romans governed first with their legions and then with Roman Law. And the British did it—governed India with, I think, a maximum of sixty thousand people. So the fact that we are what the Europeans call a hyperpower, that's a fact of life, and we have to accept it and live with it.

Thus, at the beginning of the 21st century, the terms U.S. imperialism and U.S. empire are coming into usage that was unthinkable through most of the 20th (e.g., Bacevich, 2002, 2003). However, imperialism did not suddenly descend willy-nilly onto the United States at the turn of the 21st century. For more than a century the United States administered an imperialist policy, regardless of the absence of official pronouncements denying imperialist ambitions and any evidence of outright colonial possessions.

U.S. IMPERIALISM AND MEXICO

Americans sometimes admit that imperialism did appear in the late 19th and early 20th centuries, but then cooler heads prevailed and the imperialist adventures disappeared. The claim is then extended to argue that the United States is an exception to the general imperialist conduct of economically developed nations, particularly Europe, in the 20th century. However, U.S. imperial policy resonated with European colonialism. Cuba, Puerto Rico, the Philippines, Hawaii, and Panama (a province of Colombia) were plundered from their rightful heirs. The case of Mexico is most relevant to our discussion of U.S. imperialism, in that between the end of the Civil War and the Spanish-American War, the United States expanded economically into the southern nation with a goal of "peaceful conquest," that is, the economic domination of Mexico, synonymous with economic colonization. Indeed, a groundswell of public opinion surfaced in the late 1860s calling for either the annexation of Mexico or its conquest by economic means, that is, large-scale export of capital investments into Mexico. U.S. officials and investors chose the latter route.

In the first decade of the 20th century, a policy labeled the "peaceful conquest" had been achieved (Pletcher, 1958). Classic participants in the Robber Barons era held considerable investment interests in Mexico. Daniel Guggenheim, William Randolph Hearst, J. P. Morgan, Colis P. Huntington, Jay Gould, and corporations like Standard Oil, U.S. Steel, Phelps Dodge, Union Pacific, McCormick, Atchison Topeka and Santa Fe, Doheny Oil, among others came to control Mexico (Parkes, 1970). Mexico quickly evolved into a virtual economic protectorate of the United States, which prompted muckraking journalist John Kenneth Turner to offer an insight to the transnational relation. "American capital" he contended, "has wrecked Mexico as a national entity. The United States government, as long as it represents American capital . . . will have a deciding voice in Mexican affairs" (Turner, 1911, pp. 256–257) Indeed, U.S. foreign policy dedicated itself to protecting the open door to American capital abroad. More than $1 billion of U.S. capital controlled Mexican mining, railroads, oil and significant sectors of her agriculture by 1910, and by 1930 U.S. capital enjoyed an even stronger presence (Smith, 1972). From this colonial relationship, migration to the United States and the formation of the modern Mexican-American community together with public policy applied to this community (explained later), was propelled.

Economic colonialism wrought major alterations to Mexico's demography and economy as well as its social relations and class structure. Perhaps no other activities than the construction of U.S. railroads had greater impact on Mexican society. Railroad construction proceeded directly in the path of traditional farming villages and many campesinos were forced to remove. Later, government-sponsored de-peasanting laws finished the process and uprooted several hundreds of thousands of peasants from communal farming plots leading to migrations from villages, to towns and cities, particularly Mexico City (Pletcher, 1958). For the first time in Mexico's history, a radical demographic restructuring occurred, a shift in the settlement pattern propelled by the incursion of U.S. capital. These migrants were then recruited and transported by American companies to work sites, primarily along the northern states bordering the United States. Eventually, these same internal migrants became the workforce in the oil and mining camps and in the work crews stationed along the railroads. By 1900, foreign capital, mainly from the United States, dominated the Mexican economy, while Mexicans supplied the labor power.

New social relations were instantly injected into the Mexican landscape. At least 200,000 laborers labored annually for U.S. companies by 1910,

Mexico's very first industrial working class; and new terms were injected into the productive processes such as Mexican work, meaning inexperienced cheap labor, as well as the Mexican wage, half that paid Americans for equal work. In order to attract labor, companies constructed housing at the work sites and the majority of migrating workers brought their families attracted by the same housing. But, more than just company towns appeared, these were strictly segregated towns, with Mexicans living in their own quarters separate from the American minority who resided in comfortable residences, often with recreational facilities such as tennis courts, perhaps a golf course, and community meeting hall. Many Americans brought their own families whose children were educated at the American elementary school and taught by an American teacher brought from the United States for that purpose.

The segregated social system as practiced in the United States embedded within Mexico. On the railroads, English was the official language, American Blacks served as cooks and porters, Whites managed and administered the operation. Chinese imported from the United States washed and cooked in the homes of the American personnel and their families. Segregation distinguished the American foreigner from Mexican. However, wherever Americans planted their investments and industrial work sites, they administered the production system and the company town in addition to politically dominating the nearby region (Hart, 1997).

THE CULTURE OF U.S. IMPERIALISM

Every imperial adventure manifests an imperialist mindset that identifies with and advocates for the imperialist policies. With the economic domination of Mexico, a language of imperialism constructed by Americans came to predominate discussions on Mexico. Part of the foundation for this discourse can be explained by the extension of American railroads into Mexico affording travel to Mexico City on fairly easy terms. By 1900, travelers descended on Mexico in record numbers and made possible a new genre of American writing, like that of Trumbull White, which appeared in newspapers, journals, and in books. Journalists, novelists, academicians, Protestant missionaries, and professional travelers, among others, penned accounts for a public that knew next to nothing about Mexico. However, their first images of Mexico as they stepped from their trains, which were less than approving, set the stage for what was later to come.

In a seeming unified fashion, first time travelers to Mexico expressed loathing and surprise as the crossed into Mexico. One wrote, "The Journey was made without event. Our stops were short, the country uninviting, and the natives more so" (Wilson, 1910, p. 2).

Another noted that were they transported to another world nothing would seem so strange, yet it was the economic relation between the two countries that assumed critical attention in many publications. One writer's comment captured the general colonial impression of the time: "Mexico and the United States compliment each other. . . . Something of what India is to England, Mexico could and ought to be to the United States" (Griffin, 1886, p. 210). In the pages of *Harper's New Monthly Magazine*, F. E. Prendergast's (1881) conceptualization of Mexico and Mexicans speaks to the point. "Now it is evident," he wrote,

> that any rapid progress in Mexico must come through the colonization of some higher and more progressive race, or by the introduction of capital in large amounts to develop her natural resources by the aid of native races, who are peaceable and industrious. (p. 277)

Wallace Thompson's (1921) images written in the early 1920s tell of a brash and unforgiving colonial hubris within the Tampico oil fields dominated by Doheny Oil:

> To-day there are 8,000 Americans and . . . the swaggering, free-money, noisy, busy atmosphere of the frontier, of oil fields, of the white man on his bully-ragging, destructive, inconsequential "education" of the dark brother round the world permeates the place . . . Tampico is a monument to the genius and faith of the Americans who made it great. (p. 207)

Colonialism and empire-building seemed all the rage, and discussing U.S. foreign policy in these terms few raised any objections. Mining engineer Isaac Marcossen (1916) minced no words in his article published in *Collier's Magazine*), "The vision of Harriman, the masterful ambition of Huntington, the doggedness of Palmer, the tenacity of Guggenheim, the faith of 'Boss' Shepherd, the constructive genius of half a dozen other noted empire builders all found expression in the making of Mexico" (p. 23). Another remarked, "no intelligent or responsible Mexican can hope to see his country prosper without foreign capital" (Powell, 1924, p. 169).

Some 40,000 U.S. citizens made Mexico their home and worked in the main for American enterprises, writers minced no words as they celebrated the American presence in Mexico. Several authors found that the British colonial system served as a template for describing American communities in Mexico. One compared a particular American sugar enterprise to a typical British colonial outpost and described a real colonial setting:

> It is in the heart of sugar-cane country. All the land, the sugar mills, the hotel, and most of the business firms are owned by Americans. The

> plantations are operated by modern American efficiency. The planters
> live a life that reminds one of Rudyard Kipling's stories of the life of the
> English in India. They have their tennis clubs, polo fields, gold links,
> dances, bridge parties. (Carr, 1934, p. 152)

One must keep in mind that although writing like that presented here
appeared with regularity in the United States, Blacks experienced a state-
mandated and-enforced segregation that bound them to remain a source of
cheap labor, confined to the lowest rungs of the working class.
Consequently, writers began to rationalize U.S. economic domination over
Mexico on the same fallacious concoctions that legitimized the oppression
of Blacks.

Inherent flaws in either Mexico's culture or, more often, in Mexico's
biological makeup were alleged to distinguish Americans from Mexicans.
Indians, Spaniards, and "half-breeds," or mestizos guaranteed that Mexico
would never rise above the mediocre, if that. One former U.S. diplomat put
it simply: "It must be confessed that [mestizos] often exhibit the known tendency to follow the vices and weaknesses of both sides of their ancestry
rather than the virtues" (Jones, 1921, p. 18).

Interestingly, the term Oriental was employed for the first few decades
of the 20th century as a defining characteristic of all Mexicans. Not merely
did writers refer to Mexicans as Orientals in a descriptive manner, rather the
purpose was to point out the limited mentality shared by both groups. One
Protestant missionary noted,

> Now with regard to the character of the people [of Mexico], they are as
> Oriental in type, in thought, and in habits as the Orientals themselves.
> It is true they have a veneer of European civilization; but underneath
> this veneer, on studying the people and becoming better acquainted with
> them, we find that they are genuine Asiatics. They have the same sense
> of fatalism, the same tendency for speculation on the impractical side of
> life and religion, the same opposition to the building of industries . . .
> (William Wallace, quoted in Winton, 1913, p. 2)

Shortly, the term peon, meaning common laborer in Spanish, assumed the
place formerly held by the word Oriental. However, both terms came to
mean the same thing: an adult with a child-like mental ability and corresponding behavior patterns. Not surprisingly, writers, without second thoughts,
described Mexicans as lazy, lascivious, prone to violence, inveterate thieves,
immoral, unambitious, fatalistic, plagued with the manana syndrome, to
name a few; but on the other hand Mexicans were said to be good with their
hands, artistic, musical, courteous, colorful and so on.

It is instructive that Mexicans at the turn of the 20th century were identified with the quintessential colonial subjects, the Oriental, and all that it

implied. However, as cheap and dependable labor they more than passed the productivity test for large-scale integration into the growing American industrial operations in Mexico. However, the limitations of the "Mexican mind" were to be taken into consideration for securing the greatest labor output commented one administrator of an American owned mine,

> To manage Mexican labor successfully it is necessary at the onset to take into consideration the fact that the peon is a race whose habits and characteristics are those of a simple-minded people . . . and who have not yet learned to act on their own initiative . . . the successful manager is the one who understands the limitations of the people and is willing to adapt his methods to their capabilities. (Fraser-Campbell, 1911, p. 1104)

Inherent inferiority of Mexicans implied a responsibility on part of the Americans to bring the unfortunates into the modern world without, however, changing the relations of superior to inferior. The United States candidly assumed the "White Man's Burden" in its relationship to Mexico. Americans conceived of Mexico as a nation-child, summarized in the literature as the "Mexican problem," that required foreign, meaning American, tutelage. This tutelage was commonly assumed to be a wholesale Americanization of Mexico, and writers assumed without question that such required the expansion and deepening of the economic domination over Mexico.

On the other hand, a cultural reformation was also required, a variation of the European theme of bringing civilization to the colonized peoples of the world, that is, teaching the colonized the rudiments of proper modern behavior. Professional traveler and journalist Harriet Wight Sherrat (1899) averred that Mexicans "often seem to us childish and puerile, we may, nevertheless . . . [lead] our neighbors up the steep grade of civilization" (p. 20). On the same topic, an author of an article appropriately entitled "The Americanization of Mexico" reported that, "Modernization and Americanization are almost synonymous terms," and proudly claimed that "each year the American way of living is taking a deeper hold on the Mexican people" (Conley, 1907, p. 724). Despite any amount of learned civilization by the dominated peoples, colonization never entertained an end to the process; colonization implied a permanent status and continuity of existing relations of power.

A common refrain held that the natural social condition of Mexicans equaled that of American Blacks. One American mining engineer alleged that the peon "is of mild and humble nature, much like the plantation field hands before the war . . . like the southern darkey . . . " (Rogers, 1908, p. 700). Some argued that Mexico's needs were best served with the same kind of bootstrap philosophy that Booker T. Washington. Neither group could be expected to rise above their existing condition without outside intervention.

However, the racialized ideology of imperialism worked in both the domestic and international settings by justifying continued white supremacy at home and abroad. The prescription for the salvation of Mexico, argued many a writer, can only be realized through the expansion of United States economic domination over Mexico. The ideology of U.S. imperialism abroad and the ideology of White supremacy at home were two sides of the same coin.

THE CULTURE OF IMPERIALISM AT HOME

Contrary to conventional theoretical discussions of Mexican migration, the "push–pull" model cannot explain a century of Mexican migration. Historical studies have long argued that the Mexican Revolution spurred the first large-scale migration and that poverty, unemployment, and the like have kept the momentum moving forward. However, the push–pull model and its variations, such as those emphasizing agency, social networks, and human capital cannot explain migration. For example, Mexican migration was operating on a large scale prior to the Mexican Revolution, so that by 1910 some 60,000 were crossing the border annually most crossing at El Paso, Texas. In fact, during the Revolution, the numbers of peoples coming to the United States decreased dramatically.

Rather than the violence of the Revolution, the factors propelling this transnational migration were the same that led to internal migrations within Mexico. That is, the social consequence of U. S. capitalist enterprises spurred migration within Mexico northward and from the northern region across the border. U.S. railroads and mining corporations recruited Mexican labor well within Mexico and at the border and contractors transported thousands to work sites throughout the southwest. A 1908 Department of Commerce and Labor report on Mexican labor noted the following:

> The reasons that makes El Paso the most important distributing point for Mexican immigration are its direct railway communication with the swarming States of Mexico; the presence across the border, in the State of Chihuahua, of large mines and smelters, which, in supplying their own needs, assist the southern laborer to the frontier; and the direct railway communication that the city enjoys with such chief labor-absorbing areas of the United States as the prairie grain and cotton region, the Colorado and the Territorial mining fields and California. (Clark, 1908, pp. 470–471)

By 1910, a century of immigration began, assuming a variety of forms, from state-sanctioned labor importation programs, such as the Bracero Program (1942–1964) to legal and undocumented migration. Mexican labor moved en masse and assumed work on the nation's largest capitalist enterprises, railroads, mining, and agriculture. Indeed, Mexicans were the main workforce for southwestern railroads by 1920, comprising 75% of track workers, and were the chief labor supply for agriculture, Arizona mines and Midwest sugar beet fields. As the third decade faded, approximately 750,000 Mexican immigrants integrated into the U.S. economy as cheap labor, dependable, and willing to work. Mexican settlements mushroomed across the southwest, into Kansas rail yards and midwestern steel towns. But the vast majority settled in Texas and California in what has been referred to as the Brown belt, a corridor 150 miles wide from Brownsville to Los Angeles where 85% of all Mexican migrants settled. Except for the Great Depression, Mexican migration remained constant to the present.

As immigrants settled into their communities they experienced many of the same conditions that were found in their former villages and towns where American companies operated. Residential segregation, ethnic class differentiation, the Mexican wage, company towns, company stores, and the very same racialized perceptions that Americans held of Mexico and all Mexicans welcomed Mexicans as they entered the United States. The culture of imperialism more than greeted Mexicans as they crossed the border, it also shaped in important ways public policy aimed at the Mexican community. Explaining the educational programs aimed at the Mexican community requires that we acknowledge the imperial mindset constructed by American writers writing about Mexico. When mass migration spilled into the southwest, policymakers had few clues about Mexicans in general. Consequently, experts were consulted and these were the very same authors who explained Mexico to the American public. The vast number of books and articles related to Mexico became, overnight, the keys used in public policy venues, particularly the educational establishment, for deciphering Mexican immigrants.

EDUCATION AND THE CULTURE OF IMPERIALISM

The first publications discussing Mexican immigrants appeared in the second decade of the 20th century and were little more than superficial commentaries. However, leading sociologists of the period began to refine their studies by consulting publications about Mexico. The so-called Mexican problem, which first surfaced in writings about Mexico, reappears in writing about Mexican immigrants. Essentially, there was no gap between the perceptions that Americans held about Mexico and its people and the perceptions held by Americans regarding Mexican immigrants. Once the material on Mexico became widely disseminated, it then became the prime source of information used in public policy formulation. In short order, the culture of imperialism served as a guide for policymakers as they designed public policy for Mexican immigrants. The terms *Oriental, mestizo, peon,* and the sum total of all of these terms, the "Mexican problem," once applied to only to Mexico, soon became blanket definitions for Mexican immigrants.

Pioneer in sociological studies on Mexican immigrants and graduate of the famed Chicago School of Sociology, Emory Bogardus, Professor at the University of Southern California, recommended readings in his 1919 text, *Essentials of Americanization,* for those interested in learning more about Mexican immigrants. All of the recommended publications were written about Mexico and each depicted Mexicans in a manner that defined Mexico and Mexicans as a "problem." Professor Bogardus spoke for many, including those who would later study under him, in his 1919 study. In it he contended, "In the southwestern states the 'Mexican Problem' has developed rapidly since 1900."

Bogardus was certainly not alone in adopting the term *Mexican problem* in relation to the Mexican immigrants. Protestant missionary working with the Mexican community in the U.S. penned a study of Mexican immigrants in a work titled *That Mexican! As He Really Is, North and South of the Border* published in 1928. McLean reiterated what many already concluded:

> "That Mexican" whom we have so long contemplated from north of the Rio Grande, has therefore come to live with us. With his inherited ignorance, his superstition, his habits of poor housing, his weaknesses to some diseases, and his resistance to others, with his abiding love of beauty, he has come to pour his blood into the veins of our national life. "That Mexican" no longer lives in Mexico; he lives in the United States. The "Mexican problem" therefore is no longer one of politics; it is one of people. It reaches from Gopher Prairie to Guatemala. (McLean, 1928, p. 126)

Bogardus and McLean were accompanied when advising the American public of the problem brought by the new immigrant group. Other terms supplied the same meaning particularly the use of the word *peon* for describing Mexicans. For example, in his 1919 study, Bogardus alleged that "The Mexican immigrants represent the peon, or the mixed and least developed classes of Mexico" (Bogardus, 1919, p. 179). In a later publication, he suggested that in order to fully understand the Mexican immigrant it was first necessary to "consider the Mexican immigrants in light of the family culture traits of the peon classes of Mexico" (Bogardus, 1934, p. 24). Peon seemed most appropriate for explicating the Mexican to the public. Frederick

Simpich, (1920) former U.S. consul at an Arizona border town, offered these tidbits on migrants crossing the border for popular consumption:

> the peon likes to ride. Whenever they have saved money from a few day's work, they swarm up and down these lines to border towns, carrying women, children, birdcages, blanket rolls, and family utensils, running to and fro apparently as aimless as the inhabitants of a disturbed ant-hill. (p. 63)

The word *peon* contained a clear definition of Mexican immigrants appropriated whenever necessary by those in positions of power. But, on the other hand, Mexican supplied that same meaning. In a separate article, Simpich (1924) went somewhat further in his description and depicted Mexican immigrants in a fashion typical for the period. "But the undeniable fact," he recorded, "that we do differ so widely from the Mexicans in race, in political and social habits and standards, and in history, traditions, and thinking processes, makes the settlement of the [Mexican] problem immensely difficult" (p. 238).

One can easily surmise what effects these prevalent ideas, borrowed from "authorities" on Mexico, would have on the gradually expanding public educational system. As the public school system expanded so did training programs for teachers and a cache of master's theses and doctoral dissertations on the education of Mexican immigrants appeared. No less than 25 appearing in the 1910–1950 period relied to a large extent on material written about Mexico for information related to Mexican immigrants. Given the prevalence of conceptions on the average Mexican it should come as no surprise that in her 1932 master's thesis Betty Gould found that "The majority of Mexicans in our public schools . . . represent, rather, the very lowest type, the day laborer or the peon." Later, she would claim that "the Mexican is naturally indolent, and his tendency to 'never do today what can be put off until some other time' is one of the outstanding problems with which the school is confronted" (p. 47).

Clearly, the label *peon* meant an inferior being and a potential threat to the welfare of the United States. Hence, policymakers deliberately sought resolution to the Mexican problem, which in effect meant isolating, containing, and then dominating the Mexican community. And this is precisely the objective of the educational policy as applied to the Mexican community. However, as in the case of the Black community, segregation never implied social change, on the contrary segregation efficiently reproduced the working-class position of the Mexican community as the cheapest, most exploitable labor available to the large scale capitalist system that came to depend on Mexican immigrant labor. And this is precisely how the Mexican problem, the consequence of U.S. imperial economic intervention into Mexico, was handled.

SOLVING THE MEXICAN PROBLEM: SEGREGATION, INDUSTRIAL EDUCATION, AND AMERICANIZATION

A future southern California school superintendent concluded in his master's thesis on Mexican children written at the University of Southern California, "the Mexican Problem . . . exists wherever there are Mexicans," and then detailed why segregation would be of great benefit to Mexicans and to the wider community.

> Considering the above facts, (1) because of the great social differences of the two races, (2) because of the much higher percentage of contagious diseases, (3) because of a higher percent of undesirable characteristics, (4) because of much slower progress in school, and (5) because of their much lower moral standard it would seem that:
>
> 1. Whenever numbers permit, Mexican children be segregated . . .
> 2. A special course of study be prepared to meet the needs of Mexican children. (Carpenter, 1935, pp. 27, 152)

A professor at the University of Texas recommended a similar program in his report on Texas education. "There is but one choice," he wrote, "in the matter of educating these unfortunate children and that is to put the 'dirty' ones into separate schools till they learn how to 'clean up' and become eligible to better society" (Davis, cited in Doerr, 1938, p. 1). District after district implemented this policy and in many areas deliberate segregation was practiced long after the Brown decision.

Given the wealth of information regarding the predominant characteristics of the average Mexican child, segregated schools severely limited academic training and emphasized industrial education divided into courses for boys and girls. Not infrequently, school districts concluded the education of Mexican children at the 8th Grade, others at the 10th Grade. High school was indeed a rarity. Some school districts titled the Mexican school, the Industrial School. Simultaneously, scientific racism reared its ugly head, a field of social science that argued a relationship between phenotype and intellectual ability. Not a few educators, with academic research to back them up, made the linkage between scores on IQ tests and inherent abilities of Mexican children. Many districts utilized IQ tests to track children into slow, average, and superior classes, but for the most part IQ tests were superfluous and often dispensed with because most educators already understood that vocational education was the best match given the "known" abilities of the average Mexican child. Nevertheless, IQ research into the mental ability of Mexican children, including the work of the master of scientific racism Louis Terman, produced nearly 50 studies between 1910 and

1950. Half concluded that defective genetic material caused mental inferiority, whereas an equal number held that cultural deficits caused Mexican children to score well below the average White child.

Los Angeles school district researchers found that Mexican children scored on average at the 90th percentile, a full 10 points below the mythical average. For the vast majority of Mexican children, IQ scores meant coursework for the slow to average intelligence. In his research project carried out while school superintendent in southern California, before he became director of admissions at the University of California, Berkeley, Merton Hill "discovered" that the Mexican children's ability to learn measured but 58% that of the average White child's ability (Hill, 1928). In Los Angeles in 1930, at least 50% of Mexican children were channeled into slow learner classes; nearly 30% of all children labeled educationally mentally retarded were Mexican children, although they comprised only 13% of all pupils in the schools. (Interestingly, these figures relating to Mexican children in Los Angeles public schools remained constant into 1970.) The vast majority of Mexican children entered into a schooling process that immediately defined them as good with their hands but limited in mental ability. As such, the schooling process had much in common with the educational experiences of the Black community.

The same school superintendent who found that Mexican children learned at 58% the White Anglo American child's rate connected the perceived abilities of Blacks with those of the Mexican community. Superintendent Hill confidently referred to a prevalent opinion when he wrote the following:

> Comparisons between the Mexicans and Negro pupils show that teachers consider them approximately on the same level. This is of value, for information regarding the development of Negro education should prove useful in the development of Mexican education; as industrial education for Negroes has proven most successful so should it prove for Mexican pupils. (Hill, 1928, p. 96)

If there is one thing that is certain of vocational education, it is the consequent reproduction of the Mexican community as a source of cheap labor, replicating the experience of the Black community. In short, the economic function of both communities would be preserved, the class structure of society secure. For employers, the school became a reliable source of cheap labor.

Americanization was not merely the forced the learning of English at the expense of Spanish. Segregation, vocational education, and Americanization complimented each other and were integral to the Chicano experience. The cultural cleansing greeted students in the first two grades, which were dedicated to Americanization (consequently the grades were titled Americanization rooms). Such a cultural reformation went beyond ethnicity; it aimed foremost at creating class solidarity and harmony between Mexican laborers and their capitalist employers through ridding the Mexican community of any cultural distinction with their employers. Social science theory at the time contended that a laboring community that practiced an ethnic culture at variance with the upper classes was prone to radicalism and militant unionization.

Consequently, English immersion, eliminating Spanish and Mexican cultural traits in general, while fostering American customs and traditions was considered an antidote to political radicalism within the Mexican sector of the working class. With that in mind, educators pursued the Americanization of the Mexican community with great zeal, far more than was the case in teaching vocational education. Not uncommonly, school districts rewarded those who began a cultural acculturation according to the school objectives and punished those who failed to manage the ethnic cleansing. In time, a popular identification for those who underwent a satisfactory cultural cleansing became, simply, a "good Mexican," and sometimes as a "different Mexican."

STRUGGLES TO REFORM THE SCHOOLING PROGRAM

Throughout the 20th century, the Mexican community demanded the reform of the educational system, particularly the policy of segregated schools. However, the opposition to segregation, seen as early as 1919 in Santa Ana, California, never challenged the use of IQ testing, tracking and Americanization. Despite the successful effort to desegregate schools in California in the 1947 Mendez Case, which came with the federal Appellate Court decision upholding the District Court's decision that declared the segregation of Mexican children unconstitutional, the use of IQ tests, tracking, vocational education and Americanization remained. Although segregation fell into the unconstitutional domain, implementation of the decision was never given much authority and in many instances, particularly in rural schools, segregation remained widespread. Finally, in the 1960s, the critique of testing, tracking, vocational education, and Americanization took center stage. The general questioning of wholesale dependence on testing and the emphasis on vocational education over academic preparation resulted in reforming the educational programs, but never uprooting basic approaches to the Chicano community and therefore on Chicano education.

In its fundamentals, the Chicano educational experience has not been altered since the early 20th century. The experiences of the first wave of immigrants in the 1920s have not worked themselves out and they remain to this day. The Mexican problem continues in altered forms from the "wet-back problem" of the 1950s to the "illegal alien problem" of the late 20th century, and now the "Latino problem" of the 21st (Huntington, 2004).[1] Each one of these variants warns of behavior patterns antithetical to the cultural and institutional foundations of the United States. In this setting, Americanization, testing, tracking, and vocational education remain important means to allocate education.

But, more importantly, the relationship of the United States to Mexico has deepened the domination exerted by the imperialist superpower. Today, the main employers in Mexico are more than 3,000 U.S.-owned assembly plants situated for the most part along the northern border and employ more than 1 million workers, predominantly women. Citicorp recently purchased Banamex, the largest privately owned bank in Mexico. The main investors in the Mexican stock market originate from the United States. And the North American Free Trade Agreement is ruining the Mexican countryside as the open door to American products, from corn, sorghum, and wheat to beef, chicken, and pork has destroyed the small-scale rural economy of Mexico. Farmers and ranchers are uprooted from their lands on a massive scale, and deserted villages now dot the Mexican countryside. (Cleeland, 2000; Kraul, 2000; Schrader, 1993). Today, an estimated 600 people leave the countryside each day. And where do the uprooted travel? To cities seeking work, and if none is found, to the assembly plants located along the border and from there, it is only a small trip across the border where agribusiness, hotels and middle-class professionals seeking domestics and nannies willingly employ the undocumented. Together, these migrants are treated as the growing illegal alien problem replete with debates as to whether driver's licenses are to be given them (as in California), or whether they deserve public services, such as social welfare and public education. Finally, a proposed solution to the illegal alien problem, a new guest worker program, can only create a class of indentured servants, a force of controlled labor in a society that prides itself as the epitome of freedom. But, such is the nature of imperialism.

The domination over the Mexican nation has resulted in a century of migration of peoples shoved off their lands and a century of labeling Mexican immigrants as a "problem." For more than a century, the social impact of the Mexican problem spread across the public policy spectrum, particularly in education; we are living a historical epoch that initially

---

[1]Huntington wrote: "The persistent inflow of Hispanic immigrants threatens to divide the United States into two peoples, two cultures, and two languages. Unlike past immigrant groups, Mexicans and other Latinos have not assimilated into main-stream U.S. culture, forming instead their own political and linguistic enclaves from Los Angeles to Miami-and rejecting the Anglo-protestant values that built the American dream. The United States ignores this challenge at its peril."

appeared in the first decade of the last century. The political and economic conditions imposed on the Mexican immigrant community have led to a century of struggle for democratic schooling. However, the struggle for democratic schooling is, ultimately, a struggle against imperialism.

REFERENCES

Bacevich, A. J. (2002). *American empire: The realities and consequences of U. S. diplomacy.* Cambridge: Harvard University Press.

Bacevich, A. J. (Ed.). (2003). *The imperial tense: Prospects and problems of American empire.* Chicago: Ivan R. Dee.

Bogardus, E. (1919). *Essentials of Americanization.* Los Angeles: University of Southern California Press.

Bogardus, E. (1934). *The Mexican in the United States* (University of Southern California School of Research Studies, no. 5). Los Angeles: University of Southern California Press.

Carpenter, C. C. (1935). *A study of segregation versus non-segregation of Mexican children.* Unpublished master's thesis, University of Southern California, Los Angeles.

Carr, H. (1934). *Old mother Mexico,* Boston: Houghton Mifflin.

Clark, V. (1908). *Mexican labor in the United States* (U.S. Department of Commerce and Labor, Bureau of Labor Bulletin no. 78). Washington DC: U.S. Government Printing Office.

Cleeland, N. (1997, August 3). Mexican town left behind. *Los Angeles Times,* p. 1.

Conley, E. M. (1907). The Americanization of Mexico. *American Monthly Review of Reviews, 32,* 724.

Doerr, M. F. (1938). *Problem of the elimination of Mexican pupils from school.* Unpublished master's thesis, University of Texas, Austin.

Fraser-Campbell, E. (1911). The management of Mexican labor. *Engineering and Mining Journal, 90,* 1104.

Gould, B. (1932). *Methods of teaching Mexicans.* Unpublished master's thesis, University of Southern California, Los Angeles.

Griffin, S. B. (1886). *Mexico of today.* New York: Harper & Brothers.

Hart, J. M. (1997). *Revolutionary Mexico: The coming and process of the Mexican revolution.* Berkeley: University of California Press.

Hart, J. M. (2002). *Empire and revolution: The Americans in Mexico since the civil war.* Berkeley: University of California Press.

Hill, M. (1928). *The development of an Americanization program.* Ontario, CA: Chaffey Unified School District Board of Trustees.

Huntington, S. P. (2004, March–April). The Hispanic challenge, *Foreign Affairs.* Retrieved from http://www.foreignpolicy.com/story/cms.php?story_id=2495

Jones, C. L. (1921). *Mexico and its reconstruction.* New York: D. Appleton.

Kaplan, A., & Pease, D. E. (Eds.). (1993). *Cultures of United States imperialism.* Durham: Duke University Press.

Kaplan, R. D. (2003). Supremacy by stealth. *Atlantic Monthly, 292*(1), 65–83.

Kraul, C. (2000, January 17). Growing troubles in Mexico. *Los Angeles Times*, p. 1.

Krauthammer, C. (2002, February, 20). Who needs gold medals. *Washington Post*, p. A15.

Marcossen, I. F. (1916, July 1). Our financial stake in Mexico. *Collier's Magazine*, p. 23.

McLean, R. N. (1928). *That Mexican! As he really is, north and south of the border*. New York: Fleming H. Revell.

Parkes, H. B. (1970). *A history of Mexico*. Boston: Houghton Mifflin.

Pletcher, D. M. (1958). *Rails, mines, and progress: Seven American promoters in Mexico, 1867-1911*. Ithaca, NY: Cornell University Press.

Powell, F. W. (1924). The railroads of Mexico. In R. G. Cleland, (Ed.), *The Mexican yearbook, 1922-1924*. Los Angeles: Times Mirror Press.

Prendergast, F. E. (1881). Railroads in Mexico. *Harper's New Monthly Magazine*, p. 277.

Rogers, A. H. (1908). Character and habits of Mexican miners. *Engineering and Mining Journal, 85*(14), 700.

Rusher, W. (2001, June 5). US too big for other countries to like. *Pasadena Star News*, p. A7

Schrader, E. (1993, August 24). Growing exodus turns Mexican towns glum. *Orange County Register*, p. 23.

Sherrat, H. W. (1899). *Mexican vistas seen from the highways and byways of travel*. Chicago: Rand, McNally.

Simpich, F. (1920, July). Along our side of the border. *National Geographic, 38*(1), 63.

Simpich, F. (1924). The little brown brother treks north. *The Independent, 116*, 238.

Smith, R. F. (1972). *The United States and revolutionary nationalism in Mexico, 1916-1932*. Chicago: University of Chicago Press.

Thompson, W. (1921). *Trading with Mexico*. New York: Dodd, Mead.

Turner, J. K. (1911). *Barbarous Mexico*, Chicago: Charles H. Kerr.

White, T. (1898). *Our new possessions: A graphic account, descriptive and historical, of the tropic islands of the sea which have fallen under our sway, their cities, peoples and commerce, natural resources and the opportunities they offer to Americans*. Chicago: Thompson and Hood.

Wilson, J.A. (1910). *Bits of old Mexico*. San Francisco: James A. Wilson.

Winton, G. B. (1913). *Mexico today: Social, political and religious conditions*. New York: Missionary Education Movement.

5

Educational Perversion
and Global Neoliberalism

Dave Hill

THE CONTEXTS OF EDUCATIONAL CHANGE

The current anti-egalitarian education system needs to be contextualized in
two ways: (a) the ideological and policy context, and (b) the global/spatial
context. The restructuring of the schooling and education systems across
the world is part of the ideological and policy offensive by neoliberal capital. The privatization of public services, the capitalization and commodification of humanity and the global diktats of the agencies of international
capital—backed by destabilization of nonconforming governments and,
ultimately, the armed cavalries of the United States and its surrogates—have
resulted in the near-global (if not universal) establishment of competitive
markets in public services such as education. These education markets are

marked by selection, exclusion and are accompanied by and situated within the rampant—indeed, exponential—growth of national and international inequalities.

It is important to look at the big picture. Markets in education, so-called "parental choice" of a diverse range of schools (or, in parts of the globe, the "choice" as to whether to send children to school or not), privatization of schools and other education providers, and the cutting of state subsidies to education and other public services are only a part of the educational and anti-public welfare strategy of the capitalist class.

National and global capitalisms wish to, and have generally succeeded in, cutting public expenditure. They do this because public services are expensive. Cuts in public expenditure serve to reduce taxes on profits, which in turn increases profits from capital accumulation. Additionally, the capitalist class in Britain and the United States have (a) a business agenda *for* education that centers on socially producing labor power (people's capacity to labor) for capitalist enterprises; (b) a business agenda *in* education that centers on setting business "free" in education for profit-making; and (c) a business agenda for educational businesses that allows British-and United States-based Edubusinesses and those based elsewhere to profit from international privatizing activities.

THE CURRENT NEOLIBERAL PROJECT
OF GLOBAL CAPITALISM

The fundamental principle of capitalism is the sanctification of private (or, corporate) profit based on the extraction of surplus labor (unpaid labor time) as surplus value from the labor power of workers. It is a creed and practice of (racialized and gendered) class exploitation, exploitation by the capitalist class of those who provide the profits through their labor, the national and international working class.[1]

---

[1]For a debate on, and rebuttal of, the thesis that "class is dead," and/or that the working class has diminished to the point of political insignificance, see Callinicos and Harman (1987); Callinicos (1995); German (1996); Hill (1999b); Cole et al. (2001); Hill and Cole (2001); Harman (2002b); Hill, Sanders, and Hankin (2002); Hill and Kelsh (2006). Outside the Marxist tradition, it is clear that many critics of class analysis (such as Jan Pakulski, 1995) confound class-consciousness with the fact of class— and tend to deduce the salience (some would argue, nonexistence) of the latter from the "absence" of the former. The recognition by Marx that class consciousness is not necessarily or directly produced from the material and objective fact of class position enables neo-Marxists to acknowledge the wide range of contemporary influences that may (or may not) inform the subjective consciousness of identity—but in doing so, to retain the crucial reference to the basic economic determinant of social experience.

As Raduntz (2002) argued:

> globalization is not a qualitatively new phenomenon but a tendency which has always been integral to capitalism's growth. . . . Within the Marxist paradigm there is growing recognition of the relevance of Marx's account expressed in *The Communist Manifesto* that globalisation is the predictable outcome of capitalism's expansionary tendencies evident since its emergence as a viable form of society.[2]

For neoliberals, "profit is God," not the public good. Capitalism is not kind. Plutocrats are not, essentially, philanthropic. In capitalism it is the insatiable demand for profit that is the motor for policy, not public or social or common weal, or good. With great power comes great irresponsibility. Thus, privatized utilities, such as the railway system, health and education services, water supplies are run to maximize the shareholders' profits, rather than to provide a public service, and sustainable development of Third World national economic integrity and growth. These are not on the agenda of globalizing neoliberal capital.[3]

McMurtry (1999) described "the Pathologization of the Market Model." He suggested that the so-called "free-market model" is not a free market at all, that to argue for a "free market" in anything these days is a delusion: the "market model" that we have today is really the system that benefits the "global corporate market." This is a system where the rules are rigged to favor huge multinational and transnational corporations that take over, destroy, or incorporate (hence the "cancer" stage of capitalism) small businesses, innovators, and so on, that are potential competitors.

Indeed, it is a system where the rules are flouted by the United States and the European Union (EU), which continue to subsidize, for example, their own agricultural industries, while demanding that states receiving International Monetary Fund (IMF) or World Bank funding throw their

---

[2]See also Cole (1998, 2003). It is not my purpose here to discuss contrasting theories of globalization.

[3]In the wake of a series of fatal rail disasters, it has become readily apparent that public safety has been subordinated to private profit. For example, between 1992 and 1997, the number of people employed in Britain's railways fell from 159,000 to 92,000, whereas the number of trains increased. "The numbers of workers permanently employed to maintain and renew the infrastructure fell from 31,000 to between 15,000 and 19, 000 (Jack, 2001). So capital downsizes its labor forces to upsize its profits. One result has been an unprecedented series of major fatal train crashes in Britain since the Thatcher government in Britain privatized the railways.

markets open (to be devastated by subsidized EU and US imports).[4] Thus, opening education to the market, in the long run, will open it to the corporate giants, in particular Anglo-American-based transnational companies—who will run it in their own interests.

Rikowski (e.g., 2001a, 2002a, 2002d) and others (e.g., Coates, 2001; Robertson, Bonal, & Dale, 2002; Mojab, 2001; Pilger, 2002b; Devidal, 2004; Hill, 2005, 2006a) argued that the World Trade Organization (WTO) and other "global clubs for the mega-capitalists" are setting up this agenda in education across the globe, primarily through the developing operationalizing and widening sectoral remit of the General Agreement on Trade in Services (GATS).

WHAT NEOLIBERALISM DEMANDS

The difference between classic (*laissez-faire*) liberalism of the mid-19th-century Britain, and the neoliberalism of today, based on the views of the neoliberal theorist Hayek, is that the former wanted to roll back the state, to let private enterprise make profits relatively unhindered by legislation (e.g., safety at work, trade union rights, minimum wage), and unhindered by the tax costs of a welfare state.

On the other hand, *neo*liberalism demands a strong state to promote its interests, hence Andrew Gamble's (1988) depiction of the Thatcherite polity as *The Free Economy and the Strong State: The Politics of Thatcherism.* The strong Interventionist State is needed by capital particularly in the field of education and training—in the field of producing an ideologically compliant but technically skilled workforce. The social production of labor power is crucial for capitalism. It needs to extract as much surplus value as it can from the labor power of workers, as they transform labor capacity into labor in commodity-producing labor processes.

The current globally dominant form of capitalism, neoliberalism, requires the following within national states:

- Inflation should be controlled by interest rates, preferably by an independent central bank.
- Budgets should be balanced and not used to influence demand—or at any rate not to stimulate it.

---

[4]See the film *Life and Debt*, about the effect of the World Trade Organization in effectively destroying the dairy industry in Jamaica (http://www.lifeanddebt.org. about). See also Bircham and Charlton's (2001) *Anti-Capitalism: A Guide to the Movement* and Dee's (2004) *Anti-capitalism: Where Now?*

- Private ownership of the means of production, distribution and exchange.
- The provision of a market in goods and services—including private sector involvement in welfare, social, educational, and other state services (such as air traffic control, prisons, policing, railways).
- Within education the creation of "opportunity" to acquire the means of education (although not necessarily education itself) and additional cultural capital, through selection.
- Relatively untrammeled selling and buying of labor power, for a "flexible," poorly regulated labor market, deregulation of the labor market—for labor flexibility (with consequences for education).
- The restructuring of the management of the welfare state on the basis of a corporate managerialist model imported from the world of business. As well as the needs of the economy dictating the principal aims of school education, the world of business is also to supply a model of how it is to be provided and managed.
- Suppression of oppositional critical thought and much autonomous thought and education.
- Within a regime of denigration and humbling of publicly provided services.
- Within a regime of cuts in the post-war welfare state, the withdrawal of state subsidies and support, and low public expenditure.

Internationally, neoliberalism requires the following:

- Removal of barriers to international trade and capitalist enterprise.
- A "level playing field" for companies of any nationality within all sectors of national economies.
- Trade rules and regulations to underpin "free" trade, with a system for penalizing "unfair" trade policies.

NEOLIBERALISM AND ITS EFFECTS

Neoliberal policies both in the United Kingdom and globally (see Harvey, 2005; Hill, 2005, 2006a) have resulted in (a) a loss of equity, economic and social justice, (b) a loss of democracy and democratic accountability, and (c) a loss of critical thought. Each of these effects is discussed here.

The Growth of National and Global Inequalities

Inequalities both between and within states have increased dramatically during the era of global neoliberalism. Global capital, in its current neoliberal form in particular, leads to human degradation and inhumanity and increased social-class inequalities within states and globally. These effects are increasing (racialized and gendered) social-class inequality within states, increasing (racialized and gendered) social class inequality between states. The degradation and capitalization of humanity, including the environmental degradation impact primarily in a social class-related manner. Those who can afford to buy clean water don't die of thirst or diarrhea.

Kagarlitsky (2001, cited in Pilger, 2002a, p. 5) has pointed out that "globalisation does not mean the impotence of the state, but the rejection by the state of its social functions, in favor of repressive ones, and the ending of democratic freedoms." Many commentators (e.g., Apple, 1993; Hill, 2001b) have discussed the change since the mid-1970s in many advanced capitalist economies from a social democratic/welfare statist/Keynesian state to a neoliberal state, to what Gamble (1988) has termed *The Free Economy and the Strong State*. The strong state, the repressive apparatuses of the state, have, of course, been dramatically upgraded (in terms of surveillance, control, e-privacy, policing in its various forms) in the wake of September 11, 2001.[5]

Increasing inequalities, the impoverishment and creation of a substantial underclass in Britain, has also been well documented (e.g., Hill & Cole, 2001).[6] The ratio of chief executive officer's (CEO) pay to average worker's pay stands at 35:1 in Britain. In the United States, it has climbed to 450:1 (from around 35: in the mid-1980s; Hutton, 2001). Brenner noted how the CEOs in the United States owned 2% of market capitalization in 1992, yet by 2002 they owned 12%, "the greatest of the appropriations by the expropriators" (Brenner, 2002a, see also Brenner, 2002b, 2002c).

The gap between the richest and the poorest in the United States, expressed in terms of the income of CEOs in relation to the poorest groups in society was 30:1 in 1970, 60:1 in 1990, and by 1997-1998 had grown to 500:1—without perks (Miyoshi, 2002). Susan George (2001) pointed out that "If workers had been rewarded like their chief executive officers they

---

[5]See Hill (2001a) for a discussion of various types of government and state policy: neoconservative, neoliberal, "Third Way," social democratic, socialist, Marxist. See Saltman and Gabbard (2003) and Hill (2004a) for a discussion of the increasing role of the repressive and surveillance state apparatuses in society and in education.
[6]See Gillborn and Mirza (2000) and Hill, Sanders, and Hankin (2002) for recent data on (racialized and gendered) social-class inequalities in income, wealth, and educational attainment in England and Wales—and how much inequality has increased since 1979.

would be making an average $110,000 a year, not $23,000, and the minimum hourly wage in the U.S. would be $22 not $5.15" (p. 19).

The economic apartheid nature of American capitalism has been widely exposed (e.g., McLaren, 2000). For example, the top 1% of the richest people in the United States has financial resources equal to the bottom 95%. In Brazil, the richest 10% of the population is 78 times better off than the poorest 10%, the 20 biggest landowners own more land than the 3.3 million small farmers (Socialist Worker, 2002). The current form of globalization is tightening rather than loosening the international poverty trap. Living standards in the least developed countries are now lower than 30 years ago. Three hundred million people live on less than $1 a day.

Masao Miyoshi (2002) pointed out that the growth in inequalities between the world's richest and poorest countries has been exponential in the past 30 years. In 1900, the gap in per capita wealth between the richest countries and the Third World was around 5:1 and in 1970 it was still only 7:1. By 1990, however, the gap had grown to 260–360:1 and in 2002 the wealth gap ratio was 470–500:1.

Markets in Education

Markets have exacerbated existing inequalities. There is considerable data on how poor schools have, by and large, gotten poorer (in terms of relative education results and in terms of total income) and how rich schools (in the same terms) have got richer. Whitty, Power, and Halpin (1998) examined the effects of the introduction of quasi-markets into education systems in the United States, Sweden, England and Wales, Australia, and New Zealand. Their book is a review of the research evidence. Their conclusion is that one of the results of marketizing education is that increasing "parental choice" of schools, and/or setting up new types of schools, in effect increases school choice of parents and their children and thereby sets up or exacerbates racialized school hierarchies.

In the United Kingdom, for example, while in government from 1979–1997, the Conservatives established *a competitive market* for consumers (children and their parents) by setting up new types of schools in addition to the local (state, i.e., public) primary school or the local secondary comprehensive school. Thus, new types of schools were introduced such as City Technology Colleges and Grant Maintained schools, schools that removed themselves from the control of local authorities. And to confirm this creation of a "quasi-" market in school choice, they extended the "parental choice" of schools—letting parents, in effect, apply for any school anywhere in the country.

Not only that, but the conservative governments also stopped redistributive, positive discrimination funding for schools. Decisions about funding were substantially taken out of the hands of the democratically elected local education authorities (LEAs) by the imposition of *per capita* funding for pupils/school students. So students in poor/disadvantaged areas in an LEA would receive *the same per capita funding* as "rich kids." Furthermore, this funding rose or fell according to intake numbers of pupils/students, itself affected by henceforth compulsorily publicized "league table" performance according to pupil/student performance at various ages on Student Assessment Tasks and 16+ examination results. (This "equality of treatment" contrasts dramatically with the attempts, prior to the 1988 Education Reform Act, of many LEAs to secure more "equality of opportunity" by spending more on those with greatest needs—a power partially restored in one of its social democratic polices by the New Labour government following its election in 1997.)

The result of this "school choice" is that inequalities between schools have increased because in many cases the "parental choice" of schools has become the "schools' choice" of the most desirable parents and children—and rejection of others. "Sink schools" have become more "sink-like" as more favored schools have picked the children they think are likely to be "the cream of the crop." Where selection exists the sink schools just sink further and the privileged schools just become more privileged. Teachers in "sink schools" are publicly pilloried, and, under "New Labour" the schools "named and shamed" as "failing schools," and, in some cases either re-opened with a new "superhead" as a "fresh start school" (with dismissals of "failing" teachers), or shut down (see, e.g., Whitty, Power, & Halpin, 1998).

These conservative government policies are classic manifestations of neoliberal, free-market ideology, including the transference of a substantial percentage of funding and of powers away from local education authorities to "consumers" (in this case, schools). "Ostensibly, at least, these represent a 'rolling back' of central and local government's influence on what goes on in schools" (Troyna, 1995, p. 141).

Conservative government/party policy remained and remains a mixture of neoliberalism and neo-conservatism. An aspect of its neoconservatism is its "equiphobia"—fear of equality (Myers, cited in Troyna, 1995; cf. Hill, 1997a), its hostility to agencies or apparatuses thought to be involved in promoting equality and equal opportunities—such as (democratically elected) LEA (Gamble, 1988; Hill, 1997a, 1999a, 2001c).

New Labour's education policy modifies and extends Radical Right principles and anti-egalitarianism (Hill, 1999a, 2001c, 2006b). Its policy for more *competitiveness* (between schools, between parents, between pupils/students, and between teachers) and *selection* (by schools and by universities) are a continuation, indeed, an extension, of most of the structural aspects of the 1988 Conservative Education Reform Act, in terms of the macro-structure and organization of schooling. The Radical Right principle of competition between schools (which results in an increasing inequality between schools) and the principle of devolving more and more financial control to schools through local management of schools are all in keeping with preceding conservative opposition to comprehensive education and to the powers of LEAs. As are the ever-increasing provision of new types of schools and attacks on "mixed ability teaching" and the increased emphasis on the role/rule of capital in education (see later). New Labour's neoconservatism, echoing that of the conservatives, also perpetuates "the strong state" within "the free economy" (i.e., the deregulated, low-taxed, competitive, capital ultra-friendly economy).

Governments in Britain, the United States, Australia, and New Zealand have marketized their school systems. Racialized social class patterns of inequality have increased. And at the level of university entry, the (racialized) class-based hierarchicalization of universities is exacerbated by "top-up fees" for entry to elite universities, pricing the poor out of the system, or at least into the lower divisions of higher education. And, to control the state apparatuses of education, such marketization is controlled by heavy systems of surveillance and accountability.

Thus, with respect to the United States, Pauline Lipman (2001) noted

> George W. Bush's "blueprint" to "reform" education, released in February 2001 (*No Child Left Behind*) (Bush, 2001), crystallizes key neoliberal, neo-conservative, and business-oriented education policies. The main components of Bush's plan are mandatory, high-stakes testing and vouchers and other supports for privatizing schools.

Lipman continued,

> the major aspects of this Agenda and Policy are . . . "standards, accountability, and regulation of schools, teachers and students and an explicit linkage of corporate interests with educational practices and goals."

Mathison and Ross (2002) detailed the many recommended interventions, both direct (the Business Agenda *in* education) and indirect (the Business Agenda *for* education) by capital in the U.S. environment of corporate take over of schools and universities:

> In K–12 schools some examples are school choice plans (voucher systems, charter schools), comprehensive school designs based on business principles (such as economies of scale, standardization, cost efficiency, production line strategies), back to basics curricula, teacher merit pay, and strong systems of accountability. In universities some examples are the demand for common general education and core curricula (often not

developed or supported by faculty), demands for common tests of student core knowledge, standardized tests of knowledge and skill for professional areas, promotion of "classic" education, and elimination of "new" content areas such as women's studies, post-modernism, and multiculturalism.

On an international level, diktats by the World Bank, the IMF, and other agencies of international capital have resulted in the actual disappearance of formerly free nationally funded schooling and other education (and welfare, public utility) services (Hill, 2006a).

The Growth of Undemocratic (Un)accountability. Within education and other public services, business values and interests are increasingly substituted for democratic accountability and the collective voice. This applies at the local level, where, in Britain for example, private companies—national or transnational—variously build, own, run and govern state schools and other sections of local government educational services (Hatcher, 2001, 2002; Hatcher & Hirtt, 1999). As Wilson (2002) asked,

> There is an important democratic question here is it right to allow private providers of educational services based outside Britain (and, I would add, inside Britain, too, indeed, wherever they are based). In the event of abuse or corruption, where and how would those guilty be held to account? . . . Who is the guarantor of "the last resort"? (p. 12)

This anti-democratization applies too at national levels. As Barry Coates (2001) pointed out, "GATS locks countries into a system of rules that means it is effectively impossible for governments to change policy, or for voters to elect a new government that has different policies" (p. 28).

The Loss of Critical Thought. The increasing subordination of education, including university education, and its commodification, have been well documented (CFHE, 2003; Hill, 2001b, 2002b, 2004a, 2000b; Levidow, 2002).[7] One aspect is that, other than at elite institutions, where the student

---

[7]In capitalist society, "well-being" is now equated with "well-having"—we are what we consume. In educational terms, our worth is how many years and credits we have accumulated. Indeed, being a student is now a serious game, to build up credits to get a better job. In the United States and England and Wales today, as in other advanced capitalist states, economic goals of education have sidelined social/societal/community goals, the traditional social democratic goals of education, and have also replaced education/learning for its own sake, the traditional liberal and liberal-progressive goals of education.

intake is the wealthiest and most upper class, there is little scope for critical thought. In my own work I have examined how the British government has, in effect, expelled most potentially critical aspects of education from the national curriculum, such as sociological and political examination of schooling and education, and questions of social class, "race," and gender for what is now termed *teacher training*, which was formerly called *teacher education*. The change in nomenclature is important both symbolically and in terms of actual accurate descriptiveness of the new, "safe," sanitized and de-theorized education and training of new teachers (e.g., Hill, 2001b, 2004).

McMurtry (1991) described the philosophical incompatibility between the demands of capital and the demands of education, *inter alia*, with respect to critical thought. Governments throughout the world are resolving this incompatibility more and more on terms favorable to capital. One example in England and Wales is the swathe of redundancies/dismissals of teacher educators specializing in the sociology, politics, and contexts of education following the conforming of teacher education, the imposition of a skills-based, rigidly monitored national curriculum for teacher training in 1992–1993. One dismissal was my own. At a stroke, numerous critical teacher educators were removed or displaced. So too were their materials/resources—no longer wanted by the government. Thus, at the college from which I was dismissed, the Centre for Racial Equality was closed down—its resources no longer required by the new technicist, de-theorized, anti-critical teacher training curriculum (Hill, 1997b). At a more general level, Mathison and Ross (2002) note that

> [the] university's role as an independent institution is increasingly threatened by the interests of corporations in both subtle and obvious ways. "Globalization"—which Bertell Ollman (2001) defines as "another name for capitalism, but it's capitalism with the gloves off and on a world scale. It is capitalism at a time when all the old restrictions and inhibitions have been or are in the process of being put aside, a supremely self-confident capitalism, one without apparent rivals and therefore without a need to compromise or apologize"—has transformed internal and external relations of university from teaching and research to student aid policies and pouring rights for soft drink manufacturers. Decreased funding for higher education has made universities increasingly susceptible to the influence of big money and threatens the academic freedom and direction of research.

Education, Class, and Capital

Glenn Rikowski's (2001a) work, such as *The Battle in Seattle,* develops a Marxist analysis based on an analysis of "labor power." With respect to education, he suggested that teachers are the most dangerous of workers because they have a special role in shaping, developing, and forcing *the single commodity on which the whole capitalist system rests: labor power*. In the capitalist labor process, labor power is transformed into value-creating *labor*, and, at a certain point, *surplus value* — value over and above that represented in the worker's wage — is created. *Surplus-value* is the first form of the existence of capital. It is the *life blood of capital*. Without it, capital could not be transformed into money, on sale of the commodities that incorporate value, and hence the capitalist could not purchase the necessary raw materials, means of production, and labor power to set the whole cycle in motion once more. But most importantly for the capitalist is that part of the surplus value that forms his or her *profit* — and it is this that drives the capitalist on a personal basis. It is this that defines the personal *agency of the capitalist*!

Teachers are dangerous because *they are intimately connected with the social production of labor power*, equipping students with skills, competencies, abilities, knowledge, and the attitudes and personal qualities that *can be expressed and expended in the capitalist labor process*. Teachers are guardians of the quality of labor power! This potential, latent power of teachers explains why representatives of the State might have sleepless nights worrying about the role of teachers in ensuring that the laborers of the future are delivered to workplaces throughout the national capital *of the highest possible quality*.[8]

Rikowski suggested that the State needs to control the process for two reasons. First, to try to ensure that this occurs. Second, to try to ensure that modes of pedagogy that are antithetical to labor-power production *do not and cannot exist*. In particular, it becomes clear, on this analysis, that the capitalist State will seek to destroy any forms of pedagogy *that attempt to educate students regarding their real predicament — to create an awareness of themselves as future labor powers and to underpin this awareness with critical insight that seeks to undermine the smooth running of the social production of labor power*. This fear entails strict control of teacher education and training, of the curriculum, of educational research.

---

[8]Perhaps the easiest way of understanding the concept of "national capital" is Rikowski's definition in terms of national labor markets — which is "the labour-power needs of national capitals refer to those labour-power capacities required for labouring in any labour process throughout the national capital . . . [There] is the drive [to increase] the quality (of labour-power) vis-á-vis other national capitals for gaining a competitive edge" (Rikowski, 2001b, p. 42). This particular definition points toward the national capital (when being viewed in relation to labor power) as the national labor market.

Capitalism's Business Agenda for Education

How, in more detail, do education markets fit into the grand plan for schooling and education? What is capitalism's Business Agenda for Education?

In pursuit of these agendas, New Public Managerialism—the importation into the old public services of the language and management style of private capital—has replaced the ethic, language, and style of public service and duty. Education as a social institution has been subordinated to international market goals, including the language and self-conceptualization of educators themselves (see Levidow, 2002; Mulderrig, 2002). Mulderrig showed how

> education is theoretically positioned in terms of its relationship with the economy and broader state policy (where) an instrumental rationality underlies education policy discourse, manifested in the pervasive rhetoric and values of the market in the representation of educational participants and practices.

She theorized this

> . . . as an indicator of a general shift towards the commodification of education and the concomitant consumerisation of social actors [within which] discourse plays a significant role in constructing and legitimizing post-welfare learning policy as a key aspect of the ongoing project of globalization.

And The Campaign for the Future of Higher Education slams the commodification of higher education by pointing out the following:

> Students are neither customers nor clients; academics neither facilitators nor a pizza delivery service. Universities are not businesses; producing consumer goods. Knowledge and thought are not commodities, to be purchased as items of consumption, whether conspicuous or not, or consumed and therefore finished with, whether on the hoof as take-away snacks or in more leisurely fashion. Education is not something which can be "delivered", consumed and crossed off the list. Rather, it is a continuing and reflective process, an essential component of any worthwhile life—the very antithesis of a commodity. (CFHE, 2003)

Within universities and vocational further education, the language of education has been very widely replaced by the language of the market, where lecturers "deliver the product," "operationalize delivery," and "facilitate clients' learning," within a regime of "quality management and enhancement," where students have become "customers" selecting "modules" on a pick'n'mix basis, where "skill development" at universities has surged in importance to the derogation of the development of critical thought.

Richard Hatcher (2001, 2002) showed how capital/business has two major aims for schools. The first is to ensure that schooling and education engage in ideological and economic reproduction. National education and training policies in the business agenda *for* education are of increasing importance for national capital. In an era of global capital, this is one of the few remaining areas for national state intervention—it is *the* site, suggested Hatcher, where a state can make a difference.

The second aim—the business agenda *in* schools—is for private enterprise, private capitalists, to make money out of it, to make private profit out of it, to control it.

The Business Agenda *for* Schools

Business wants education fit for business—to make schooling and higher education subordinate to the personality, ideological, and economic requirements of capital, to make sure schools produce compliant, ideologically indoctrinated, pro-capitalist, effective workers.

This first agenda constitutes a broad transnational consensus about the set of reforms needed for schools to meet employers' needs in terms of the efficiency with which they produce the future work force. The business agenda *for* schools is increasingly transnational, generated and disseminated through key organizations of the international economic and political elite such as the Organization for Economic Cooperation and Development (OECD). In that global context there is a project for education at the European level, which represents the specific agenda of the dominant European economic and political interests. It is expressed in, for example, the various reports of the European Round Table (ERT) of industrialists, a pressure group of 45 leaders of major European companies from 16 countries, and it has become the motive force of the education policies of the European Commission and its subsidiary bodies. Monbiot (2001) quoted the ERT as saying "the provision of education is a market opportunity and should be treated as such" (p. 331; see also Hatcher & Hirtt, 1999).

The Business Agenda *in* Schools

Second, business wants to make profits from education and other privatized public services such as water supply and healthcare.

The work of Molnar (2001), Monbiot (2000, 2001, 2002), Robertson et al. (2002) in the United States and in Britain by Rikowski (2001a, 2002a,

2002b, 2002c, 2002d, 2003a) and Hill (1999a, 2006b) highlight another aspect of what national and multinational Capital wants from schooling and education—it wants profits through owning and controlling them. Thus privatization of schools and educational services is becoming "big business" (so, too, are libraries—see R. Rikowski, 2002). As the weekly radical newsletter *Schnews* exclaims, in an April 2000 article entitled "The Coca-Cola Kids,"

> "Education in the West is fast becoming indistinguishable from any other industry." Privatization of education was this week put in the spotlight with the National Union of Teachers threatening strike action not just over performance related pay, but also over big business moving in on the classroom. But what the hell is "Best Value," "Out-sourcing," "Action Zones," and the "Private Finance Initiative"? Shall we peer into the New Labour Dictionary of Gobbledee Gook to find out just what it all means?
>
> How about "Privatization, privatization, privatization." Yes, New Labour is busy selling off everything—they just dress it up in fancy jargon to try and pull the wool over our eyes. Still, why would private companies want to move into education? McDonalds' "operations manual" gives us a clue: "Schools offer excellent opportunities. Not only are they a high traffic (sales) generator, but students are some of the best customers you could have." And with £38 billion spent on education a year, there's a lot to play for. ("The Coca Cola Kids,", 2000)

Of course, ultimate responsibility within private company-owned schools and colleges and libraries is not to children, students or the community—it is to the owners and the shareholders.

Such privatization and loss of tax/publicly funded clean water, clinics and schools results directly in death, disease and dumbing down (Bircham & Charlton, 2001).[9]

The Business Agenda Internationally

Rikowski (2002a) examined the gathering pace of GATS and the British government's role in seeking to give British companies the lead in educational privatization internationally.

---

[9]This is an important claim, that privatization and loss of tax/publicly funded clean water, clinics, and schools result directly in death, disease, and dumbing down. Many of the chapters in Bircham and Charlton (2001) give examples of this. So, too, with respect to global society, do Monbiot (2000); Klein (2001, 2002); Mojab, (2001); Hill and Cole (2001); Hill, Sanders, and Hankin (2002); Pilger (2002a); Cole (2003); and Hill (2004b).

He pointed out that since February 2000, a whole series of GATS negotiations have taken place. These discussions were consolidated in March 2001 through an intensive series of meetings, and there was a final deadline of December 2004 for an agreement on a strengthened GATS process. This explains the urgency regarding privatization of public services in the United Kingdom today. As Matheson noted:

> Backed by the US and UK Governments, the WTO aims to liberalise the service sector further. The immediate impact would be the privatization of some services that have so far been provided by governments. Governments would be obliged to sell off such services as housing, education and water. (p. 9, cited in Rikowski 2002d, p. 14).

The drive to privatize public services is powered by a number of forces, but in terms of the GATS the urgency derives from two main considerations. First, home-grown operators need to be nurtured—and quickly—so that when a more powerful GATS process exists, U.K. operators in education, health, social services, and libraries can fend off foreign enterprises. This is not just because the government believes that more of the profits from these privatized public services are likely to remain in the United Kingdom; it is primarily because of the need to "sell" the idea of private companies running schools, hospitals, libraries and social services to the British public. Although French companies might be tolerated in providing electricity or water, the U.K. government perceives there may be more of a problem with American or other nations' companies running schools as profit-making ventures.

Second, as Monbiot (2002) indicated, drawing on the work of Hatcher (2001), the government is also mightily concerned that the fledgling U.K. businesses currently taking over our public services can develop rapidly into export earners. This is already happening. For example, the education business Nord Anglia is already exporting its services to Russia and the Ukraine as well as running schools and local education authority services in the United Kingdom. Many U.K. universities have franchised operations and a whole raft of deals with other colleges and universities in other countries. U.K. university schools of education generate income through consultancies that advise countries like Chile, Poland, and Romania on how to restructure school systems. The government is keen to maximize this export potential across all the public services.

The WTO has identified 160 service sectors, and British and U.S. businesses would benefit particularly if the GATS could liberalize trade in services still further by incorporating currently "public" services into their export drives.

In 2000, Britain exported $117 billion worth of services. New education, health, library, and social services business would provide "new opportunities for this export trade to expand massively" (Tibbett, 2001, p. 11). Thus, "international businesses have now seized on service provision as a money-making opportunity" (Matheson, 2000, p. 9). As the WTO Services Division Director David Hartridge said in a speech in 2000, "[GATS] can and will speed up the process of liberalization and reform, and make it irreversible" (Matheson, 2000, p. 9).

The pressure from corporations on the U.S., British and other EU governments to deliver on the GATS is colossal. As Allyson Pollock (2001) argued, "[business] sponsors and the Treasury are clear that the future of British business rests on trading in public services on an international scale regardless of the social costs."

Finally, the leading capitalist powers (the "Quad"—the United States, EU, Japan, and Canada), driven on by major corporations and business interests, are

> trying to revise GATS so it could be used to overturn almost any legislation governing services from national to local level. . . . Particularly under threat from GATS are public services—health care, education, energy, water and sanitation. . . . A revised GATS could give the commercial sector further access and could make existing privatizations effectively irreversible. (Sexton, 2001, p. 1)

This helps explain the British government's determination to push through privatizations, to provide deregulatory frameworks for state services (e.g., 2002 Education Act and the 2005 Education White Paper; DES, 2005) and to nurture the growth of indigenous businesses that can virus public sector operations (see Rikowski, 2003b, 2005a, 2005b, for commentary).

Neoliberal Theory and Policy Perverting Education

This section discusses some theoretical and academic aspects of some neoliberal arguments and suggest where they fall down. Neoliberals such as James Tooley (2000, 2001) draw a number of unwarranted implications or conclusions about the role of the state in education and about the role of the market in education. These relate to their assumption that the market/privatization is compatible with education.

But education is not a commodity to be bought and sold. One can buy *the means* to an education, but not the hard graft of autonomous learning itself. John McMurtry (1991), among others, noted that education and the capitalist market hold opposing *goals, motivations, methods,* and *standards of excellence.*

1.   *The goals of education.* McMurtry (1991) noted that private prof-
     it is acquired by a structure of appropriation that excludes others
     from its possession. The greater its accumulation by any private
     corporation, the more wealth others are excluded from in this
     kind of possession. This is what makes such ownership "private."
         Education, in contrast, is acquired by a structure of appropri-
     ation that does not exclude others from its possession. On the
     contrary, education is furthered the more it is shared, and the
     more there is free and open access to its circulation. That is why
     learning that is not conveyed to others is deemed "lost," "wast-
     ed" or "dead." In direct opposition to market exchanges, educa-
     tional changes flourish most with the unpaid gifts of others and
     develop the more they are not mediated by private possession or
     profit.

2.   *Opposing motivations.* McMurtry noted that "the determining
     motivation of the market is to satisfy the wants of whoever has
     the money to purchase the goods that are provided. The deter-
     mining motivation of education is to develop sound understand-
     ing *whether it is wanted or not*" (italics added). "The market by
     definition can only satisfy the motivations of those who have the
     money to buy the product it sells.
         The place of education, on the other hand, remains a place of
     education insofar as it educates those whose motivation is to
     learn, independent of the money-demand they exercise in their
     learning." In addition, "development of understanding is neces-
     sarily growth of cognitive capacity; wherein satisfaction of con-
     sumer wants involves neither, and typically impedes both."

3.   *Opposing methods.* "The method of the market is to buy or sell
     the goods it has to offer to anyone for whatever price one can
     get. . . . The method of education is never to buy or sell the item
     it has to offer, but to require of all who would have it that they
     fulfill its requirements autonomously" . . . "Everything that is to
     be had on the market is acquired by the money paid for it.
     Nothing that is learned in education is acquired by the money
     paid for it."

4.   *Opposing standards of excellence.* "The measures of excellence
     in the market are (1) how well the product is made to sell; and
     (2) how problem-free the product is and remains for its buyers.
     The measures of excellence in education are (1) how disinterest-

ed and impartial its representations are; and (2) how deep and broad the problems it poses are to one who has it" . . . The first works through "one sided sales pitches . . . which work precisely because they are not understood," the second "must rule out one-sided presentation, appetitive compulsion and manipulative conditioning."

The last critical theoretical point I make here in analyzing the relationship between neoliberalism and education is that the market suppresses critical thought and education itself. Clearly, some aspects of the market wish to promote learning—the learning of skills considered appropriate to different strata in the labor market. The point here is that capital seeks to repress those aspects of critical thought, such as those embodied in critical pedagogy, in socialist/Marxist analysis, which are inimical to its own continuation.

Thus, there is the suppression and compression of critical space in education today (Rikowski, 2003a). On the one hand, capital requires educated and flexible workers, but on the other hand, it cannot countenance that workers should be thinking *fundamental critique* for themselves—or coming across it in schools, vocational education or universities. So free thinking, and oppositional thinking, has been chopped, curtailed, circumscribed.

Critical space for critical education studies and research is being compressed through curriculum control, through the remaking of human personality, and through a gamut of ideological and repressive state apparatuses. This is especially so for fundamental critique: "how the core processes and phenomena of capitalist society (value, capital, labor, labor power, value creation, and capital accumulation, and so on) generate contradictions and tensions in everyday life—for individuals, groups, classes, societies and on an international scale" (Rikowski, 2003a).

Part of this repression is *The Naturalisation of Capital and the Denaturalisation of Dissent* (Hill, 2004). As Peter McLaren (2000) noted, one of its greatest achievements is that capital presents itself as natural, free and democratic,

> as if it has now replaced the natural environment. It announces itself through its business leaders and politicians as coterminous with freedom, and indispensable to democracy such that any attack on capitalism as exploitative or hypocritical becomes an attack on world freedom and democracy itself. (p. 32)

McMurtry (2001) considered "America's New War" to be the latest expression of a much deeper and wider terrorist campaign of an emergent totalitarian pattern of instituting world corporate rule with no limit of occupation or accountability beyond itself. He forcefully claimed that the United States has effectively created a new form of totalitarianism. The old totalitarianism culture of the "Big Lie" is marked by "a pervasive overriding of the distinction between fact and fiction by saturating mass media falsehoods." This Big Lie is an omnipervasive lie that "is disseminated by round-the-clock, centrally controlled multi-media which are watched, read or heard by people across the globe day and night without break in the occupation of public consciousness instead of national territories." McMurtry wrote that "in the old totalitarian culture of the Big Lie, the truth is hidden. In the new totalitarianism, there is no line between truth and falsehood. The truth is what people can be conditioned to believe."

McMurtry (1991) concluded his analysis of the relationship between education and the market powerfully: "this fundamental contradiction in standards of excellence leads, in turn, to *opposite standards of freedom.* Freedom in the market is the enjoyment of whatever one is able to buy from others with no questions asked, and profit from whatever one is able to sell to others with no requirement to answer to anyone else. Freedom in the place of education, on the other hand, is precisely the freedom to question, and to seek answers, whether it offends people's self-gratification or not."

McMurtry (1991) succinctly related his arguments to the "systematic reduction of the historically hard won social institution of education to a commodity for private purchase and sale" (p. 216). "The commodification of education rules out the very critical freedom and academic rigor which education requires to be more than indoctrination (p. 215).

Much of my own work calls for critical education and for the development of teachers as critical transformative intellectuals. Big business and their government agents now call most of the shots in university research—hence the potential importance of independent radical think-tanks and research units. Important, too, are the collective efforts of radical egalitarian and socialist political organizations and their publications and demonstrations—their fight back against exploitation and oppression.[10]

---

[10]Independent Marxist and left-radical think-tanks and research and campaigning groups include the Institute for Education Policy Studies (http://www.ieps.org.uk) and radical groups such as, in Britain, the Hillcole Group of Radical Left Educators (see http://www.ieps.org.uk), the Campaign for the Future of Higher Education (http://www.cfhe.org.uk), and the Socialist Teachers' Alliance (see www.socialist-teacher.org/). In the United States, see the Rethinking Schools collective and publishers/activists (http://www.rethinkingschools.org), and The Rouge Forum (http://www.rougeforum.org)

RESTRAINING AND RESISTING
NEOLIBERALISM

There are three major restraining forces on the activities of neoliberalism: infrastructural, consumer-related regulation, and legitimation.

Infrastructural Restraints

The first restraining force is the need for an educational, social, transport, welfare, housing, infrastructure to enable workers to get to work, to be trained for different levels of the work force, to be relatively fit and healthy. This restraint, however, is *minimal*—it can cope with extreme poverty and the existence of billions of humans at the margins of existence. It is a basic needs provision that says nothing. It has no implications at all for equality in society or in education. Indeed, as Pilger (2002b) pointed out, it has no implications even for the maintenance of human lives. In effect, the depredations of neoliberal globalizing capital condemns millions—in particular those in the Third World displaced by the collapse of national agricultural industries that are of no use as either producers or consumers—to death.

Regulating Capital

The second restraint on capitalism is consumer dissatisfaction and consumer protection in the form of regulations. These, and inspectors of various sorts are criticized as "red tape" and as bureaucrats. Yet without regulation, and enforcement in Britain, BSE (i.e., mad cow disease") and foot-and-mouth disease have flourished and been exported to continental Europe, and, following the privatization of railtrack in Britain, with its subsequent reduction of a maintenance work force and monitoring of safety, the number of dead in rail accidents has shot up.

State regulation operates against the freedom of capitalism to do totally as it pleases. Hence, in Britain, Conservative Party policy on schools and universities is to deregulate them, to "set them free," to allow them to charge what they want and run their own affairs. Similarly, the "anti-bureaucracy" policies of the Republican Party in the United States and its demands for privatized "public sector" education and for education vouchers is a similar case.

The regulatory model can be weak or strong, although the state is far from neutral with respect to capital, seeking to maximize the profits and profitability of national capital.[11] It can demand only basic standards (perhaps failing to inspect regularly, and frequently open to corruption) or it can demand strong controls, including controls over profits, as, rarely, during some periods of social democratic rule by the Labour Party in Britain.

It is interesting that in a number of states such as Britain, some of the most vigorously enforced current standards are those in education, as noted with respect to the United States by Hursh (2001), Lipman (2001), and Mathison and Ross (2002)—testimony perhaps to the crucial nature of the state apparatus of schooling, as noted by Rikowski (2001a).

Resistance to and Delegitimation of Capital

The third and most powerful restraint is that capital (and the political parties they fund and influence) needs to persuade the people that neoliberalism—competition, privatization, poorer standards of public services, greater inequalities between rich and poor—is legitimate. If not, there is a delegitimation crisis: government and the existing system are seen as grossly unfair and inhumane. The government and existing system, nationally and globally, may also be seen as being in the pocket of the international and/or national ruling classes, impoverishing millions while "fat cat" bosses and their politicians consume the surplus value produced by sweat shop deregulated workers—indeed the working classes per se, throughout the world.

To stop delegitimation and to ensure that the majority of the population consider the government and the economic system of private monopoly

---

[11]The state is not neutral with respect to capital—but some state regulation is, to a greater or lesser extent, in the interests of national capital. In some respects national capital needs to regulate individual firms and enterprises, "rogue" capitalist operations in the interests of national capital as a whole. Clearly, much of this regulation is voluntary (as with the Stock Exchange in Britain and with the Press Complaints Commission in Britain), and clearly this regulation is often not only weak, but also ineffective (as, e.g., in the Enron scandal, or, indeed, globally, the Chernobyl, Bhopal and other toxic/nuclear escape disasters).The interests of capital are clearly contradictory—for example, capital requires an efficient and cheap transport system for transporting labor and goods. This interest is in contradiction to its desire not to pay for it through taxation on profits. How this works out historically and in different national settings relates to the balance of class forces and their political expression. Similarly, although politically usually acting in concert against the forces and interests of the working classes, there are different interests between different fractions of capital, for example finance capital and manufacturing capital, and between national and international/transnational capital.

ownership as legitimate, the state uses the ideological apparatuses such as schools and universities to "naturalize" capitalism—to make the existing status quo seem "only natural" to hegemonize its "common sense" (e.g., Mathison & Ross, 2002).

Chapters such as this one are written to contest the legitimacy of government policy and its subordination to and participation in the neoliberal project of global capital. Clearly, for the European and North American eco-warriors Rikowski (2001a) described as *The Battle of Seattle* and for various groups of socialists, trade unionists, social movements, greens, and groups such as the World Development Movement, Attac, and Globalise Resistance, the current system is not legitimate.

Nor is it so for groups of workers and others throughout the world who see their governments bowing before the might of international capital, who see their national government elites and accompanying military cavalries and riot police seeking to ensure that all spheres of social life are incorporated within the orbit of global capital. Educators are implicated in the process, like everyone else. The school or university and other areas of cultural and ideological reproduction (such as newsrooms and film studios) are no hiding place.

Increasingly, across the globe, educational debate is turning in the economically rich world from debates about "standards" and "school effectiveness" to wider questions such as "what is education for? And in the economically poorer world to questions of free access to schooling and higher education—and why they do not have it any more where once it existed.

The Resistant Role of Critical Cultural Workers. The Brazilian educator and political activist, Paulo Freire, argued that although there are exceptional academics and a handful of organizations dedicated to conducting research that serves egalitarian ends, not enough academics are working as critical "cultural workers" who orient themselves toward concrete struggles in the public and political domains in order to extend the equality, liberty, and justice they defend (Freire, 1998). Freire maintained that "[t]he movements outside are where more people who dream of social change are gathering," but points out that there exists a degree of reserve on the part of academics in particular, to penetrate the media, participate in policy debates, or to permeate policy-making bodies (Shor & Freire, 1987, p. 131).

Freire argued that if scholars, researchers, or educators want to transform education to serve democratic ends, they cannot simply limit their struggles to institutional spaces. They must also develop a desire to increase their political activity outside of the schools. To engage as critical cultural workers would require academics to politicize their research by becoming social actors who mobilize, develop political clarity, establish strategic alliances, and work closer to the nexus of power, or the "real levers of trans-formation" (Shor & Freire, 1987, p. 131).

Critical transformative intellectuals seek to enable student teachers and teachers (and school students) to critically evaluate a range of salient per-spectives and ideologies—including critical reflection itself—while showing a commitment to egalitarianism. For McLaren (2000), "critical pedagogy must . . . remain critical of its own presumed role as the metatruth of educa-tional criticism" (p. 184). This does not imply forced acceptance or silencing of contrary perspectives. But it *does* involve a privileging of egalitarian and emancipatory perspectives.

It is necessary to be quite clear here. This *does* mean adhering to what Burbules and Berk (1999) defined as *critical pedagogy*, as opposed to *critical theory*. The difference is that the claim of *critical thinking* is the importance of thinking critically. For many critical thinkers, critical thinking is not nec-essarily about thinking politically. In contrast, for critical pedagogy, and for revolutionary critical pedagogy, this is a false distinction. That is, for critical pedagogues and revolutionary political pedagogues, disinterested critique/deconstruction, or indeed committed ethical moral critique and critical theory, need to be enacted politically. As Giroux and McLaren (1986) articulated, a transformative intellectual is someone "who is capable of artic-ulating emancipatory possibilities and *working towards their realization*" (emphasis added). In more detail, Giroux and McLaren gave their definition of a "transformative intellectual" as:

> one who exercises forms of intellectual and pedagogical practice which attempt to insert teaching and learning directly into the political sphere by arguing that schooling represents both a struggle for meaning and a struggle over power relations. We are also referring to one whose intel-lectual preferences are necessarily grounded in forms of moral and eth-ical discourse exhibiting a preferential concern for the suffering and the struggles of the disadvantaged and oppressed. Here we extend the tradi-tional use of the intellectual as someone who is able to analyse various interests and contradictions within society to someone capable of artic-ulating emancipatory possibilities and working towards their realiza-tion. Teachers who assume the role of transformative intellectuals treat students as critical agents, question how knowledge is produced and dis-tributed, utilise dialogue, and make knowledge meaningful, critical, and ultimately emancipatory. (p. 215)

Giroux (1988) emphasized the interrelationship between the political and the pedagogical as follows:

> Central to the category of transformative intellectual is the necessity of making the pedagogical more political and the political more pedagog-

ical. . . . Within this perspective, critical reflection and action become part of a fundamental social project to help students develop a deep and abiding faith in the struggle to overcome economic, political and social injustices, and to further humanise themselves as part of this struggle. (pp. 127–128)

McLaren (2000) extended the "critical education" project into "revolutionary pedagogy, "which is clearly based on a Marxist metanarrative. Revolutionary pedagogy "would place the liberation from race, class and gender oppression as the key goal for education for the new millennium. Education . . . so conceived would be dedicated to creating a citizenry dedicated to social justice and to the reinvention of social life based on democratic socialist ideals" (p. 196; see also McLaren & Farahmandpur, 2005).

Arenas of Resistance. What is to be done? In brief, there are at least *three arenas* of activity for critical intellectuals and oppositional educators.

The first arena, as Peter McLaren analyzed powerfully (Aguirre, 2001; McLaren, 2000, 2003b), is education, and, indeed, within other sites of cultural reproduction. Paula Allman (2001) put it this way:

education has the potential to fuel the flames of resistance to global capitalism as well as the passion for socialist transformation—indeed, the potential to provide a spark that can ignite the desire for revolutionary democratic social transformation throughout the world.

However, the question of how far this transformative potential can be realized is the subject of considerable debate, for contemporary theory as well as practice. The autonomy and agency available to individual teachers, teacher educators, schools and other educational institutions is particularly challenged when faced with the structures of capital and its current neoliberal project for education (as I argue in Hill, 2001b). It is necessary to highlight the phrase "potential to fuel the flames of resistance," in Allman's quote. Considerable caution is necessary when considering the degree of autonomy of educators (and, indeed, other cultural workers such as journalists and filmmakers) who attempt to fuel the flames of resistance.

I do not underestimate the limitations on the agency and autonomy of teachers, teacher educators, cultural workers and their sites, and indeed, to use concepts derived from Louis Althusser (1971), the very limited autonomy of the education policy/political region of the state from the economic region of the state. There are, in many states, increasing restrictions on the ability of teachers to use their pedagogical spaces for emancipatory purposes. The repressive cards within the ideological state apparatuses are stacked against the possibilities of transformative change through initial teacher education and through schooling. Within school and universities in the United States and England/Wales and other states, there has been the following:

- Increasing *concentration* of/on pro-capitalist formal curricula (in England and Wales this includes rigorously monitored and assessed formal national curricula in schooling and in "teacher training"; in the United States it includes what is, in effect, the national curricula of "high-stakes testing" and the tyranny of the approved textbook,
- Increased *marginalization* of resistant/anti-(capitalist) hegemonic alternative/oppositional curricula, texts, programs,
- Increasing *concentration* of/on pro-capitalist hidden/informal curricula and pedagogy,
- Increased *marginalization* of resistant/anti-(capitalist) hegemonic alternative/oppositional of resistant/anti-(capitalist) hegemonic alternative/oppositional education and educators—the compression and suppression of critical space.

Currently, the capitalist class is ratcheting up the use of ideological state apparatuses in the media and education systems in particular to both "naturalize" and promote capitalist social and economic relations on the one hand and to marginalize and demonize resistant/anti-(capitalist) hegemonic oppositional ideologies, actions, and activists. In the current period of capitalism there is increasing and naked use of repressive economic, legal, military force globally to assert capital, and ensure compliance and subordination to multinational capital and its state agents. This includes repressive state apparatuses such as the police, prison, and legal systems, as well as surveillance procedures (Cole, Hill, McLaren, & Rikowski, 2001).

And for those who do protest, who do stick their heads above the parapet, they sometimes get them blown off—in dramatic or in undramatic but effective ways. In the period prior to and since the United States-led invasion of Iraq, oppositional school students, college students and faculty have suffered something of a witch hunt in the United States (McLaren, 2003a; McLaren, Martin, Farahmandpur, & Jaramillo, 2004). McLaren et al. detailed what they termed witch hunting by teachers against students who participated in anti-war protests such as organizing teach-ins in both K–12 and higher education, witch hunts against students who express opinions critical of U.S. policy. They gave examples of disciplinary actions taken by school managements and by the police.

At a less dramatic, but more pervasive level, Gabbard (2003) described the drip-drip, repression and sidelining of "those who have challenged the viability of the market as a mode of social organization." They receive no (positive) attention. "Neither does the school afford the vast majority of children the opportunity to study the lives of people like themselves, much less the opportunity to study their *own* lives (p. 71).

There is, however, space for counterhegemonic struggle—sometimes (as now) narrower, sometimes (as in western Europe and North America, the 1960s and 1970s) broader. Having recognized the limitations, however, and having recognized that there is *some* potential for egalitarian transformative change, whatever space does exist should be exploited. Whatever we can do, we must do, however fertile or unfertile the soil at any given moment in any particular place. But schools, colleges, and newsrooms are not the only arenas of resistance.

The success of critical educators and cultural workers will be limited if their work is divorced from other arenas of progressive struggle. Successful resistance to neoliberalism necessitates the development of pro-active debate both by, and within, the radical left. But debate alone is not sufficient. Successful resistance demands direct engagement with ideologies and programs of both liberal pluralists (modernist or postmodernist) and with radical right in all the areas of the state and of civil society, in and through all the ideological and repressive state apparatuses.

The ideological intervention of teachers and other educators and cultural workers is likely to have a different impact than that of sections of the work force less saliently engaged in ideological production and reproduction. But, by itself activity of transformative intellectual cultural/ideological workers, however skillful and committed, can have only a limited impact on an egalitarian transformation of capitalist society.

Working outside of the classroom on issues relating to education and its role in reproducing inequality and oppression is the second arena of resistance. Unless critical educators' actions within classrooms are linked to a grammar of resistance, such resistant and counterhegemonic activity is likely to fall on relatively stony ground. Hence, using educational sites as arenas of cultural struggle and education as a vehicle for social transformation needs to conservative/capitalist times is premised on a clear commitment to work with communities, parents and students, and with the trade unions and workers within those institutions.

When I say working "with," I do not mean simply "leading" or "talking at." Working with means "learning from" as well, from the daily, material existence of the exploited classes. Ideally, it means fulfilling the role of the organic intellectual, organically linked to and part of those groups. This also means working with communities—and their own hope, despair, and anger—in developing the perception that schools, education, and the media are sites of social, economic, and ideological contestation. They are not "neutral" or "fair" or "inevitable," but sites of economic, cultural, and ideological domination, of class domination. It is, of course, important to develop awareness of the role of education in capital reproduction and in the reproduction of class relations—and of whatever counterhegemonic and resistant potential it has.

Although I do not share Rikowski's view that educators are "*the* most dangerous of workers", they/we can certainly be dangerous to capital and have effect in the struggle for economic and social justice.

Globally and nationally, societies are developing, to a greater or lesser degree, critical educators, community activists, organic intellectuals, students, and teachers whose feelings of outrage at economic and social class and racial and gender oppression fuel activism. Thus, the *third arena* for resistance is action across a broader spectrum, linking issues and experience within different economic and social sectors, linking different struggles.

Educators participating in mass (or mini-) actions as part of a broader movement for economic and social justice is a key arena of resistance that must not be overlooked or underestimated. Ideological intervention in classrooms and in other cultural sites can have dramatic effect, not least on some individuals and groups who are "hailed" by resistant ideology. However, actualizing that ideology—that opposition to an oppressive law, state or capitalist action; feeling the solidarity, feeling the blood stir, feeling the pride in action and joint learning that comes from that experience—can develop individual as well as collective confidence, understanding, commitment.

For example, protest by the 2 million strong people over the deregulation of labor laws by workers in Italy in March 2002 and follow-up strikes in October 2005—as well as similar actions in Spain, South Korea, and the United Kingdom over proposed labor deregulation and over low pay and pension "reform"—were massive learning experiences for the participants.

The mass protests against the WTO in Seattle, Genoa, London, and Barcelona, together with the various mass events associated with the European Social Movement (such as the 400,000 strong march against the war on Iraq on November 8, 2002) and World Social Forum in Porto Alegre (see Mertes, 2002; Sader, 2002), serve as a key context for linking the work of critical educators to broader movements for economic and social justice. In election after election in Latin America, people are voting out neoliberal parties—in Brazil, Ecuador, Venezuela, Bolivia—and the economic meltdown of a former beacon of neoliberalism, Argentina, is helping create an anti-neoliberal bloc of governments (see Saunois, 2002). In the United Kingdom, the growing militancy of trade unions—not only over low pay but also against privatization and pension rights—has led to the re-emergence of the Socialist Campaign Group, the election of a new left-wing breed of trade union leaders in Britain, and levels of strike action in Britain unprecedented since 1979 (Bambery & Morgan, 2002).

These events have been and continue to be a learning experience for those who thought such mass actions—whether internationally or nationally—were a product of a bygone age (Pilger, 2002a).

CRITICAL ACTION

Although critical political dispositions and analyses such as those espoused by Marx and Freire can provide political direction in the struggle for social change, they have been challenged on a number of points. Of course, conservatives permanently challenge such ideas, but they are also challenged from positions that also claim a radical mantle. For example, among feminist critiques, critical theory and some of the endeavors it supports have been accused (famously, by Ellsworth, 1992) of "repressive myths." In this critique, a notion such as "empowerment," for instance, can be imbued with paternalism and perpetuate relations of domination whether it be in the classroom, in academic discourse, or in everyday life.

This type of criticism is frequently made. Thus, in their *Reflective Teaching: An Introduction*, Zeichner and Liston (1996) determinedly avoided taking a position on critical reflection (see Hill, 1997c; Zeichner & Liston, 1987), offering it as one of a range of types of reflection only. In their book there is absolutely no indication that critical reflection should be privileged or pursued. They claimed that teacher education "needs to be fair and honest" and that "we have not written these texts to convince you to see schools and society as we do but rather to engage you in a consideration of crucial issues" (p. x). They continued:

> When students and faculty engage in discussions of the social and political conditions of schooling and the effects of these conditions on students and schools, it is likely that the talk will be lively and that controversies will emerge. In this area there are no absolutely "right" or "wrong" answers. (p. xi)

Certainly, none are given in their book. It is for that reason that in many respects, this tradition could be termed liberal-pluralist, albeit potentially of a progressive, egalitarian variety. It certainly debars them (and others) from advancing programs for transformation!

Aronowitz and Giroux (1991) associate some radical educators with critical pedagogy that:

> at its worst . . . comes perilously close to emulating the liberal democratic tradition in which teaching is reduced to getting students merely to express or access their own experiences. Teaching collapses in this case into a banal, unproblematic notion of facilitation, self-affirmation and self-consciousness. (p. 117)

It is not enough for teachers merely to affirm uncritically their student's histories, experiences, and stories—this is to run the risk of idealizing and romanticizing them (Aronowitz & Giroux, 1991).

> Education workers must take seriously the articulation of a morality that posits a language of public life, of emancipatory community, and individual and social commitment. . . . A discourse on morality is important . . . it points to the need to educate students to fight and struggle in order to advance the discourse and principles of a critical democracy. (p. 108)

In this enterprise,

> educators need to take up the task of redefining educational leadership through forms of social criticism, civic courage, and public engagement that allow them to expand oppositional space—both within and outside of school—which increasingly challenges the ideological representation and relations of power that undermine democratic public life. (Aronowitz & Giroux, 1991, p. 89)

Zeichner and Liston's "neutrality" stance within the classroom abdicates the responsibility and potential they otherwise display in various of their analyses as committed radicals. But their neutrality is, of course, a political position. The commitment I am defending here is clearly at odds with the *apparent* disinterest (as noted earlier).

In my own teaching to undergraduate and postgraduate students, I make it quite clear that I am a Marxist with a class perspective. So, clearly, do many educators. But not enough. When, occasionally (around once per year) a student suggests/asks if I am brainwashing him or her, I ask the student group just how many Marxist teachers they have ever been taught by, just how many Marxist publications—newspapers, books, magazines—they have read, and, on the other hand, just how many teachers and books and newspapers they have come across that do *not* present Marxist/socialist analysis and arguments. Numerous books, such as David Hursh and E. Wayne Ross's (2000) *Democratic Social Education: Social Studies for Social Change* (2000) and Peter McLaren's (2003b) *Life in Schools* promote teachers and university educators to use Marxist analyses and to call on teachers at all levels to themselves call on their/our students to study, consider, and, if in agreement, adopt and act on those analyses. Thus, to take one example, Hursh and Ross attempted to guide social studies educators as to what they can do to help build a democratic society in the face of current antidemocratic impulses of greed, individualism and intolerance. And in the writings of the Hillcole Group in England, aimed at school and university teachers, there are explicit delineations of a socialist education policy (Hillcole Group, 1991) and an explicit development of socialist principles for education (Hillcole Group, 1997).

The efforts to empower people in certain contexts can simultaneously strengthen the privileged position of those dispensing it. In the same sense, a Freirean approach to permeating policymaking contexts *may* involve a form of imposition by cultural workers, whereby representation, organization, and collective struggle may not necessarily build understanding or political efficacy among groups of people, but merely essentialize or exoticize the other.

Finally, the work of the intellectual left and those who advance more radical forms of democracy is often criticized for being driven by a "politics of hope" that has lost its appeal. The desire for researchers and academics to become cultural workers and the struggle toward political mobilization of the Freirean nature is often nothing more than an unrealized ideal for those whose progressive ideas are continuously stifled in a political milieu overwhelmingly ruled by an egocentricity of elite culture and by an ideology of efficiency and control.

However, the concepts of critical cultural worker, of critical transformative intellectual and of revolutionary pedagogy, extend the possibilities for dealing with policy conflicts (primarily but not irreducibly, class conflict) and are essential to building a generation of citizens who struggle to mitigate and *to transform* a society rife with economic and social injustice and oppression. Mike Cole, Glenn Rikowski, Peter McLaren and I, along with Marxist feminist writers such as Helen Colley, Teresa Ebert, Rachel Gorman, Jane Kelly, and Shahrzad Mojab, have challenged the claims of postmodernist and postmodernist feminist writers such as Patti Lather in the United States and Elizabeth Atkinson in the United Kingdom that postmodernism and poststructuralism can be forces for macro-social change and social justice. We argue that Marxism—not postmodernism, fundamentalist religion, liberalism or neoliberalism, conservatism—or indeed, social democracy—remains the most viable option in the pursuit of economic justice and social change (Hill, McLaren, Cole, & Rikowski, 1999, 2002).

By engaging in critical transformative practice, we can work in solidarity with others as well as individually to mitigate and replace unjust policies and educational inequalities, and in doing so, build a fuller and richer democracy.

In keeping aloft ideals of plurality of thought, of economic and social justice and of dissent, teachers, teacher educators, and the community must resist the ideological hijacking of our past, present, and future. Teachers and teacher educators are too strategically valuable in students' education to have slick media panaceas and slanted ministerial programs attempting to dragoon them into being uncritical functionaries of a conservative state and of the fundamentally and essentially anti-egalitarian and immoral society and education system reproduced by the capitalist state and its apparatuses.

Such radical cultural workers advocate education as an aspect of anti-capitalist social transformation where social justice, respect for difference, is not enough—we can respect the beggar in the street as a human being. That does rather less for her/his future and the future of humanity in general than an economic system *not* based on the exploitation of labor power by ever-burgeoning capitalist expropriation of surplus value and ever increasing global immiseration and the imperialism of global capital and its governmental and supra-governmental agencies.[12]

Well-organized and focused nonsectarian campaigns organized around class and anti-capitalist issues, which are also committed to economic and social equality and justice and environmental sustainability, can help shape an understanding that we are part of a massive force—the force of the international working class—with a shared understanding that, at the current time, it is the global neoliberal form of capitalism that shatters the lives, bodies, and dreams of billions. And that it can be replaced. As Harman (2002b) suggested, "what matters now is for this (new) generation (of activists) to connect with the great mass of ordinary workers who as well as suffering under the system have the collective strength to fight it" (p. 40).

---

[12]Social justice by itself is not enough. There cannot be social justice in a capitalist society, in situations of gross economic inequality. Human degradation through poverty, the relative poverty/life style that results from the class nature of a capitalist society; the social class-based power relationships that result from capital—exhibiting themselves, for example, in the differential values placed on different cultural capitals, flowing from current and historical patterns of class domination and different historical and current patterns of economic capital—mean that social justice can only ever be partial. It is contingent on economic justice and injustice. The creation of true social justice within capitalism is not viable. Furthermore, no capitalist class is going to give up its economic and political power willingly. Improvements in the relative position of the working class are brought about by class struggle, not by appeals to social justice, however much such appeals might aid that struggle in particular circumstances.

REFERENCES

Aguirre, L. C. (2001). The role of critical pedagogy in the globalization era and the aftermath of September 11, 2001. Interview with Peter McLaren. *Revista Electronica de Investigacion Educativa, 3*(2). Retrieved from http://www.redie. ens.uabc.mx/vol3no2/contenido-coral.html

Allman, P. (2001). Foreword. In M. Cole, D. Hill, P. McLaren, & G. Rikowski (Eds.), *Red chalk: On schooling, capitalism and politics* (pp. 10-14). Brighton, UK: Institute for Education Policy Studies.

Althusser, L. (1971). Ideology and ideological state apparatuses. In L. Althusser, *Lenin and philosophy and other essays*. London: New Left Books.

Apple, M. (1993). *Official knowledge: Democratic education in a conservative age.* London: Routledge.

Aronowitz, S., & Giroux, H. A. (1991). *Postmodern education: Politics, culture and social criticism.* Minneapolis: University of Minnesota Press.

Bambery, C., & Morgan, P. (2002, November). Anger into action? *Socialist Review, 268,* 9–11.

Bircham, E., & Charlton, J. (2001) *Anti-capitalism: A guide to the movement.* London: Bookmarks.

Brenner, R. (2002a, November 3). Global instability: Speech at the Conference Politics Culture Resistance: Globalisation and its Discontents 2. University of Brighton, UK.

Brenner, R. (2002b) *The boom and the bubble: The US in the world economy.* London: Verso.

Brenner, R. (2002c) The economy after the boom: A diagnosis. *International Viewpoint: News and Analysis for Socialists Worldwide, 342,* 24–33.

Burbules, N., & Berk, R. (1999). Critical thinking and critical pedagogy. In T. Popkewitz & L. Fendler (Eds.), *Critical theories in education: Changing terrains of knowledge and politics* (pp. 45-65). London: Routledge.

Bush, G. W. (2001). No Child Left Behind. U. S. Department of Education. Retrieved January 29, from http://www.ed.gov/inits/nclb

Callinicos, A. (1995). *The revolutionary ideas of Karl Marx* (2nd ed.). London: Bookmarks.

Callinicos, A., & Harman, C. (1987). *The changing working class.* London: Bookmarks.

Campaign for the Future of Higher Education (CFHE). (2003). Retrieved from http://www.cfhe.org.uk

Coates, B. (2001). GATS. In E. Bircham & J. Charlton (Eds.) *Anti-capitalism: a guide to the movement* (pp. 27-42). London: Bookmarks.

The Coca Cola kids. (2000, April 28). *Schnews, 257.* Retrieved from http://www. schnews.org.uk/archive/news257.htm#Top

Cole, M. (1998) Globalisation, modernisation and competitiveness: A critique of the New Labour project in education. *International Studies in the Sociology of Education, 8*(3), 315–332.

Cole, M. (2003). New Labour, globalization and social justice: The role of education. In G. Fischman, P. McLaren, H. Sünker & C. Lankshear (Eds.) *Global conflicts, critical theories, and radical pedagogies* (pp. 3-22). Lanham, MD: Rowman & Littlefield.

Cole, M., Hill, D., McLaren, P., & Rikowski, G. (2001). *Red chalk: On schooling, capitalism and politics*. Brighton: Institute for Education Policy Studies.

Dee, H. (Ed.). (2004). *Anti-capitalism: Where now?* London: Bookmarks.

Department for Education and Skills. (2005). Higher standards: Better schools for all (White Paper). Norwich, England: The Stationary Office. Online at http://www.dfes.gov.uk/publications/schoolswhitepaper/

Devidal, P. (2004). Trading away human rights: The GATS and the right to education. *Journal for Critical Education Policy Studies, 2*(2). Online at 222.jceps.com

Ellsworth, L. (1992). Why doesn't this feel empowering? Working through the repressive myths of critical pedagogy. In C. Luke & J. Gore (Eds.), *Feminisms and critical pedagogy* (pp. 90-119). New York: Routledge.

Freire, P. (1998). *Teachers as cultural workers.* Boulder, CO: Westview Press.

Gabbard, D. A. (2003). Education *is* enforcement: The centrality of compulsory schooling in market societies. In K. Saltman & D. Gabbard (Eds.) *Education as enforcement: The militarization and corporatization of schools* (pp. 61-78). New York: Routledge.

Gamble, A. (1988). *The free economy and the strong state.* London: Macmillan.

George, S. (2001). Corporate globalisation. In E. Bircham & J. Charlton (Eds.), *Anti-capitalism: A guide to the movement* (pp. 11-41). London: Bookmarks.

German, L. (1996). *A question of class.* London: Bookmarks

Gillborn, D., & Mirza, H. (2000) *Educational inequality: Mapping race, class and gender.* London: Ofsted.

Giroux, H. A. (1988). *Teachers as intellectuals: Toward a critical pedagogy of learning.* Granby, MA: Bergin & Garvey.

Giroux, H. A., & McLaren, P. (1986). Teacher education and the politics of engagement: The case for democratic schooling. *Harvard Education Review, 56*(3), 213–238.

Harman, C. (2002a, November 2). Brazil: A country divided between rich and poor. *Socialist Worker, 1824.* Retrieved from http://www.socialistworker.co. uk/article.php4?article_id=4392

Harman, C. (2002b). The workers of the world. *International Socialism, 96,* 3–45.

Harvey, D. (2005). *A brief history of neoliberalism.* Oxford: Oxford University Press.

Hatcher, R. (2001). Getting down to the business: Schooling in the globalised economy. *Education and Social Justice, 3*(2), 45–59.

Hatcher, R. (2002). *The business of education: How business agendas drive labour policies for schools.* London: Socialist Education Association. Retrieved from http://www.socialisteducation.org.uk

Hatcher, R., & Hirtt, N. (1999). The business agenda behind labour's education policy. In M. Allen, C. Benn, C. Chitty, M. Cole, R. Hatcher, N. Hirtt, & G. Rikowski (Eds.), *Business, business, business: New Labour's education policy* (pp. 12-23). London: Tufnell Press.

Hill, D. (1997a). Equality and primary schooling: The policy context intentions and effects of the conservative "reforms." In M. Cole, D. Hill, & S. Shan (Eds.), *Equality and the national curriculum in primary schools* (pp. 15-47). London: Cassell.

Hill, D. (1997b). Brief autobiography of a Bolshie dismissed. *General Educator, 44,* 15–17.

Hill, D. (1997c). Reflection in initial teacher education. In K. Watson, S. Modgil, & C. Modgil (Eds.), *Educational dilemmas: Debate and diversity, vol. 1: Teacher education and training* (pp. 193-208). London: Cassell.

Hill, D. (1999a). *New Labour and education: Policy, ideology and the third way.* London: Tufnell Press.

Hill, D. (1999b). Social class and education. In D. Matheson & I. Grosvenor (Eds.), *An introduction to the study of education* (pp. 84-102). London: David Fulton.

Hill, D. (2001a). Equality, ideology and education policy. In D. Hill & M. Cole (Eds.), *Schooling and equality: Fact, concept and policy* (pp. 7-34). London: Kogan Page.

Hill, D. (2001b). State theory and the neoliberal reconstruction of teacher education: A structuralist neo-marxist critique of postmodernist, quasi-postmodernist, and culturalist neo-marxist theory. *British Journal of Sociology of Education, 22*(1), 137–157.

Hill, D. (2001c, September). *The third way in Britain: New Labour's neoliberal education policy.* Paper presented at the Conference Marx 111, Universite de Sorbonne/Nanterre, Paris. Retrieved from http://www.ieps.org.uk

Hill, D. (2002a). Global capital, neoliberalism, and the growth of educational inequality, *The School Field: International Journal of Theory and Research in Education, 13*(1/2), 81–107.

Hill, D. (2002b). The radical left and education policy: Education for economic and social justice. *Education and Social Justice, 4*(3), 41–51.

Hill, D. (2004). Books, banks and bullets: Controlling our minds—the global project of imperialistic and militaristic neoliberalism and its effect on education policy. *Policy Futures, 2*(3&4). Retrieved from http://www.wwwords.co.uk/pfie/

Hill, D. (2005). Globalisation and its educational discontents: Neoliberalisation and its impacts on education workers' rights, pay and conditions. *International Studies in Sociology of Education, 15*(3), 257-288.

Hill, D. (2006a). Education services liberalisation. In E. Rosskam (Ed.), *Winners or losers? Liberalising public services.* Geneva: International Labour Organisation.

Hill, D. (2006b). *New labour education: Ideology, (in) equality and capital.* London: Tunell Press.

Hill, D. (2006c). Six theses on class, global capital and resistance by education and other cultural workers. In O.-P. Moisio & J. Suoranta (Eds.), *Education and the spirit of time.* Rotterdam, Netherlands: Sense Publishers.

Hill, D., & Cole, M. (2001). Social class. In D. Hill & M. Cole (Eds.), *Schooling and equality: Fact, concept and policy* (pp. 137-159). London: Kogan Page.

Hill, D., McLaren, P., Cole, M., & Rikowski, G. (Eds.). (1999). *Postmodernism in educational theory: Education and the politics of human resistance.* London: Tufnell Press.

Hill, D., McLaren, P., Cole, M., & Rikowski, G. (Eds.). (2002). *Marxism against postmodernism in educational theory.* Lanham, MD: Lexington Press.

Hill, D., Sanders, M., & Hankin, T. (2002). Marxism, class analysis and postmodernism. In D. Hill, P. McLaren, M. Cole, & G. Rikowski (Eds.). *Marxism Against postmodernism in educational theory* (pp. 159-194). Lanham, MD: Lexington Books.

Hillcole Group. (1991). *Changing the future: Redprint for education*. London: Tufnell Press.

Hillcole Group. (1997). *Rethinking education and democracy: A socialist alternative for the twenty-first century*. London: Tufnell Press.

Hursh, D. W. (2001). Neoliberalism and the control of teachers, students, and learning: The rise of standards, standardization and accountability. *Cultural Logic*, 4(1). Retrieved from http://www.eserver.org/clogic/4-1/4-1.html

Hursh, D., & Ross, E. W. (2000). *Democratic social education: Social studies for social change*. New York: RoutledgeFalmer.

Hutton, W. (2001). *The world we're in*. London: Little, Brown.

Jack, I. (2001, April 3). Breaking point. *The Guardian*, p. G2.

Klein, N. (2001). *No logo*. London: Flamingo.

Klein, N. (2002). *Fences and windows: Dispatches from the front lines of the globalization debate*. London: Flamingo.

Levidow, L (2002, January). Marketizing higher education: neoliberal strategies and counter-strategies. *The Commoner*, 3. Retrieved from http://www.commoner.org.uk/03levidow.pdf

Lipman, P. (2001). Bush's education plan, globalisation and the politics of race. *Cultural Logic*, 4, 1. Retrieved from http://eserver.org/clogic/4-1/lipman.html

Matheson, M. (2000). Are you being served? WDM in Action. London: World Development Movement.

Mathison, S., & Ross, E. W. (2002). The hegemony of accountability in schools and universities. *Workplace: a Journal for Academic Labor*, 5(1). Retrieved from http://www.louisville.edu/journal/workplace/issue5p1/mathison.html

McLaren P. (2000). *Che Guevara, Paulo Freire and the pedagogy of revolution*. Lanham, MD: Rowman & Littlefield.

McLaren, P. (2003a). The dialectics of terrorism: A Marxist response to September 11 (Part 2: Unveiling the past, evading the present). *Cultural Studies/Critical Methodologies*, 3, 103–132

McLaren, P. (2003b). *Life in schools: An introduction to critical pedagogy in the foundations of education* (4th ed.). Arlington, MA: Allyn & Bacon.

McLaren, P., & Farahmandpur, R. (2005). *Teaching against global capitalism and the new imperialism*. Lanham, MD: Rowman and Littlefield.

McLaren, P., Martin, G., Farahmandpur, R., & Jaramillo, N. (2004). Teaching in and against empire: Critical Pedagogy as Revolutionary Praxis. *Teacher Education Quarterly*, 31(3), 131–153.

McMurtry, J. (1991). Education and the market model. *Journal of the Philosophy of Education*, 25(2), 209–217.

McMurtry, J. (1999). *The cancer stage of capitalism*. London: Pluto Press.

McMurtry, J. (2001). *Why is there a war in Afghanistan?* Speech at Science for Peace Forum and Teach-In How Should Canada Respond to Terrorism and War? Retrieved from http://scienceforpeace.sa.utoronto.ca/Special_Activities/McMurtry_Page.html

Mertes, T. (2002). Grass-roots globalisation. *New Left Review*, 17, 101-110.

Miyoshi, M. (2002). Education, culture, globalisation. Speech at the Conference Politics Culture Resistance: Globalisation and its Discontents. University of Brighton, UK, November 3.

Mojab, S. (2001). New resources for revolutionary critical education. *Convergence*, *34*(1), 118–125. Retrieved from http://www.ieps.org.uk.cwc.net/mojab2002. pdf

Molnar, A. (2001). *Giving kids the business: The commercialization of America's schools* (2nd ed.). Boulder, CO: Westview.

Monbiot, G. (2000). *Captive state: The corporate takeover of Britain.* London: Pan.

Monbiot, G. (2001, July 17). How to rule the world: Rich nations should stop running the planet and give way to global democracy. *The Guardian*, p. 20. Retrieved from http://www.guardian.co.uk/globalisation/story/0,7369,522903, 00.html

Monbiot, G. (2002, June 19). Public fraud initiative. *The Guardian*, p, 20. Retrieved from http://society.guardian.co.uk/futureforpublicservices/comment/0,8146, 739525,00.html

Mulderrig, J. (2002). Learning to labour: The discursive construction of social actors in New Labour's education policy. Retrieved from http://www.jceps.com/ index.php?pageID=article&articleID=2

Ollman, B. (2001). *How to take an exam . . . and remake the world.* Montreal: Black Rose.

Pakulski, J. (1995). Social movements and class: The decline of the marxist paradigm. In L. Maheu (Ed.), *Social movements and social classes* (pp. 55-86). London: Sage.

Pilger, J. (2002a, November 4). The new protest movement: Something is stirring among the people. *New Statesman*, pp. 11–12. Retrieved from Znet at http:// www.zmag.org/content/showarticle.cfm?SectionID=15&ItemID=2579

Pilger, J. (2002b). *The new rulers of the world.* New York: Verson.

Pollock, A. (2001). Private sector lured by £30bn public gold rush. *The Observer Business* (London), p. 5.

Raduntz, H. (2002). Personal communication.

Rikowski, G. (2001a). *The battle in Seattle.* London: Tufnell Press.

Rikowski, G. (2001b). Education for industry: A complex technicism. *Journal of Education and Work*, *14*(1), 29–49.

Rikowski, G. (2002a). *Globalisation and education.* Paper prepared for the House of Lords Select Committee on Economic Affairs, Inquiry into the Global Economy. Retrieved from http://www.ieps.org.uk%20or%20rikowski@tis-cali.co.uk

Rikowski, G. (2002b). Schools: Building for business. Retrieved from http://www. ieps.org.uk/

Rikowski, G. (2002c). *Schools: The great GATS buy.* Retrieved from http://www. ieps.org.uk/

Rikowski, G. (2002d). Transfiguration: Globalisation, the World Trade Organisation and the national faces of the GATS. *Information for Social Change*, *14*, 8–17.

Rikowski, G. (2003a). *The suppression and compression of critical space in education today.* Paper presented at University College Northampton.

Rikowski, G. (2003b). Schools and the GATS enigma. *Journal for Critical Education Policy Studies*, *1*(1). Online At http://www.jceps.com/index.php?pageID=article&articleID=8

Rikowski, G. (2005a). The Education White Paper and the marketisation and capitalisation of the schools system in England. *The Volumizer*. Online at http://journals.aol.co.uk/rikowskigr/volumizer

Rikowski, G. (2005b). *Silence on the wolves: What is absent in New Labour's five year strategy for education*. Occasional paper published by the Education Research Center, University of Brighton, UK.

Rikowski, R. (2002). *The WTO/GATS agenda for libraries*. Available on www.ieps.org.uk

Robertson, S., Bonal, X., & Dale, R. (2002). GATS and the education service industry: The politics of scale and global re-territorialization. *Comparative Education Review, 46*(2), 472–496.

Sader, E. (2002). Beyond civil society, the left after Porto Alegre. *New Left Review, 17*, 87-99.

Saltman, K., & Gabbard, D. (Eds.). (2003). *Education as enforcement: The militarization and corporatization of schools*. New York: Routledge.

Saunois, T. (2002). Radical Latin America. *Socialism Today, 70*, 6–7.

Sexton, S. (2001, July). Trading health care away? GATS, public services and privatisation. *The Corner House*, Briefing 23.

Shor, I., & Freire, P. (1987). *A pedagogy for liberation: Dialogues on transforming education*. South Hadley, MA: Bergin & Garvey.

Socialist Worker. (2002). Brazil: A country divided. 2 November.

Tibbett, S. (2001). It's shocking all over the world. *Tribune, 65*(30), 10-11.

Tooley, J. (2000). *Reclaiming education*. London: Cassell.

Tooley, J. (2001). *The global education industry* (2nd ed.). London: Institute for Economic Affairs.

Troyna, B. (1995). The local management of schools and racial equality. In S. Tomlinson & M. Craft (Eds.), *Ethnic relations and schooling* (pp. 140-154). London: Athlone.

Whitty, G., Power, S., & Halpin, D. (1998). *Devolution and choice in education: The school, the state and the market*. Buckingham: Open University Press.

Wilson, C. (2002, September 12). Assault on our rights. *Morning Star*, p. 3

Zeichner, K., & Liston, D. (1987). Teaching student teachers to reflect. *Harvard Educational Review, 57*(1), 23–48.

Zeichner, K., & Liston, D. (1996). *Reflective teaching: An introduction*. Mahwah, NJ: Erlbaum.

6

Schools and the GATS Enigma[1]

Glenn Rikowski

The World Trade Organization's (WTO) General Agreement on Trade in Services (GATS) of 1994 seems to have a strange kind of social existence. It appears to be a shadowy force, with massive potential to disrupt, undermine, and transfigure public services—yet distanced from their privatization. The GATS' substantive impact is in some doubt, as many governments—especially the United Kingdom—seem hell bent on nurturing the business

---

[1]This chapter began life as a paper presented at the Education Policy Research Unit (EPRU) Seminar, *Education for Profit: Private Sector Participation in Public Education,* which was convened by Professor Stephen Ball at the Institute of Education, University of London on November 27, 2002. In 2003, a version of the original paper was published in the *Journal for Critical Education Policy Studies,* 1(1). This chapter is a revised and extended version of that article.

takeover of public services, GATS or no. In short, GATS is an enigma. As Grieshaber-Otto and Sanger (2002) argued:

> At first glance, the GATS does not appear to pose serious or immediate threats to public education . . . [Yet it] . . . would be wrong to conclude, however, that WTO rules do not affect public education. The treaty already casts a long shadow over it. The effects of the current treaty, already significant in themselves, can be expected to become more important in the future. (p. 45)

This chapter brings GATS into focus a little more, to get a clearer view of the monster casting a shadow over state schools in England.

A common way to approach the relationship between GATS and public services is to do an "impact" assessment, as the Association of University Teachers has undertaken for U.K. higher education, and as some Canadian GATS critics have done for Canadian schools. Although having tremendous value, such impact assessments are partially speculative—developing scenarios regarding what might or could happen through the application of GATS imperatives and disciplines.

However, this is only half the picture and the relation between GATS and public services ideally needs to be approached on the basis that it is a two-way thing, and that government policies affect differentially the nature of the relation for each service, and for each country. This chapter explores the relation between schools and the GATS in England today. The opening two sections provide brief outlines of the WTO and the GATS.

The World Trade Organization[2]

While World War II was still raging, in 1943 the U.S. and British governments embarked on a series of bilateral discussions aimed at designing a post-war international trading system free of the protectionism of the inter-war years (Cohn, 2000). In Autumn 1945, the U.S. State Department floated a document on trade and employment that was to be the basis of multilateral negotiations. It constituted an outline for a proposed International Trade Organization (ITO). This document was developed as the basis for the Havana Charter that was discussed by 23 leading capitalist countries in March 1948. Meanwhile, in 1946, the same 23 nations met to discuss the much narrower issue of tariff reduction. At this meeting, it was decided to

---

[2]This section was adapted from Section 1 of *The Battle in Seattle: Its Significance for Education* (Rikowski, 2001), and also draws from Rikowski (2002c).

meet up the following year in Geneva to negotiate to reduce tariffs on about a fifth of the world's trade. Thus, in October 1947 the first round of the General Agreement on Tariffs and Trade (GATT) resulted in these 23 countries signing up to the agreement, which became effective on January 1, 1948 (MSN Encarta, 2000a). Furthermore, the signatories agreed to accept some of the trade rules enshrined within the draft ITO charter (ahead of the forthcoming meeting in Havana) in order to protect the tariff reductions negotiated in Geneva.

Thus, the GATT emerged after World War II as a charter for the ITO, which was envisioned as an agency of the United Nations (MSN Encarta, 2000a). The ITO was to complement the World Bank and the International Monetary Fund (IMF) in establishing international trade rules and co-operation (DTI, 1999). However, it was at the meeting in Havana in March 1948 that this broader scenario started to unravel. The main aim of the meeting was to attain agreement to the formation of a permanent ITO. The 1947 GATT agreement was to be incorporated within the ITO. The ITO charter was to have had "an ambitious agenda" (DTI, 1999, p. 1). It was to cover not just trading relations but also employment, international investment, economic development, services, competition, restrictive practices, and commercial policy and commodity agreements. It also included the administrative arrangements for a permanent ITO (Cohn, 2000; DTI, 1999; Penrose, 1953; Reisman, 1996). As Tabb noted, "The ITO was to impose order on the world trading system, in order to avoid the kind of protectionist downward spiral in trade which occurred in the 1930s" (p. 4).

The ITO was not ratified at Havana (or thereafter). Cohn (2000) presented the ITO as a dog's breakfast, with complex rules and "numerous escape clauses and exceptions in the charter [that] would interfere with trade liberalization" (p. 205). He also noted the disruptive effects for the ITO charter of the strong U.S. protectionist lobby. Yet Tabb (2000) argued that it was the possibility of the ITO providing substantive protection on labor standards and meeting the needs of developing countries that effectively sank it. From a U.S. perspective, the ITO framework for regulating international trade yielded too much to workers' rights and Third World countries' yearnings for preferential treatment in trade, and set too tight a leash on big corporations' market power (promising anti-trust laws; Tabb, 2000). On this score, the United States dragged its heels over ratifying the ITO. In 1950, the ITO failed to win ratification in the U.S. Congress and was consigned to history. The GATT, meanwhile, remained in use to regulate international trade.

From its "provisional" status as precursor to the ITO in 1948, the GATT provided a legal and institutional framework for international trade and tariffs until 1995 (DTI, 1999). Its participants were "contracting parties" rather than members; the GATT was never formally constituted. It aimed at nondiscrimination in the sense that all participants were to be treated equally, such that when a country reduced trade tariffs for one GATT participant it had to do so for all. Second, there was a clause that enabled a GATT participant to withdraw its tariff reduction if it "seriously harmed" its domestic producers (MSN Encarta, 2000a). This was a loophole that GATT participants were keen to exploit, pointing toward a need for a more formal trade dispute mechanism. GATT participants sponsored eight "trade rounds" in all. The "Kennedy Round" (1962–1967) established a set of trade negotiation rules when parties disagreed. The Tokyo Round (1973–1979) established a series of non-tariff barrier codes of practice in the areas of government procurement, customs valuation, subsidies and countervailing measures, antidumping, standards, and import licensing (Antweiler, 1995).

The final "Uruguay Round" (1986–94) broadened the GATT agreement further by limiting agricultural subsidies and including trade in services and intellectual property within its scope. This round also established the WTO. The GATT and the WTO co-existed throughout 1995, and the former was wound up in December 1995. Trade agreements established by the GATT became incorporated within the WTO agreement (MSN Encarta, 2000b). In 1995, GATT's functions were taken over by the WTO.

The WTO is based permanently in Geneva and is controlled by a General Council comprising member states' ambassadors (who also serve on WTO committees). The Ministerial Conference meets every 2 years, and appoints the WTO's director general. It had a budget of £48 million and 500 staff in 1999 (Legrain, 2000, p. 30), and by 2001 a budget of $78 million and a staff of 530 (*Economist*, 2001).[3] The Seattle meeting in 1999 was the third Ministerial Conference. There were 135 member countries represented at Seattle, and a further 35 nations had observer status there. By 2001, the WTO had 142 member nations (Tibbett, 2001), and by 2004 it had 147 members (Elliott, 2004).

As Bakan (2000) noted, the WTO extends far the remit of the old GATT. It includes a series of other agreements, for example:

- Trade Related Investment Measures (TRIMS)
- Trade Related Intellectual Property Measures (TRIPS)
- General Agreement on Trade in Services (GATS)
- Sanitary and Phyto-sanitary Standards Agreement (SPS) (setting restrictive standards on government policies regarding food and safety and animal and plant health)

---

[3] As *The Economist* notes, the WTO's budget is "about half what the World Bank spends on travel, [and] the WTO is the poor relation among international organizations. But it is the centre of negotiations that could have a far bigger impact on global prosperity than any decision made in more imposing buildings" ("Playing games with prosperity," 2001).

- Financial Services Agreement (FSA)—designed to remove all obstacles to financial services
- Agreements on agriculture, information technology, and telecommunications.

Furthermore, the WTO incorporates a complex Dispute Settlement Process. Tribunals operate in secret to settle disputes between member states. Only national governments are allowed to participate, and there is no outside appeals procedure (Working Group on the WTO/MAI, 1999). Rulings generate three possibilities. First, losing countries have a set time to comply and they must change their laws to conform to WTO stipulations. Second, if they refuse to do this then they pay permanent compensation to the winning country. The third possibility is that they face non-negotiated trade sanctions. As Smith and Moran (2000) noted:

> What distinguishes the WTO among international agreements is its Dispute Resolution Panel. The panel possesses far-reaching sanctioning powers over member countries, which it uses to ensure compliance with WTO commitments. No other international body has such strong enforcement capabilities. (p. 66)

The WTO is "the only global institution that even the US and the [European Union] are supposed to obey," whereas the World Bank and the IMF have influence only over "weak developing countries," noted Martin Wolf (1999), a journalist for the *Financial Times*.

On disputes other than trade, the WTO operates on a system of "consensus," but in practice this process is driven by the "Quad"—the United States, the EU, Japan, and Canada—whose representatives meet daily in Geneva to address these non-trade issues (Bakan, 2000). Representatives from the Quad are lobbied heavily by transnational corporations. Furthermore, representatives from transnational corporations "sit on all the important advisory committees" deciding detailed policy and set the agenda (Price, Pollock, & Shaoul, 1999). Thus, the WTO provides an "enforceable global commercial code" based on close relations with transnational capital, making it "one of the main mechanisms of corporate globalization" (Working Group on the WTO/MAI, 1999, p. 1). It is a "forum for trade rights of capital, on terms negotiated by the agencies of governments that represent the interests of capital. No other rights count" (Tabb, 2000, p. 6). Trade barriers are essentially "*anything* that can limit profits made via trade or investment" (Puckett, 2000, p. 14). Major corporations have lobbyists settled permanently at the WTO's lair in Geneva, and representatives of corporations sit on some of the many WTO committees and working groups.

The outlook underpinning the WTO is deregulation, with incremental "freedom for transnational capital to do what it wants, where and when it

wants" (Tabb, 2000, p. 5). As Tabb noted, the "WTO's fundamental postu-
late is that trade and investment liberalization lead to more competition,
greater market efficiency and so, necessarily, to a higher standard of living"
(p. 5). In practice, standards of living for many countries in the poorer South
have declined absolutely or relatively (compared to the richer Northern
nations) in recent years. These principles and propositions are the essence of
the concept of "neoliberalism" in international economy. However:

> While its proponents say it is based on "free trade," in fact, the WTO's
> 700-plus pages of rules set out a comprehensive system of corporate-
> managed trade. Under the WTO's system of *corporate-managed trade*,
> economic efficiency, reflected in short-term corporate profits, domi-
> nates other values. The neoliberal ideological underpinning of corpo-
> rate-managed trade is presented as TINA—"There Is No
> Alternative"—an inevitable outcome rather than the culmination of a
> long-term effort to write and put in place rules designed to benefit cor-
> porations and investors, rather than communities, workers and the envi-
> ronment. (Working Group on the WTO/MAI, p. 1)

The anger directed at the WTO's third Ministerial meeting in Seattle late
November–early December 1999 was underwritten by more than 50 years
of capital-friendly developments in organizational changes in the international trading infrastructure. Yet Seattle was an instant within a series of acts
of resistance to global capital. These included landless peasants (NST) movements in Brazil, Mexico's Zapatistas, the farmers of India's Karnataka state,
a 50,000 strong demonstration in the Niger Delta, Jubilee 2000, the J18
Carnival Against Capitalism in London 1999, and more besides (Bakan,
2000; Madden, 2000). McLaren (2000) reminds us that 10,000 protesters
picketed the WTO's Second Ministerial Meeting in Geneva in May 1998.
Ward and Wadsworth (2000) argued that: "Seattle was not the beginning, but
the result of many small to medium movements that have been gathering
strength for over two years" (p. 4).

The Seattle Ministerial was set up to produce an agenda for the next
"Millennial Round" of negotiations. When the "Millennial Round" opened
in Seattle on November, 30, 1999, the ministers and delegates were confronted by 40,000 anti-WTO protesters, which was more than the "20–30,000
thousand that shut down Interstate 5 to protest about the Vietnam War"
(Tabb, 2000, p. 1). The protesters represented around 800 trade union and
activist organizations from more than 75 countries (Tabb, 2000). The vibran-
cy, creativity, and courage that they incorporated into their strategies for
shutting down the Seattle Ministerial were stunning. Despite being shot at
with rubber bullets, tear-gassed and pepper-sprayed, the mass of protesters
prevented ministers and the WTO *entourage* from addressing their agenda;
they "left Seattle in disarray" (Bakan, 2000). As some have noted (e.g.,

Mandel & Magnussen, 1999), the limited discussions that did take place in Seattle merely showed up serious rifts within the WTO as some Third World countries set out to block proposals for the next trade round. Furthermore, some countries made pledges to "free trade" while lobbying seriously for rules favorable to their own economies (Mandel & Magnussen, 1999). Finally, Marshall (1999) pointed toward familiar EU/U.S. splits in Seattle. Even without the protesters it would have been no picnic. The Doha Ministerial of November 2001 attempted to pick up the pieces and drive trade liberalization forward once more.

THE GENERAL AGREEMENT ON TRADE IN SERVICES

The GATS seeks to open up 160 services sectors to international capital. Specifically, it aims to create a "level playing field" thereby avoiding discrimination against foreign corporations entering services markets. The process of trade liberalization in services (including currently public ones) is progressive; it will be deepened and strengthened over time, and Part IV of the GATS Agreement makes this clear. In this scenario, "public" services will progressively be turned into internationally tradable commodities. U.K. government claims that public services are exempt from the GATS have no firm foundation. Once a service has been committed to the GATS there is no possibility of reversing the position (Kelk & Worth, 2002).

As Kelk (2002) noted, the GATS cuts deepest into services trade regulation through its National Treatment (NT), Most-Favored Nation (MFN), and Market Access (MA) disciplines. The NT trade rule requires that foreign services providers be "treated at least as well as domestic service providers" (Kelk, 2002, p. 26). The MFN rule means "the best treatment accorded to any foreign service provider must be accorded 'immediately and unconditionally' to all foreign service providers" (Grieshaber-Otto & Sanger, 2002, p. iv). The MA GATS rule means that governments are prevented from "introducing quantitative restrictions on the amount of trade activity in a sector" (Grieshaber-Otto & Sanger, 2002, p. iv). Hence, member states' economic policy options are curtailed by the MA rule. Finally, the transparency rule stipulates that member governments must publish details of all measures—local, regional, and national—that may affect the operation of the GATS treaty (Grieshaber-Otto & Sanger, 2002). These "top–down" rules are supplemented by "bottom–up" bilateral commitments, in which individual members agree to open up service sectors to GATS disciplines, and can request that other members do so too. The current GATS 2000 negotiations are well under way in this horse-trading process.

International trade law lecturer Markus Krajewski (2002) has analyzed the GATS Agreement in detail. He concluded that the Agreement makes it impossible to tell whether public services are included under GATS. This makes the GATS fiendishly difficult to combat on the basis of what is actually written down in the Agreement. On the one hand, if it was clear that public services were included under the GATS then governments, corporations and pro-GATS lobbyists could give no assurances that the "GATS has nothing to do with privatisation," as they do currently. Their reassurances to concerned organizations and their patronising arguments that anti-GATS folk are merely scare mongering would not be taken seriously, as they sometimes are today. On the other hand, if it were clear that public services were excluded from GATS provisions then two things would be obvious. First, anti-GATS activists and trade unions could defend public services from the GATS monster on the basis of international trade law, and corporations attempting to argue that public services were incorporated within the GATS would clearly be on a loser. Anti-GATS forces could confront corporations that attempted to use the GATS to further their interests in public services by using the actual Agreement against them. Second, it would be clear that UK's New Labour is really keen on the business takeover of public services, and is not being forced or cajoled into it by trade rules framed by some distant, business-friendly institution such as the WTO.

Meanwhile, the opacity of the GATS is cunning indeed. It has the potential to intellectually disarm GATS critics. Anti-GATS activists have no firm footing for critiquing the Agreement.

The current round of GATS negotiations at the WTO headquarters in Geneva started up in February 2000; almost directly after the WTO Ministerial Meeting in Seattle late-1999 broke up in disarray following the anti-WTO protests there. An overall deal had to be brokered for December 2004, to come into force in 2005. So for anti-GATS activists, trade unions, and defenders of public services there was some urgency. The following section focuses specifically on the relationship between the GATS and the business takeover of schools.

SCHOOLS AND THE GATS

A good starting point for exploring the relation between schools and the GATS is the GATS Agreement itself, together with the Schedule of Commitments for education in relation to the EU. The U.K.'s GATS commitments are incorporated within those for the EU, although there are a few national differences (see WTO, 1994). On information gleaned from the EU GATS Infopoint, it appears education has already been lost to the GATS. For primary education, 20 countries committed themselves to GATS disciplines in 1994, and for secondary education 22 countries took the plunge. The EU is GATS-committed for both primary and secondary education.

The GATS incorporates four modes of service supply. Mode 1 is "cross-border" supply, the "supply of a service from the territory of one Member to a consumer in the territory of another" (EU GATS Infopoint, n.d., p. 1). Mode 2 supply is concerned with "consumption abroad," where "the consumer of the service travels to the service supplier" (p. 1.). Mode 3, "commercial presence" is "where the service suppliers establishes in the foreign market as a legal entity in the form of a subsidiary or a branch" (p. 1). For all of these modes of supply, the EU's commitments for primary and secondary education are "none"—which is the *opposite* of what it sounds. "None" means that a country is committing itself to ensuring that there are "no restrictions which are inconsistent with GATS rules covering participation in the market by foreign service suppliers" (EU GATS Infopoint, n.d., p. 2). In relation to U.K./EU GATS commitments on primary and secondary education, there are two aspects to this. First, for the United Kingdom, there are no barriers regarding "Limitations on Market Access" (although a few EU countries have some limitations on market access incorporated into the EU Schedule for either primary or secondary education). Thus, U.K. primary and secondary education "markets" appear to be open to foreign suppliers. WTO members committing themselves to opening up primary and secondary education through GATS (as the EU has) must show any limitations on access for foreign suppliers—and then these are open to challenge through the WTO Disputes Panel by a corporation's national government, if they are WTO members. Only national governments that are WTO members can participate in the complex WTO Dispute Settlement Process (Rikowski, 2001). Corporations would have to lobby and persuade national governments to go through with this if there was any reluctance among trade ministers and officials to pursue the case.

Furthermore, as the United Kingdom (via the EU) has signed up to the GATS regarding primary and secondary education, then those services are also subject to the "Limitations on National Treatment" provision. Under this GATS rule, member states must acknowledge any limitations in the treatment of foreign suppliers that puts them in a less favorable position than their domestic counterparts. For example, Edison Schools (from the United States) must be alerted to any differences in the ways they are being treated as compared with U.K. education services suppliers if they enter the U.K. schools market. Failure to provide the necessary information might result in a foreign supplier seeking recompense through the GATS via their national government taking the case through the WTO Dispute Settlement Process. Transparency is the issue here. The United Kingdom has no limitations on the provision in the EU Schedule either. Finally, only in Mode 4 supply, the "presence of natural persons" from another country does some limitation regarding foreign primary and secondary education suppliers possibly apply. Mode 4 supply is "unbound" for EU primary and secondary education. *Unbound* means a country is making no commitment either to open up its market or to keep it as open as it was at the time of accession into the WTO. Practically, what this means for Mode 4 supply is that if Edison Schools wanted to set up operations in the United Kingdom then the company would probably have to use U.K. employees, as general immigration rules would still apply. It is likely that teachers from the United States could not be just flown in to work in Edison U.K. schools regardless. However, the nature of the unbound status on Mode 4 supply muddies the picture, with no clear barrier to U.S. teachers being jetted into Edison U.K. schools established on the basis of the EU GATS Schedule.

From the account just given, it might appear that the United Kingdom (via the EU) has a pretty much "open-door" policy regarding the foreign supply of primary and secondary education services. It seems that education activists and trade unionists are 10 years too late on GATS rules for education services that are technically irreversible. Yet this is a misleading impression, which is exposed as such on deeper examination of the EU's Schedule of Commitments for education services under GATS (WTO, 1994). Section 5 of the EU Schedule of Commitments indicates that in relation to education, the GATS refers to "privately funded education services." From this, it might seem that the only education services in relation to schools under threat from the GATS are independent and private schools. Why should we get too agitated if only Eton, Harrow, and Roedean and their ilk are under threat from GATS rules? They are clearly in the "education market," so must take the consequences and face competing foreign providers.

However, once again, the GATS language is cleverly crafted. The Schedule does not pinpoint private education "institutions," but privately funded education "services." It is not the case that a whole education institution has to be a for-profit outfit for the GATS to apply. Any of its constituent services—from frontline ones such as teaching, to cleaning, school meals services and the school library—could fall under the GATS if private capital is involved. Furthermore, private sector operators in school improvement, equal opportunities and recruitment and other schools' services previously supplied by the local education authority (LEA), also fall under the GATS.

It could be argued this misses the point: Are not these services still "publicly funded" even though education businesses like Nord Anglia and school meals providers like Initial Services are delivering the service? It could be argued they are not basically "privately funded" education services. A number of points are relevant here.

First, this argument assumes that "public" money remains "public" even when transferred to a private sector service deliverer ruled by profit generation. However, it could be argued that once the contract is signed to deliver frontline teaching, school management, or school improvement services the "public money" undergoes transformation into private capital. This is the magic of money, the illusion on which New Labour and GATS protagonists' arguments rest. At a meeting in a church hall in Newham following the Trade Justice Movement lobby of Parliament on June 19, 2002, Stephen Timms (former U.K. Schools Minister, now at the Department for Trade and Industry) said the private sector was being brought in to improve standards. He argued that it was not "privatization" as the pertinent services were still being publicly funded. This argument is naïve at least, and positively misleading.

Second, for some New Labour schools policies, private finance forms an element of start-up capital. In the city academies, or just academies now under Education Act 2002 (see Her Majesty's Government, 2002, Part 5, pp. 45–47), for specialist schools and also for some education action zones, private capital forms part of the start-up fund. The foundational significance of private capital is even clearer in the case of schools built under the Private Finance Initiative (PFI), where money to build the school is raised at commercial rates in the money markets by private companies. In all these cases, it would seem that the involvement of the private sector opens up schools or, at a minimum these *educational services*, to the GATS. These are private education services that have virused public money through running various public education services.

Third, under the Education Act 2002, school governing bodies can set themselves up as companies (see Her Majesty's Government, 2002, Chapter 3). They then have the power to invest in other companies. Furthermore, school companies can merge to form "federations"—chains like McDonalds—to gain economies of scale, thereby increasing profit-making capacity. In September 2002, David Miliband (Schools Minister) indicated that business leaders running school federations did not need teaching qualifications (Kelly, 2002). Schools can enter into deals with private sector outfits. They can also sell educational services to other schools. The 2002 Act gives the Secretary of State new powers to form companies for involvement in any area of school or LEA life. Finally, under the Act around 1,000 schools are to be given the freedom to vary the curriculum and change teachers' pay and conditions. These powers result from the new "earned autonomy" status that top performing schools can gain. This gives private sector operators some control over staff costs through manipulating teachers' contracts of employment. Overall, the 2002 Act provides a deregulatory framework for the business takeover of schools, and hence also for the virusing of GATS throughout our school system. Of course, New Labour can still argue that the school system is "publicly funded," but in specific instances of outsourcing, PFI and strategic partnerships with companies, the previously public finance is transfigured into private capital. Sponsorship by private companies involves injections of corporate cash. Through these mechanisms, schools are exposed to the GATS.

THE BUSINESS TAKEOVER OF SCHOOLS

Private school group to run City Academy in Moss Side

A Christian Independent schools company, denounced by teachers as having a "white, middle-class ethos," looks set to be given the management of a £5m government-backed City Academy in one of Britain's most deprived urban areas.
Financial Times, 1 April 2002.

Corporations, Corporations, Education

Walsall recently contracted out most of its education services to Serco, whose other contracts include asylum seeker detention centres and the electronic tagging of criminals.
Corporate Watch Newsletter, Issue 7, Jan-Feb 2002.

Private sector to run worst schools

Private sector operators will help manage some of the country's worst schools, under plans to be published on Wednesday. Initially, about 30 secondary schools with chronic problems will form the potential market for companies – but with more than 300 schools said to be failing, the market could grow considerably if the measure proves a success.
Financial Times, 3 September 2001.

Fourth, directly after the General Election victory in 2001, Schools Minister Stephan Timms and Sports Minister Richard Caborn promoted a series of "partnerships" between private and state schools. Thirty-four Independent/State School Partnerships were established on July 3, 2001. Dissolution of the barriers and distinction between public finance and private capital muddy the issue of whether schools services are either state financed or "privately funded." The insurgence of private schools into the state sector could well be dragging the GATS in its wake.

Fifth, the Department for Education and Skills (DfES) recently published its *Five Year Strategy* for education (DfES, 2004). At the heart of the strategy for secondary schools (for children aged 11–16) is business sponsorship. Specialist schools, which will supersede comprehensive schools, require up to £50,000 in business sponsorship. Another category of schools that will expand under the Five Year Strategy will be academies. These will require up to £2 million from the private sector sponsors and philanthropists for start-up costs. Apart from the grammar schools (which are ignored in the Five Year Strategy), it is envisaged that all state secondary schools will have some form of business sponsorship. This policy opens up secondary schools in England to GATS disciplines and rules further still.

Finally, as Belgian teacher and education activist Nico Hirtt (2000) indicated, only education systems financed solely by the state and with total exclusion of any commercial operations are excluded from the GATS. This point underscores the previous five: the greater the business involvement in state schools and state education services, the more they are opened up to GATS and a future as internationally tradable commodities. On this account, policies and mechanisms that nurture the business takeover of schools can be viewed as the *national faces of the GATS* (for more on this see Rikowski, 2002a, 2002b, 2002c). These are the national, local, and school-level GATS *enablers* that facilitate the business takeover of schools by turning educational services into internationally tradable commodities. In England, the national faces of the GATS include PFI, outsourcing, long-term strategic partnerships with companies and information and computer technology deals. The Office for Standards in Education is transfigured into a GATS-facilitator every time it locates a "weak" school ripe for business takeover.

CONCLUSION

Rather than a Geneva-based GATS monster forcing the U.K. government to embrace GATS, every time the private sector enters, deepens and expands its involvement in our schools it opens up those "educational services" to the GATS. The fight against the business takeover of schools is simultaneously the struggle against GATS and our education services being catapulted into international education markets. New Labour's education policy is virusing the GATS into our schools and LEAs. One day, a company in Detroit or Vancouver that focuses primarily on the bottom-line could control a local secondary school in England. Now, that would certainly stretch the notion of a "community school" and the concept of democratic accountability.

On the question of why the business takeover of school is happening, I have located four inter-linked explanations (see Rikowski, 2003). First, there is no doubt that education business leaders and companies selling educational services have put considerable pressure on successive U.K. Education Ministers in the last 10 years or so to open up schools to business interests. Second, New Labour is actively seeking to build up U.K. education service companies as export earners. Part of this strategy includes nurturing U.K. businesses in the schools sector. Third, the business takeover of schools sits well with New Labour's economic vision of the knowledge economy. Education services businesses are a significant element in a model of the economy where knowledge is viewed as the key factor of production, supplanting labor, land, and capital as the core elements. Education businesses produce a range of "knowledge products" that can be sold and traded internationally. Of course, this model of an emerging knowledge economy can be critiqued easily. But its significance as a guide to New Labour economic policy was established in the 1998 White Paper, *Our Competitive Future—Building the Knowledge Driven Economy* that originated from the Department of Trade and Industry while Peter Mandelson was minister there. Finally, the GATS intensifies the previous three factors, especially given that a strengthened GATS Agreement was to be established on January 1, 2005. The GATS timetable generates urgency regarding the establishment of a vibrant and sustainable U.K. education services sector. This partly explains New Labour's rush to push through "modernization" in schools and to open school doors to U.K. education services businesses as quickly as possible.[4]

However, following the collapse of the WTO Cancun Ministerial meeting in September 2003, the GATS timetable is in disarray. The Cancun meeting failed to agree on cutting agricultural subsidies paid to U.S. and to EU farmers by their governments. These subsidies discriminated against agricultural exports to these countries by the G90 group of developing countries, argued representatives of the G90. This situation had the effect of stalling WTO agreements in other areas, such as the GATS, as many of the G90 refused to consider these until the rich nations of the North had agreed to a deal on agriculture. WTO members are currently aiming to break the deadlock at a series of emergency meetings in Geneva. They are seeking to generate a draft framework for taking forward the Doha "development round" of November 2001. The deadline for agreement on the draft framework was July 31, 2004. However, Frances Williams (2004) has reported that: "global negotiations to open services markets to foreign competition . . . could take two years or more, even if current bottlenecks over agriculture were overcome." Thus, anti-GATS activists may have more time to protest a strengthened GATS agreement than previously anticipated.

There is, however, a more general explanation regarding why the business takeover of schools is occurring. This is based on the fact that we live in capital's social universe (Rikowski, 2002b). One feature of our existence in this social universe is that all aspects of our lives are potentially open to invasion by capital—for this is one way in which the social universe of capital expands (Rikowski, 2002c). The business takeover of schools is an aspect of this, and future work will make the necessary connections.

---

[4]These explanations are given more space in Rikowski (2003).

REFERENCES

Antweiler, W. Jr. (1995). *A brief history of the General Agreement on Tariffs and Trade.* Retrieved from http://pacific.commerce.uba.ca/trade/GATT-rounds.html

Bakan, A. (2000). After Seattle: The politics of the World Trade Organization. *International Socialism, 86*(Spring), 19-36.

Cohn, T. (2000). *Global political economy: Theory and practice,* Harlow: Longman.

DfES. (2004). *Department for Education and Skills: Five year strategy for children and learners.* July, Cm.6272, Norwich: The Stationery Office. Retrieved from http://www.dfes.gov.uk

DTI. (1999). *The World Trade Organisation and international trade rules: An introduction to the World Trade Organisation (WTO).* Available from the Department of Trade and Industry, UK. Retrieved from http://www.dti.gov.uk/worldtrade/intro.htm.

Elliott, L. (2004, July 26). Geneva talks aim to end trade deadlock. *The Guardian,* p. 20.

EU GATS-Infopoint. (n.d.). *Opening world markets for services: Legal texts and commitments.* Retrieved from http://gats-info.eu.int/gats-info/gatscomm.pl?MENU=hhh

Grieshaber-Otto, J., & Sanger, M. (2002). *Perilous lessons: The impact of the WTO Services Agreement (GATS) on Canada's public education system.* Ottawa: Canadian Centre for Policy Alternatives.

Her Majesty's Government. (2002, July 24). *Education Act 2002.* Norwich: The Stationery Office.

Hirtt, N. (2000). The "Millennium Round" and the liberalisation of the education market. *Education and Social Justice, 2*(2), 12–18.

Kelk, S. (2002, November). Higher education: A GATS disaster zone in waiting. *Red Pepper, 101,* 26–27.

Kelk, S., & Worth, J. (2002). *Trading it away: How GATS threatens UK higher education.* Oxford: People & Planet. Retrieved from http://www.peopleandplanet.org/tradejustice/tradingitaway.asp

Kelly, J. (2002, August 5). Business people may run state school federations. *Financial Times,* p. 4.

Krajewski, M. (2002, September). *Public interests, private rights and the "constitution" of GATS.* Paper presented at the workshop on "GATS: Trading Development?" Centre for the Study of Globalisation and Regionalisation, University of Warwick.

Legrain, P. (2000, May). Against globophobia. *Prospect,* 30–35.

Madden, R. (2000, Spring). If capitalism is pants, what are you wearing under your trousers? *Corporate Watch, 10,* 17–19.

Mandel, M., & Magnussen, P. (1999, December 13). Whose world is it, anyway? *Business Week,* pp. 38–41.

Marshall, A. (1999, December 4). US bypasses Third World as trade talks fail. *The Guardian,* p. 16.

McLaren, P. (2000). *Che Guevara, Paulo Freire, and the pedagogy of revolution,* Lanham, MD: Rowman & Littlefield.

MSN Encarta. (2000a). *General Agreement of Tariffs and Trade.* Retrieved from http://encarta.msn.com/encyclopedia_761565898/General_Agreement_on_Tariffs_and_Trade.html

MSN Encarta (2000b). *World Trade Organization.* Retrieved from http://encarta.msn.com/encyclopedia_761579951/World_Trade_Organization.html

Penrose, E. (1953). *Economic planning for peace.* Princeton, NJ: Princeton University Press.

Playing games with prosperity. (2001, July 28). *The Economist,* p. 14.

Price, D., Pollock, A., & Shaoul, J. (1999). How the World Trade Organisation is shaping domestic policies in health care, *The Lancet, 354*(27), 1889-1892.

Puckett, J. (2000, April-May). An activist's dictionary for translating WTO-speak (Orwellian to English). *Nexus, 7*(3), 14.

Reisman, S. (1996). The birth of a World Trading System: ITO and GATT. In O. Kirschner (Ed.), *The Breton Woods-GATT system: Retrospect and prospect.* Armonk, NY: Sharpe.

Rikowski, G. (2001). *The Battle in Seattle: Its significance for education.* London: Tufnell Press.

Rikowski, G. (2002a). *Globalisation and education.* Paper prepared for the House of Lords Select Committee on Economic Affairs, Inquiry into the Global Economy, January 22, ATTAC Britain. Retrieved from http://www.attac.org.uk

Rikowski, G. (2002b). The Great GATS buyout. *Red Pepper, 101,* 25–27.

Rikowski, G. (2002c). Transfiguration: Globalisation, the World Trade Organisation and the national faces of the GATS. *Information for Social Change, 14,* 8–17. Retrieved from http://libr.org/ISC/.

Rikowski, G. (2003) The business takeover of schools. *Mediactive: Ideas Knowledge Culture, 1,* 91–108.

Smith, J., & Moran, T. (2000, Spring) WTO 101: Myths about the World Trade Organization. *Dissent,* 66–70.

Tabb, W. (2000, March). The World Trade Organization? Stop world take over, *Monthly Review, 51*(10), 1–18.

Tibbett, S. (2001, July 27). It's shocking all over the world. *Tribune, 65*(30) 10–11.

Ward, R., & Wadsworth, R. (2000, May). A16, Washington DC: The battle after Seattle. *International Viewpoint, 321,* 4–7.

Williams, F. (2004, July 6). World trade talks on services markets "may last years." *Financial Times,* p. 9.

Wolf, M. (1999, December 8). In defence of global capitalism. *Financial Times,* p. 29.

Working Group on the WTO/MAI. (1999). *A citizen's guide to the World Trade Organization: Everything you need to know to fight for fair trade* (From a temporary web site for Seattle '99).

WTO. (1994, April 15). *European communities and their member states—Schedule of specific commitments, World Trade Organization, GATS/SC/31.* Retrieved from http://docsonline.wto.org

7

Reading Marxism

Patrick Shannon

Progressive educators note an alarming increase in the regulation of teachers' and students' actions during elementary school reading programs (Allington, 2003; Coles, 2001; Dudley-Marling & Murphy, 2001; Strauss, 2001). They identify the following:

- A definition of learning to reading as the ability to score well on tests.
- Pressure for teachers to employ scientifically based core reading programs with scripted lessons.
- The concentration of those programs among three large publishing companies that monopolize the market.
- Business and government leadership in these changes.

Most remark that these mandates and events are changing the rationale for reading instruction from its goals to develop individuals' abilities to use text effectively for specific purposes and to express themselves clearly popular in the 1980s and early 1990s, to one that treats reading ability as a commodity that will increase students' market value after graduation. Many remark that these changes have turned students away from using reading and writing to engage actively in civic life, reducing the quality and quantity of public democratic discourse. All lament these changes and call for teachers to become political in order to oppose these trends.

Most of this writing lacks a coherent social framework that locates these changes within an understandable context. Although the authors rage against the constitutionality of federal interference in school curricular matters, the influence of business practices on humane developmental process of reading, and the consequences for teachers and children, they fail to offer plausible explanations for why and how business, science, and the federal government have become the predominant powers in reading instruction in the United States. This neglect severally limits the possibilities of teachers marshalling effective resistance to the regimentation of their lives at school. In this chapter, I use Marxism to provide a historical and theoretical explanation for the changes, to explain the commodification of literacy, and to offer explicit suggestions on what teachers and others might do (Shannon, 1992, 2001).

SOME HISTORICAL CONTEXT

The current efforts to make reading instruction more efficient and effective through business principles began nearly 100 years ago during the "progressive" era. At the same time that Congress was passing laws to curb the excessive behaviors of business (e.g., the Meat Inspection Act, the Hepburn Act to regulate the railroads, and the Mann-Elkins Act placing telephone and telegraph companies under the jurisdiction of the Interstate Commerce Commission), government officials, journalists, and professional organizations found business management principles simply irresistible. Pundits and the public became enamored with industries' capability to produce goods cheaply; their abilities to forge technological solutions of industrial problems; and the power of a few industrialists to amass huge fortunes. Celebrated by the media, these industrialists urged all social institutions to adopt business principles of economy and technology. If they would, the industrialist promised more social efficiency and great prosperity for all. This mindset has directed the education of school personnel, the planning and organization of schools, and the expectations of the public since that time (Apple, 2000; Callahan, 1962; Curti, 1935; Giroux, 1983).

The efficiency movement in reading instruction began during the first two decades of the 20th century (Shannon, 1989). "Primarily schooling is a problem of economy; it seeks to determine in what manner the working unit may be made to return the largest dividend upon the material investment of time, energy, and money" (Bagley, 1911, p. 2). Beginning in 1914, the National Society for the Study of Education's Committee for the Economy of Time in Education applied means–ends rationality to all elementary school subjects, culminating in three reports in 1919 (Principles of Methods as Derived from Scientific Investigation: Teaching Writing, Teaching Spelling, and Teaching Reading). These reports offered rules for the design and practice of curriculum and instruction in elementary schools. Curriculum was set as testable skills with speed and accuracy as the primary criteria for success.

During the 1920s, textbook publishers combined these rules for efficient curriculum with E. L. Thorndike's laws of learning to establish the basal reading series—now called a core reading program—a set of graded anthologies, practice books of skills for students, and teacher's manuals for the correct use of the anthologies and teaching of skills. Basals became the official technology of reading instruction that would standardize teachers' practices according to scientific principles in order to ensure efficiency in and control over the quality of student learning. The teacher's manuals listed the skills to be taught in order to ensure readiness, the workbook guaranteed skill exercise, and the correct answers supplied in teacher's manuals encouraged teachers to reinforce students' accurate responses. Since the 1920s, most teachers and administrators have accepted basal teacher's manuals as the correct stimulus to evoke the appropriate standard response from teachers in order to ensure that students received businesslike, scientific instruction.

In fact, many state education departments and school districts mandated their use. In a survey during the 1960s (Austin & Morrison, 1965), 95% of elementary school teachers acknowledged that they used basal materials to direct all of their reading instruction. According to a National Assessment of Educational Progress in 1994, students reported that 80% of elementary teachers used commercially produced instructional materials to drive their instruction. Across the century, programmed learning, criterion-referenced testing, mastery learning, teacher and school effectiveness, and now curriculum standards and high-stakes testing have been proposed as variations on the theme of ensuring that teachers follow the prescribed teacher guides closely in order to make the outcomes of their instruction more predictable and less dependent on teachers.

In the light of this history, the recent trends in reading education in American classrooms are not new or even changes. Rather they are the logical extensions of a 100-year-old project to spread the logic of business to the production of literate workers and the harnessing of science and the state to accomplish that goal.

COMPELLING TEACHERS TO FOLLOW SCRIPTS

Marxist thought can help us to understand the reasons behind the proliferation of business practices in reading programs and to comprehend teachers' apparent welcoming of these practices. Both are expected consequences of the expansion of the capitalist economic system. "The mode of production of material life conditions the social, political, and intellectual life process in general" (Marx, 1978, p. 4). The "rationalization" of reading instruction is only part of the spread of capitalist logic throughout public and private life. According to capitalist logic in order to reduce the risk to capital and to maximize profits, all aspects of business must become predictable. This is not as easy as it might seem because production requires people, raw materials, the environment, and capital. At one time and by some people, each of these contributors were invested with spiritual significance, requiring deference to their natural characters.

In order to render production more predictable and profitable, capitalist theorists exploited the Christian and the Enlightenment's "disenchantment" of nature, separating feelings and spirits from raw materials and the environment. Moreover, these theorists posited that work is a rational process devoid of spirituality and emotion, which can become more productive if organized accordingly. When people enter into a capitalist production process, which they must do in order to survive, they exchange their labor for wages and the relationship among people become one of exchange. These two steps render the dissimilar (people, the environment, and artifacts) comparable according to abstract, value-free laws (both physical and human). In this way, raw materials, the environment, and workers become simply factors in the planning and organization of production— none of which require any special consideration or treatment. (It is the application of this logic that allows the Brookings Institution's educational policy analyst Diane Ravitch to exclaim "teachers don't need creativity. They need to follow proven methods" (cited in Morse, 2000, p. 60). Capitalist logic promises that if all of society could be organized in a similar fashion, then society would run like a business, creating the best conditions for production, technological advance, and accumulation. The allure of this promise drives the efforts to rationalize more and more aspects of public and private life.

Accordingly modern institutions, social norms, and even individual actions are developed and judged according to objective scientific and meritocratic business principles in order that they can be entered safely as factors into the calculus of modern life. Hierarchical relationships of authority, means–ends analyses, and continuous regulation are intended to ensure this predictability in institutions and everyday matters. Rationalization, then, treats human beings as variables to be manipulated along with materials, time, and space to ensure predictable products and profits from material, ideational or social manufacturing. Marcuse (1941) described the human consequences of this rationalization:

> The private and public bureaucracy thus emerges on an apparently objective and impersonal ground, provided by the rational specialization of function. For, the more the individual functions are divided, fixated, and synchronized according to objective and impersonal pattern, the less reasonable it is for the individual to withdraw and withstand. The material fate of the masses becomes increasingly dependent upon the continuous and correct functioning of the increasingly bureaucratic order of private capitalist organizations. The objective and impersonal character of rationalization bestows upon the bureaucratic groups the universal dignity of reason. The rationality embodied in the giant enterprises makes it appear as if men, in obeying them, obey the dictum of an objective rationality. The private bureaucracy fosters a delusive harmony between the special and the common interests. Private power relationships appear not only as relationships between objective things but also as the rule of rationality itself (p. 151)

The conditions of life in contemporary elementary schools provide an example of this rationalization process. The justification for scripted lessons and high-stakes testing is the logic of production. Simply they make the production of student test scores more predictable. Scripts provide the division of function with teachers becoming factors in the implementation of the curricular designs of others; they fix the actions of teachers across classrooms, schools, and districts; and they synchronize the actions of teachers and students toward the abstracted exchange value of student test scores. These scores now define teachers' success, become students' cultural capital, legitimize administrators' plans, and raise property values in communities.

Using science as the objective and impersonal logic behind the rationalization of reading instruction in elementary schools (see Edmondson & Shannon, 2002), the entire process appears natural and inevitable. Inside the logic of rationalized reading programs it makes sense to follow the scripts in order to increase the chances of higher test scores, and few inside or outside of elementary schools object to the rationalization of reading instruction. Those that do object are dismissed as irrational or political (see Pressley, 1994). According to Marxist theory, then, the scripted programs for reading instruction are simply an expression of capitalist logic.

Marxist theory also helps us to understand why so many individuals—teachers, administrators, and taxpayers—now accept this rationalization. Within attempts to secure student learning through the specialization of teaching functions, individuals lose sight of the human process of teaching and learning (and the scientific study of same). Teachers' teaching, and students' learning—once the very expression of their generic being—now confronts them as things apart from them. Teachers' teaching and students' learning are reified in the scripted programs, which now direct teachers' actions and students' learning and knowledge. Marx refers to this separation of individuals from their actions as alienation—in this case, the subordination of the teachers and students to the reified product of their activities. The dialectic between reification and alienation helps explain why teachers become complicit in the rationalization of reading instruction and provide a more specific definition of what becoming political might mean.

Reification is the treatment of an abstraction as a concrete object or an immutable procedure. Many teachers, administrators, and taxpayers reify the many possible ways of teaching others to read as the systematic application of the scripted commercial materials and programs. Perhaps the best evidence of reification of reading instruction of these materials is seven decades of schools districts exchanging one scripted program for another when they find that their students do not learn to read in a timely fashion. History, educational experts, and business encourage this reification, promoting these commodities as the tools of teaching and learning reading. Commercial publishers enlist the support of educational scientists to develop and endorse the scripted programs for the broadest possible market without any regard for the emotional and social context of any particular classroom. Although the ideas for the scripts originate with teachers, the programs are produced far from the daily practices of teachers and students. The programs divide, fixate, and synchronize teachers' instructional behaviors during reading instruction, reducing them to technical support for the actions required in the scripts. Teaching without these scripted commodities, then, appears to be the irrational act.

Reification has at least three consequences which recycle as causes with newcomers to teaching. First, when teachers and administrators reify reading instruction, they lose sight of the fact that reading instruction is a human process. Second, reification of the scientific study of reading instruction as the commercial programs means that teachers' and administrators' knowledge of reading and instruction is frozen in a single technological form. Third, teachers' and administrators' reification of learning as test scores requires that they define the teaching and learning of reading to be a closed system of production. Although rationalization creates the social conditions to remove the emotion and thought from teaching, reification of teaching as application of scripted lessons and of reading as test scores develops the psychic conditions.

Alienation is the process of separation between people and some quality assumed to be related to them under natural circumstances. This process can be consciously recognized (subjective alienation) or it could be beyond the control of the individual (objective alienation). The rationalization of reading instruction relies on both types of alienation through policies which require the use of scripted programs. The scripts' standardize teachers' statements and actions, objectively separating teachers from natural association with students and limiting their thoughts and actions to those encoded in the scripts. The content of the scripts defines students' learning to read, rendering moot all students' thoughts and behaviors that are not scripted to bring higher test scores. Yet, limiting student learning to what will be tested devalues most of what they do, say, and desire.

Reducing teachers and students to factors in the scripted system of test score production requires that both lose, at least officially, emotional, cultural, and social attachments to the process of teaching and learning. It separates them from each other. To achieve such detachment within the space of a classroom demands a subjective separation of teachers from teaching and students from learning. This does not mean that alienated teachers are uncaring or that alienated students lack engagement. Rather it means that the nature of that engagement is subsumed under the process of rationalization and the possibilities of teaching and learning are artificially directed and severely restricted.

A Marxist reading of the current conditions of reading instruction in elementary schools, then, suggests that capitalist rationalization continues to increase its control of teachers' and students' lives through the processes of reification and alienation. State and local interpretations of the federal No Child Left Behind (NCLB) educational law and the Reading First Initiative bind teachers and students to script driven programs designed to deliver universal proficiency on world-class academic standards. These conditions are not unique to reading instruction or schools because rationalization of public and private life are a consequence of the expansion of capitalism. And capitalism is expanding rapidly and overtly since the 1990s. Many institutions and industries are being remade along these lines or plowed under. "The bourgeoisie cannot exist without constantly revolutionizing the instruments of production, and thereby the relations of production, and with them the whole of relations of society" (Marx, 1978, p. 38). Some critics have argued that NCLB is a pretext to privatizing public education by setting unreachable goals for public schools (Goodman, Shannon, & Goodman, 2004).

Under these conditions, teachers' attempts to compose curriculum for their classrooms and to improvise during their teaching in order to tailor their work to particular students in particular contexts are acts of resistance to the rationalization of reading education, the consequent reification of reading instruction as commercial programs, and their objective alienation from their work as teachers. By composing and improvising, teachers pursue the goal of Marx's (1844/1956) historical project—to secure the conditions that would allow, encourage, and support the "universal right to be freely active, to affirm ourselves, to be spontaneous in our activity, and to pursue the free development of our physical and mental energy" (p. 75).

During the 1980s and 1990s, as the possibilities of composing new curricula and improvising instruction increased, teachers and teacher educators who encouraged them should have expected reactions from the forces of rationalization. And the "empire" did strike back with all its forces. First, textbook publishers absorbed the rhetoric of this resistance into their scripted programs, and the state assimilated the language of resistance into policies without making any accommodations in the expected tested outcomes. Second, philanthropic organizations brokered a consensus that these changes in teaching threatened not only the future of current students, but the economic future of the country as well. Third, business leaders chimed in that they couldn't find skilled workers for the high-wage/high-skill jobs they had open. Fourth with this consensus, government officials called for the reestablishment of standards and accountabilities, and, then, funded research to prove the need for both. Finally, many educational psychologists were quick to the funding trough, providing scientific reports discrediting composed curricula and improvised teaching and reaffirming the scientific basis of the commercial scripted programs. Through NCLB and the Reading First Initiative, the federal government offered underfunded school districts financial incentives to comply.

These acts were intended to (and did) restore capitalist rationalization in schools, to support the reification of reading and learning as scripts and tests, and to promote the alienation of teachers from teaching and students from learning.

LITERACY FOR SALE

Because literacy (however defined) is valued as a cultural, social, and economic possession, which gives its owner a head start in the race for success within groups and society, corporations, companies, and individual entrepreneurs have produced literacy (or part of it) as a commodity (see Shannon, 2000, for a more elaborate treatment of the commercialization of reading and reading education). Because there are several alternative definitions of literacy and differing conceptions of its value, companies have produced many literacy commodities from which to choose. And educators and citizens have purchased those commodities to either enhance their own cultural, social, and economic capital (computer literacy, anyone?) or to increase the same for students. In this sense, people acquire literacy as a commodity in order to improve their value as a cultural, social, or economic commodity themselves.

This is the crux of critics concern about the commodification of literacy and learners. The forces of capitalism have turned reading and readers into things for sale. Marxist theory can deepen an understanding of how this happens and demonstrate the likely consequences.

> The wealth of those societies in which the capitalist mode of production prevails presents itself as an immense accumulation of commodities — its unit being a single commodity. Our investigation must therefore begin with the analysis of a commodity. (Marx, 1967, p. 35)

A commodity appears to be just an object, however, it has a double nature. Commodities have use value (bringing utility and/or pleasure to people) and exchange value (commanding other objects or money in transactions of daily life). Although use values are a product of both social and physical properties, exchange values are purely social constructs, which are established as ratios of comparable labor among the objects to be exchanged. In order to make labor comparable across commodities, it must be reduced to a common kind, as undifferentiated and measurable as any other thing involved in commercial production. This requires a conversion of value from labor to money. The human activity of work then must be separated from personal expression or development (the disenchantment) in order to become one of many comparable factors to be considered in the manufacture of things for sale. This need for "abstract" labor requires a particular set of circumstances in which profit is the highest priority in the production of commodities.

That set of circumstances is capitalism, a system which organizes production in order to increase the chances for profits. This profit motive impels capitalist manufacturers to rationalize production, reducing individualized and differentiated work into routine and regular acts, creating new efficiencies. Under capitalism, even labor becomes a commodity — a thing that individuals possess, develop, and sell in order to survive, and perhaps, thrive. Marx (1967) wrote, a "definite social relation between men themselves assumes the fantastic form of a relation between things" (p. 165). Capitalism's moral character is based on this distortion of reality to make profit off the work of others. Despite their simple appearance as objects, commodities represent all these invisible social relationships.

Marx called the invisibility of these relationships "the fetishism of commodities" (an extension of reification) in which people lose sight of the social character of commodities and act as if the physical properties of the commodity itself commands a price. Many, even some economists, believe that the thing itself sets its price and that it has productive powers. The confusion between social relations and the physical reality of production obscures the workings of capitalism from public view. It appears that the commodities are remunerated with profits for their contribution and not their owners who are accumulating profits. In a sense, however, the transaction is really an act of stealing. The raw materials during production are transformed from one state of matter to another, but the surplus value which labor creates (beyond laborers' remuneration) is taken from the laborers. Under capitalism, this government-sanctioned robbery is deemed acceptable (even necessary) according to the scientific laws of capitalism (Heilbronner, 1985). Through what they call scientific research, economists discover and interpret such laws as the nature of the capitalist system. With government and science behind it, capitalism projects the illusion that it is the natural state of civilization which we must preserve at all costs and which is inscribed in the U.S. Constitution as "the pursuit of happiness." Once environment, capital, and labor are transformed into commodities and those commodities are fetishized, all opportunities for subversive interpretations of the system disappear.

Each commodity can teach us about capitalism as a socially constructed, historical system of production. There is nothing eternal or natural about capitalism (although there are universals within it and a recognizable order to its system). The social values directing each transformation of practices, things and ideas into things for sale include the central role of profits in the structures and practices of our daily life, the rights of owners of the means of production to all the profits from commodity exchange, the notion that laborers must be alienated from their work in order to achieve the highest exchange value for commodities, and the fact that any thing, one, practice or idea can become a commodity.

At a cultural level, commodities represent the values of their manufacturers (Schor, 2000). The thing for sale is an embodiment of not only the generalized values of capitalism, but also of what manufacturers want in the world and how they wish to live with others. Manufacturers produce commodities for profit, of course, but also enter production to make the world better (according to their vision of better). This may seem hard to accept with so many apparently cynical commodities on the market (chocolate cereals, hand guns, cigarettes, Elvis statues). Yet, cereal manufacturers point to the importance of choice in the development of individuals and to the aid that they bring to parents who struggle to get their children to eat breakfast. Hand gun producers trot out the second and fourth amendments to the U.S. Constitution as their moral justification. Each commodity expresses its manufacturer's commitment to freedom of choice, to quality of life, and to an ideal of how the world should work (Lear, 1994). Even manufacturers who consciously make and sell products they know to be harmful display their values about how the world should work and their elevated position in that world. As Widemann (1995) suggested about those who propose barbaric prison conditions, these manufacturers do not believe that their products or the conditions under which they are produced are for people like themselves.

To understand the commercialization of reading instruction, then, we must examine the commodities offered, the markets created and the values promoted through the extension of capitalism into elementary schools. Consider the Open Court reading program published by the Science Research Associates (SRA), which thousands of schools and school districts have adopted across the United States. Similar to other commercially prepared reading programs, Open Court provides anthologies of children's stories, a scope and sequence of skills to be taught as students work their way through the anthologies, many forms of practice and assessment of those skills, and a teacher's guidebook to direct teachers on how to coordinate the use of all the materials across each grade level. Open Court is a scripted program, which means that the teacher's guidebook includes explicit directions for both teachers and students on what they are to do and how that are to do it each day during reading instruction. As one California principal reports, Open Court assures that "what is happening in one class is happening in another. Teachers work from detailed instructional guides, scripted down to the very examples they are to write on the board" (Anderluh, 1998, p. A1). For example, the teacher's guidebook for Grade 1 opens with these words:

> Choose one or more of the following activities to focus the children's attention and to review some of the concepts they have been learning.
>
> Sound Review: Name a family spelling card and call on a child to say the sound the card represents. The child should then give a word that contains the sound and identify where the sound is heard in the word. That child then names a new card and calls on another child to say the new sound and a new word. Continue in this manner.
>
> Identify Rhymes: Write the three words on the chalkboard.

The tone and register of these directions continue throughout the first-grade teacher's guidebook, across the guides for the practice activities, and through the sixth-grade guidebook to the last lesson. At every moment, it is clear what teachers should do and who is in charge of the instruction.

At the beginning of each teacher's guidebook, SRA lists Open Court's authors and prints its mission statement. The authors of the first grade edition are well known educational psychologists who have published widely on reading, writing, and instruction. After the authors names, lists of consultants both university- and school-based are presented to demonstrate that many educators have looked at the materials and found them worthy. Because Open Court is a commodity, however, it hides the true producers of the final product. The authors listed for Open Court wrote few of the stories, lessons, instructions, practices, or assessments. They may have written none. What they did was provide a template of what the skills should be, the order that made logical sense to them, the format for the lessons, the orientation of the lessons, and perhaps the modes of assessment. They negotiated a framework for the program among themselves, and probably reviewed a selected sample of the finished product. Between their establishment of the framework and the completed programs, scores of scribes and editors worked on the actual pages of the Open Court program. That's not to mention the layout production and the actual printing crews.

Moreover, the framework that was negotiated isn't really the authors' production either. Rather it is an abstracted form of the lessons that these authors have observed experienced teachers presenting. This is not to imply that the authors stole the framework from any one teacher. They regularized the practices of teachers who they have defined as good teachers and suggested that SRA package them for other teachers to buy. This intention to sell the lessons reduces the possible use value of those original lessons that unnamed teachers devised for their students at a certain time in a certain place. The exchange hides the original use value and the human labor behind the colorful pages.

This cloak—the fetishism of commodities as Marx called it—makes it seem as if the materials are responsible for students learning to read. SRA encourages this assumption among teachers and the public:

> Students who experience Collections for Young Scholars: learn how to read and respond to a variety of texts; acquire strategies for accessing information and for explaining concepts from many areas of knowledge including some that do not even exist today; learn how to communicate effectively using both oral and written language; learn how to work both independently and collaboratively; and give sustained effort to thinking and problem solving. (p. 10)

This statement suggests that the scripted program, and not the interaction of teacher and students around text, produce learning. Because the lessons are scripted, teachers become extensions of the program. Because the students' route through the program is also scripted, they become extensions of the program as well. The human essence of reading, teaching, and learning are lost from view.

Although Open Court may be a more explicit tool in its rationalization of reading instruction than other core basal reading programs, they are not different in kind. All core basal reading programs are commercial endeavors and must rationalize and carry the social entailments of capitalism with them into classrooms. The fetishism of these commodities instantiates a morality that is at odds with the possibilities of literacy. While literacy can be domesticating as we see when the teacher reads the scripts, it can also be liberating, allowing teachers and students to compose and improvise their own scripts. This language of possibilities for the right to be freely active, to affirm ourselves, to be spontaneous, and to pursue free development of ourselves is present in SRA's philosophical statement about the powers of their commodity—the Open Court reading program. However, the scripts and the rationalized logic behind the scripts contradict these possibilities at least in the classroom.

PROJECTS OF POSSIBILITY

Rejecting the current forms of rationalization of reading education, critics celebrate teachers who resist and call for teachers and parents to become political concerning mandates for scripted lessons in NCLB and the Reading First Initiative. The critics seek a cultural politics committed to creating specific forms of schooling that encourage and foster the realization of differentiated human capacities. This politics requires a dialectical effort to change the minds and social conditions of teachers, administrators and taxpayers. This is what Marx meant by praxis, the bond between thinking and doing in which ideas and ideals can only be vindicated and validated by some kind of activity. According to Marx, reality is not merely what is, but what we make of it. Marxist educational praxis, then, is intended to provide more than an understanding of politics or schooling or whatever historical circumstance. It is intended to serve as a guide for making politics, schooling, and history. By illuminating past and current efforts to rationalize teachers' and students' lives, Marxism can help teachers understand the cognitive, social, and physical structures of the past congealed in the present, opening teachers' awareness to unsuspected aspects of their social existence. A Marxist understanding of rationalization of instruction and commodification of reading changes the terms by which teachers accept the present and thereby changes their abilities to shape the future.

Becoming political, then, requires that teachers judge all past, present and future school structures by their moral unfolding, or more precisely, their orientation toward human freedom. Inquiry into the structures of reading instruction (or any other practice) must center on a commitment to the idea of human emancipation. In this way, the contradiction between the rhetoric of Open Court concerning the possibilities of literacy and the actual scripted social relations of that reading program which turn teachers and students into things can serve as an opening for what Roger Simon (2001) called "projects of possibility":

> I am using the term "project" as an activity determined by both real and present conditions, and conditions still to come which it is trying to bring into being. In this sense a project of possibility begins with a critique of current realities. This critique suggests that a contradiction exists between the openness of human capacities that we encourage in a free society and the social forms that are provided and within which we must live our lives. It is this contradiction which is the starting point for a project of possibility and defines its broad aim: the transformation of the relation between human capacities and social forms. More particularly the project requires both the expansion of forms to accommodate capacities and the expansion of capacities to make the realization of new forms possible. Such a project would reject the resolution of this contradiction between capacities and forms through narrowing of capacities to fit existing forms or through the narrowing of forms to fit preconceived, fixed, "naturalized" notions of capacities. (pp. 141–142)

The social form of Open Court's tight scripting of teachers' and students' words and actions during reading instruction contradicts the openness of literacy, teaching, and learning. Despite the talk of higher test scores, efficient instruction, and systematic learning, the program cannot lead to human emancipation. Although it may be argued that a tightly controlled beginning will eventually lead students to greater futures, this line of reasoning suggests the narrowing of social forms to fit preconceived, fixed and naturalized notions of what their capacities might be in the future. Some may overcome the controlled beginning to use literacy to open opportunities in their lives, but some will also internalize the process of control, limiting the potential of their development. And, of course, the scripted lives are all there is offered to teachers. They are never allowed to develop as teachers. Neither teacher nor students is likely to make possible the realization of a variety of differentiated human capacities.

This contradiction does not lie in the scripts themselves, but in the forces of rationalization that attempt to standardize reading programs in order to make them predictable factors in the productive industrial equations. Those forces rely on the reification of all possible social structures and means for teaching reading as the commercially produced, scientifically validated scripted programs. Rationalization and reification result in the alienation of teachers from their work and their students because the fetishism of the commodified programs makes it appear as if the materials are the agents of teaching and learning.

Similar contradictions can be found in more and more aspects of our public and private lives, all of which have been rationalized in order to ensure that capitalism endures and expands. In this way, the composers and innovators in education are linked with the composers and innovators in other fields of work—child care and health care workers, agricultural workers, service workers, and many others.

Teachers becoming political from a Marxian standpoint means raising our own and others' consciousness about the root causes of scripted lessons, high-stakes testing, and commercialization of schools and schooling. This is by no means an easy task because the structures of rationalization and commodification are cognitive, social, and physical. Those cognitive structures weigh heavily on even the innovative teacher. Harder still may be learning to act in conjunction with other workers suffering under increased pressures of rationalization in their work. Until those alliances are made, the chances for effective politics in education are limited. To really address the essence of the issue and not continue to stagger from opposition of one rationalized solution to another, we must stop the unmediated expansion of capitalism into social institutions (see Shannon, 1998, for an elaboration on this point). This means teachers should join the movements toward livable minimum wages, national health insurance, affordable housing, and repeal of the North American Free Trade Agreement and General Agreements on Tariffs and Trade. They should make their presence know at the protests of the World Trade Organization and the International Monetary Fund. These are large projects of possibility that show promise on a large scale.

On a smaller scale, the local, state, and national movements concerning high-stakes testing are projects of possibility. Attempts to incorporate choice about methods at a district and school level keeps open the possibilities of reading instruction, allowing at least some composition of curricula and improvisation in teaching. Wrestling control of time away from 42-minute periods and 180-day sentences at a grade levels and space away from isolated rooms and individual desks undercuts the standardization of reading instruction. Working with other adults (parents, custodians, librarians, local business owners, etc.) as co-teachers expands the possibilities of literacy and learning for all involved. Each of these acts rejects the rationalization of schools, the reification of reading instruction and science, and the alienation of teachers from their teaching and students from their learning. Each is directed by a commitment to human emancipation.

REFERENCES

Allington, R. (2003). *Big brother and the national reading curriculum*. Portsmouth, NH: Heinemann.

Anderluh, D. (1998, February 1). Building with words: City schools hope phonics boosts reading. *Sacramento Bee*, p. A1.

Apple, M. (2000). *Official knowledge*. New York: Routledge.

Austin, M., & Morrison, C. (1965). *The first r*. New York: Wiley.

Bagley, W. (1911). *Classroom management*. New York: Macmillan.

Callahan, R. (1962). *Education and the cult of efficiency*. Chicago: University of Chicago Press.

Coles, G. (2001). *Misreading reading: The bad science that hurts children*. Portsmouth, NH: Heinemann.

Curti, M. (1935). *The social ideas of American educators*. New York: Scribner.

Dudley-Marling, C., & Murphy, S. (2001). Changing the way we think about language arts. *Language Arts, 79,* 574–578.

Edmonson, J., & Shannon, P. (2002). The will of the people. *Reading Teacher, 55,* 452–456.

Giroux, H. A. (1983). *Theory and resistance in education*. South Hadley, MA: Bergin & Garvey.

Goodman, K., Shannon, P., & Goodman, Y. (2004). *Save our schools: The dangerous trap of no child left behind*. San Francisco, CA: RJR Books.

Heilbronner, R. (1985). *Understanding capitalism*. New York: Norton.

Lear, J. (1994). *Fables of abundance*. New York: Basic Books.

Marcuse, H. (1941). Some social implications of modern technology. In A. Arato & E. Gebhardt (Eds.), *The essential Frankfort School reader* (pp. 187-201). New York: Monthly Review.

Marx, K. (1844/1956). *Economic and philosophical manuscripts*. Moscow: Progress Publishers.

Marx, K. (1967). *Capital (Vol. 1)*. New York: International Press.

Marx, K. (1978). *The Marxist reader* (R. Tucker, Ed.). New York: Norton.

Morse, J. (2000, March 6). Sticking to the script. *Time*, pp. 60–61.

Pressley, M. (1994). Problems with the other side. In C. Smith (Ed.). *Whole language: The debate* (pp. 155-172). Bloomington, IN: ERIC.

Schor, J. (2000). *Do Americans shop too much?* Boston, MA: Beacon Press.

Shannon, P. (1989). *Broken promises: Reading instruction in 20th century America*. South Hadley, MA: Bergin & Garvey.

Shannon, P. (Ed.). (1992). *Becoming political: Reading and writings in politics of literacy education*. Portsmouth, NH: Heinemann.

Shannon, P. (1998). *Reading poverty*. Portsmouth, NH: Heinemann.

Shannon, P. (2000). *iSHOP, you shop: Raising questions about reading commodities*. Portsmouth, NH: Heinemann.

Shannon, P. (Ed.). (2001). *Becoming political too*. Portsmouth, NH: Heinemann.

Simon, R. (2001). Empowerment as a pedagogy of possibility. In P. Shannon (Ed.), *Becoming political too* (pp. 142-155). Portsmouth, NH: Heinemann.

Strauss, S. (2001). An open letter to Reid Lyon. *Educational Researcher, 30,* 25–31.

Widemann, J. E. (1995, October 30). Doing time, marking race. *The Nation*, pp. 502–503.

8

Paulo Freire and Revolutionary Pedagogy for Social Justice

Rich Gibson

AN INTRODUCTION TO FREIRE
(A Life and Work Abridged)

Paulo Freire, the radical Brazilian, was the most widely known educator in the world. He died on May 2, 1997, in Sao Paulo, Brazil, at the age of 75.

Freire drew upon Catholic liberation-theology and Marxist ideas to forge a concept of popular literacy education for personal and social liberation. So formidable was his work that the *Harvard Educational Review* published a recapitulation of his essays in 1999.

Freire proposed that the use of his "see–judge–act" student-centered methods could lead to critical consciousness, that is, an awareness of the necessity to constantly unveil appearances designed to protect injustice which, he said, then serves as a foundation for action toward equality and democracy. For Freire, no form of education could be neutral. All pedagogy is a call to action. In a society animated by inequality and authoritarianism, he sided with the many, and exposed the partisanship of those who claimed to stand above it all.

Freire became a world figure after he was jailed for using literacy methods developed by Catholic communities working against communists among poor peasants. He was driven from his native Brazil by a rising dictatorship in 1964. He fled to Chile to work with the democratically elected Allende government that fell to a CIA-manufactured coup. He spent the next 15 years in what he called exile, working at Harvard and for the World Council of Churches in Geneva, organizing and writing books for social justice (Gibson, 1994).

In 1989, shortly after he returned to Brazil as a leader of the social-democratic Workers' Party, Freire was named secretary of education in Sao Paulo, a city of 13 million people. He served for 2 years.

In the early 1970s, Freire's *Pedagogy of the Oppressed* and *Education for Critical Consciousness*, swept the globe. These books and nearly two dozen others that followed propose that education, although in inequitable societies predominantly a tool of elites, is also a democratic egalitarian weapon. Freire recommended pedagogical methods that recognized the experience and dignity of students and their culture, techniques calling into question the assumptions that lay at the base of their social systems. Freire's pedagogy sought to reunite the curriculum, grasping that the not-always seamless fabric of learning is made alien by teaching methods that split it into irrational pieces. Freire's geographic literacy involved mapping problems, not memorizing borders.

Freire criticized "banking" educational methods, seeing students as empty accounts to be filled with deposits of knowledge. He practiced a transformational style, the student becoming a subject in gaining and experimenting with knowledge. Truth became an examination of social understandings, not a doctrine determined by testing services. Motivation came from demonstrations that education is linked to power. For the process to work, the educator-leader had to be deeply involved in the daily lives of the students.

In Latin America, for example, a typical Freirean social inquiry method would trace the path of (a) a careful study of students' surroundings and everyday lives, followed by (b) a "codification session" with students where key factors of life were drawn as pictures. Then (c) students would be urged to look at the pictures not as simply reality, but as problems: first as individual problems, then as collective problems with underlying reasons. As codification led to problem solving, relevant words were linked with the students' drawings of the world, and reality repositioned as a human creation. Finally, (d) students were called on to use their newly won literacy as a way to make plans for change.

Specifically, a picture of a peasant's hut and a bountiful hacienda would be paired with a drawing of a peasant hoeing and a patron at rest. Why does he rest in the hacienda while we sweat and live in huts? Especially in the developing world, Freire was seen as a leader in a movement that could connect a sometimes awkward four-part formula for social justice: literacy, social insight, revolution, and national economic development.

There are problems with Freire's work. He became, against his mild protests, an icon, idolized by dramatically different sectors of education, business, and liberation movements. A miniature publishing industry, a cabal often steeped in the hubris of trendy postmodernist verbiage of word inventors who claimed that language stands above and makes reality—high priests of left-Versace academia—developed in the entrepreneur sense from uncritically praising a purportedly humble man whose life was social criticism.

The Freire-postmodernists, who surrounded his work in the English-speaking world, sought to emancipate theory from life. They attained limited academic prominence in lifting the divorce of mental and manual labor to a source of reverence (and became the butt of academic jokes, like Sokol's hoax). No social movement of any consequence, or threat to power, ever emanated, or could emanate, out from them although each Hubris sometimes had his Echo, in the form of fawning, uncritical, graduate students. Ignoring the transcendent human struggle for freedom from necessity, the postmodernist Freireites elevated what they considered identity, not as a construction of social relations, but to the point where each person became a personification of their own separate tiny little capital, with each element of the processes of capital embodied in them, every little hierarchy, every little nationalism, every neurosis a central issue—and then they worshiped the suppurations ("Professor Sokol's transgression," 1996).

Their campus postmodernism, really sheer opportunism demonstrated in their truckling praise and subsequent marketing of Freire's work, helped create an atmosphere in academia where students learned that one idea is as good as the next, since all is sheer perspective and discourse—social practice discounted as a source of truth-finding. Corresponding to that paralysis came the idea that all forms of oppression are equivalent, so dozens of splintered self-oriented sects became to be seen as superior to a mass, class-based, organization—leaving the student anti-capitalist movement weak and divided at the onset of the development of fascism. Or student-academics adopted the other stand: Dominance is completely encapsulating; cultural seduction, surveillance, and repression, wins. Either way, students, academics, and community activists could find an infinite variety of excuses in the many opportunist interpretations of Freire to avoid the centrality of class struggle—which would leave them unready to face 21st-century crises. Selfishly exploiting Freire, in any case, mattered.

The reality of endless world imperialist war may be an effective message from material existence—that it is there, and it may toll the end of fashionable postmodernism (Breisach, 2003). The intensification of exploitation, inequality, segregation, and irrationalism within the whole of capital's system, still grinning and dripping blood in its many self-made crises, may be signal enough to show that the idea of language determining life was just another market move of the petty bourgeoisie, and their threatened existence in academia created their most recent, hardly new, howl, "religion with an angry cloak" (p. 16). Still, the selling of one-sided interpretations of Freire continues and needs to be condemned.

As an icon, Freire indeed became a commodity. His work was purchased, rarely as a whole, but in selective pieces, which could further the career of an academic, propel the interests of a corporation—or a state-capitalist "revolutionary," party. Many of his enthusiasts called his work "eclectic," and let it go at that (Freire, 1998c, p. 7).

But Freire called himself a contradictory man. His politics were often seemingly at odds. As seen here, the Marxist Freire urged the analysis of labor and production. But, like the entire socialist project, was unable to resolve the incongruity of human liberation and elite demands for inequality in order to motivate national economic development. The Catholic-humanist postmodern Freire denied the centrality of class and focused on deconstructing culture and language. In both cases, Freire had to rely on the ethics of the educator-leader to mediate the tensions between middle-class teachers and profoundly exploited students.

So, with a little effort, his works were stripped of their politics and simultaneously appropriated by the government of Sweden, then adopted by what became the authoritarian socialist movements in Guinea Bissau and Grenada, and by reformist poverty programs in the United States, and, later on, by neoliberals in the garb of the African National Congress (ANC) working for the privatization of natural resources in South Africa. Yet Freire's work was often also used in the struggle for South African liberation, later betrayed by the ANC (Center for Community Development, 2001; Gibson, 1994; Nkomo 1999). It may be that Freire's life is an example of David Harvey's (1992) pessimistic take on a key problem of Marxism, "it is fair to say that the duality of the worker as an object of capital, and as living creative subject, has never been adequately resolved in Marxist theory" (p. 114). Late in his life, defending his classic *History and Class Consciousness*, the great Hungarian Marxist philosopher Georg Lukacs (2000) also said the decisive question of Marxism is the relationship of subjectivity overcoming objectivity.

This challenge is well-summed in Marx third thesis on Feuerbach: The materialist doctrine concerning the changing of circumstances and upbringing forgets that circumstances are changed by men and that it is essential to educate the educator himself. This doctrine must, therefore, *divide society into two parts, one of which is superior to society.*

The coincidence of the changing of circumstances and of human activity or self-changing can be conceived and rationally understood only as revolutionary practice. (p. 112, italics added)

I hope to demonstrate, via Freire, that Harvey's view is not sufficiently historical (there have been revolutions led by self-actualizing workers who were later defeated, life being uneven and education impermanent), and thus undialectical—but at the same time the crux of the challenge to those who struggle for reason and equality today.

Freire, conservative in many ways, in practice supported conventional school grading systems, traditional approaches to literacy instruction like flash-cards, and the use of postrevolution textbooks, routinely coded in the creed of the party—and beyond critique. His later books were diluted with extraneous transcriptions of his discussions over a glass of wine. He was compelled to apologize to feminists and others who objected to the male-centered language of his early books. His final work is so full of, well, perkiness ("I never left my house without a purpose in my step") that a critical reader must wonder about his repeated insistence on his own probity (Freire, 1994, 1998a; Gibson, 1994).

Nevertheless, Freire's focus on the role of consciousness, critique, and a utopian vision, the need for imaging a better future before it can be achieved, the critical role of education for social justice, and the vital necessity of leadership fully at one with the people, should deepen the practices of movements for social change (Freire, 1973). His grasp of the reciprocal interactions of class, race, sex, and nationality as simultaneously pivotal to conscious action for change predated both feminism and postmodernism. (It can, of course, be argued that there was little new in both, so predating them may be only a minor achievement.)

Still, Freire's methods could instigate a process in which students examine both their potential roles as self-liberators and—in the hands of a conscious activist—the history of people who cease to be instruments of their own oppression.

Paulo Freire embodied the wisdom of the man he admired most, Che Guevara: "At the risk of seeming ridiculous, the true revolutionary is, motivated by love." Freire also embodied Che's limitations. Sometimes Freire simply protested too much: "(I am not) full of myself" (Freire, 1998a, p. 129).

WHERE SHALL WE GO
AND HOW SHALL WE GET THERE?

This is an effort to critique Freire in theory and practice, using the central role he played in the development of education systems in the Grenadian revolution of 1979–1983 as a lens into the implications of his work. It will be useful to travel this route with a story in mind. The theoretical work can be thick. Perhaps a story will lighten the journey.

In 1996, I returned from a Fulbright research trip to Grenada where I met with the minister of education, installed after the 1983 U.S. invasion, and the leaders of the former revolutionary New Jewel Movement of Grenada, now held in a 17th-century prison—sentenced to life.[1] Both the minister of education and the New Jewel prisoners asked me about techniques that might build an ethic of democracy through literacy and citizenship education. They offered to demonstrate to me how they link—in society and in jail—methods of education, especially literacy education, with democratic activist citizenship and technological or economic progress. Both were interested, for practical and historical purposes, in how the work of Paulo Freire might weave their interests together. Indeed, the jailed top New Jewel leader, Bernard Coard, said they relied heavily on Freire's direction, not only for educational advice but for political direction, during their brief stint in power (Gibson, 1994).

Richmond Hill Prison, a tepid, dank jail, with a stench baked in for more than 200 years, is perched on one of Grenada's most beautiful mountains, overlooking the capital, St. George's harbor. The jail is the scene of many ironies. In 1997, Winston Courtney, the Prison Commissioner, was the key civilizing influence in the jail, holding back guards who told me they had tortured the Grenada 17 prisoners for years before his arrival. Courtney had himself been jailed as a counter-revolutionary during the New Jewel government. One of the most reputable journalists in the country, the editor of the *Grenadian Voice*, now lobbies for the release of the Grenada 17. He, too, served more than 1 year in the jail—as a guest of its current inhabitants (Gibson, 2004b).

---

[1] I omit names where I feel there is any possibility that naming might damage the hopes of a subject. I also wish to criticize a section of my earlier work on Grenada, which I now think suffers from an incomplete analysis of the Grenadian revolution and the later invasion (Gibson, 1994). I have posted on my web page, cited later, an analysis by a jailed New Jewel leader, John Ventour, which offers the basis for a better examination of the crises in Grenada. I also wish to underline the horrific injustice of the continued incarceration of the New Jewel members, the Grenada 17, who are innocent as charged, and who have served 16 years in a 17th-century prison.

The irony of the two educational positions—Bernard Coard and his New Jewel colleagues running a school for liberation and literacy in a 17th-century prison and the minister of education operating a school system in the midst of a collapsing economy abandoned in post-Soviet globalism—and the questions they asked drove home to me the notion that literacy, and education for citizenship, has potential both as a domesticating tool and as a force for liberation. Indeed, in some cases, literacy, critical citizenship, and democracy have little in common. Slaves could be taught to read simply so they would become better workers (Stuckey, 1993).

Surely, it is paradoxical that other nations might look to the United States for hints about the relationship of democracy and literacy. If Jonathan Kozol is still right, the U.S. suffers from a functional illiteracy rate of about 25%, color-coded unemployment, the collapse of its social service safety net, official promises of perpetual war, an all-out assault on the conditions of work among those who still have jobs, the collapse of civil liberties, a consumer-based casino culture creating an ever more obese citizenry, a representative government that can only conduct elections via millionaires, and a twist of very literate scholarship that elevates the geneticist arguments of Murray and Hernstein's *Bell Curve* to the focal point of public discourse (Kozol, 1985; Shannon, 1998).

The peoples' movement in Grenada could be an illuminating practical ground for North Americans interested in linking literacy with democratic citizenship projects. Although some, like Ann Hickling-Hudson, think otherwise, I believe the literacy campaigns were systematic, met many of the problems literacy work usually meets, and, importantly, followed the path Freire himself mapped. While the Grenadian literacy campaigns were fraught with problems that might be predicted in an African-Caribbean nation trying to build socialism under a host of offended imperial eyes, it remains that the reading project drew leadership from all over the world, including Freire's. Whether the literacy effort met, or could meet, the goal of literacy for liberation is the issue I seek to untwine (Gibson, 1994; Hickling-Hudson, 1988).

But, at that moment, I was the Fulbright fellow who wrote a dissertation on Freire, and I wanted to respond to the Grenadians questions succinctly, with subtle elegance. I found that I could not. So what follows is in part an investigation sparked by their inquiries. Could Freire's literacy for critical consciousness answer questions like: what must people know and, equally significant, how they must come to know it, in order to overcome exploitation and alienation? Can human creativity be unleashed in an increasingly undemocratic world? Can consciousness leap past exploitation—or repression? How do we spot lies? Can revolutionary pedagogy foment revolutionary social change, incorporating forms of consciousness that can also overturn the rise of new bosses, so we do not become what we set out to oppose? What might pedagogy have to do with overturning the subject–object split, the habitual subservience created both by capital and revolutionary organizations, that both Harvey and Freire, and the late George Lukacs, all said was central?[2]

"THE RICH ARE NOT FOREVER, AND WILL THE CROWN LAST TO EVERY GENERATION?"
(Proverbs 27:24)

Freire insisted, repeatedly, that no system of education is neutral. Bias is inherent in any selection and ordering of facts, the common project of social educators. One's understanding of how the democratic possibilities of citizenship might be achieved depends on a partisan assessment of current conditions, and where one wants to go: a political standpoint. Any appraisal of the prospects of democratic education through literacy, a literacy that reads both the word and the world, must start from an articulated standpoint, on expressed terrain. Just what is the current situation? What should be done about it?

It is only fair to confide, in quick-march, my own outlook. Global systems of production, exchange, communications, and technology drive people together in a social world, yet divisive and deadly ideologies persist (irrationalism, nationalism, racism, sexism—foundation stones of imperialism— contempt for disabled people, etc.). Immediate material interests estrange people from their work, creative potential, and one another; especially the interests of savage greed and fear that are rooted in a fickle system of capital that cares nothing even for its loyal personifications, but betrays one for the next in the ruthless quest for more still. These factors sum up a world of humanity that is at once potentially united and practically split to pieces— ever at war.

Our world produces abundance—enough for all. At issue is not scarcity, but inequality. In each hemisphere, we function at the brink of a world depression that began in embryo about twenty years ago and has grown

---

[2]Freire, constrained by his viewpoint that focuses on appearances, has an extraordinarily thin understanding of the revolution in Grenada and the years of preparation that preceded it—even though he was an active participant in the post-revolutionary government. Counter to Freire, revolutions do not "wait to happen," and this one was years in preparation. Both Freire and I erred in our criticism of the crisis in Grenada in 1983, iconicizing Maurice Bishop and demonizing Bernard Coard, a critique that missed the complexity of events (Freire, 1994).

uninterruptedly. Beneath the apparently steady grip of capital is, at once, the extension of social being—the unity of all people caused by capital's movement to produce, exchange, and distribute everywhere—and an underlying cauldron of the results of a system, and its representatives, that must keep people apart: irrationalism, hunger, epidemic, joblessness and idle time, imperialism, despair: incipient fascism. Democracy meets inequality and loses. Criticism meets authoritarianism and is defeated. This imbalance, as Giovanni Arrighi and others suggest, will not long persist. The crisis of overproduction, on the one hand, and the social debt of unremitting repression on the other, easily boils over into economic collapse, political upheavals, and open war (Arrighi, 1994; Greider, 1997; Kaplan, 1995).

There is no place that the goal of those in power is to create a thinking, active work force or citizenry. "It would be naive to expect the dominant classes to develop a type of education which would enable subordinate classes to perceive social injustices critically" (Freire, 1985, p. 102). Instead, all poor and working people, including educational workers, are ever more segregated by class and race, degraded and de-skilled while they are charmed by dream censors, curricula regulators, with stories of teacher empowerment and the commonality of their interests with their national ruling class—a vulgar if historically triumphant way to turn people into more willing instruments of their own oppression. Concurrent with the rise of inequality and tyranny is the rebirth of irrationalism, a convulsion of organized and unorganized superstition, turns to faith, and mysticism of one form or another (Anyon, 1998; Harvey, 2003; Johnson. 2003; Lipman, 1999; Shannon, 1990).

Throughout the world, we witness privileged voices calling for the national unity of government, corporations, and the organizations of working people—an appeal to all-class unity that has ominous affinities with similar corporatist projects in the late 1920s and 1930s, that is, organized social disintegration under the banners of national interest—and war preparation. Societies promising their youths perpetual war make peculiar demands on schools.

Nevertheless, it has been in times of historical crisis, like the one I think we have entered, that people interested in democratic citizenship and social justice have made the greatest gains. For example, during the U.S. depression, people won the now evaporating 8-hour day, the right to form unions and bargain, and social security laws. Each world war engendered a revolution. It is extraordinarily clear today that the choice is some form of revolutionary communism, or barbarism.

Even so, today, any struggle for democracy must incorporate a reasoned grasp of the failure of socialism as well (Gibson, 1998). The collapse of the Soviet Bloc underscored the crisis of resistance while it simultaneously revealed the frailty of the modern bureaucratic state—and the failure of socialism to create a new class-conscious generation. Although today's world democratic movements have fought back and struggled for social justice in electoral arenas, around environmental questions, and sometimes won (although on-the-job fights in North America have been losers), those movements have changed little or nothing of essence. Although I cannot agree with those who suggest that socialism did nothing but nationalize the working class, which ignores the remarkable historical high-water marks of equality that those struggles embraced, it is sadly true that no one has yet escaped capitalism, which socialism set up as the base for industrialization, with a benevolent party in the lead.

Clearly, an economic and political system whose bellwether, the United States, jails 1 in 250 of its citizens, does not work especially well. The socialist alternative has not worked either. Nevertheless, the material base for shared abundance and deepened democracy exists in the world. What trails behind is the political, class, consciousness of people—and organizing for change. Still, the spreading processes of reality are relentless, grinding away illusions. People, even in imperial America, fight back because they must, just to live. Even modest radicals in education, like Michael Apple, are rediscovering the central roles of labor and social class in progressive change—and integrating that focal point with the lessons of what Freire liked to call, "progressive post-modernism." Given the de-industrialized nature of North America, the repositioning of schools as the focal points of social life, the permanence of war, the deindustrialization of the United States stripping the working class of its organizations, educators—whose jobs of gaining and testing knowledge are hard to outsource—are centripetal to hopes for social change. Elites, right now, have little to fear from a UAW-disciplined strike at General Motors. They have plenty of concern about another 1992 Los Angeles rebellion—or the reverberations of school to work from France in 1968. The young activist leaders of that uprising came from schools (Apple, 1999; Freire, 1998a, 1998b, 1998c, 1998d; Gibson, 1999b, 2004a, 2004b; Mishel & Bernstein, 1999).

FREIRE AS A SEXTANT FOR CHANGE "GOD LED ME TO THE PEOPLE . . . AND THE PEOPLE LED ME TO . . . MARX"
(Freire, cited in Mackie, 1980, p. 126)

It is in this context that many educators and agents for change—as well as those who want to construct hegemony in new ways—now turn to Freire, the individual who defined radicalism and revolution in education. Freire designed the educational programs in revolutionary Grenada (as well as mirror image campaigns in Guinea-Bissau) and was key in developing their political programs as well. It is Freire, and his Promethean promises of liberation, who I hope to problematize.

Freire invited educators to mix his intriguing four-part formula of literacy, critical consciousness, national economic development, and revolution to create a new practice of democracy. Freire suggested we can see, judge, and act—and become nearly impenetrable to lies—if we follow the form and content of critical pedagogy he has conceived (Dewitt, 1971). People who apply this formula typically run into the fact that Freire is a paradigm shifter, willing to enclose postmodernism, Catholicism, Marxism, and liberalism, a person far more complex than many of those who appropriate his work.

Freire is also reified. To invoke his name is to conjure radicalism, revolution in education—an embryonic phantom image like a Che Guevara t-shirt. The forbearer of late 20th-century educational criticism remains, for the most part, beyond sharp critique. His few public critics, like Paul Taylor (1993), who concluded that Freire is finally just a Christian, chide him only from strict textual references, and, for most others than Taylor, in only the most generous ways. The absence of criticism of his theoretical foundations and social practice allows his complexity and internal contradictions to be ignored, and his own counsel, to develop a fully critical outlook for social change rooted in the examination of social applications, to be denied.

Freire is rarely historicized, although some have noted his proximity to parts of John Dewey. A historical understanding would not only locate Freire through his life, in Brazil, Chile, the United States, Switzerland, and so on, but would also place him beside, for sake of close comparison, Mao Tse Tung, for example, whose earlier pedagogical and practical contradictions are remarkably similar (Chu, 1980).

Worse, Freire's work is easily and often stripped of whatever emancipatory political base it may hold and used as an rudimentary training method in, for example, Total Quality Management programs in Sweden which crudely unite Freire's student-centeredness and sense of collective work with the mind-stripping project of Frederick W. Taylor's stop-watch scientific management. Freire is artful in his application of multiple analytical models to social analysis; yet Freire is sometimes applied as a template on reality by those who he actually urges to be crafty (Taylor, 1993).

My theoretical view may be as contradictory and idiosyncratic. I seek to ground my thinking in dialectical materialism in the tradition of Marx's sense of the study of human agency as a part of matter in motion, the Hungarian philosopher-activist Georg Lukacs' and Istvan Meszaros' insistence on the interpenetrating role of the material world and class consciousness—as a prerequisite for fundamental social change, Fredy Perlman's and I. I. Rubin's (1972) investigation of reification and alienation in political economy, Situationist Guy Debord's (1995) study of capital's empty—if hypnotic—appearances, Foucault's (1979) study of reciprocal discipline from mind to body, Wilhelm Reich's (1972) suggestion of the role of the fear of sexuality in obsequiousness, and the dialectical agency outlined by North American, Bertell Ollman (1971, 1992). With Lukacs, I think the key to dialectical materialism, the action of change in the material world, is the transformation of the subject and object, that is, revolution (Lukacs, 2000). I agree with Lukacs, and Marx, that revolution, and revolutionary consciousness, demand organization. Dialectical materialism is a spacious paradigm that Freire also claims as his own. Dialectical materialism, very simply put, is the partisan study of change in the world.

PAULO FREIRE: OBJECTIVE IDEALIST
"BLESSED IS THE ONE WHO READS THE WORDS"
(Revelation 1:3)

In order to understand how it is that Freire can call himself a "totality," yet can say he believes in original sin on one page, and feel no need to criticize his support for the mechanically orthodox regimes in Grenada and Guinea Bissau on another page, it is necessary to take a detour to investigate some philosophical options, in this case two options, each with important subsets (Freire, 1994). The two key options are *idealism* and *materialism*. The subsets that I simplify and make understandable are subjective and objective idealism, on the one hand, and mechanical and dialectical materialism on the other.

Idealism is most easily presented in misusing Descartes', "I think therefore I am." Or, in the bible, "In the beginning was the Word. The word was in God's presence, and the word was God" (John 1:1). Idealism suggests that the world is a construction of the mind. Subjective idealism, briefly put, is the notion that nothing exists but the mind, and all else is apparitions. No one could be a full-blown subjective idealist and function, worrying at every step that the body might fly off into space—gravity being a problem if forgotten.

Objective idealism, told well with the tale of Plato's cave, his story of the people for whom images on a wall are the reality of the world, is the belief that while all begins with the mind, or god, there is indeed a world which is of interest to the mind, or god, and is likely to be a manifestation of a microcosm of the mind. God, in this view, would be interested in class struggle. Objective idealism was later codified by the great systematizer, Hegel. For the idealist, the external world is a creation of the mind, if it exists at all. For the subjective idealist, really nothing can change. For the objective idealist, Hegel, the motor of change is necessarily the mind—

which sets up all the change that follows. For a subjective idealist, there is really no possibility for historical change, as one could never tell, the only test being in one's own head. For an objective idealist, there can be history, and it can be relatively factual, if taken as the progress of the mind. At the end of the day, any form of idealism is a closed system, a turn to faith for proofs, a decision to be irrational. Irrationalism, the decision to worship the gap between what is known and what is not known, in a world of exploitation and inequality, is a partisan position (Lukacs, 1952).

Materialism is perhaps summed up well with this counter-quote to the Bible from Mary Coomes, "In the beginning was the world. Then came people. Then came the struggle for life and production, and reproduction, the deed. Ideas developed in social practice" (Gibson, 1994, p. 61). Mechanical materialism, probably best or most popularly represented by what has become known as Orthodox Marxism (an oxymoron for Marx), or Kautskyism, or Stalinism, the vision of the Second International later adopted by Bolshevism, is a belief in the inevitability of change through incremental additions: add up X amount of productive capacity and you get socialism. Marx attacked mechanical materialism in his Theses on Feuerbach, in which he emphasized, "human sensuous activity, *practice.*" Marx repeatedly insisted that the greatest productive force is class consciousness, class struggle, but honest, and dishonest, revolutionaries ran into what they saw as the irreconcilable contradiction of consciousness, and productive economic development for abundance-sharing later.

Dialectical materialism, the study of change in the material world, is the idea that things do indeed exist external to you or me, although we are clearly part of the world, and that things change, and that human agency, including conscious agency, is a key part of social change.

I suggest in the paragraphs to come that Freire can only be considered a Hegelian objective idealist, and that as such, he represents, as did Hegel, a vital contribution to the understanding and necessity of change, but that his advice is finally a cul-de-sac from which people interested in equality and democracy must at some point depart. Hegel's contributions are monumental, as Freire's borrowing from him demonstrates. Hegel, however, lived two centuries before Freire.

While Freire wants to locate himself in the complexities of dialectical materialism, outside the bounds of either the idealists or mechanical materialists, it remains that he cannot go further than to examine the world as a creation of his mind, and to reduce the world to the dichotomies, the appearances, that his mind initially is able to comprehend, not the richness of the material world as it transforms. While Freire's language is full of discourse about domination and oppression, he is never able to transcend this key understanding and reach into the content of these factors in labor, exploitation, or sexual oppression. He is able, in pedagogy and in print, to take up questions of a central issue of life, the construction of knowledge, but he can eclectically pass but a glance at the sources of the enemy of wisdom: irrationalism (Freire, 1998b).

There is little evidence that Freire had a good grasp of history, or historiography. Like many academic educators, he was rooted in philosophy and pedagogy, something of a hollow shell for a Marxist. The absence of historical understanding may have deepened Freire's objective idealism. He had few clear suggestions on how to get from what is to what should be, mostly an intellectualized denunciation of what is, and a utopian vision of where to be. Because of this his abstraction is pure abstraction, distanced from the complexity of material circumstances, and his ability to break out complex internal relations is mainly theory, quasi-religion, representative of educators with thin substantive backgrounds, who focus on pedagogical forms—absent history—and venture that one pedagogical emptiness slips into philosophy, and back again. With a limited grasp of history, for example, Freire is left analyzing racism in the common place terms of the right wing of multiculturalism—as a system of nasty ideas with no particular material base. He suggests that reason can overcome exploitation.

Allow me to pass beyond subjective idealism, since no one functioning in our world could fully adopt it and take a step with any confidence, and try to examine objective idealism more deeply through Hegel, who I think is Freire's forefather.

For the mature Hegel, not necessarily the anti-clerical Hegel who supported the violence of the French Revolution, but the Hegel of *The Logic*, the world is a totality, an unlimited whole, and its motive force is the absolute, ever-lasting Mind, "and whose outer form is but the manifestation of the Mind—such manifestation culminating in conscious units identical with nature in the mind. *That is all.*" Hence, people walk not because of their evolutionary relationship with the world, but because they *will* it (Bryant, 1971, pp. 21, 31). The world exists, things change, but things as they change are the product of an Absolute Spirit directing change to and from itself. Truth is in the Absolute spirit, and is in microcosm within the developing minds which are headed toward the Spirit. Because Hegel posited the existence of a world in change, and because he exhausted incredible, if sometimes undecipherable, discipline in examining its changes, Marx was able later to find and transcend the "rational kernel" inside Hegel's shell. Indeed, Lenin would later say that no one could understand Marx without having read, and understood, Hegel's *Logic*, making a problem of all he, Lenin (1976), wrote earlier, like *What is to Be Done?*

Narcissism is imbedded in any form of idealism—as anyone who knows Freire's postmodernist fan club has probably noticed. If all one can be sure of is the mind, all one can really be sure of is one's own mind, a propensity that leads to the fetishism about the self in some forms of postmodernism, and in parts of Freire (1998c). Flowing outward from the idealist's consciousness, the representative of consciousness, language, above and predating, preempting, labor and sexuality, becomes central. It make sense that if the mind is principal, then its communicative processes constitute the key to the processes of change. This goes to the fascination of right-wing postmodernism with discourse analysis—abstracted from the processes of the material world. It follows, as well, that an idealist position will posit an eternal ethics, as distinct from ethics derived from a material analysis of social conditions, and insist that if there is to be hope, it must be couched in the language of those ethics, finally, a battle between good and evil (Freire, 1998c). As Marx repeatedly suggested, criticism of religion is always helpful in critiquing our world, and it is in Freire's.

Freire made this analysis an uneasy one. He occasionally appropriated ideas of "over-determination," to demonstrate the relationship of culture, language, and economic structures. Yet, like Althusser, Freire remained bound in their dualism and impenetrability, rather than probing deeply into their interrelationship. Freire, as an objective idealist, is left with language, culture, and mythology, over-determining life (Dewitt, 1971; Freire, 1998b, 1998c; Palmer 1990). Sometimes in Freire, we find clues of the distortion of Gramsci's (and many others) views of the semi-autonomous nature—and the predictable next move, the autonomous nature—of the state, when in fact it is not mainly the state that is semi-autonomous, but capital.

" . . . AND DISTRIBUTION WAS MADE TO EVERYONE, ACCORDING AS HE HAD NEED"
(Acts 4:35)

While recognizing Hegel's profound contribution with the study of consciousness and transformation, and the efforts of a later philosopher, Feuerbach, Marx sought to address the question of subjectivity and objectivity through a careful examination of the material world and social practice. He suggested that the answers lay not in further theoretical contemplation: "Their resolution is therefore by no means merely a problem of knowledge, but a real problem of life, which philosophy could not solve precisely because it conceived this problem merely to be a theoretical one" (Tucker, 1978, p. 89). Here Marx began to build the notion that it is not possible to be dialectical, to understand how things change, without being a materialist, without positing the primacy of the external material world—and the interaction of, human, ideas.

Marx dug into Hegel's notions of labor in order to demonstrate this thesis. "Hegel conceives labor as man's act of *self-genesis*—conceives man's relation to himself as an alien being and the manifesting of himself as an alien being to be the coming-to-be of *species-consciousness and species-life.*" Marx suggested that Hegel's is an examination of the mind, "formal and abstract," and is at once superficial and incapable of offering a solution, an annulment, other than in thought (Tucker, 1978, p. 121). Yet Lenin's (1976) reading of Hegel demonstrates that Hegel did indeed offer Lenin the chance to understand transformation through contradiction, as a transition of thorough-going difference, overcoming, grasped in the material world, beyond ordinary imagination.

Nevertheless, Marx credited Hegel with identifying labor as the essence of human life, seeing the alienation of people from their creative lives as a critical problem in existence, and with the understanding that the genesis of human life is in relation to labor. Hegel apprehended moreover, the beginning of the philosophy of contradictions, negativity, at the heart of that process (Tucker, 1978). Hegel, in his world constructed in the mind, a world in motion toward the absolute spirit, understood that things change, and in studying how things change, his profoundly systematic honest investigation concluded, philosophically, that things change because they are composed of a unity and struggle (unity temporary, struggle permanent) of oppositions: contradictions.

Dialectical materialism, counter to Lenin (and even some of Marx) does not simply invert Hegel's notion of the Idea as the beginning of matter and motion. It does not simply turn Hegel on his head. Perhaps a better metaphor would be to turn Hegel inside out. Metaphors, in this case, though, may not work well at all. To shift from the Idea to the material world, is not to merely replace one initiating agent with another, one shell with another, but to introduce an entirely new set of complexities, a compass with much greater capability than the beginning point offered in Hegel. It means, too, to replace the test of truth in Hegel, theory (the application of an abstract truth to manipulate the collection of facts) with the test of truth in Marx, praxis, social practice.

This ends the linear dualism of thesis/anti-thesis/synthesis in Hegel, and suggests a sense of history best represented graphically by a spiral. Furthermore, this makes possible a study of relationships, the unity and struggle of complex opposites, in both form and content, while Hegelian objective idealism remains stuck in deep contemplation of appearances, forms—abstracted or estranged from their related content. In practice, the left-Hegelian mechanical socialists rooted truth inside the central committee; right-Hegelian irrationalists locate truth in god, mysticism. Dialectical materialism locates truth, as a simultaneously relative and absolute phenomena, in social praxis, the developing relationships of understanding and concrete tests. Since theory trails (and sometimes leaps ahead of) practice, dialectical materialism, in contrast to idealism is an open system, recognizing the incomplete nature of understanding. The material world always holds more to be discovered. To reiterate and abridge, it is not possible to be dialectical without being a materialist, and vice-versa (Korsch, 1970; Sartre, 1982). Idealism closes the system (even against Freire's many protests that his system remains unfinished), while dialectical materialism grasps, and opens it (Freire, 1998b). Things change, ceaselessly.

To expand, in his first and fourth thesis on Feuerbach (early philosopher of mechanical materialism), Marx offered his initial warnings that it is not possible to be dialectical, to understand change, without being a thorough-going materialist, grounded in the understanding that being initiates consciousness—which reverberates back and recreates being—that the material world exists in a relationship with the mind, neither preempted by the other. He suggested that Feuerbach detaches himself from a material understanding, then contemplates his own singular ideas within the limits of his mentally constructed, dogmatic, contradictions. Marx urged a project that is rooted in the reciprocal interaction of change and the material world, of ideas and things, each creating and recreating the other.

In his critique of religion, Marx sought to do more than counter it, but to examine and surpass it, a dialectical materialist transformation. So, too, against Feuerbach, Marx wrote of the working class as the class that is "superior to society," the class that can consciously transform its conditions, not to reproduce domination, but because of the material interests of that class as the interests of all of humanity, to end domination.

Georg Lukacs sews this thread as a theme into most of his work. In "The Young Hegel," Lukacs (1975) indicated that, "contradiction is the profoundest principle of all things. . . ." However, he continued, "this doctrine of contradiction can only be worked out adequately and consistently within a materialist dialectic in which it can be regarded as the intellectual mirroring of the dynamic contradictions of objective reality" (p. 218). Surely the great Hungarian dialectical philosopher would agree that the mirroring involves mutuality, reflecting, recreating, making profound, and reflecting back upon—and transforming.

Lukacs identified Hegel as an "objective idealist" and describes how Hegel's dialectics had to play out.

> There can only be an objective idealist dialectics (a) if we may assume the existence of something that goes beyond the consciousness of individuals but is still subject-like, a kind of consciousness, (b) if amidst the dialectical movement of the objects dialectics can discern a development which moves toward a consciousness of itself in this subject, and (c) so if the movement of the world of objects achieves an objective and subjective, a real and conscious union with knowledge. Thus the identical subject object is the central pillar of objective idealism, just as the reflection in human consciousness of an objective reality subsisting independ-

ently of consciousness is the crux of materialist epistemology.[3] (Lukacs, 1975, p. 270)

Now let us return to Marx attacking the Young Hegelians: (They) "consider conceptions, thoughts, ideas, in fact all of the products of consciousness, to which they attribute an independent existence, as the real chains of men . . . it is evident (they) have to fight only against those illusions of consciousness . . . they are fighting only against 'phrases.' They forget that to these phrases they themselves are only opposing other phrases, in no way combating the real existing world when they are merely combating the phrases of the world" (Tucker, 1978, p. 149).

Moreover, a fundamental understanding of historical or dialectical materialism (in which nothing comes from nothing) is that the elements of hope for a new or better world reside in the old, including the ideas necessary to forge a bridge, really a leap, from one to the next: critical imagination as distinct from dreamy imagination. It follows that a deep study of particulars, coupled with transformative practice guided by that study, is both the source and the route toward social change. Lukacs (1975) suggested that the objective idealist stance, in a sense, subverted Hegel's project of understanding what makes people continuously allow themselves to be turned into agents of their own subjugation, that is, Hegel's inability to probe deeply into understanding alienation.

Bertell Ollman (1992) believes that the route to the solution of the concept–object paradox is through the process of abstraction.

> Marx claims his method starts from the real concrete and proceeds through abstraction (the intellectual activity of breaking this whole down into mental units with which we think about it) to the "thought concrete" (the reconstituted and now understood whole present in the mind). The real concrete is simply the world in which we live, in all its complexity. The thought concrete is Marx's reconstruction of that world in the theories of what has become known as "Marxism." The royal road to understanding is said to pass from one to the other through the process of abstraction. (p. 24)

---

[3]Lukacs (1975). Here Lukacs marginally follows Lenin in his critique of Berkeley, in which Lenin suggests that Berkeley's notions of representation have no materiality, existing only on the plane of consciousness; see Lenin (1989). While the APA style of avoiding footnotes except in near-crisis situations is adopted here, there is an extensive bibliography for the reader interested in exploring the ideas, especially relating to dialectics and materialism, addressed in this chapter. For those interested in introductory texts I suggest, from the left, Gollobin (1988), and from the right, Wetter (1963). John Dewitt's (1971) unfortunately unpublished dissertation on Freire is a gem.

Ollman, then, underscored the relationship of ideas to the material world rather like a numerator and denominator in a fraction whose whole would evaporate in the absence of either.

For Freire (1998b), filled with a lifetime of radical Roman Catholicism, the material world is subordinate to, and plays itself out in, the world of ideas and religion. Abstraction often comes from first examining the processes of the mind—which can never be as fertile as the "real concrete." Because the mind of a serious objective idealist combines a gaze that must be finally both consummate and omnipotent with real respect for the material world, Freire is able to present himself as a totality, not a dichotomy, yet present a philosophy of appearances and clear, irreconcilable, contradictions.

Consider the obvious parallel of reading the word, the world, critical consciousness, and revolution, with reading the word and revelation, "Blessed is he that readeth the words for the time is at hand" (Revelation 1:3). In Freire's framework, like Hegel's, where the word often comes first, God would be attentive to dialectical materialism. And reading the word would necessarily be the pathway to liberation.

Freire is no subjective idealist, one who would argue that the material world is simply an enchantment of the mind. In Freire's work, the world and the mind exist, but finally as territory in the mind of a god. This is what makes it possible for Freire to presume both a belief in original sin and in revolution (Freire, 1998c). However complex and contradictory—for Hegel could hardly be considered a patron of traditional organized Christianity—Christianity and Hegelianism are at the heart of a significant sector of Freire's theoretical base. These factors are the sources of his ideal-ism—which Lukacs identified as *objective idealism*. Freire commented that he never lost Jesus when he discovered Marx. Christianity and Hegelianism, both well-springs of Marxism, are also the foundations for Freire's rever-ence for equality and the importance of leadership and ideology (Gibson, 1994).

Objective idealism leads Freire to easily resolve, or personify, an appar-ently impossible binary: Literacy for liberatory consciousness becomes lit-eracy for national economic development (Freire, 1978). This, at the end of the day, was the project of the Grenadian New Jewel Movement, Cabral's Guinea Bissau, and one of the rocks that shipwrecked orthodox socialism. The goal, once critical consciousness and a self-actualizing working class dedicated to end the long history of the master–slave relationship, quickly became national economic development, with the party leadership at the head, living in the best houses around. Freedom was abandoned for the long grinding out of Taylorized industrial necessity. Critique of alienation became confused with the promotion of the gross national product. Concern about exploitation, which never extended into an honest study of surplus value, shifted to a preoccupation with greater output—in the name of socialist equality (Gibson, 1994). A world view that necessarily focuses on appearances, objective idealism, does not go deeper than concern about domination and oppression, "the fundamental theme of our epoch is domination, which implies its opposite, liberation," into the essence of the creation of value, labor, and reproduction, sexuality (Freire, 1980, p. 93). Therefore, in practice, this world view resolves appearances, and fails to get to the heart of things—and ideas. One of Freire's great contributions goes to this issue: that element of liberation that addresses the role of class consciousness as a precondition of social change (Freire, 1980). Also implied is the role of class consciousness in maintaining change.

Still, in the absence of a profound sense of materialism, Freire can only be superficially dialectical. Consciousness itself is never as rich and complex as the objects and subjects with which it interacts. In other words, Freire embodies a contradiction, a contradiction flowing from the binary created by his objective idealism: He believes ideas change the world, or on the other hand that national technological/economic development changes the world—and he does not comprehend the interactions of a contradiction in which the power of one element overwhelms the other. Either we become what we wish, that is, a correct reading of the world creates a just world; or we become what the nation can develop, a form of Bolshevik-socialist mechanical materialism. This brittle binary, again, rises from Freire as an objective idealist, one who finally privileges consciousness over being and whose interest in dialectical materialism is subordinate to his beliefs in God and abstractions about reason. Freire rarely made commonly materialist claims. The words *political economy* or *surplus value* received little attention in his works, although he did occasionally affirm or deny the pivotal role of class struggle, depending on what one reads. Freire was at once the modest dialectician and educator, often humbly imperious about his abilities. For Freire, an understanding of the infinite complexity of the real world was, in theory and practice, reduced to a naive binary, as opposed to the multitude of interrelating contradictions that are available to the materialist view.

Lukacs (1988) is especially helpful, "The theoretical cul-de-sacs of the bourgeoisie idealist philosophy, which are continually re-emerging, very often originate in an abstract and antinomic contrast between the material and the mental, the natural and the social, which inevitably leads to the destruction of all genuine dialectical connections and thus makes the specific character of social being incomprehensible" (p. 107). Lukacs' contribution is to demonstrate the framework that captures Freire. The caged bird helps build its own cage.

Freire, in both his earliest and his most recent works, tried to defend against this criticism. Indeed, he parried caricatures of the arguments of both the mechanists and the dreamy idealists. He countered those who have, unfairly and superficially I think, called him a keeper for capitalism in crisis

(Freire, 1974, 1994, 1998c). It is possible, but unlikely, as Martin Carnoy seems to think, that reading Freire is going to be especially good for progressive sectors of capital (Freire, 1998b). We shall see. But Freire remains stuck, in theory and in practice. The annulment of alienated consciousness, the way an estranged mind is overcome, following Freire's philosophical origins and path, is that progressives should fight for national "economic development, and to limit the size of the state." The guiding hand here should be God's, "a God on the side of those with whom justice, truth, and love should be" (Freire 1998b, pp. 34, 35, 103).

Although Freire recognized a democratic and egalitarian utopian goal, he urged paths—liberatory consciousness linked to national development—idealism or mechanical materialism—which in practice have repeatedly been in harsh opposition to each other and yet are twins of the same mother, as we shall see. In practice, national economic development has never played second fiddle to equality and democracy; most certainly beacon issues to the movement for critical consciousness.

In practice, the jailed New Jewel leaders and the minister of education in Grenada agreed on the purpose of pedagogy, but lost interest in critically democratic citizens, because national economic development was far more important to them than critical consciousness, at least as long as the former held power. National economic development, moved to the role of the highest priority, means that criticism of the construction of profits, or surplus value, that is, the exploitation of labor on the shop floor or in the agricultural field, must take second shrift.

Alienation is, in part, the estrangement of people from other people and their work because they do not control the product or process of production. Human social relations and human creativity, a unity possible today more than ever before, are split apart. Social relations are estranged by ideological systems rooted in opportunist interests—and exploitation. The potential for collective creativity in work becomes an authoritarian relationship—and boredom. Work becomes apart from real life. Work sucks.

Alienation inserts an additional insult: The more working people engage in the central aspect of what might or should be their human creativity—work—the more they empower, enrich, those who own—those who simply want them to work harder, faster, less thoughtfully—and this accelerates the construction of their own oppression. The more that is produced inside this framework, the less human people become.

Really critical literacy that addresses hierarchy and injustice is linked by Freirean magic, objective idealism, to technological national economic progress—rarely the catalyst for deconstructing inequality. Critical consciousness, which must at some point connect with the deeper realities of alienation, the creation of surplus value by work forces that do not control the process or products of their labor, is submerged by promises for justice delayed. Critical consciousness is buried in the productive forces—national economic development.

In Grenada, calls for national economic development meant considerable sacrifice for many people, even though the New Jewel Movement did have a reasonably honest system of national economics. The New Jewel Movement had programs for medical care, the local control and production of local goods and foodstuffs, a plan to build technology through education that predated the Asian Tigers, and a sensible scheme to boost tourism via an international airport. But people remained alienated from the literacy programs that were clearly designed to buttress the New Jewel Movement economic campaign. People walked away, slept in class. They felt the literacy project was coercive, unconnected to their lives (Gibson, 1994). Moreover, the same pattern of alienation from school and work, despite the calls to sacrifice for the national economy, continues under the current government, which ironically turned to Fidel Castro to finance a local sports stadium. Cuban assistance with the Grenadian international airport was a key excuse for the 1983 U.S. invasion, and the imprisonment of the New Jewel Movement leaders.

The main phrase used to sell national economic development is that, "we are all in this together." The socialist project promised that abundance would be on the horizon, and once abundance was achieved through worker sacrifice for national economic development, it would be shared. The line of today's global capital is much the same, except the promise of sharing some day is spoken much more softly, if at all. The belief that we are one, all in the same boat, is Hegelian, a remnant of objective idealism and is fully taken up by Freire. His followers, even those like Martin Carnoy with proud records of taking apart the workings of capital, are thus left with making calls to humanize the culture of the globalization of capital, a social system which Meszaros rightly calls a "giant sucking pump of surplus value" (Carnoy, 1974, 1985; Freire, 1998b; Meszaros, 1995).

Freire's objective idealism on the one hand *produces*, and *recreates* mechanical materialism on the other hand—a contradiction among many Freire is willing to live with—allowing his admirers to uncritically appropriate only parts of him, without addressing his clear contributions in their complexity. Some adopt Freire's humanism and ignore his politics, others adopt his politics and abuse his humanism. The Grenadian and Guinea Bissau revolutions appropriated Freire for national economic development and abandoned his ideas about equality and democracy. Others, like Carnoy, lift his humanist and constructivist approaches to literacy, and hush his revolutionary politics. Objective idealism manufactures this binary, and allows Freire to live with his own contradictions.

Still, within Freire's objective idealism is also the sense that dialectical materialism, which privileges the primacy of class struggle and social practice, constitutes a coherent way to comprehend and act on the world. His demands for a critique of praxis create a fair ground for examining his own ideas and those of others. Moreover, Freire's insistence on the importance of ideas (critical consciousness) and leadership inextricably linked to the masses in any struggle for social change and education lays the basis to explore the possibilities of ideology linked to material equality (Freire, 1980). Freire said critical consciousness is, "Something which implies to analyze. It is a kind of reading the world rigorously . . . of reading how society works. It is to better understand the problem of interests, the question of power . . . a deeper reading of reality . . . common sense goes beyond common sense" (Freire, 1998c, p. 9).

PAULO FREIRE FOR BEGINNERS: THE PARADIGM SHIFTER
"THERE WILL BE EQUALITY, AS IT IS WRITTEN:
HE WHO GATHERED MUCH DID NOT HAVE TOO MUCH,
AND HE WHO GATHERED LITTLE DID NOT HAVE TOO LITTLE"
(Corinthians 8:13)

Let's look at a simplified approach to how the unity and struggle of opposites (dialectics) within Freire works. What I pose is but two useful photos of what should be better seen as a complex film always in motion, the Idealist Freire riding on the same tracks as the Mechanically Materialist Freire.

I pose two Freires. In the first instance, I summarize, in a brief format, Freire's analytical process as it appears in his theoretical work. This addresses Freire as an objective idealist (Catholic humanist), with Freire answering questions like: What is the motive force of history? How do we know this? Who is positioned to make change? How will they do that? What kind of pedagogy do you propose? Why? What is the source of alienation and exploitation, and what shall we do about it? Who are our friends? Where does the government come from and who does it serve? Where does racism come from? What shall we do about that? How shall we fight? How will we know when we win? What do we need to know to avoid recreating the mistakes of the past, to act anew?

Under the second heading, I apply similar questions to Freire's practice, where we see the most orthodox of mechanical materialisms. The binary I am proposing, which Freire's objective idealism allows him to encircle, is most easily seen in two of Freire's works, *Pedagogy of the Oppressed* and *Pedagogy in Process: Letters to Guinea Bissau*, the former representing the humanist tilt and the latter the mechanist side. His most recent books, *Politics and Education, Pedagogy of Freedom*, and *Pedagogy of the Heart*, perhaps more even than others, are rife with the contradictions I outline here.

The Objective Idealist Freire

1. All of history is seen as "a process of human events" (Freire, 1973, p. 147). The "fundamental theme of our epoch is domination, which implies its opposite, liberation" (Freire, 1973, p. 93). Oppression equals "dehumanization" (Freire, 1980, p. 28).
2. Culture and language are the primary indicators of this process. Silence is a prime indicator of oppression (Freire, 1985, 1994).
3. Hence, to grasp history, analyze culture and language . . .
4. . . . through literacy achieved via cultural investigation and dialogue.
5. Middle-class leaders and teachers are motivated, and linked to the masses and students, by respect, benevolence, dialogue, and love, which overcomes inequality. This requires the "class suicide," of the teacher-leaders (Freire, 1978, p. 103).
6. Literacy classes are student-centered, texts rise from student experience.
7. Inequality is examined as dehumanization, "spiritual weariness, historical anesthesia," cultural invasion (Freire, 1994, p. 123).
8. Change is achieved through new consciousness gained through literacy, and new approaches to language. Coming to voice becomes change: education for freedom (Freire, 1985, p. 78).
9. The state, government, is mediated terrain, a potential ally (Freire, 1993).
10. In political activity, pluralism, such as Freire's Workers Party of Brazil, national culture and economic development are privileged.
11. False consciousness is defeated by critical analysis (Freire, 1973).
12. Alienation is annulled by deconstructing hegemony. *Will* defeats might (Freire, 1994).
13. Truth is located within Freire's mind, or God's. The test for truth is in theory (Freire, 1973).
14. In theory: this is the postmodernist Freire; sex-gender, race, class, nation, are simultaneously pivotal. "Class struggle is not *the* mover of history, but it is certainly one of them" (Freire, 1994, p. 91).
15. Racism is analyzed primarily as an ideological system—or an ethical problem.
16. Resistance, revolution, or praxis is equated to literary deconstruction.
17. Inequality is overcome by heightened consciousness. The oppressors are liberated (Freire, 1980).

In summary, the outline just presented amounts to traditional social democracy.

Next, I pose (again, for sake of exposition, urging the reader to see that this is an interplay that is presented as a frozen moment) the questions noted previously to the revolutionary Freire, the Freire who advised the Grenadian and Cabral revolution of Guinea Bissau. This is the mechanist side of Freire. It should be clear that this Freire is no stranger to the idea that violence is the mother of social change (Gibson, 1994, p. 326).

The Mechanically Materialist Freire

1. All history is the history of the struggle for production, then class struggle. "Relationships can never be understood except in the light of class analysis" (Freire, 1978, p. 8).
2. Production and technology are the primary indicators/motivative forces (Freire, 1978).
3. Hence, to transform reality; analyze and achieve national production . . . (Freire, 1973, p. 32; 1978, p. 47).
4. Through literacy won via directive and steered dialogue: re-education (Freire, 1978).
5. Teachers and leaders are motivated by love, party or leader-worship, and national economic development. Personality cults rise: Cabral, Maurice Bishop in Grenada, Castro, etc. (Freire, 1994, 1980).
6. Inequality is checked via revolution and the vanguard revolutionary party.
7. Change is achieved via revolution and the vanguard party.
8. The state, government, is to be smashed, then appropriated. (In the case of Chile, failure to conduct this activity made counter-revolution possible.)
9. False consciousness is defeated by national commitment to revolutionary national economic/technical development (Freire, 1978).
10. Alienation is annulled in praxis by revolution, then economic improvements. National development requires support for the national bourgeoisie (Freire, 1978).
11. "Democratic" centralism in politics (i.e., New Jewel, Guinea Bissau, Cuba, etc.).
12. In theory, class is pivotal; race, sex-gender, nation secondary. (Subverted by emphasis on national development.)
13. Racism is analyzed as system of exploitation, usually overcome by the revolution (Cuba).

14. Resistance is guerrilla or revolutionary war.
15. Truth resides within, and is tested by, usually, the central committee.
16. Inequality is purportedly defeated by technological change that creates abundance, that is, by the restoration of capitalist relations. The party bourgeoisie, red experts, etc., promise an egalitarian future.

In summary, this amounts to dogmatic, vulgar, or mechanical Marxism.

Social democracy as seen in Allende's Chile, and vulgar, doctrinaire, dogmatic strains of Marxism, as seen in caudillo Castro's Cuba, charismatic Bishop's Grenada, not-Communist China, or the collapsed Soviet Union, are failed systems. I characterize these systems as idealism in power, and mechanical materialism in power. Within the left, the history of what can be properly called right (Chile) and left (U.S.S.R.) Hegelianism, the elements of Freire's contradictions, both of which rely heavily on the good will of intellectuals and the postponement of equality in exchange for abundance, will not get anyone to critical democratic citizenship. In Freire's day-to-day life after his exile from Brazil, it is fairly clear that he was a liberal reformer wherever he actually lived, and not necessarily, but often, a socialist revolutionary where he did not.

Grenadian efforts to build an economy rooted in new technology and to create a workforce technologically capable and disciplined, were built on worker sacrifices and a party-centered educational system which sought to mask its alienating efforts in the language of national self-determination. The party leadership retained decision-making power, and the results of labor-producing surplus value. In the minds of the far-seeing leadership, the educational system had to be motored by the goals of the economy. These goals were certainly within the framework of traditional socialism, and in many ways in Grenada, under Bernard Coard's New Jewel Movement leadership, predated the Gorbachev Glasnost and perestroika projects (Gibson, 1994). For a worker in the fields, or in the new fruit-processing plants, however, the burden of alienated work, of work out of workers' control, creating unpaid value beyond the reward, value that boomerangs back and empowers those in charge; that estrangement remained in full force. The promise of better days lagged and lagged—and vanished. In socialist practice, it is evident that abundance alone will never lead to equality, the bedrock to democracy. Consciousness alone will never lead to democracy. You simply cannot get there from here on either singular route. Yet no movement for fundamental change can leap ahead if the ideas of the people have not hurdled their current conditions, if the people have not discovered that they are superior to their circumstances, if they are unable to locate their often utopian hopes in seeds of the present. The slave cannot get rid of the master, and all of domination, without first envisioning life without the master—and combating the inner slave as well. Absent Guevara's quixotic vision, that the dozen or so loving revolutionaries could win, there would be no Cuban socialism to learn from. Without revolutionary theory, there is no revolutionary practice (Lenin, 1990; Lukacs, 1971). The question remains: What do people need to know in order to end exploitation and alienation? What must we see today to construct freedom tomorrow? What if revolutionaries will never inherit abundance, but must teach people to share suffering for awhile?[4]

Freire failed to recognize in depth the importance of his own call for the centripetal role of critical consciousness, which, is the role of ideas as a material force—especially the idea of equality. Just as literacy does not necessarily have anything to do with liberation or democracy, neither does development or abundance lead to democratic equality or social justice. But democratic egalitarianism is a powerful notion, with deep historical roots (Birchall, 1997). Freire was distracted from this profound principal by traveling into another mechanical and dogmatic cul-de-sac.

Freire in social practice relied heavily on the theory of productive forces, both in the idealist Freire and the doctrinal Freire. This theoretical model within dogmatic threads of Marxism (left-Hegelianism) overestimates the role of technique of production and privileges technological advance far above the social relations of production. In other words, the theory of productive forces insists that in order for democratic and egalitarian citizenship to become a reality, it is necessary to create abundance. To construct abundance requires rapid industrialization or technological development, which in turn demands material rewards for political and technical experts—and well-rewarded party leaders—to make the decisions for the rabble. This requires and reintroduces official ideas and practices supporting inequality—which promises, someday, to become equality. The unquenchable thirst of surplus value that is capital is re-introduced, as a Trojan Horse or a Prometheus, carrying the promise of social justice. Working people tithe to the party. This is not to reduce to a single theory the many rocks that have shipwrecked socialism: caudillo cults of personality, nationalism hidden in socialist cloth, party leaders' privileges, the repeated failure of justice-oriented movements to address questions of sexism, the use of professional armies

---

[4]For a brief parenthetical discussion of how this operated, see E.H. Carr (1967). Here the Soviets tried to resolve the problem, "We Russians have to do with still primitive human material. We are compelled to adapt the flying machine to the type of flyer who is at our disposal. To the extent which we are successful in developing a new man, the technological development of the material will be perfected." The new man, however, was not to critique Soviet hierarchy or inequality, but to develop in relation to technology (p. 191).

as hooligans of new elites. The theory of productive forces is, however, a mostly uncharted rock. Remarkably, all of the socialist revolutions of the century were made with armies that were more or less egalitarian and democratic, but conquering regimes almost immediately installed a new undemocratic privileged aristocracy in the name of promoting economic development for, postponed, equality (Mao Tse-tung, 1977). In the world of theory, addressing merely the appearances of domination and oppression does not get to the sources in exploitation and authoritarianism.

Freire's embodiment of contradictions in his theoretical work, and his contradictory practice, really demonstrates the twin relationship of what leftists know as sectarianism and opportunism. Both rise, if we are to estimate that the agents of change are reasonably honest and not simply huckster-opportunists, out of a limited, one-sided, analysis of the material world, rooted in a similar philosophical error.

Sectarianism and opportunism are twins of the same mother, two faces of opposition to real critical and democratic citizenship. Both reify truth, locating truth outside the realm of tests in social practice. The sectarians usually locate truth inside the party's central committee, for the opportunists, truth is in God's hands, really their minds. Opportunists abandon the interests of the many for the interests of the few. Sectarians confuse the interests of the few with the interests of the many. Both sectarianism and opportunism are based at once in deep fear of the people, elitism, contempt for mass struggle; and in support of privilege, hero iconicization, mesmerized mass action, or passivity. Once the party of revolution is in power, stop wondering about equality or the division of surplus value; wait for the promised land of abundance. Then we will share, from benevolence. Sectarianism overestimates the primacy of the material world, making it appear that matter changes only at its own reified pace—the mechanically materialist Freire. Opportunism contends that matter is only changed through the force of ideas, often individual ideas, not concrete, analytical, egalitarian mass struggle—the idealist Freire. Sectarianism and opportunism combine to form the fatalistic belief that the world, matter, will surely change in ways we desire. Both finally limit or deny the significance of fully reflective human agency—grasping and transforming the world at its political and economic roots. We have seen these mis-estimations quickly turn into the opposites of their civic claims far too often. For left Hegelianism, sectarianism, and right Hegelianism, opportunism, change happens along a line of accumulated, predictable, nearly inevitable, ingredients, or change happens because we wish it so. Both reality and/or change are constructs of the mind, usually the Mind in charge. Meet the new boss, same as the old boss (Freire, 1980, pp. 20-25).

The resolution of this is a deep probe into the intersections of mind and matter, in the construction of everyday life, in using critical theory to make the reproductive veils of capital transparent, and to grasp what useful elements of the future are built into the present—and to look into the future.[5]

IF WE LIVE, WE LIVE TO TREAD ON KINGS
(Shakespeare, Henry IV)

There are ways out of Freire's dilemma, understanding that social practice is tentative, experimental, partial, yet ineluctable. The untenable contradiction of national economic development and democracy could be resolved by uniting them under the rubric of the moral and material imperative of equality—in both the mode (decision making) and means (equality in distribution) of production: ethical ideas as a material force. Freire's work is riddled with calls for ethics. But his ethics are idealist, religious, falling from the sky. A dialectically material ethic rises from a concrete grasp of historical materialism, ethics won in struggle over time (Freire, 1998b). This does not mean equality as a dogmatic abstraction, but equality as a necessary common goal, recognizing that the starting points of people are simply not equal. As elements of Freire's work suggest, we must not only examine discourse and culture, but that we pay particular attention to the creation and distribution of surplus value—both in terms of the creation of goods and the *creation and distribution of surplus time*—which relates to the foundations of creating culture. Decision-making power as a form of alienation, or liberation, must be considered a part of this process of critique as well.

Freire's objective idealist focus on appearances, in this instance the appearance of oppression, as indicated above, limits the routes to liberation. Istvan Meszaros offers a deepened understanding of what must be understood in order to reach into a more democratic and egalitarian future. He underlined the necessity of grappling with dialectics, studying the processes of change in a thorough-going materialist fashion, and suggests that capital (whose life blood is exploitation and alienation) has a lot of defenses, what he called second-order mediations, including the following:

---

[5]Here Lukacs and I, leaving from the same starting point, cross paths, but I think the thought is very similar: "most of the deviations from Marxism follow one of these paths in their methods and revoke Marx's supersession of a false antimony in a bourgeoisie sense . . . it should be noted that sectarian dogmatism generally takes the path of fetishization of reason, whereas opportunist revisions of Marxism commonly show the tendency to an empiricist fetishization" (Lukacs, 1988, p. 107). For a fine discussion of the masks of capital as a "natural force," see Fredy Perlman (1992).

1. The nuclear family (a center of reproducing authoritarian relations).
2. Alienated means of production, distribution, and consumption.
3. Fetishist (as opposed to humanist) production objectives.
4. Labor structurally divorced from control.
5. Capital's nation status—and its fickle willingness to follow the sweet smell of surplus value from one nation to the next. Nationalism is a secondary interest to capital.
6. The uncontrollability of the market (Meszaros, 1995).
   To which I add:
7. Cultural hegemony.
8. The fragmentation of labor—workers split by unions, trade, skill, race, and so on.
9. The continuing appeal of nationalism (Perlman, 1985).
10. And to which Wilhelm Reich (1970) would add: the role of sexuality and the family in preparing people for an irrational oppressive world.

Guy Debord, the situationist anarcho-communist, enraged on every stinging page of *The Society of the Spectacle* demonstrates, with his colleague Fredy Perlman and I. I. Rubin (1990), that revolutionary change must penetrate into every area of body and mind, to unchaining every aspect of human creativity. Listen to Debord (1995) raise his fist:

> No quantitative relief of its poverty, no illusory hierarchical incorporation, can supply a lasting cure for its satisfaction, for the proletariat cannot truly recognize itself in any particular wrong it has suffered; nor therefore, *in the righting of any particular wrong*—nor even in the righting of many such wrongs; but only in the righting of the unqualified wrong that has been perpetrated upon it—the universal wrong of its exclusion from life. (p. 85)

Now, return to Meszaros, "what determines ideology more than anything else is the imperative to become *practically conscious* of the fundamentals of social conflict—from the mutually exclusive *standpoint*s of the hegemonic alternatives that face on another in the given social order—for the purpose of *fighting it out*" (Meszaros, 1989, p. 11).

Here is how Bertell Ollman (1979) lined this up:

> First, workers must recognize that they have interests. Second, they must be able to see their interests as individuals in their interests as members of a class. Third, they must be able to distinguish what Marx considers their main interests as workers from other less important economic interests. Fourth, they must believe that their class interests come prior to their interests as members of a particular nation, religion, race, etc. Fifth,

they must truly hate their capitalist exploiters. Sixth, they must have an idea, however vague, that their situation could be qualitatively improved. Seventh, they must believe that they themselves, through some means or other, can help bring about this improvement. Eighth, they must believe that Marx's strategy, or that advocated by Marxist leaders, offers the best means for achieving their aims. And, ninth, having arrived at all the foregoing, they must not be afraid to act when the time comes.

Freire and I (and I suspect an older Ollman) would reject the call for hatred. There is enough of that, and it is as much a cul-de-sac as binary opposition to religion. Hatred does not overcome, but recreates, the dichotomy of the master and the slave, as does the reification of violence that is usually the consequence of hatred. But the commonality of the remainder of the project should be clear.

Let us give Marx his say, from *The German Ideology*:

> Both for the production on a mass scale of this communist consciousness, and . . . the alteration of men on a mass scale is necessary . . . a revolution; this revolution is necessary, therefore, not only because the ruling class cannot be overthrown in any other way, but also because the class overthrowing it can only in a revolution succeed in ridding itself of all the muck of ages and become fitted to found society anew. (Tucker, 1978, p. 134)

Wilhelm Reich saw the struggles of life as centered, from necessity, on love, work, and knowledge. Detroiter Raya Dunayevskaya (1999), translator of Marx's *Economic and Philosophical Manuscripts*, offers to add to our vision with her reading of Hegel and Marx: the struggle for freedom.

In summary, the way out must at once address the totality of human creativity and the particular methods that are used to imprison it. No one can reasonably suggest a grasp of the totality, or, hence, all of its components. But it is possible, recognizing the simultaneously absolute and relative nature of truth, to go out the door and take informed, critically conscious, action.

It might appear that what I have written here creates a Freire that is profoundly pessimistic, a fellow whose language of love and understanding is undermined simultaneously by a view that people are born in sin, or that people must have corrupt and coercive direction to move forward. As a subset of Freire's ideas that has gone mostly uncriticized, there is some truth in that. But that is a caricature of my interpretation, a fraction of the story. This chapter seeks to take Freire at his word, to critically address aspects he "may not have perceived" (Freire, 1980, p. 24). This is a reasonably respectful work.

Listen to Freire's (1998c), idea of good teaching: "There is no more ethical or truly democratic road than one in which we reveal to learners how we think, why we think the way we do, our dreams, the dreams for which we will fight, while giving them concrete proof that we respect their opinions, even when they are opposed to our own" (p. 40). Who does this better than Freire? The objective idealist Freire is a worthy starting point for pedagogy for the common good.

Freire, even in his objective idealism, still understands that things exist, things change, and he is able to put together an admirable pedagogical outlook to participate in transformation. Freire's contributions around the pivotal nature of praxis as the testing ground for knowledge, the centrifugal role of honest leadership, and the importance of the unity of leaders and educators with the masses and students alone are worth the complex encounter that occurs when assaying the fellow who calls himself the Vagabond of the Obvious—Paulo Freire. A prescient tribute from Lenin in his reading of Hegel, "At ought, the transgression beyond finitude, infinity, begins" (Lenin, 1976).

Nevertheless, what is clear at this historical moment, is that the people of the world have never been as educated and as technologically advanced as they are now. The history of oppression demonstrates that where there is oppression there is always resistance. Oppression is both ideological and material: Princess Diana worship and Patriot missiles, standardized educational curricula, layoffs at Levis, and the Daimler-Chrysler merger, promises to empower teachers and the takeover of the Detroit public schools by the banks and casino powers, all interacting with one another. What lies behind language is not merely technique, but power, the iron fist under the velvet glove.

Discourse analysis in the tradition of the idealist Freire will not supply the social forces necessary to make change. It will not bring about a society that privileges relations between people over relations between things. Postmodernist discourse analysis taken alone, as it too often is, has demonstrated, by now, that it simply creates a new class of priests, offering new words, driving new cars, hypnotized by the processes of power, unable to lead revolution.

Still, what drives production is not sheer technology but social relations—again imbued with imbalances of power—a process that the doctrinal Freire undervalues. Freire does offer a chance to underline Lukacs' position, interestingly ratified later by Maoist economics, that consciousness rising out of social relations must, at some point, strip ahead of the development of technologies in the means of production. Within Freire's contribution about the importance of ideology is the hint that equality might overcome the contradiction, not by overlapping idealism with materialism, but simply with a new understanding rising from a mostly social, rather than mostly technologically mechanical vision.

Educators concerned about citizenship and the common welfare are being urged by elites to join them in their efforts to tamp down the democratic expectations of the mass of people, to help children to understand and accept that they will not likely do as well as their parents, that the high-stakes tests they are taking really prepare them for a multitude of alienated jobs in a world where employer loyalty is a one-way street. School workers are being told to tell kids that war is the only alternative. For any educator to play along is to ignore the old revolutionary adage that an injury to one only precedes an injury to all: to join in the organization of decay is to eventually organize one's own rot. Educators who tacitly support the stratification of children by class, sex, and race, will themselves find their wages tied to the parental incomes of those they teach. Moreover, passive educators, or partisans who opt to oppose the valuable contributions of Freire's work on education for transmission or transformation, will be unable to unpack the alienation they themselves will build and feel in classrooms driven by standardized curricula, national examinations, and burgeoning class size counts—and the invasion of military recruiters on the necrophiliac rut for new bodies (Anyon, 1998; Gibson, 1999a, 1999b; Lipman, 1999).

We who profess to stand for education toward revolution against barbarism, for a full overturning, must make problematic the intersections of power and inequality that block our best laid plans. The key area of agreement, for example, of the U.S.-installed minister of education in Grenada and the former revolutionary New Jewel leaders now in prison, was that education must serve national economic development. The implications of that decision are labyrinthine. As both sides of this struggle are intensely aware, ideas have consequences. The New Jewel leaders have been unjustly held as political prisoners in a 17th-century prison since 1983, for crimes that, after a careful review of evidence, I believe they did not commit. Tragically, at the conclusion of a cold war conducted primarily by white folks, the last prisoners of that war are African-Caribbeans.

Grenada's minister of education really has no desire to take either of Freire's paths toward liberatory consciousness, not the examination of domination, not real national development. The current government is busy selling passports and seeking top-of-the-line tourist development. In contrast, the New Jewel leaders, still thinking of themselves as patriots, have guided the prison education program so well that it has the top test scores on the island—to boost the national economy.

So, we who look to education seriously as a passage to social justice must determine just where it is we want to go and how we hope to get there. Now, more than ever, what teachers do matters. There are now about 49 million children in the public schools of the United States, 24 million in middle and secondary school, all of whom will be draft age by 2010. If the future must be forged by people who at least make new errors, what do those people need to know to be immune to lies, to be inoculated against submissiveness—and how should they learn it? If we are to understand Freire at all: things change. Capital is temporal. We are accountable for what is next.

Late in their lives, both Georg Lukacs and Paulo Freire wrote last books. Lukacs' *A Defense of History and Class Consciousness: Tailism and the Dialect*, drives home three key ideas that Freire's last work, *Pedagogy of Freedom*, takes up as well. Freire's book, unfortunately, is available in English only in a terrible translation, and he died before he could finish the editing. However, in each instance, two things are clear from the two writers. First, overcoming the contradiction of subject and object requires the conscious action of the critically curious subject. Second, justice demands organization. Only through a revolutionary political organization can such a conscious become truly a movement. Third, within this, "revolutionary passion," is vital, key (Lukacs, 2000, p. 67). I do not share Lukacs' or Freire's sense of what the organization should look like—or at least not Lukacs' tacit support of Stalin's Russia, and Freire's leadership in the opportunist Workers Party of Brazil, about to recreate all the old problems of socialism. Still, I think their common idea is correct. The negation of the negation, the idea that things change and what is new is always in re-creation, and the profound optimism built within it, requires organization. Organization splits off opportunism, which is all for the good—and is not necessarily the fountainhead of sectarianism. Opportunism, and related factors of racism, ignorance, and cowardice, are the driving forces of the North American school work force. At issue is not to just identify those forces, but to fully understand and overcome them. That task demands organization, which I have urged should center in schools in de-industrialized North America. What makes Marxist practice possible is organizational form. That task is before us, in embryo in groups like the Rouge Forum (Gibson, 2003; Lukacs, 2000).[6]

---

[6]In Marx and to one degree or another those who followed him, there has always been a recognition that labor, the mode and means of production, science, the class struggle, and ideas have all been related to one another. How this plays out is a problem in many arenas.

Lenin quotes Marx from the *Manifesto* in Lenin's *State and Revolution* (written, I note, after his encounter with Hegel's *Logic*, which seems to have reformed Lenin less than others, like Dunayevskaya, I suspect). Marx argues that the first step of a revolution is to raise the proletariat to the level of the ruling class, then, "to raise the level of productive forces as rapidly as possible" (Lenin, 1990). Mao Tse-tung (1964) made a tangential point in his *Where Do Correct Ideas Come From?*

Some Marxists, like Marty Glaberman of the Johnson-Forrest Tendency, led by C.L.R. James and Raya Dunayevskaya, believe that no idea exists before it takes place somewhere in social practice (Glaberman, 2002).

Others, like David Harvey, suggest that ideas do indeed leap ahead of social practice, using Marx's analogy of the bridge builder who imagines the bridge, designs it, and puts the design into practice. Indeed, Marx felt that this was one element that distinguished people from animals.

Such an organization does need, as Freire often suggested, an ethic that people understand and can use to judge what they do, what the organization is, where they have been, and where they are headed. This is what I have developed, based on what I think are vital lessons from the struggles of millions of people who have gone before us.

Things change; a fact and an ethic. This means revolution always seen on our horizon. Perhaps a counter-question might offer a benchmark to test: Do masses of people, individually and collectively, understand that things change, and how, and why, better, because of a given action or even a lesson plan? Did people become, in shorthand, more class-conscious? Did they see themselves as part of things changing? Or did they learn better to do what they are told to do?

There is also an ethic behind the next social change, not a religious ethic but an ethic drawn from painful historical experiences of betrayal, an ethic that can give revolutionary action a vision, a body, a collective, and a practice:

This debate has serious implications. For example, Lukacs argued (in many ways like Glaberman, even though they have fundamental differences) that there is such a thing as "Imputed consciousness" (i.e., the consciousness that the working class has, and/or should have, as a class, arguing that this consciousness bursts forth in certain periods). Glaberman, on a smaller scale, points to a worker at a machine who, seeing her comrades moving toward her and the exit door, in mass, when it is not time for lunch or a break, puts down her tools and walks out in solidarity, only asking what is up when the shop is empty and work stopped (Glaberman, 2002; Lukacs, 2000).

All agree that there is in fact an object class consciousness rooted in a careful, dialectical examination of concrete circumstances. Lukacs (2000) used the analogy of Marxists rejecting scabbing, knowing that a scab is wrong, as proof of objective class consciousness.

The implications of these differing positions on class consciousness are, of course, enormous, and at the end of the day, questions of life and death.

What to do? Glaberman suggests patience, and that it will be up to the working class itself, in its daily activity in opposition to exploitation and alienation, to discover its own class consciousness, and when it does, it will act. Glaberman, more or less, follows the path set by Anton Pannekoek and many others, anarchists and communists alike, who argued against the direction of a vanguard party–or at least Lenin's Bolshevik vanguard party (Pannekoek, Workers' Councils, 1970). It is, however, a little surprising that Glaberman, a close associate of Raya Dunayevskaya who translated Marx's Economic and Philosophical Manuscripts and relied heavily on them to guide her, and his, work, did not take note of the section of the Manuscripts that says, "We must consider it an advance that we have previously acquired an awareness of the limited nature and the goal of historical development, and can see beyond it."

Lenin and Lukacs both attacked Glaberman's position, unfairly I think, as a theory of spontaneity. This is not a theory of spontaneity, but a theory of the inexorable working out of class struggle on the job and off, based on the idea that people must fight to live, every day, and that fight over time takes on the aspect of a class strug-

- We can, as a class-community, understand and change our world.
- Reason, to gain and test knowledge in the struggle for the truth, over mysticism and fear.
- Equality: from each per commitment to each per need; exploitation is unethical.
- All Must Rise: We have a right to rebel with deepening wisdom, and under every social system to demand control over the products and processes of our work, meaning class struggle does not end.
- Freedom—for curiosity, radical criticism, sensual inquiry, and the right to err.
- Solidarity, an injury to one is an injury to all.
- Aesthetics, beauty . . . the right to art, pleasure, sensuality, creativity, music, dance
- Communist democracy, related to mass critical consciousness.
- Resistance and direct action in the least alienating ways possible.
- Education, to raise our understanding of the whole, and its parts.

gle, and that in that working out, class consciousness comes to being as, above all, a struggle for freedom. Pannekoek accused Bolshevism as only being interested in training obedient followers—not a conscious class. There is truth in this, but it is insufficient as, I think, Lenin is correct, with Lukacs, in saying that this will not become revolutionary class consciousness, and that the organization necessary to conduct a revolution cannot be merely based in disparate workers' councils, easily split, left incommunicado, etc.

Harvey suggested, in 2004, that we choose liberal capitalists over conservative capitalists, in order to stave off fascism, thus beginning the old debate that was finalized in the seventh world congress of the Comintern in the mid-1930s, when the Comintern took a similar path—in opposition to people like R. Palme Dutt (1972) who urged that the Comintern attack capitalism, not conservatives.

Lukacs, whose arguments I think hold the greatest weight, says that class consciousness must be embodied in the social practice of a leading party. He is not insisting, as the Bolsheviks, Chinese Communists, and most others did, that truth resides within the central committee; but that truth resides in the interactions of the mass of people, the party, and the class struggle. This not-seamless interaction of ideas, organization, and social action, can be best planned (to face a ruthless and organized opposition) by a party, can be corrected by the self-criticism of the party and its members—who have the ability, then, to look back and judge what they set out to do, using an outline of what was attempted. The parallel to pedagogy should be obvious (Tailism, pp. 76–79). However, it is equally obvious that one advantage that a party has over workers' councils, the ability to maintain a secret wing that is not so easily obliterated, has its own problems: an underground wing must be made up of people who take direction, for the most part.

- Courage, the ethic that says: You are what you do.
- Internationalism, anti-racism, anti-sexism.
- Revolution, struggle: We are not all in this together.
- To overcome capitalism in total.
- For survival, inclusion, community, and love—harmony for the first time ruling disharmony.

We will win. Over time, we will win. In the master–slave relationship, it is too easy to see defeat after defeat. We need to remember that in our struggle, we win by defining ourselves and remaining sane, but in the long term, we win as well. But justice demands organization.

REFERENCES

Anyon, J. (1998). *Ghetto schooling*. New York: Teachers College Press.

Apple, M. (1999). *Official knowledge*. New York: Routledge.

Arrighi, G. (1994). *The long twentieth century*. London: Verso.

Birchall, I. (1997). *Spectre of Babeuf*. New York: Palgrave McMillan.

Breisach, E. (2003). *The future of history: The postmodernist challenge and its aftermath*. Chicago: University of Chicago.

Bryant, W. M. (1971). *Hegel's educational ideas*. New York: AMS Press.

Carnoy, M. (1974). *Education as cultural imperialism*. New York: McKay.

Carnoy, M. (1985). *Schooling and work in the democratic state*. Stanford, CA: Stanford University Press.

Carr, E. H. (1967). *What is history?* New York: Vintage.

Center for Community Development. (2001). *Human development in further education and training in South Africa*. Capetown: ABC Press.

Chu, D-C. (1980). *Chairman Mao: Education of the proletariat*. New York: Philosophical Library.

Debord, G. (1995). *The society of the spectacle*. New York: Zone Books.

Dewitt, J. (1971). *An exposition and analysis of Paulo Freire's radical psycho-social andragogy of development*. Unpublished doctoral dissertation, Boston University, Boston, MA.

Dunayevskaya, R. (1999). *The power of negativity*. Lanham, MD: Rowman & Littlefield.

Dutt, R. P. (1972). *Fascism and social revolution*. New York: Freide.

Foucault, M. (1979). *Discipline and punish*. New York: Vintage.

Freire, P. (1973). *Pedagogy of the oppressed*. New York: Seabury.

Freire, P. (1974). *Education for critical consciousness*. New York: Crossroad.

Freire, P. (1978). *Pedagogy in process*. New York: Seabury.

Freire, P. (1980). *Pedagogy of the oppressed*. New York: Continuum.

Freire, P. (1985). *Politics of education*. New York: Bergin and Garvey.

Freire, P. (1993). *Pedagogy of the city*. New York: Continuum.

Freire, P. (1994). *Pedagogy of hope*. New York: Continuum.

Freire, P. (1998a). *Pedagogy of freedom*. Lanham, MD: Rowman and Littlefield.

Freire, P. (1998b). *Pedagogy of the heart*. New York: Continuum.

Freire, P. (1998c). *Politics and education*. Los Angeles: UCLA Latin American Studies.

Freire, P. (1998d). *Teachers as cultural workers*. Boulder, CO: Westview.

Gibson, R. (1994). *The promethean literacy, Paulo Freire's pedagogy of reading, praxis, and liberation*. Unpublished doctoral dissertation, Penn State University, State College. Retrieved from http://www.pipeline.com/~rgibson/gibson.htm

Gibson, R. (1998). The Michigan social studies standards: Beware the dream censors. *Cultural Logic 1*(1), Fal. Retrieved from http://eserver.org/clogic/1-1/gibson.html

Gibson, R. (1999a, Winter). Ghetto schooling. *Review of Pedagogy and Cultural Studies*. Retrieved from http://www.pipeline.com/~rgibson/anyon.htm

Gibson, R. (1999b). The theory and practice of constructing hope: Detroit teachers wildcat strike. *Cultural Logic, 2*(2). Retrieved from http://eserver.org/clogic/2_2/gibson.html

Gibson, R. (2003). *What do people need to know, and how do they need to come to know it, in order to be free?* Retrieved from http://www.pipeline.com/%7Ergibson/free.htm

Gibson, R. (2004a). The California grocery strike. *Cultural Logic*. Retrieved from http://eserver.org/clogic/2004/gibson.html

Gibson, R. (2004b, June 5-6). The last prisoners of the cold war are black. *Counterpunch*. Retrieved from http://www.counterpunch.org/gibson06052004.html

Glaberman, M. (2002). *Punching out and other writings*. Chicago, IL: Charles Kerr.

Gollobin, I. (1988). *Dialectical materialism*. New York: Petras Press.

Greider, W. (1997). *One world ready or not*. New York: Simon & Schuster.

Harvey, D. (1992). *Limits to capital*. Oxford: Blackwell.

Harvey, D. (2003). *New imperialism*. Oxford: Oxford University Press.

Harvey, D. (2004). *New imperialism*. London: Oxford University Press.

Hickling-Hudson, A. (1988). Toward communication praxis. *Journal of Education, 170*, 9–38.

Johnson, C. (2003). *Sorrows of empire*. New York: Metropolitan.

Kaplan, R. (1995). *The ends of the earth: Journey to the ends of anarchy*. New York: Vintage.

Kozol, J. (1985). *Illiterate America*. New York: Doubleday.

Korsch, K. (1970). *Marxism and philosophy*. New York: Monthly Review Press.

Lenin, V. I. (1976). *Selected works, vol. 38*. New York: Progress Publishers.

Lenin, V. I. (1989). *Materialism and empiro-criticism*. New York: International Publishers.

Lenin, V. I. (1990). *State and revolution*. New York: International Publishers.

Lipman, P. (1999). *Race, class, and power in school restructuring*. Albany: State University of New York Press.

Lukacs, G. (1952). *Destruction of reason*. Atlantic Highlands, NJ: Humanities Press International.

Lukacs, G. (1971). *History and class consciousness*. Cambridge, MA: MIT Press.

Lukacs, G. (1975). *The young Hegel*. London: Merlin.

Lukacs, G. (1988). *The ontology of social being* (Vols. 1–3). London: Merlin.

Lukacs, G. (2000). *A defense of history and class consciousness: Tailism and the dialectic.* New York: Verso.

Mackie, R. (1980). *Literacy and revolution.* London: Pluto Press.

Mao T-t. (1964). *On practice, on contradiction, where do correct ideas come from?* Peking: Foreign Language Press.

Mao T-t. (1977). *A critique of soviet economics.* New York: Monthly Review Press.

Meszaros, I. (1989). *The power of ideology.* New York: New York University Press.

Meszaros, I. (1995). *Beyond capital.* London: Merlin.

Mishel, L., & Bernstein, J. (1999). *The state of working America, 1998-99.* New York: M. E. Sharpe.

Nkomo, M. (1999). *Pedagogy of domination: Toward a democratic education in South Africa.* Trenton, NJ: Africa World Press.

Ollman, B. (1971). *Alienation: Marx's conception of man in a capitalist society.* Cambridge: Cambridge University Press.

Ollman, B. (1979). Toward class consciousness in the working class. In *Social and sexual revolution: Essays on Marx and Reich.* Cambridge, MA: South End Press. Retrieved from http://www.pipeline.com/%7Erougeforum/towardclassconsciousness.htm

Ollman, B. (1992). *Dialectical investigations.* New York: Routledge.

Palmer, R. (1990). *Descent into discourse.* Philadelphia: Temple University Press.

Pannekoek, A. (1970). *Workers' Councils.* Chicago: AK Press.

Perlman, F. (1985). *The continuing appeal of nationalism.* Detroit: Black & Red.

Perlman, F. (1992). *The reproduction of everyday life.* Detroit: Black & Red.

Professor Sokol's transgression. (1996, June). *New Criterion, 14*(10). Retrieved from http://www.newcriterion.com/archive/14/june96/june-nc.htm

Reich, W. (1970). *The mass psychology of fascism.* New York: Touchstone.

Reich, W. (1972). *Sex-pol: The essays of Wilhem Reich, 1929-1934.* New York: Random House.

Rubin, I. I. (1972). *Essays on Marx's theory of value.* Detroit: Black & Red. Retrieved from http://www.marxists.org/subject/economy/rubin/index.htm

Sartre, J-P. (1982). *Critique of dialectical reason.* London: Verso.

Shannon, P. (1990). *The struggle to continue.* Portsmouth, NH: Heinemann.

Shannon, P. (1998). *Reading poverty.* New York: Longman.

Stuckey, J. E. (1993). *The violence of literacy.* Portsmouth, NH: Boynton-Cook.

Taylor, P. (1993). *The texts of Paulo Freire.* Philadelphia: Open University Press.

Tucker, R. C. (Ed.). (1978). *Marx–Engels reader* (2nd ed.). New York: Norton.

Wetter, G. A. (1963). *Dialectical materialism.* New York: Praeger.

9

The Unchained Dialectic

Critique and Renewal
of Higher Education Research

John F. Welsh

Only that which is an object of freedom may be called an Idea.

—G. W. F. Hegel (1796)

RESEARCH AND PURPOSE

Commentaries on the scope and status of research on higher education consistently confront a fundamental contradiction: Higher education itself is entrusted with a singular and major societal responsibility to preserve, extend, and apply the body of human knowledge. However, the body of knowledge about higher education, taken as a whole, fails to meaningfully inform the higher education community, much less the society it serves, about the instructional, curricular, financial, and organizational dynamics of the higher learning.

Among the laments catalogued in studies and commentaries on higher education research by David Leslie (2002), Marvin Peterson (2000), George Keller (1985), Kezar and Eckel (2000), and Yvonna Lincoln (1991) are a sense that inquiry into higher education has become too technocratic, too narrow, too specialized, too self-serving, too inwardly focused, and irrelevant to public policy and social practice. Analysts of the status of research in higher education are particularly perplexed as to why policymakers and administrators seem uninterested in applying the body of knowledge about higher education to existing problems. The lack of interest in higher education research by policymakers and administrators may be secondary to more fundamental questions about the purpose of research about higher education. Is the primary purpose to inform organizational and managerial elites about the social dynamics of the higher learning, or is it to contribute to society's knowledge of itself and its processes of self-organization? Perhaps we need to add to the list of concerns the observation that precious little research is either critical of higher education or employs research methodologies that open new vistas into how this major societal institution can become more responsive to human interests.

Typifications of higher education research reflect the domination by positivistic and interpretive methodologies that fail to situate themselves and higher education in macro-level, sociohistorical contexts. The consequence of the domination by positivistic and interpretive methodologies is that critical dimensions of social thought and practice are rarely the priorities of discourse about social relations in higher education. There are both epistemological and ontological grounds for offering a critique and alternative to these meta-analyses of research on higher education.

The epistemological critique is that inquiry into higher education is almost entirely based on a concept of society as *Substance* and not as *Subject*. This Hegelian distinction is useful in the analysis of higher education research because it emphasizes the difference between a view of people as passive receptacles of external stimuli in their social relations and not as reflective and active producers of their environment. The content and methodological approach in higher education research seem to matter very little; knowledge about higher education is routinely gathered through methodologies that assume that human reality is an inert "out there," and that the *telos* of this knowledge is its application by policymakers and administrators to correct or fix the infinite array of conflicts and contradictions in the social organization of the higher learning. Because society is assumed to be Substance and not Subject, it is thought that the implementation of an appropriate methodological canon in any inquiry will produce an identity or correspondence between the thought and the object.

The epistemological foundation encourages, entails, and promotes important ontological assumptions about higher education. For instance, it legitimates a division of manual and mental labor in the process of the self-organization of this major social institution. Much of the discourse about higher education assumes that scientifically or scholarly generated knowledge about its operations can and should be employed as instruments by policy and managerial elites to improve the effectiveness and efficiency of colleges or universities, or of units or actors within them. The basic ontological concept of much research on higher education is that social relations within colleges and universities must be externally transformed by the scientific, policy, and managerial elites who possess special knowledge about the social reality of higher education. Ontologically, this division of labor also tends to reinforce existing hierarchies and prevailing patterns of distribution of social *desiderata*.

The epistemological assumption that social inquiry seeks to establish an identity between thought and object is the goal of positivistic, interpretive, and some postmodernist methodologies. The ontological assumption that the goal of inquiry into higher education is the external transformation of social relations by scientific, policy, and managerial elites is also shared by many positivistic, interpretive, and postmodernist researchers.

Opposed to the correspondence theory of truth and an externally mediated theory of social action is a philosophy of liberation that maintains that human freedom, which can be understood as self-conscious self-determination, is the goal of inquiry into social relations and the knowledge process. It is important to contrast the basic elements of dialectical thought with the prevailing methodological approaches in research on higher education and to appreciate positivistic and interpretive research as moments in the dialectical understanding of the social relations in the higher learning.

This argument is pursued in three sections in this chapter. The first section discusses the basic forms of research about higher education based on Jürgen Habermas' categories of scientific interest as a way of understanding the important distinctions among methodological approaches in higher education research. This section briefly discusses examples of research that demonstrates elements of each category. The second section explores the basic elements of a dialectical approach to research on higher education. This section specifically examines "immanent critique" as the core of critical, dialectical, and emancipatory approaches to social research. The final section extends this discussion by exploring the philosophic roots of a dialectical approach to research in higher education. In this section, Hegel's concept of the "Absolute Idea" is examined as a basis for understanding the epistemological, ontological and methodological elements of a dialectical methodology in higher education research.

TYPIFICATIONS OF RESEARCH IN HIGHER EDUCATION

Critical Dimensions in Research

Peterson's (2000) study of research cultures in higher education counterposes a traditional, conservative, and "social fact" paradigm against a cultural, radical and "social definition" paradigm. The qualities he used to distinguish the two research cultures were basically epistemological in nature. One paradigm is based on a positivist view of knowledge, the other is based on an interpretive view of knowledge. One paradigm is focused on structures and patterns, the other is focused on emergent processes and dynamics. The measurement strategy of one paradigm is quantitative, the other is qualitative. Although this is a familiar typification of research approaches in higher education (Tierney, 1991), it is a restricted vision because it is focused exclusively on how the researcher knows about the social world. It does not address issues that pertain to the researcher's interaction with the social world. In brief, it does not address the ontological questions about knowledge and society and, thus, limits our understanding of the full range of theoretical and methodological options for scholarly research on higher education.

Largely through the work of Jürgen Habermas (1971; McCarthy, 1978; Schroyer, 1973), critical social theory has identified three forms of research, each of which entails assumptions or principles about the nature of knowledge and human activity. These three forms of research operate to constitute and support specific social and political interests because they entail legitimations or justifications of social practices. Critical theorists from Horkheimer to Marcuse to Habermas have argued that when researchers adopt a theoretical perspective or methodological approach to a research problem, they must ask, whose interests are served if this theory or method is situated in the social world? Despite his modernist agenda, Habermas insisted that theoretical perspectives and social research strategies are not politically or socially neutral but have an impact on social life in that they either critique or legitimate the social practices under study. Habermas maintained that theoretical perspectives and research strategies can be grouped into three categories, each with a corresponding legitimation of social practice.

In delineating the three categories of scientific interests, Habermas utilized two analytic dimensions that can be understood as questions that are asked about the particular theoretical orientation and research strategy. The first dimension is epistemological and concerns the response to how the perspective views its subject matter: people acting within an educational context. Are people and their social relations understood as the passive receptacles of the external stimuli or of immutable social structures? Or, are they understood as the actual or potential creators of their external behavioral environment? These are typically questions of knowledge or epistemology and they address the issue of whether people are capable of reflecting upon themselves and directing their own behavior. Schroyer (1973) referred to the first dimension articulated by Habermas as "epistemological reflexivity."

The second dimension is ontological and is concerned with how the theoretical perspective and methodological approach views its own relationship to the object of its analysis: people acting in an educational context. The basic question is whether the perspective understands itself as neutral toward and detached from the social world. Or, does it understand itself as necessarily engaged and existing in a reciprocal or interactive relationship with the social world? What is the relationship between the intellectual and the social world he or she studies? These are typically questions about the relationship of scientific knowledge and social being. They address the issue of what are the social and political problems and responsibilities of science. Schroyer (1973) referred to Habermas' second dimension as "ontological reflexivity." Precious little of the research in and about higher education has understood itself as part of the social process it studies.

Scientism and Technical Control

Scientism, the first form of scientific interest identified by Habermas, is reflexive neither epistemologically nor ontologically. Scientism is concerned with the production of general laws and the prediction and control of human behavior, which contributes to the critical analysis of society and its major institutions by producing knowledge of existing social relationships, patterns, and conflicts. Scientism is conceived as a mode of inquiry that produces information that assumes the interests of certainty and technical control. It is empiricist, based on a positivist epistemology, assuming that knowledge is inherently neutral and that the quantitative precision of the natural sciences constitutes the only appropriate route to understanding the social world. What is essential about this mode of inquiry is that, although it sees itself as socially and politically neutral, it is actually a form of inquiry that has the theoretical interest and societal consequence of maintaining technical control of knowledge and organization (Schroyer, 1973).

Research about higher education is dominated by the scientistic form of inquiry. One of the three major research journals in higher education in the United States, *Research in Higher Education*, is exclusively devoted to positivistic, quantitative forms of research. Articles appearing in the *Journal of Higher Education* and the *Review of Higher Education* are also largely scientistic in their methodological orientations. Although the two latter journals also include some studies employing more qualitative forms of inquiry, most of the research is quantitative and employs positivist assumptions about the nature of knowledge and society. When they are not writing conceptual pieces about higher education, many, arguably most, of the leading researchers in the field consistently employ quantitative methodologies. Success as a scholar and the arrival of higher education as a content area appear dependent on the adoption of a single theoretical paradigm that elevates the methods of the natural sciences as the only appropriate approach to understanding social relations in higher education.

Hermeneutics and Intersubjective Understanding

The second mode of inquiry identified by Habermas is hermeneutics or interpretive inquiry. This form of research provides a potent challenge to the positivistic presentation of the social reality of the higher learning. The hermeneutic approaches are concerned with the processes of the social construction of everyday life. According to Habermas and Schroyer (1973), the hermeneutic sciences are conceived as "that mode of interpretation that yields an understanding of the socio-cultural life-world and that presupposes the interests of extending intersubjective understanding" (p. 215). The intent of the hermeneutic approaches, which include symbolic interactionism, phenomenology, and much postmodernist discourse, is to define the object of analysis in educational research from a more humanistic and interactive perspective by focusing on intersubjective structures. The hermeneutic approaches are reflexive in an epistemological sense as they assume that social reality is constructed by conscious, willful agents and seek to discover the processes by which humans make sense of their environments.

However, these qualitative approaches are not reflexive in an ontological sense. Qualitative, humanistic, and postmodernist researchers tend not to situate their work in the social context, or to see their work as affecting the structures of social reality, but merely apprehending, describing and reflecting the social dynamics of higher education. Habermas (1971) noted that the hermeneutic sciences have a "scientific consciousness" in that they share the methodological imperative of "describing a structured reality within the horizon of the theoretical attitude" (p. 303). Because they do not accept the notion that scientific knowledge has a constitutive effect on social relationships, the hermeneutic sciences have become "the positivism of the cultural and social sciences." The hermeneutic or interpretive perspectives cannot be conceived to be ontologically reflexive since they maintain that social relationships are created by active human agents, but either insist on political disinterest and the social disengagement of scientific practice, or do not articulate a relationship between a political stance and their methodological approach.

For instance, the research of Anna Neumann (2000), Estella Bensimon (Bensimon, Neumann, & Birnbaum, 1989), and Robert Birnbaum (1988) entails the clear use of hermeneutic or interpretive methods to study organizational leadership in higher education, but each fails to articulate a political stance on the structure of social relationships within colleges and universities. The discourse that emerges in their studies of leadership is oriented toward incremental improvements in the organization's hierarchy; they do not challenge or seek to transform the relationships between the leaders and the led. Similarly, the extensive research of William Tierney (1991, 1993) on leadership and organization in higher education has a clear interpretive foundation. Tierney himself claimed that he is "on the Left" and identified his perspective as a type of critical postmodernism, but Wilms and Zell (2003) demonstrated that his use of categories such as "high performance" suggest that his work is well within the theoretical and cultural horizon of capitalist organizational theory.

Societal Critique and Emancipation

Critical social thought generally insists on an epistemological break with the more traditional and conservative social theories and methodological approaches. Max Horkheimer (1972), one of Habermas' precursors in the Frankfurt Institute for Social Research, distinguished critical from traditional theory by noting the critical theorist's awareness of his or her social partiality. Critical approaches reject the value-neutral and presumed objective self-understanding of the scientistic and hermeneutic approaches by affirming the interactive, dialectical relationship between knowledge and society. Social reality, as the scholar's object of cognition, is transformed by social knowledge from a thing-in-itself to a thing-for-itself. In contrast to the claims of scholars who argue that the research enterprise is only an academic effort somehow existing independently of social reality, the critical approaches in human and behavior sciences take the perspective that sociological theory and research are intellectual definitions of the situation and structure social action.

From a critical standpoint, the social reality of higher education is what it is to some degree because of what educational research says about it, or how it is defined by cultural, managerial, and scientific elites. Intellectual definitions of the situation have a socially self-fulfilling character to them, particularly if they are able to attract political and organizational power in their service. Educational theory and research, thus, must be understood as socially situated vocabularies of motive that lay a foundation for social and political action (Mills, 1940). The critical or emancipatory interest in educational research views knowledge and definitions of reality as not only emerging out of a specific sociohistorical milieu, but also as affirmations or critiques of the sociohistorical milieu. Knowledge has a social base and social knowledge legitimates or helps transform the social base.

The critical form of inquiry, although it finds little support in research on higher education in North America, contributes to the emancipatory interests of human knowledge because it comprehends the constitutive role of science and because it affirms the notion that human beings must participate as self-conscious, self-determining agents in the social construction of reality, or else the resulting social formations lose their human and social character. Following the critical work of Hegel, Marx, Lukacs, Marcuse, Habermas, Giroux, and McLaren, the emancipatory thrust of educational research is particularly important in situations where structural obstacles to full social participation have been erected. In its emancipatory mode, according to Lukacs (1971), social research is the intellectual expression of social revolution. Or, the role of research in opposing and transforming capitalist commodity relations, and statist or bureaucratically administered relationships, into fully social, fully participatory relationships is the political expression of critical science.

The scientistic perspective is a major form of legitimation for the social formations and cultural representations of state power and advanced capitalism. The critical approach maintains that the predominant uses of educational research include the legitimation of hierarchical organizational relationships, exclusionist managerial practices, and institutional goals that reinforce capitalist exchange relationships. The task of the emancipatory forms of educational research is to critique the methods and content of the dominant modes of educational research and to challenge the social reality they constitute. The emancipatory forms of educational research reject the necessity of historical modes of domination and seek to understand processes of conflict, change, reality construction, and emancipation. Critical forms of educational research emphasize that human emancipation is firmly grounded in processes of self and social reflection on the legitimacy accorded existing social formations. Critical knowledge about the higher learning potentially augments human self-knowledge and encourages human participation in societal processes, but cannot be used for the managerial or exploitive purposes of one entity toward another.

There are two important points about this schematic delineation of research orientations. First, it is absolutely important to understand that there are more options than those identified by Peterson (2000), Keller (1985), and other commentators on the scope of research in higher education. Second, it is important to focus more attention on the defining elements and characteristics of the dialectical and critical perspectives as alternatives to positivistic and interpretive research.

IMMANENT CRITIQUE AND HIGHER
EDUCATION RESEARCH

The method of immanent critique is arguably the core of critical and dialectical inquiry. It unites such disparate thinkers as Hegel, Marx, Lukacs, Gramsci, and Marcuse (Antonio, 1981; 1983). Immanent critique enables its user to restore authenticity and actuality to false appearances by first expressing what a social formation holds itself to be and contrasting that with what in fact it is or what it is becoming. In his reformulation of the Hegelian dialectic, Marx was able to show that the false appearance of reciprocity, or the false equivalence of exchange between labor and capital, was negated by the structural tendencies of capitalist exchange relations, which, in some respects, generate human exploitation and alienation (Marx, 1954). Antonio (1981) noted, "Immanent critique attacks social reality from its own standpoint, but at the same time criticizes the standpoint from the perspective of historical context" (p. 338). Similarly, the critical analysis of higher education attempts to unmask the false presentations of this major social institution by contrasting the phenomenal appearance generated by scientistic and hermeneutic research with the in-itself reality. The elaboration of the opposition of the ideological claim and the real social entity is oriented toward social emancipation because the ideal is converted by the researcher into a tool to transform the real. The false correspondence of the ideal and the real is elaborated in the first instance as a method of social analysis, but it has a political meaning as well: to make the ideal a reality.

Marx understood that the ruling ideas of any era were the ideas of the ruling class, which means, in part, that the dominant ideas about social relations benefit those who rule by legitimating their power, irrespective of whether the dominant ideas are generated by religion, science, or the mass media. The emancipatory interests of inquiry and society are advanced by examining the ruling ideas of an historical period. If dehumanizing, alienating dimensions can be demonstrated in the ruling ideas, then these help illuminate the dehumanizing, alienating dimensions of a social formation.

Scientistic and hermeneutic research assumes that the goal of inquiry is the development of a correspondence or identity between the in-itself reality and the phenomenal appearance of objects of cognition. Qualitative ethnographers, for instance, assume a consensus social ontology in which social interaction consists of subjective meaning tied to objective gestures, and that the overt presentation is an accurate reflection of that which is hidden from public view. Similarly, the quantitative researcher assumes, or strives to demonstrate, that the markings or responses on a survey instrument adequately reflect the in-itself reality of the respondent's motives or perceptions. However, phenomenal presentations often mystify the thing-in-itself.

Marx (1954) demystified the reciprocity of labor and capital by showing that the expropriation of surplus value contradicted the notion of equal exchange underlying all social relations in capitalist society. The notion of equal exchange functioned as a presentation that mystified the reality of the process of capital accumulation since the latter depends on the extraction of surplus value, or the exploitation of the worker. The survival of capitalism depended, in part, upon the continued acceptance by the workers of the "equality" or "reciprocity" of labor and capital. When there is a mismatch between the thing-as-presented and the thing-in-itself, then a form of distorted communication has occurred. In the first volume of *Capital*, Marx described the distorted communication as "Commodity Fetishism." The distorted communication reinforces the alienation of the objective and subjective realities and subverts full human participation in the social construction of reality. The method of immanent critique operates to expose fetishistic, distorted communication in human interaction as an alienative, exploitative process, and it explores how human agents can fully participate in reality construction.

Antonio Gramsci (1971) developed further the basic concepts of critical inquiry in higher education research. Gramsci insightfully noted that power and domination in alienated social environments is maintained not only by material forces of coercion and repression but also within the consciousness of people. With the concept of "ideological hegemony," Gramsci argued that the ruling class always seeks to legitimate its power through the creation and imposition of a worldview that stresses the need for order, authority, and discipline. The ruling class consciously attempts to subvert potential for opposition by subordinate social categories. Capitalism controls its contradictions and manages its objective crises by "taking captive" the minds of those victimized by alienation and exploitation. Ideological hegemony depends upon the ruling class seizing and controlling the means of communication or the means of the production of culture and knowledge. The unseen power of the ruling class is enhanced in the schools, the workplace, and in the creation and dissemination of scientific knowledge.

Independent of the work of Gramsci, the Hegelian-oriented Marxism of Georg Lukacs affirmed the ability of the ruling class to maintain its hegemony through the control of consciousness. The central problematic of his *History and Class Consciousness* (Lukacs, 1971) is that socialist revolutions failed because Marxism failed to focus attention on the processes through which the ruling class controlled its subject populace through ideas. Lukacs' notion of "reified consciousness" emphasizes that the consciousness of people is managed by an elite for the purposes of capital accumulation and political legitimacy.

For Lukacs, the interest in maintaining the status quo of the capitalist totality is fulfilled by a process in which the human-made world of culture and society are viewed in terms that affirm their independence from humans. Objective social relations are viewed as "things" and are understood as immutable parts of the natural world. Reification is the personification of things and the "thing-ification" of persons. Reification is a dangerous departure from the normal social objectification of cultural artifacts and social bonds in that it inverts subjects and objects in order to create a docile populace. Reification must be overcome if human agents are to participate in the social construction of reality in a reflexive, reciprocal manner. The relationship of the work of Lukacs with that of Marx and Gramsci can be summarized by saying that, in class societies, domination and exploitation can be maintained or extended through asymmetrical prerogatives to define reality on behalf of the superordinate classes. Under capitalism, the problems of capital accumulation and political legitimacy are addressed by class and organizational elites by maintaining false impressions of reciprocity and the necessity of order, authority, and discipline, or a reified view of social relations. Social and behavioral research into major social institutions, such as higher education, is an important progenitor of reification when the social interest of critique is divorced from the interests in description and understanding.

This is not to suggest that there are no examples of immanent critique in the analysis of higher education in North America, but to argue that this work is a limited slice of research on higher education. Among the critical research on culture and ideology in higher education is an important example of the use of immanent critique in Gary Rhoades' (2000) analysis of managerial ideology and strategic activity in higher education. In this study, Rhoades clearly employed a critical methodology by counterposing "managerial myths" of strategic activity with evidence that contradicts their premises. He also placed a discussion of the managerial myths in a more macro-level sociohistorical context that illuminates their sources and impacts. The managerial myths are shown to be reifications that are oriented toward generating organizational discipline and protecting institutional hierarchies.

TOWARD A DIALECTICAL FOUNDATION
FOR HIGHER EDUCATION RESEARCH

The social origins of positivistic and hermeneutic research on higher education lie in the milieu of the professionalization of social and behavioral science in which scientific thought was both shaping and being shaped by the methodologies and organizational forms of advanced state capitalism. The philosophic origins of research in higher education can be traced back to

Aristotle's philosophy of mind, although its contemporary expressions in positivism and hermeneutics are rooted in empiricism and Kantianism.

Kant's Methodology

Despite their many and important differences, particularly in method, empiricism and Kantianism share a similar attitude toward the objective world and a correspondence theory of truth, in which the goal of inquiry is assumed to be the establishment of an identity between thought and the object. Immanuel Kant was the philosopher who conceded the most to empiricism and who was most repulsed by its conclusions, especially in the skepticism pursued by David Hume. Kant could not accept the empiricist route to knowledge nor its assumption that scientific determinism is compatible with personal freedom. John Locke, David Hume, and the positivists who followed them all denied that human actions can ever have the status of uncaused events. All insisted that human actions are subsumable under general scientific laws, no less than natural events. Kant, on the other hand, maintained that there is in human individuals a faculty capable of initiating a new causal series in the world.

In making concessions to the empiricists, and in distancing himself from them, Kant most clearly laid the foundation for the application of scientific knowledge to social life by delineating the boundaries for the noumenal and phenomenal worlds. Necessity, determination and scientific certainty, in Kant's (1998b) formulation, are found in only the phenomenal world, whereas freedom, human agency, and ethical behavior are found in only the noumenal world (Kant, 1998a). For Kant, the attempt to save both science and religion, necessity and freedom, meant that science can know nothing about human freedom nor human values, and that ethics and politics can never be grounded in anything better than the good intentions of individual humans. Thus, pure and practical reason are forever separated in Kant's thought.

Kant is not to be discarded but is to be studied for the clarity with which he saw the problems of empiricism and the alienation of pure and practical reason. However, the philosophic development of almost all educational research stops dead in its tracks with the Kantian alienation of pure and practical reason. The qualitative or interpretive approaches to higher education research are no less captive to the limits of Kantianism, than the quantitative or positivist approaches are captives of empiricism. The distinction between pure and practical reason has been institutionalized theoretically and methodologically in social and behavioral research on the higher learning. As a form of social inquiry, the study of higher education has not progressed beyond Kant because it has not progressed beyond the correspondence theory of truth and a concept of society as Substance.

Hegel's Dialectic

Kant's successor in the German idealist tradition, Georg Wilhelm Friedrich Hegel, was profoundly concerned with the issues Kant articulated. Hegel developed a philosophic position that is both a summation and transcendence of both the empiricist and Kantian traditions on society and on the relationship between thought and the object. Hegel provided a philosophical foundation for transforming our understanding of the alienation of knowledge from human agency, or of pure and practical reason. It is most unfortunate that Dewey, the "scientific" Marxists, and the postmodernists have largely gone unchallenged in the interpretation and judgment of Hegel they have rendered.

A pivotal contribution of Raya Dunayevskaya's study of the Hegelian dialectic is the notion of an "unchained dialectic," which, by insisting that there is no *terminus* to the historical process, shatters the Kantian notion of the eternal separation of pure and practical reason. Her books *Philosophy and Revolution* (1973) and *The Power of Negativity* (2002) are particularly important for understanding Hegel's centrality in social thought. Dunayevskaya emphasized that social inquiry can only transcend Kant's methodology by working through the structure of Hegel's thought and plunging into his Absolutes, unapologetically and unafraid. Otherwise, Hegel is not understood and we have not learned what he has to offer in understanding and transforming ourselves and the world. From Dunayevskaya's perspective, neither Dewey, nor Lukacs, nor Althusser, nor Habermas, nor Marcuse has dealt with Hegel adequately because none explored his Absolutes. Her argument is applicable to discourse on educational research by appreciating Hegel as a critic of the correspondence theory of truth and as a philosopher of liberation. Lenin's (1981) *Conspectus on Hegel's "Science of Logic,"* Fanon's (1967) *Black Skins/White Masks*, and Dunayevskaya's (1973) *Philosophy and Revolution* variously identified the social and analytical relevance of Hegel's Absolutes. Hegel's concept of the Absolute Idea as a critique of the correspondence theory of truth and as a ground for a philosophy of liberation should be brought to the center of discourse on the study of higher education.

The Absolute Idea

Kant refused to speak of pure reason and freedom simultaneously. But, Hegel, the philosopher whose intellectual foundation was the French Revolution, insisted that pure reason and freedom must be spoken of simultaneously. Hegel argued that the ultimate test of knowledge is not in its correspondence to an inert "out there," but in its contribution to human freedom. For Hegel, freedom means that the agent is self-consciously self-determining. No other concept is more central to Hegel's philosophy than his concept of freedom. He referred to "freedom realized" as the absolute end and aim of the world. His political philosophy (Hegel, 1952) is a discussion of freedom as "both the substance of right and its goal," whereas the system of right is the realm of freedom made actual.

Freedom is also the central concept in his philosophy of history: "World history is progress of the consciousness of freedom" (Hegel, 1956, p. 24). Because, in Hegel's view, "Geist" is not merely the human's basic nature, but also the fundamental principle of reality, freedom is the defining characteristic of the most fundamental philosophic category, the Notion. For Hegel (1977), the "Notion" is the principle of freedom, the power of substance self-realized. Hegelian commentators, even critical theorists such as Marcuse, stopped prior to the Doctrine of the Notion, which, in Hegel's system, is merely the threshold of the Absolute. These scholars are still operating within the Kantian separation of necessity and freedom, knowledge and society, pure and practical reason. This realization helps us understand why Marcuse could applaud student, black and women radicals during the 1960s and 1970s, but cannot not reconcile his enthusiasm with his one-dimensionality thesis, which emphasized that such self-conscious, self-determining opposition was impossible in advanced, industrial society.

A similar problem is apparent in Tierney's (1991) concept of critical theory. One of the basic principles he used to differentiate "logical positivism" and "critical theory" is the idea that "critical theory views the production of knowledge as socially and historically determined and as a consequence of power" (p. 6). Although there is ample reason to argue with his assertion that knowledge is socially and historically "determined," the primary focus here is on his failure to situate his concept of critical theory in a sociohistorical context. If knowledge is socially and historically determined, and if it is a consequence of power, how is critical theory possible? Is critical theory also socially and historically determined and a consequence of power? If so, then how can it negate, challenge or propose alternatives to existing social relations in higher education?

If not, then his premise about critical theory cannot be universally valid since it does not apply to itself. In essence, Tierney's concept is that he and those who possess the special ability to theorize critically, somehow stand outside of society and history and that their knowledge is somehow not a consequence of power. This is a Kantian separation between pure and practical reason, not the interaction of the two. Like Marcuse, Tierney argued that critical theorists see the world in pure, undistorted terms, while others are puppets of society, history, and power. The dialectical foundation for critical thought outlined by Hegel challenges these Kantian antinomies and the division of mental and manual labor in society it conceptualizes.

In his discussion of the Absolute Idea in the *Science of Logic*, Hegel (1969) proved himself to be an enemy of methodological systems and distinguishes his concept of the Absolute from that of other philosophers. For Hegel, the Absolute Idea does not refer to any *terminus* to the historical process nor is it a quietistic legitimation of an oppressive Prussian state. For Hegel, it is both a summation of what has transpired historically and a ground for a new human beginning. In the *Science of Logic*, Hegel spent 250 pages separating his dialectic of thought and practice from that of Kant. But the great divide between Hegel and Kant is reached in the final chapter of this work, where we find that not only is the Idea of freedom Absolute, but so is the dialectical Method. This chapter contains some real shockers to anyone who thought that practice and thought would continue on their separate paths.

The very first sentence of the chapter reads: "The Absolute Idea has now turned out to be the identity of the Theoretical and Practical Idea; each of these by itself is one-sided." Neither can pass beyond the contradiction. Anyone who is looking for an absolute end to all contradictions will not find it in Hegel. Hegel stated unequivocally that the "Absolute Idea contains the highest opposition within itself." In the same paragraph, he said that the "Absolute Idea alone is Being, imperishable Life, self-knowing Truth and the whole of Truth." But far from stopping there, he turns to self-conscious self-determination, which is both Method and Idea. "The self-determination, therefore, in which the Idea is, is to hear itself speak."

Hegel's political philosophy, which has been mistakenly thought to be an oblation to the Prussian state, also develops the critical dimensions of the Absolute Idea in the realm of political and social formations. In the *Philosophy of Right*, Hegel (1952) offered what Avineri (1972) called an "oblique critique" of the Prussian state and a statement on the relationship between inquiry and existing regimes. In the Preface to his political philosophy Hegel introduced his famous epigram about the rational and the actual, inquiry and existence: "What is rational is actual and what is actual is rational" (p. 10). This epigram has been taken to reflect Hegel's conservatism. It is assumed to be an argument that existing political and social forms are rational because they are actual. The implications of this interpretation include the idea that it is futile or irrational to challenge or critique the state and the social base it protects.

But Hegel (1952) continued to say that the "great thing" is to apprehend the "infinite wealth of forms, shapes, and appearances" actuality takes once the Idea enters external existence. His discussion produces an epiphenomenal admission about the limits of inquiry,

> Whatever happens, every individual is the child of his time; so philosophy too is its own time apprehended in thoughts. It is just absurd to

fancy that a philosophy can transcend its own contemporary world as it
is to fancy that an individual can overleap his own age. (p. 11)

Hegel's statements supposedly reflect an apparent admission about the
historicity of knowledge and a conservative resignation to the status quo.
However, there is in the preface to *The Philosophy of Right* an important
message about the role of critical inquiry. If philosophy and inquiry cannot
overleap the contemporary world, and if the task of inquiry is to apprehend
the infinite wealth of forms, shapes, and appearances of actuality, then the
role of critical inquiry is to tell existing social and political formations that
their time is up. For researchers on higher education, our ability to comprehend our own world already points to its demise. As Avineri indicated, our
interpretation of the world changes it; our interpretation tells the world that
its historical period is over. From this vantage point, Hegel's argument on
the historicity of knowledge is an intellectual subversion of existing social
and political formations.

The Unchained Dialectic

Progressive educators today are more concerned with the self-determination
of ethnic and linguistic groups, classes and gender, but the goal, human freedom, and "the path of self-construction" by which to achieve it are not
removed from the self-determination of the Idea. From this vantage point,
we can understand that as Hegel spoke of the "Self-Thinking Idea" and the
"Self-Bringing Forth of Liberty" he is not inverting Subject and Substance,
as many Marxists and critical theorists assert. Hegel's philosophic point of
departure was the French Revolution, not the academic study of philosophy.
He consistently argued that philosophy is grounded in sociohistorical
events.

One example of the "Self-Bringing Forth of Liberty" from American
labor history may be the coal miner's strike of 1950 in which workers
protested not only against their bosses but against the government that
ordered them back to work, the union bosses who betrayed them, and the
onset of automated working conditions with the introduction of the continuous miner. In education, one example of the "Self-Bringing Forth of
Liberty" may be the resistance to high-stakes testing. In higher education,
examples of the "Self-Bringing Forth of Liberty" may be the conflict and
struggle over increased accountability, increased faculty workloads, and
increased state intervention into curricular, instructional and administrative issues. Student protests against tuition increases, cuts in financial aid,
and the use of standardized tests in admissions decisions may be other
examples.

One test of the adequacy of the philosophic foundations of inquiry is how we respond to the closing statement of Marx's (1988) essay, "Private Property and Communism," which appears in the *Economic and Philosophic Manuscripts of 1844*: "Communism is the necessary form and the energetic principle of the immediate future, but communism is not as such the goal of human development, the form of human society—which goal is the structure of human society" (p. 114). This statement is frequently left out of analyzes of Marx's early thought, or is explained away as youthful exuberance over Hegel's dialectic. But, Marx, like Hegel, asserts no end to human history, philosophy or inquiry. For Hegel, the Prussian state is not the goal of sociohistorical development. In dialectical thought, history, philosophy and inquiry remain open.

When we replace the word *communism* in the latter half of Marx's quote with words such as *bureaucracy, sexism, racism, capitalism, imperialism*, and *statism* we begin to get a handle on the real lesson Hegel and dialectical thought offer: the dialectic is not a mechanical triad of thesis–antithesis–synthesis, which was never Hegel's nor Marx's formulation anyway. Instead, the dialectic is the ceaseless movement of ideas in human history. There is no end to the development of forms of human thought or human practice.

This is a conception that the work of philosophy, sociology, and inquiry are not done. We do not know all that we need to know either about method or the social relations of higher learning. We cannot understand the totality of history because new forms of liberation and new forms of oppression are always possible. And we need more than empirical observations, intersubjective understandings, or managerial techniques so that trustees and administrators can straighten out the classroom, the administration, society, and the world. The goal of inquiry must be more than developing recommendations to assist university presidents, boards of trustees, and state governments in their control and management of colleges and universities.

The "unchained dialectic" of Hegel, Marx, and Dunayevskaya is pertinent to the critique of higher education research, in as much as it entails a concept of society as Substance and not Subject, and a correspondence theory of truth. An important point of departure for scholars and educators who seek to understand the role of higher education in our contemporary sociohistorical context is to acknowledge both method and society as Subject, not Substance. The methodological challenge is not to generate knowledge that can be uncritically applied by administrators and policymakers to fix the world, but to identify and learn from those forms of social and educational practice that are self-consciously self-determining.

REFERENCES

Antonio, R. (1981). Immanent critique as the core of critical theory: Its origins and development in Hegel, Marx and contemporary thought. *British Journal of Sociology, 32*, 330–345.

Antonio, R. (1983). The origin, development and contemporary status of critical theory. *The Sociological Quarterly, 24*, 325–351.

Avineri, S. (1972). *Hegel's theory of the modern state.* London: Cambridge University Press.

Bensimon, E., Neumann, A., & Birnbaum, R. (1989). *Making sense of administrative leadership: The "L" word in higher education.* Washington, DC: The George Washington University.

Birnbaum, R. (1988). *How colleges work: The cybernetics of academic organization and leadership.* San Francisco: Jossey-Bass.

Dunayevskaya, R. (1973). *Philosophy and revolution: From Hegel to Sartre and from Marx to Mao.* New York: Delacorte Press.

Dunayevskaya, R. (2002). *The power of negativity: Selected writings on the dialectic in Hegel and Marx.* Lanham, MD: Lexington Books.

Fanon, F. (1967). *Black skin, white masks.* New York: Grove Press.

Gramsci, A. (1971). *Prison notebooks.* New York: International Publishers.

Habermas, J. (1971). *Knowledge and human interests.* Boston: Beacon Press.

Hegel, G. W. F. (1952). *The philosophy of right.* London: Oxford University Press.

Hegel, G. W. F. (1956). *The philosophy of history.* New York: Dover Publications.

Hegel, G. W. F. (1969). *Science of logic.* Amherst, NY: Humanity Press.

Hegel, G. W. F. (1977). *Phenomenology of spirit.* London: Oxford University Press.

Horkheimer, M. (1972). *Critical theory.* New York: The Seabury Press.

Kant, I. (1998a). *Critique of practical reason.* Cambridge: Cambridge University Press.

Kant, I. (1998b). *Critique of pure reason.* Cambridge: Cambridge University Press.

Keller, G. (1985). Trees without fruit. *Change, 17*(1), 7–10.

Kezar, A., & Eckel, E. (Eds.). (2000). *Making higher education research useful.* New Directions for Higher Education. San Francisco: Jossey-Bass.

Lenin, V. I. (1981). *Philosophic notebooks* (Vol. 38). Moscow: Progress Publishers.

Leslie, D. (2002). Thinking big: The state of scholarship on higher education. In W. Tierney & L. Hagedorn (Eds.), *From research to policy to practice to research* (pp. 1–7). Los Angeles: Center for Higher Education Policy Analysis, University of Southern California.

Lincoln, Y. (1991). Advancing a critical agenda. In W. Tierney (Ed.), *Culture and ideology in higher education: Advancing a critical agenda* (pp. 3–16). New York: Praeger Publishers.

Lukacs, G. (1971). *History and class consciousness: Studies in Marxist dialectics.* Cambridge, MA: MIT Press.

Marcuse, H. (1964). *One-dimensional man.* Boston: Beacon Press.

Marx, K. (1954). *Capital, volume 1.* Moscow: Progress Publishers.

Marx, K. (1988). *Economic and philosophic manuscripts 1844.* Amherst, NY: Prometheus Books.

McCarthy, T. (1978). *The critical theory of Jürgen Habermas.* Cambridge, MA: MIT Press.

Mills, C. W. (1940). Situated actions and vocabularies of motive. *American Sociological Review, 5,* 904–913.

Neumann, A. (2000). The social construction of resource stress. In C. Brown (Ed.), *Organization and governance in higher education* (pp. 389–405). Boston: Pearson Custom Publishing.

Peterson, M. (2000). Emerging developments in postsecondary organization theory and research: Fragmentation or integration. In C. Brown (Ed.), *Organization and governance in higher education* (pp. 71–82). Boston: Pearson Custom Publishing.

Rhoades, G. (2000). Who's doing it right? Strategic activity in public research universities. *The Review of Higher Education, 24*(1), 41–66.

Schroyer, T. (1973). *The critique of domination: The origins and development of critical theory.* Boston: Beacon Press.

Tierney, W. (1991). Border crossings: Critical theory and the study of higher education. In W. Tierney (Ed.), *Culture and ideology in higher education: Advancing a critical agenda* (pp. 3–16). New York: Praeger.

Tierney, W. (1993). *Building communities of difference: Higher education in the twenty-first century.* Westport, CT: Bergin & Garvey.

Wilms, W., & Zell, D. (2003). Accelerating change in the academy: Balancing new demands while protecting core values. *On the Horizon, 11*(3), 16–22.

10

Marketizing Higher Education

Neoliberal Strategies and Counterstrategies

Les Levidow

> *Underlying the market orientation of tertiary education is the ascendance, almost worldwide, of market capitalism and the principles of neoliberal economics.*
>
> —Johnstone, Bruce, Arora, and Experton (1998)

MARKETIZATION AGENDAS

Higher education has special stakes for capitalist rule. Universities define the skills of professional workers for labor markets, reinforce ruling ideologies, and represent the needs of the state and industry as those of society. Despite that prevalent role, students and staff often succeed in creating spaces for critical citizenship, even for overt challenges to capitalist agendas.

That tension has been played out on several fronts. Student numbers have increased, whereas teaching has been underresourced and so appears as an "inefficiency" problem, to be solved by standardizing curricula. Knowledge has been packaged in textbook-type formats, so that students become customers for products. Moreover, higher education has become more synonymous with training for employability, for example, skills to solve problems, which are set by one's superiors. As a U.S. critic once remarked, "the various universities are competitors for the traffic in merchantable instruction" (Veblen, 1918, p. 65).

Recent tendencies have been called *academic capitalism*. Although university staff are still largely state funded, they are increasingly driven into entrepreneurial competition for external funds. Under such pressure, staff devise "institutional and professorial market or market-like efforts to secure external monies" (Slaughter & Leslie, 1997).

Beyond simply generating more income, higher education has become a target for marketization agendas since the 1980s. Universities are urged to adopt commercial models of knowledge, skills, curriculum, finance, accounting, and management organization. They must do so in order to deserve state funding and to protect themselves from competitive threats, we are told. These measures threaten what many people value in universities (e.g., the scope for critical analysis and broad social access), and thus provoke new forms of resistance. An extreme case was the 1999–2000 student occupation of the Autonomous National University of Mexico, which became a test case for potential privatization of all public services.

Recent conflicts over educational values have been amplified by the emergence of information and communication technology (ICT). ICT is designed and used in ways that can favor some agendas rather than others, although the precise link remains open to struggle. In the ruling ideology, marketization is attributed to the socioeconomic imperatives of ICT.

Those developments can be analyzed within wider neoliberal strategies for reshaping society in the image of a marketplace. The neoliberal project seeks to undo past collective gains that limited labor exploitation and maintained public goods, instead fragmenting people into vendors and consumers. As this chapter argues, neoliberal strategies for higher education have the following features:

- Marketization is justified as self-defense by dealing with all relevant constituencies as business relationships.
- Educational efficiency, accountability, and quality are redefined in market terms.
- Courses are recast as instructional commodities.

- Student–teacher relationships are mediated by the consumption and production of things (e.g., software).

Neoliberal strategies have been devised for marketizing higher education on a global scale. Each region provides an extreme case and component of more general tendencies. These must be analyzed globally in order to develop effective counterstrategies and alternatives. Toward that aim, this chapter has the following structure:

- The "information society" as a paradigm for ICT.
- The World Bank "reform agenda" for the self-financing of higher education.
- Africa, where higher education is being forcibly marketized and standardized through financial dependence.
- North America, where some universities attempt to become global vendors of instructional commodities.
- Europe, where state bodies adopt industry agendas of labor flexibilization under the guise of technological progress.
- United Kingdom, where ICT design becomes a terrain for contending educational agendas; and implications for global counter-marketization strategies.

INFORMATION SOCIETY PARADIGM

Central to the neoliberal project is the information society. According to this paradigm, the management, quality, and speed of information become essential for economic competitiveness. Dependent on highly skilled labor, we are told that ICT will be used in order to increase productivity and to provide new services.

A related concept is the "knowledge economy." This suggests that greater "human capital" will be necessary to enhance worker creativity, to use information productively, to raise the efficiency of the service economy, to achieve economic competitiveness, and thus to maintain employment. The human capital concept individualizes skills that can exist only in a social collectivity or network (for a critique, see Fine, 2000).

In the knowledge economy, however, jobs will have a greater requirement for "transferable skills" and cognitive capacities. Labor markets will face a skills shortage, and workers will need reskilling so that they remain flexibly employable in a labor market beset by insecurity. Therefore, societies must invest more in human capital.

Yet there is evidence that jobs are following contrary trends. "Knowledge" workers face an overload of information to evaluate, spend more time dealing with it, and thus may have even lower efficiency than before. An information overload may even reduce capacity for new ideas. In any case, it is difficult to demonstrate such input–output correlations in practice (Garnham, 2000)

Moreover, job specifications have generally not increased the requirement for cognitive capacities. Nevertheless, many employers have required workers to have qualifications beyond those needed to carry out the job. As one U.K. student lamented, "You have to work harder to get a worse and worse job" (quoted in Ainley & Bailey, 1997).

This qualification inflation is due to excess supply rather than any inherent demands of the job. In the United States, for example, skill levels have risen while wage levels have fallen for comparable jobs (Gottschalk, 1998). Indeed, job structures often reduce knowledge to information processing, rather than require the skill of evaluating information, much less producing new knowledge.

Further to neoliberal ideology, universities must raise their own productivity in order to survive. They must package knowledge, deliver flexible education through ICT, provide adequate training for "knowledge workers," and produce more of them at lower unit cost. Although this scenario portrays universities as presciently guiding social change, there is evidence of a reverse tendency: They are becoming subordinate to corporate-style managerialism and income maximization. For neoliberal strategies, the real task is not to enhance skills but rather to control labor costs in the labor-intensive service sector (e.g., education; Garnham, 2000).

ICT usage can define skills and restructure education in various ways. It can help to democratize educational access (e.g., by helping students to learn at their own pace, or by creating "virtual communities" of interest in particular issues). Alternatively, it can help to commodify and standardize learning (e.g., by extending the authoritative approach of textbook-based knowledge; Johnston, 1999).

According to some educators who design Internet-based courses, their use can lower personal contact and thus reduce student motivation: "Many students need the personal interaction." Thanks to ICT, however, "We have cleverer ways in which we can search for information, but it still needs to be filtered, sifted," that is, interpreted (interviews cited in Newman & Johnson, 1999). This illustrates a long-standing issue, although rarely debated as such: how to define the societal problems for which information should be sought and evaluated, and therefore how to design technology.

Indeed, computer systems are designed by selecting a metaphor (rather than others) and translating it into hardware or software: "And this is where technology can become ideological: if you believe that information technology as such inevitably brings markets, or hierarchies, or freedom, or modularity, or conflict, or God-like control over human affairs, then you may not even recognize that you have choices" (Agre, 1999).

In such a way, the information society paradigm plays an ideological role. Some current tendencies are projected into an inevitable future, to which we must adapt—or else suffer. That future is represented as an inherent property of technology. Relationships between people take the form of relationships between "transferable skills" and ICT, for example.

In that vein, the information society has similarities with capitalist ideology in general. Through commodity exchange, social relations are actively reified as relations between things. "To the producers, the social relations between their private labors *appear as what they are*, i.e., they do not appear as direct social relations between persons in their work, but rather as material relations between persons and social relations between things" (Marx, 1976, p. 166, italics added). This appearance may seem natural in capitalist society, yet it is always an unstable result of attempts at extending commodity exchange to more areas of social activity.

As another pervasive feature of capitalist society, people's knowledge is codified and embedded in technologies. As human qualities take the fetishized form of properties of things, those things acquire human-like qualities (e.g., smart weapons, environmentally clean products, precise techniques, efficient technologies, etc.). This fetishism is not merely a false appearance; it is a real material process of investing qualities in things.

Like commodity exchange, efficiency too can be analyzed as a class relation. According to Herbert Marcuse (1978), "rational, 'value-free' technology is the separation of man from the means of production and his subordination to technical efficiency and necessity—all this within the framework of private enterprise" (p. 222). Modern bureaucracy homogenizes diverse, heterogenous qualities into universally comparable ones, thus allowing social qualities to be quantified. This process is "the precondition of calculable *efficiency*—of universal efficiency" (p. 205).

As Marcuse further argued, technology is specially designed for such purposes: "Specific purposes and interests . . . enter the very construction of the technical apparatus" (p. 224). Through pretense of neutral technical efficiency, social values are both embedded and concealed in technology. As various critics have argued, technologies have been specially designed for managing, disciplining, exploiting, and/or expelling human labor.

We can ask: Efficiency for what kind of society? "Information" for whose interests and control? With such questions in mind, key terms can be analyzed as both ideological and material. They provide weapons to naturalize, impose, and legitimize a future scenario of marketizing social relations.

World Bank "Reform Agenda"

In the neoliberal worldview, trade liberalization generates a virtuous circle of market access, technology, efficiency, and so on. For example:

Markets promote efficiency through competition and the division of labour—the specialisation that allows people and economies to do what they do best. Global markets offer greater opportunity for people to tap into more and larger markets around the world. It means that they can have access to more capital flows, technology, cheaper imports, and export markets. (International Monetary Fund [IMF], 2000)

On the contrary, as many critics have argued, trade liberalization is generally designed to serve capitalist profitability. It throws people into more intense competition with each other on a global scale, thus preventing people from deciding collectively "what they do best" and what kind of economic relations to develop with each other. Prime agents are the IMF and World Bank, which elaborate the strategies of their paymasters in the dominant Organization for Economic Co-operation and Development (OECD) countries. In the neoliberal project, U.S. capital serves both as a prime driving force and as a model for its imitators or partners elsewhere.

For several years, the World Bank has been promoting a "reform agenda" on higher education. Its key features are privatization, deregulation, and marketization. According to a World Bank report,

The reform agenda . . . is oriented to the market rather than to public ownership or to governmental planning and regulation. Underlying the market orientation of tertiary education is the ascendance, almost worldwide, of market capitalism and the principles of neo-liberal economics. (Johnstone et al., 1998, quoted in CAUT, 1998b)

From a neoliberal standpoint, what is the problem—and opportunity? As a private good, higher education is in limited supply, not demanded by all, and is available for a price. Consumers (business and industry) are "reasonably well informed," whereas the providers (administrators and faculty) are "often ill informed—conditions which are ideal for market forces to operate." Fulfilling the demand therefore requires measures to make higher education completely self-financing.

Having defined the problem in this way, the report identifies the traditional university and its faculty members as the main obstacles to a solution:

Radical change, or restructuring, of an institution of higher education means either fewer and/or different faculty, professional staff, and support workers. This means lay-offs, forced early retirements, or major retraining and reassignment, as in: the closure of inefficient or ineffective institutions; the merger of quality institutions that merely lack a critical mass of operations to make them cost-effective; and the radical alteration of the mission and production function of an institution—which means radically altering who the faculty are, how they behave,

the way they are organized, and the way they work and are compensat-
ed. (Johnstone et al., 1998)

This diagnosis identifies teachers and their traditional protections as the
obstacle to market-based efficiencies. In its future scenario, higher education
would become less dependent on teachers' skills. Students would become
customers or clients. As the implicit aim, private investors would have
greater opportunities to profit from state expenditure, while influencing the
form and content of education. Business and university administrators would
become the main partnership, redefining student–teacher relationships.

The World Bank report soon became a political weapon for recasting
academic freedom as a commitment to neoliberal futures. University administrations have sought to characterize academic freedom as a duty "to
uphold the balance" between "the spiraling demand for higher education on
the one hand, and the globalization of economic, financial and technical
change on the other." At a UNESCO conference in October 1998, this conflict was ultimately fudged by declaring that faculty members should enjoy
"academic freedom and autonomy conceived as a set of rights and duties,
while being fully responsible and accountable to society" (cited in CAUT,
1998a).

Presumably, the university administrations meant responsibility to a
neoliberal globalization agenda, not to the forces resisting it. Indeed, academic "accountability" often means subordination to accountancy techniques. In response to these attacks, professional societies have defended
academic freedom as a right of free expression, as if it could mean autonomy from all political-economic pressures. When academics pose research
questions or set curricula, however, these cannot be entirely autonomous
from the wider struggle over public resources, ruling ideologies, and class
interests.

Although the World Bank agenda has little support among educators,
some aspects may be implemented. Indeed, it may describe proposals that
are being driven by wider political-economic forces and already implemented around the world. We need to analyze their various practical forms, how
they may complement each other, and how they appropriate ICTs. Let us
survey Africa, North America, and Europe as different examples and components of a neoliberal globalization project.

AFRICA: STRUCTURAL ADJUSTMENT PROGRAMS
FOR RECOLONIZATION

Higher education has become a casualty of the overall neoliberal policies
imposed on highly indebted countries of the south. By the late 1970s, these

countries faced a "balance of payments" deficit for many reasons (e.g., because their main exports suffered a world decline in prices, while oil imports became more expensive). As these countries could no longer repay even the interest on their national debt, their currency lost value, and they were denied credit for further imports.

The IMF and World Bank turned these national debts into an opportunity to impose structural adjustment programs (SAPs) in the 1980s. Indebted governments were required to reduce spending, to privatize industry and services, to cheapen labor, to open up markets to multinational companies, to relax controls on capital movements, to weaken environmental and labor protection laws, to devalue their currencies and so on.

"Growth-oriented loans" were granted to countries that accepted those "conditionalities." According to the World Bank, such measures would help governments to reduce budget deficits, reduce the balance-of-payments deficit, control inflation, and thus create conditions for resumed growth. In practice, local industries were driven out of business, many jobs were lost, rural people lost their access to cultivable land, and fees were imposed for health and education services. The main "growth" has come from people working more in order to pay more than before for goods or services—apart from the "growth" of multinational companies buying up local assets on the cheap (see examples in FGS, 2000).

Consequently, higher education has suffered in all Southern countries, especially in Africa, which was singled out for special treatment. According to World Bank reports on African countries, investment in higher education was benefiting mainly the social elites there, and it had a lower social return than investment in primary education. As yet another conditionality, therefore, they were told to reduce funding of higher education, in the name of both egalitarian and efficiency criteria. Thanks to SAPs, governments would have an opportunity to "increase the efficiency of resource use," declared World Bank consultants.

That attack had different motivations than the publicly stated ones. African governments were regarded as too weak to discipline labor for foreign investors and thus as inadequate managers of public services. More importantly, university faculty and students there were foremost critics of SAPs, often catalyzing wider political opposition. In many cases, universities were invaded by repressive forces or simply shut down (Federici, Caffentzis, & Alidou, 2000).

Given the great resistance, the neoliberal strategy was to create means by which African universities could be intellectually recolonized, in at least two senses. The general effect of SAPs, combined with tuition fees, effectively limited university access to an elite—far more so than beforehand. Eventually, the World Bank acknowledged the worsening quality of African higher education, although not its own responsibility for this outcome. As a remedy, the World Bank promoted "capacity building" there through direct funding. Through this financial dependence, African universities could be pressurized to change their educational content along lines acceptable to the World Bank (Federici et al., 2000).

Under neoliberal constraints, then, universities substitute new staff, standardize pedagogical materials, and marginalize local knowledges. Meanwhile, governments repress any resistance such "reforms." Moreover, these changes potentially create customers for global educational commodities—hardly the sort of "growth" that was promised. Within Africa and elsewhere, resistance has been publicized by solidarity activists through the Campaign for Academic Freedom in Africa.

NORTH AMERICA:
INSTRUCTIONAL COMMODITIES

In North America, many universities have adopted entrepreneurial practices. They act not only as business partners, but also as businesses in themselves. They develop profit-making activities through university resources, faculty, and student labor (Ovetz, 1996).

Within an entrepreneurial agenda, universities have developed online educational technology (i.e., electronic forms of course materials). Of course, this medium could be used to enhance access to quality education, and to supplement face-to-face contact, as some European universities have been doing for a long time. In North America, however, the aims were clearly different (namely, to commodify and standardize education).

Those aims have been resisted by students and teachers. For example, in 1997, the University of California, Los Angeles, established an Instructional Enhancement Initiative that required computer Web sites for all its arts and sciences courses. Its aims were linked with a for-profit business for online courses, in partnership with high-tech companies. Similar initiatives at York University led to a strike by staff, backed by the students. They raised the slogan, "the classroom versus the boardroom" (Noble, 1998).

What problem was the new technology supposed to solve? After university rules were changed to permit profit-making activities, their research role was commodified. Substantial resources were shifted from teaching to research activities that were expected to result in patents and royalties. With less staff time devoted to teaching, student–teacher ratios increased, thus increasing the burden on them both. This result of profit-seeking was represented as an inherent problem of educational inefficiency.

From that standpoint, the logical solution is to increase efficiency by standardizing course materials. Once lectures are submitted to administrators and posted on web pages, these materials can be merchandised to other universities. Better yet, the course writing can be outsourced on contract to non-university staff. By transferring control to administrators, the technology can be designed to discipline, deskill, and/or displace teachers' labor.

This approach changes the role of students, who become consumers of instructional commodities. Student–teacher relationships are reified as relationships between consumers and providers of things. This marginalizes any learning partnership between them as people.

Students readily become objects of market research. In Canada, for example, universities have been given royalty-free licenses to Virtual U software in return for providing data on its use to the vendors. When students enroll in courses using this software, they are officially designated as "experimental subjects," who grant permission for the vendor to receive all their "computer-generated usage data" (Noble, 1998).

A marketization model can be extended to sell courses, potentially to anyone in the world. Even third parties can sell new commodities that redefine educational skills. For example, by 1998, IBM's Lotus Corporation had already sold its Total Campus Option software to more than 1 million students. The company hoped that these future workers would thereby acquire "a Lotus brand preference and relevant skills: the campus is the starting point of the sales cycle to the corporate world with whom we conduct business."

EUROPE: ICT FOR FLEXIBLE LEARNING

The European education debate has been ideologically framed by the supposed imperatives of an information society. This is conceptualized differently by "market" models versus "social" models of Europe (de Miranda & Kristiansen, 2000). So far, dominant has been a neoliberal agenda of individual flexibilized learning for labor-market needs.

European Round Table Agenda

A neoliberal agenda has been promoted effectively by the European Round Table (ERT) of Industrialists since the 1980s (Balanyá et al., 2000). Its problem definitions have been adopted by leading politicians and European Union officials. In particular, the ERT has sought to change the form and content of education.

The ERT has regarded education and training as "strategic investments vital for the future success of industry." European business "clearly requires an accelerated reform" of educational programs. Unfortunately, however, "industry has only a very weak influence over the programs taught," and teachers "have an insufficient understanding of the economic environment, business and the notion of profit" (ERT, 1989; cf. ERT, 1998).

They further argued: "As industrialists, we believe that educators themselves should be free to conduct the same kind of internal searches for efficiency without interference or undue pressures exerted on them." European industry has responded to globalization, but "the world of education has been slow to respond," the authors lamented. As a remedy, "partnerships should be formed between schools and local business" (ERT, 1995). More recently they have promoted ICT as an essential learning tool—in schools today and for work tomorrow. As the key virtues cited, ICT opens up the world of knowledge, allows individual enquiry, and powerfully motivates learning (ERT, 1997).

ICT has a more specific role in the neoliberal business agenda, as critics have argued (Hatcher & Hirtt, 1999). First, it facilitates the individualized and flexibilized learning that is required for the modern worker, who must become individually responsible for managing his or her own human capital in the workplace. Second, ICT diminishes the role of the teacher—a desirable change (e.g., because teachers have "an insufficient understanding" of business needs, and because their present role hinders "internal searches for efficiency").

European Commission: Industry Needs

As president of the European Commission (EC), Jacques Delors basically accepted a neoliberal diagnosis in his 1993 White Paper on "Growth, Competitiveness, Employment." Identifying the future as an information society, it counseled adaptation to inexorable competitive pressures: "The pressure of the market-place is spreading and growing, obliging businesses to exploit every opportunity available to increase productivity and efficiency. Structural adaptability is becoming a major prerequisite for economic success," for example by disseminating the skills essential for ICTs (CEC, 1993, pp. 92–93).

Moreover, the paper mandated the public authorities "to remove the remaining regulatory obstacles to the development of new markets." Although not specifically mentioning education, it welcomed marketization of public services:

> The ordinary citizen can have access to "public services" on an individual basis, and these will be invoiced on the basis of the use made of them. Transferring such services to the market-place will lead to new private-sector offers of services and numerous job-creation opportunities. (CEC, 1993, p. 94)

Within that framework, EC documents and official speeches put forward arguments similar to the ERT's. According to the chief of the directorate-general, which funds research, the ICT market is "too weak and penalizes our industry." Therefore, support is necessary to "give our market the dimension which our industry needs" (Cresson, 1995). With such language, society's needs are either ignored or else are equated with industry's needs.

Soon the supposed threat was made more explicit: "It is doubtful if our continent will keep hold of the industrial place it has achieved in this new market of multimedia if our systems of education and training do not rapidly keep pace" (CEC, 1996). For the solution, government must subsidize the European ICT industry.

Moreover, official documents foresee and welcome a decline in the dominant role of educational institutions:

> Even within the schools and colleges, the greater degree of individualization of modes of learning—which are flexible and demand-led—can be considered as supplanting the formulas that are too heavy and dominated by the provider. It announces the consequent decline in the role of the teacher, which is also demonstrated by the development of new sources of learning, notably by the role of ICT and of human resources other than teachers. (CEC, 1998)

Through such language, the empowerment of vendors and business partners is represented as greater freedom for students. A student–teacher learning relationship is potentially replaced by an individual consumer–producer relationship.

UNITED KINGDOM: UNIVERSITY AS A BORDERLESS BUSINESS

As the vanguard of the neoliberal project in Europe, the United Kingdom epitomizes pressure toward marketizing higher education. As academics there have found since the 1980s, many developments have "eroded the protection from pressures to render their work more commensurable with the commodity form of value" (Wilmott, 1995, p. 995).

The government has pressed for a substantial increase in student numbers, while providing little increase in funds. Under pressure from the Research Assessment Exercise, many university departments have shifted resources from teaching to research, while seeking more research funds from industry. For both those reasons, there have been fewer resources for student–teacher contact, and thus greater pressure to standardize curricula and assessment criteria. Similar pressures come from formal assessment exercises that require teachers to produce explicit "learning aims and outcomes."

Students have become more subject to accountancy versions of educational values. In the late 1990s, the government abolished maintenance grants for most students and introduced tuition fees. As these changes led students into greater debt than before, they felt under pressure to choose academic programs that would lead to more highly-paid jobs, rather than arts or humanities programs, for example. Student protests have opposed tuition fees, while linking this burden to more general dependence on private finance. For example, "In providing this funding, business is assuming more direct and indirect control of our education system. . . . Students should not be forced to choose on the basis of what [courses] businesses are prepared to make available" (CFE, 2000).

U.K. marketization agendas link two business meanings of flexibility. First, student-customers (or their business sponsors) seek learning for flexible adaptation to labor-market needs (e.g., through "transferable skills" for employability). Second, universities face threats from global competitors that flexibly design and sell courses according to consumer demand.

For many years, such a competitive threat has been linked with ICTs. "In due course, just-in-time electronic education, delivered to your living room by commercial companies, will undermine the most hallowed names in higher education" (Prowse, 1995, p. 16). As an Australian vice-chancellor warned his U.K. counterparts, non-universities will provide electronic courses, offer degrees, and not bother with being accredited, "thus competing with universities in the education market" (cited in McLeod, 2000). To protect themselves, they must further commodify educational goods as individual learning packages.

Taking that logic further, one neoliberal militant has declared: "Higher education is now a no-value commodity unrelated to real costs and no basis whatsoever for an effective and efficient business . . . the future is always best left in the hands of discerning customers close to the marketplace" (Hill, 1999). Again, university corporatization is represented as greater freedom for the student as customer.

According to the U.K.'s committee of university executives, the solution is to abolish borders between the university and business, as well as those between domestic and international "markets" for educational goods. The executives promote internet-based delivery as a key means to become a "borderless business." Going further than the ERT diagnosis, they describe the university as already a business, albeit a deficient one which must be fixed according to corporate principles:

> [Universities must create] new systems of operation which disaggregate function, increase specialisation and where outsourcing is a strong fea-

ture. It follows that universities need to give priority to identifying their core business, niche opportunities and specialist functions . . . (e.g.) consistent delivery through a customer-focused approach to education and training; a widening of educational values to include company certification, learning outcomes relevant to the workplace, personal development and flexibility. (CVCP & HEFCE, 2000)

According to the executives' chief, Professor Howard Newby (1999), universities "are an integral part of the knowledge-based economy," thus echoing a neoliberal paradigm. "At present we seem to be rather like the British motor industry in the 1960s—on the brink of participating in a global market, but poorly organized to take advantage of the opportunities available." He identifies changes in undergraduate delivery: from a "just-in-case" general intellectual training, to a more flexible "just-in-time" ethos, and then to "just-for-you" forms of learning.

Newby emphasized opportunities as much as threats. In his account, critical analytical skills are to be supplanted by lifelong adjustment to the needs of a flexibilized labor market. Extending the business logic, he advocates government investment in higher education as "a sector that is absolutely central to the development of the U.K. as a prosperous and competitive knowledge-based economy." He also advocates performance-related pay in order to modernize "our human resources management."

Thus, educational dividends are to be quantified as human capital. Once the "investment" metaphor is reified, it can become literal. Universities may be held accountable for delivering the goods in measurable terms (Demeritt, 2000, p. 309).

In planning an electronic university, some educators emphasize that high quality cannot be achieved at low cost. Partly for this reason, many U.K. universities have formed consortia for jointly providing and evaluating prospective course material, so that they do not compete among themselves for students. At the same time, a private-sector partner will handle "the commercial aspects of content procurement to match demand," among other aspects (McLeod, 2000). Companies may play a role in defining students as "market demand" for some types of content rather than others. Such arrangements readily conflate the needs of business and society (e.g., through "flexible learning" for the labor market).

Electronic media have a double-edged potential. They can broaden access to quality material and social networks that enhance critical citizenship, provided that the design includes resources for creative student–teacher and student–student interaction. Given the political will, argues one academic, scholarly values "may survive in the multi-media environment. But the tension between digitized means and these values may sharpen as learning becomes more commodified" (Harris, 2000). The effect on education depends on social design of electronic media.

CONCLUSION: WHAT GLOBAL COUNTERSTRATEGIES?

In order to develop effective counterstrategies, it is necessary to analyze the various forms of marketization.

Marketization Strategies

Marketization strategies should be understood as both ideological and material at the same time. As analyzed earlier, here are some key features follow.

Efficiency As Progress. In neoliberal ideology, employment insecurity is attributed to a deficiency of human capital appropriate for the information society. This problem is cited to justify pedagogical changes for adapting students to labor-market needs. Educational "reforms" are presented as universal progress on grounds that they enhance efficiency, extend access, flexibly customize the content for individual needs, facilitate learning through ICT, provide accountability to students and society, yield a better return on state investment, and so on. These benefits are to be measured according to human capital criteria, or even according to money transactions. Whether they are literal or metaphorical, accountancy methods define the efficiency of educational progress, thus naturalizing marketization.

Commodification. Prospective students are represented as customers/markets in order to justify commodifying educational services. Knowledge becomes a product for individual students to consume, rather than a collaborative process for students and teachers. Individualized learning both promotes and naturalizes lifelong re-skilling for a flexibilized, fragmented, insecure labor market. By standardizing course materials, moreover, administrators can reduce teachers to software-writers or even replace them with subcontractors. Through ICT, neoliberal agendas take the apparently neutral form of greater access and flexible delivery. In all these ways, student–teacher relationships are reified as relations between things (e.g., between consumers and providers of software).

Globalization. A global competitive threat and opportunity is invoked to justify commodifying all institutional arrangements. People are actively linked around the world through new market relations—as business partners, competitors, patrons, clients, customers, assessor-consultants, and so on. This neoliberal internationalism is promoted within and across countries. As SAP conditionalities forcibly marketize and standardize higher education in Third World countries, people there may become more willing customers for instructional commodities elsewhere (e.g., through distance education). Perhaps as a self-fulfilling prophecy, this marketization intensi-fies (or even creates) the competitive pressures from which universities needed protection in the first place.

Counterstrategies

In response, what counterstrategies are being developed? As a defensive approach, teachers' organizations have re-asserted their professional prerog-atives as experts in educational content, and they have defended academic freedom against state interference disguised as societal "responsibilities." Students have opposed plans to replace human contact with software prod-ucts, while demanding educational access as a right rather than a commodity. More imaginative efforts will be needed to counter the neoliberal agenda.

Demonstrating Links Among Various Measures. Marketization meas-ures extend far beyond formal requirements of SAPs. The pressures take more subtle forms (e.g., ideological language, funding priorities, public–pri-vate partnerships, tuition fees, cost–benefit analysis, performance indicators, curriculum changes, new technology), which often conceal the ultimate implications. Critics need to demonstrate how all these aspects are linked, how they change the content of academic work and learning, and how they arise from efforts to discipline labor for capital, as part of a global agenda.

Linking Resistances Across Constituencies and Places. Neoliberal strate-gies are turning us all into fragments of a business plan (e.g., competitors, partners, customers, etc.). In response, we need an international network for several purposes: (a) to link all targets of the neoliberal attack worldwide, (b) to circulate analyses of anti-marketization struggles, (c) to enhance solidari-ty efforts, and (d) to turn ourselves into collective subjects of resistance and learning for different futures. Such networks need to span all relevant con-stituencies (teachers, students, nongovernmental organizations), as well as the geographical regions that are supposedly competing with each other.

De-Reifying Information and Communication Technology (ICT). ICTs can be designed in ways that either facilitate a marketization agenda (e.g., by reifying student–teacher relations) or else hinder marketization (e.g., by enhancing critical debate among students and with teachers). In that vein, we need to distinguish between various potential designs for ICT, in order to dereify them as social relations. For example, computer-supported coopera-tive learning techniques are being developed to retain the collective aspects of learning at a distance. Although ICTs are widely used for distributing critical analyses, we need to ensure that these are included and used imagi-natively in accredited courses.

Developing Alternatives. It is inadequate simply to oppose marketization or to counterpose whatever existed beforehand. Resistance would be strengthened by developing alternative pedagogies that enhance critical citizenship, for example, debate over the collective problem definitions of society (e.g., Hill, 1999; McLaren, 2000). If we advocate educational methods and content along those lines, then we can link academic freedom with responsibility to public debate over potential and desirable futures.

ACKNOWLEDGEMENTS

My interest in these issues was stimulated by "Reclaim our Education", a conference of the Campaign for Free Education in August 2000 at the University of East London. This conference led me to emphasize higher education in a later talk, "Neoliberal Technologies and Collective Resistance", at the INPEG Counter-Summit (Initiative against Economic Globalization), in September 2000 in Prague, just before the IMF–World Bank meeting there. I would like to thank the organizers for the opportunity of presenting my ideas there. For helpful comments on the text, I would like to thank Liz Delowee, Anne Gray, Alv de Miranda, David Harvie, David Margolies, Korinna Patelis and Glenn Rikowski.

REFERENCES

Agre, P. E. (1999). The distances of education, *Academe 85*(5), 37–41. Retrieved from http://dlis.gseis.ucla.edu/pagre

Ainley, P., & Bailey, B. (1997). *The business of learning: Staff and student experiences of further education in the 1990s.* London: Cassell.

Balanyá, B., Doherty, A., Hoedeman, O., Ma'anit, A., Wessel, E., & Wesselius, E. (2000). *Europe Inc.: Regional & global restructuring and the rise of corporate power.* London: Pluto Press.

Campaign for Free Education (CFE). (2000). *Winning the arguments. A briefing by the campaign for free education.* Retrieved from http://members.xoom.com/nus_cfe,%20email%20cfe@gn.apc.org

Canadian Association of University Teachers (CAUT) (1998a). *UNESCO declaration puts academic freedom at risk.* Retrieved from http://www.caut.ca/English/CAUTframe.html

Canadian Association of University Teachers (CAUT) (1998b). *World Bank promotes its agenda in Paris.* Retrieved from http://www.caut.ca/English/Bulletin/98_nov/lead.htm

Commission of the European Communities (CEC). (1993). Growth, competitiveness, employment: The challenges and ways forward into the 21st century. *Bulletin of the European Communities* (Suppl. 6/93). Brussels: Commission of the European Communities.

Commission of the European Communities (CEC). (1996). *Rapport du Groupe de Reflexion sur l'Éducation et la Formation, 'Accomplir Europe par l'Éducation et la Formation* [Achieve Europe through education and training]. Brussels: Commission of the European Communities.

Commission of the European Communities (CEC). (1998). L'apprentisage de la Citoyenneté Active. Brussels: Commission of the European Communities.

Committee of Vice-Chancellors and Principals (CVCP) & Higher Education Funding Council for England (HEFCE). (2000). *The business of higher education: UK perspectives*. London: Committee of Vice-Chancellors and Principals. Retrieved from http://www.cvcp.ac.uk and http://www.hefce.ac.uk

Cresson, E. (1995, March 3). Speech on Socrates programme, Tours.

de Miranda, A., & Kristiansen, M. (2000, December 1–3). *Technological determinism and ideology: The European Union and the information society*. Paper presented at Policy Agendas for Sustainable Technological Innovation, POSTI 3 conference, London. Retrieved from http://www.esst.uio.no/posti/workshops/miranda.html

Demeritt, D. (2000). The new social contract for science: Accountability, relevance, and value in US and UK science and research policy. *Antipode, 32*(3), 308–329.

European Round Table (ERT). (1989). *Education and competence in Europe*. Brussels: European Round Table of Industrialists. Retrieved from http://www.ert.be

European Round Table (ERT). (1995). *Educations for Europeans: Towards the Learning Society*. Brussels: European Round Table of Industrialists.

European Round Table (ERT). (1997). *Investing in knowledge: The integration of technology in European education*. Brussels: European Round Table of Industrialists.

European Round Table (ERT). (1998). *Job creation and competitiveness through innovation*. Brussels: European Round Table of Industrialists.

Federici, S., Caffentzis, G., & Alidou, O. (Eds.). (2000). *A thousand flowers: Social struggles against structural adjustment in African universities*. Trenton, NJ: Africa World Press.

Fine, B. (2000). *Social theory and social capital*. London: Routledge.

Focus on Global South (FGS). (2000). *Prague 2000: Why we need to decommission the IMF and the World Bank*. Bangkok: Author.

Garnham, N. (2000). "Information society" as theory or ideology. *Information, Communication & Society, 3*(2), 139–152.

Gottschalk, P. (1998). Cross-national differences in the rise of earnings inequality: Market and institutional factors. *Review of Economics and Statistics, 80*, 489–503.

Harris, M. (2000). HE of the future. *AUTLOOK, 215*, 10–11. London: Association of University Teachers.

Hatcher, R., & Hirtt, N. (1999). The business agenda behind Labour's education policy. In M. Allen, C. Benn, C. Chitty, M. Cole, R. Hatcher, N. Hirtt, & G. Rikowski (Eds.), *Business business business: New labour's education policy* (pp. 12–23). London: Tufnell Press.

Hill, D. (1999). *New Labour and education: Policy, ideology and the third way*. London: Tufnell Press.

International Monetary Fund (IMF). (2000). *Globalisation: Threat or opportunity?* Washington, DC: Author.

Johnston, R. (1999). Beyond flexibility: Issues and implications for higher education. *Higher Education Review 32*, 55–67.

Johnstone, D. B., Arora, A., & Experton, W. (1998). *The financing and management of higher education: A status report on worldwide reforms* [departmental working paper]. Washington, DC: World Bank.

Marcuse, H. (1978). Industrialization and capitalism in the work of Max Weber. In *Negations: Essays in critical theory* (pp. 201–26). Boston: Beacon Press.

Marx, K. (1976). The fetishism of the commodity and its secret. In *Capital* (Vol. 1, pp. 163–177). London: Penguin.

McLaren, P. (2000). *Che Guevara, Paulo Freire, and the pedagogy of revolution.* Lanham, MD: Rowman & Littlefield.

McLeod, D. (2000, November 28). Clever business. *The Guardian.* Retrieved from http://www.guardian.co.uk/guardianeducation/story/0,,403498,00.html

Newby, H. (1999, March). *Higher education in the 21st century: Some possible futures.* London: Committee of Vice-Chancellors and Principals of the Universities of the United Kingdom.

Newman, R., & Johnson, F. (1999). Sites for power and knowledge? Towards a critique of the virtual university. *British Journal of Sociology of Education, 20*(1), 79–88.

Noble, D. (1998). Digital diploma mills: The automation of higher education, *Monthly Review, 49*(9), 38–52.

Ovetz, R. (1996). Turning resistance into rebellion: Student struggles and the global entrepreneurialization of the universities. *Capital & Class, 58*, 113–52.

Prowse, M. (1995, November 20). Endangered species. *Financial Times*, p. 16.

Slaughter, S., & Leslie, L. L. (1997). *Academic capitalism: Politics, policies and the entrepreneurial university.* Baltimore, MD: Johns Hopkins University Press.

Veblen, T. (1918). *Higher learning in America: A memorandum on the conduct of universities by businessmen.* New York: Hill & Wang.

Wilmott, H. (1995). Managing the academics: Commodification and control in the development of university education in the UK. *Human Relations, 48*(9), 993–1027.

11

Critical Pedagogy and Class Struggle in the Age of Neoliberal Globalization*

Notes From History's Underside

Peter McLaren

THE CRISIS OF THE EDUCATIONAL LEFT IN THE UNITED STATES

Part of the problem faced by the educational left today is that even among the most progressive cadres of educators there appears to exist an ominous resignation produced by the seeming inevitability of capital, even as financial institutions expand capacity in inverse proportion to a decline in living standards and job security. It has become an article of faith in the critical

*This chapter was previously published in *Democracy and Nature*, 9(1), 65-90, 2004, and also in Peter McLaren, *Capitalists and Conquerors: A Critical Pedagogy Against Empire*, 19-74, 2005. Lanham, MD: Rowman and Littlefield Publishers.

educational tradition that there is no viable alternative to capitalism. When class relations are discussed, they are rarely ever talked about in the Marxist sense of foregrounding the labor/capital dialectic, surplus value extraction, the value form of labor, or the structure of property ownership; instead, the conversation is directed toward consumption, lifestyle politics, theories of social stratification in terms of access to consumption, or job, income, and cultural prestige. The swan song for Marxist analysis apparently occurred during the intellectual collapse of Marxism in the 1980s after the Berlin Wall came crashing down and along with it a bipolar imperialist world. Capitalism was loudly proclaimed to be the victor over socialism. The globalization of capital was the designated savior of the world's poor and powerless. But as we have begun to observe, its function, far from supplicatory or transitive, has been deadly alienating. Gobbling up the global life world in the quest for an endless accumulation of surplus value, capital has produced some world-historical excretory excesses, turning the world into a global toilet of toxic waste while adding legions to Marx's reserve army of labor. The cutbacks in government expenditure on health, education, and housing investment, the creation of shantytowns in urban industrial areas, the concentration of women in low-wage subcontracted work, the depletion of natural resources, the rampant de-unionization, the growth of labor discipline, the expansion of temporary and part-time labor, the progressive diversion of capital into financial and speculative channels—what some have called "casino capitalism" on a world scale—the pushing down of wages, and the steady decline of decent working conditions have all proceeded apace but the rule of capital is rarely challenged, only its current condition.

In Russia today, the *prikhvatizatisiya* (grabitization) that has been bequeathed to the masses by a kleptocratic capitalism that dragged itself out of the carrion house of economic shock therapy has led to *blitzkrieg liquidations*, the destruction of industry, the disappearance of health benefits and housing, the slashing of salaries, and the transfer of wealth to a dozen or so private owners who now commandeer one public property. As poverty shifts from 2% to 50%, Western free-market fundamentalists keep reminding the Russians how awful it must have been to live under communism. Western countries that had established their economic fiefdoms by protecting key industries and subsidizing some domestic producers continue to preach the gospel of free trade and deregulation to other countries. Even when the messianic monopoly fantasies of chief executive officers from Enron, WorldCom, and Global Crossings culminate in bankruptcy disasters that shake the very pillars of the hallowed marketplace, the belief in the sanctity of the market remains undisturbed. Capital stealthily hides behind Nietzsche's unsullied veil, maintaining its secret of reversibility (i.e., that its economic assistance to the Third World reproduces underdevelopment and ensures the continuity of dependency).

The belief in the single-model neoliberal alternative had pullulated across the global political landscape before the fall of the Soviet Union and the Eastern Bloc, attaching itself like a fungus to regional and national dreams alike. The winds of the Cold War had spread its spores to the farthest reaches of the globe. After laying dormant for a decade, these spores have been reactivated and have seemingly destroyed our capacity to dream otherwise. Today, most nations celebrate capital as the key to the survival of democracy. Watered by the tears of the poor and cultivated by working-class labor, the dreams that sprout from the unmolested soil of capital are those engineered by the ruling class. Ploughed and harrowed by international cartels of transnational corporations, free-marketeers, and global carpetbaggers poised to take advantage of Third World nations in serious financial debt to the West, the seeds of capitalism have yielded a record-breaking harvest. The capitalist dream factories are not only corporate board rooms and production studios of media networks that together work to keep the capitalist dream alive, but a spirit of mass resignation that disables the majority of the population from realizing that capitalism and exploitation are functional equivalents, that the globalization of capital is just another name for what Lenin (1951) termed *imperialism*. U.S. imperialism—what Tariq Ali (2002, p. 281) called "the mother of all fundamentalisms"—has decamped from its Keynesian position of pseudoliberalism to fully embrace a fanatical neoliberalism. The grand mullah of neoliberalism, von Hayek, an avatar to both Thatcher and Reagan,

> favored military actions to defend U.S. interests abroad. On the domestic front he favoured the invisible magic of a manipulated market. No state intervention against the interests of capital was to be tolerated. But the state was vital to undertake military operations in the sphere of international relations. (Ali, 2002, p. 286)

Furthermore, von Hayek's neoliberal followers

> were staunch defenders of the Vietnam war. They supported the U.S.-backed military coup in Chile. In 1979, Hayek favoured bombing Tehran. In 1982, during the Malvinas conflict, he wanted raids on the Argentinian capital. This was the creed of neo-liberal hegemony most favoured by its founder. (Ali, 2002, p. 286)

The fact that neoliberalism—the midwife to the return of a fanatical belief in non-state intervention into capital movements that was spawned by 19th-century libertarianism—has resoundingly defeated the bureaucratic state capitalism of the former Soviet "evil empire", creating a seismic shift in the geopolitical landscape. Michael Parenti (2002) grimly commented that the overthrow of the Soviet Union has abetted a reactionary "rollback" of democratic gains, public services, and common living standards around the world as the U.S. continues to oppose economic nationalism and autonomous development in Asia, Africa, and Latin America, primarily through enforcing debt payments and structural adjustment programs imposed by the World Bank and the International Monetary Fund (IMF). Particularly hard hit have been the so-called Third World countries. The Soviet Union's collapse has opened the political floodgates of United States imperialism, permitting the U.S. to pursue virtually uncontested an agenda of "arrogance and brutality." The United States is no longer faced with a competing superpower that imposed constraints on the dream of U.S. global dominance. Parenti (2002) offered this disillusioned comment:

> The record of U.S. international violence just in the last decade is greater than anything that any socialist nation has ever perpetrated in its entire history. U.S. forces or proxy mercenary forces wreaked massive destruction upon Iraq, Mozambique, Angola, Nicaragua, El Salvador, Guatemala, East Timor, Libya, and other countries. In the span of a few months, President Clinton bombed four countries: Sudan, Afghanistan, Iraq repeatedly, and Yugoslavia massively. At the same time, the U.S. national security state was involved in proxy wars in Angola, Mexico (Chiapas), Colombia, East Timor, and various other places. And U.S. forces occupied Macedonia, Bosnia, Kosovo, and Afghanistan, and were deployed across the globe at some 300 major overseas bases—all in the name of peace, democracy, national security, counter-terrorism, and humanitarianism. (p. 44)

Today's international political economy is the toast of the global ruling class, and the bourgeoisie see it as their biggest opportunity in decades to join their ranks. Free-marketeers have been given the New World Order's *imprimatur* to loot and exploit the planet's resources with impunity and to invest in global markets without restriction. The menacing concomitant of capital's destructive juggernaut is the obliteration of any hope for civilization, let alone democracy. While liberals are plumping for fairer distribution of economic resources, the working class are taught to feel grateful for the squalid working conditions of the *maquiladoras* that are now sprouting up in countries designated to provide the cheap labor and dumping grounds for pollution for the Western democracies. The poor and powerless are taught that socialism and communism are congenitally evil and can only lead to a totalitarian dictatorship. In short, capitalism and the legitimacy of private monopoly ownership has been naturalized as common sense.

It is no longer just the capitalists who believe that they are the salvation for the world's poor, but the workers themselves have become conditioned to believe that without their exploiters, they would no longer exist. The entrails of the eviscerated poor now serve as divining mechanisms for the soothsayers of the investment corporations. Even many trade unions have served as little more than adjuncts of the state, reimposing the discipline of capital's law of value. Those who wish to avoid both Communist-type centralized planning and the disequilibrium and instability of *laisséz-faire* capitalism have turned to a type of market socialism through labor-managed firms, but have done little to challenge the deep grammar of capital itself.

Everywhere we look, social relations of oppression and contempt for human dignity abound. It is not that workers are being press-ganged to serve in the social factory; it is more like they are being made to feel grateful that they have some source of income, as meagre as that may be. As the demagogues of capitalist neoliberal globalization spin their web of lies about the benefits of "global trade" behind erected "security" walls, protesters are gassed, beaten, and killed. As the media boast about the net worth of corporate moguls and celebrate the excesses of the rich and famous, approximately 2.8 billion people—almost half of the world's people—struggle in desperation to live on less than $2 (U.S.) a day (McQuaig, 2001).

As schools become increasingly financed by corporations that function as service industries for transnational capitalism, and as bourgeois think-tank profiteerism and educational professionalism continues to guide educational policy and practice, the U.S. population faces a challenging educational reality. Liberals are calling for the need for capital controls, controls in foreign exchange, the stimulation of growth and wages, labor rights enforcement for nations borrowing from the United States, and the removal of financial aid from banking and capital until they concede to the centrality of the wage problem and insist on labor rights. However, very few are calling for the abolition of capital itself.

The commercialization of higher education, the bureaucratic cultivation of intellectual capital—what Marx referred to in the *Grundrisse* as the general intellect or social brain—and its tethering to the machinery of capital, the rise of industrial business partnerships, the movement of research into the commercial arena of profit and in the service of trade organizations and academic–corporate consortia, have all garnered institutions of higher learning profound suspicion by those who view education as a vehicle for emancipation. In the hands of the technozealots, teachers are being re-proletarianized and labor is being disciplined, displaced, and deskilled. Teacher autonomy, independence, and control over work are being severely reduced, whereas workplace knowledge and control is given over more and more to the hands of the administration.

The educational left has unloaded its impotence in a concern with identity politics over class politics and is finding itself without a revolutionary agenda for challenging in the classrooms of the nation the effects and consequences of the new capitalism. As a result, we are witnessing the progressive and unchecked merging of pedagogy to the productive processes within advanced capitalism. Education has been reduced to a subsector of the economy, designed to create cybercitizens within a teledemocracy of fast-moving images, representations, and lifestyle choices brought powered by the seemingly frictionlessness of finance capital. Capitalism has been naturalized as commonsense reality—even as a part of nature itself—whereas the term *social class* has been replaced by the less antagonistic term, *socio-economic status.*

THE TRANSNATIONAL CAPITALIST CLASS

Robinson (2001) made a convincing argument for the appearance of a transnationalist capitalist class. By employing a renewed historical materialist conception of the state in this current epoch of neoliberal globalization, Robinson was able to achieve two important results. First, he was able to de-reify the state–nation-state binarism in order to identify the social classes operating within formal state institutions and, second, he was able to analyze the constellation of social forces in cooperation and in conflict as they develop historically. Robinson argued for a conception of globalization that transcends the nation-state system. He effectively reconceptualized the dominant Weberian conception of the state through a Marxist problematic as the institutionalization of class relations around a particular configuration of social production in which the economic and the political are conceived as distinct moments of the same totality. Here, the relation between the economy and states is an internal one.

There is nothing in this view that necessarily ties the state to territory or to nation-states. Although it is true that, seen in aggregate nation-state terms, there are still very poor countries and very rich ones, it is also true that poverty and marginalization are increasing in so-called First World countries, whereas the Third World has an expanding new strata of consumers. The labor aristocracy is expanding to other countries such that core and periphery no longer denote geography as much as social location. The material circumstances that gave rise to the nation-state are, Robinson argued, being superceded by globalization such that the state—conceived in Marxist terms as a congealment of a particular and historically determined constellation of class forces and relations (i.e., a historically specific social relation inserted into larger social structures)—can no longer simply be conceived solely in nation-state-centric terms. Robinson's argument—that a transnational state apparatus is emerging under globalization from within the system of nation states—rests on the notion that the production process itself has become increasingly transnationalized as national circuits of accumulation become functionally integrated into global circuits.

Neoliberal globalization is unifying the world into a single mode of production and bringing about the organic integration of different countries and regions into a single global economy through the logic of capital accumulation on a world scale. Non-market structures are disappearing as they are fast becoming penetrated and commodified by capitalist relations. Global class formation has involved the accelerated division of the world into a global bourgeoisie and a global proletariat. The transnationalized fractions of dominant groups have become the hegemonic fraction globally. Social groups and classes are central historical actors rather than "states" as power is produced within the transnational capitalist class by transnationally oriented state-managers and a cadre of supranational institutions such as the World Bank, the World Trade Organization, the Trilateral Commission, and the World Economic Forum. Of course, there is still a struggle between descendant national fractions of dominant groups and ascendant transnational fractions. The class practices of a new global ruling class are becoming condensed in an emergent transnational state in which the transnational capitalist class has an objective existence above any local territories and polities. The purpose of the transnational ruling class is the valorization and accumulation of capital and the defense and advance of the emergent hegemony of a global bourgeoisie and a new global capitalist historical bloc. This historical bloc is composed of the transnational corporations and financial institutions, the elites that manage the supranational economic planning agencies, major forces in the dominant political parties, media conglomerates and technocratic elites. This does not mean that competition and conflict have come to an end or that there exists a real unity within the emergent transnational capitalist class. Competition among rivals is still fierce and the United States is playing a leadership role on behalf of the transnational elite, defending the interests of the emergent global capitalist historical bloc.

Marxists have long recognized the dangers of the rule of capital and the exponentially of its expansion into all spheres of the lifeworld. Today, capital is in command of the world order as never before, as new commodity circuits and the increased speed of capital circulation works to extend and globally secure neoliberal capital's reign of terror. The site where the concrete determinations of industrialization, corporations, markets, greed, patriarchy, technology, all come together (i.e., the center where exploitation and domination is fundamentally articulated) is occupied by capital. The insinuation of the coherence and logic of capital into everyday life—and the elevation of the market to sacerdotal status, as the paragon of all social relationships—is something that has successfully occurred and the economic restructuring that we are witnessing today offers both new fears concerning capital's inevitability and some new possibilities for organizing against it. Critical pedagogy is, we maintain, a necessary (but not sufficient) possibility.

NEOLIBERALISM AND EDUCATION

Neoliberalism ("capitalism with the gloves off," or "socialism for the rich") refers to a capitalist domination of society that supports state enforcement of the unregulated market, engages in the oppression of nonmarket forces and antimarket policies, guts free public services, eliminates social subsidies, offers limitless concessions to transnational corporations, enthrones a neomercantilist public policy agenda, establishes the market as the patron of educational reform, and permits private interests to control most of social life in the pursuit of profits for the few (i.e., through lowering taxes on the wealthy, scrapping environmental regulations, and dismantling public education and social welfare programs). It is undeniably one of the most dangerous politics that we face today.

Hill and Cole (2001) noted that neoliberalism advocates a number of pro-capitalist positions: that the state privatize ownership of the means of production, including private sector involvement in welfare, social, educational and other state services (such as the prison industry); sell labor-power for the purposes of creating a flexible and poorly regulated labor market; advance a corporate managerialist model for state services; allow the needs of the economy to dictate the principal aims of school education; suppress the teaching of oppositional and critical thought that would challenge the rule of capital; support a curriculum and pedagogy that produces compliant, pro-capitalist workers; and make sure that schooling and education ensure the ideological and economic reproduction that benefits the ruling class. Of course, the business agenda for schools can be seen in growing public–private partnerships, the burgeoning business sponsorships for schools, business mentoring and corporatization of the curriculum (McLaren & Farahmandpur, 2001a, 2001b), and calls for national standards, regular national tests, voucher systems, accountability schemes, financial incentives for high-performance schools, and quality control of teaching. Schools are encouraged to provide better value for money and must seek to learn from the entrepreneurial world of business or risk going into receivership. In short, neoliberal educational policy operates from the premise that education is primarily a subsector of the economy.

It is growing more common to hear the refrain, "education is increasingly too important to be left to the educators," as governments make strong efforts at intervention to ensure schools play their part in rectifying economic stagnation and ensuring global competitiveness. And standardized tests are touted as the means to ensure the educational system is aligned well with the global economy. There is also a movement to develop international standardized tests, creating pressures towards educational convergence and standardization among nations. Such an effort, noted Davies and Guppy (1997), provides a form of surveillance that allows nation-states to justify their extended influence and also serves to homogenize education across regions and nations. School choice initiatives such as voucher programs have dramatically expanded their scope, sapping the strength of the public school system and helping to spearhead further educational privatization.

Because capital has itself invaded almost every sphere of life in the United States, the focus of the educational left has been distracted for the most part from the great class struggles that have punctuated this century. The leftist agenda now rests almost entirely on an understanding of asymmetrical gender and ethnic relations. Although this focus surely is important, class struggle is now perilously viewed as an outdated issue. When social class is discussed, it is usually viewed as relational, not as oppositional, not as liberatory or emancipatory. Privatization initiatives have secured a privileged position that is functionally advantageous to the socially reproductive logic of entrepreneurial capitalism, private ownership, and the personal appropriation of social production by the transnational ruling elite. This neoliberal dictatorship of the comprador elite has re-secured a monopoly on resources held by the transnational ruling class and their allies in the culture industry. The very meaning of freedom has come to refer to the freedom to structure the distribution of wealth and to exploit workers more easily across national boundaries by driving down wages to their lowest common denominator and by eviscerating social programs designed to assist laboring humanity.

CRITICAL PEDAGOGY AND THE PRIMACY OF POLITICAL STRUGGLE

It is impossible to disclose all the operative principles of critical pedagogy. To penetrate the glimmering veil of rhetoric surrounding it would require an essay of its own. Suffice it here to underscore several of its salient features. First and foremost, it is an approach to curriculum production, educational policymaking, and teaching practices that challenges the received "hard sciences" conception of knowledge as "neutral" or "objective" (i.e., epistemological positivism) and that is directed toward understanding the political nature of education in all of its manifestations in everyday life as these are played out in the agonistic terrain of conflicting and competing discourses, oppositional and hegemonic cultural formations, and social relations linked to the larger capitalist social totality. Critical pedagogy has its importance in understanding the mechanisms of oppression imposed by the established order. But such an understanding is approached from the perspective of the dispossessed and oppressed themselves. It is an encounter with the process of knowledge production from within the dynamics of a concrete historical movement that transcends individuality, dogmatism, and certainty. Only within the framework of a challenge to the prevailing social order en toto is it possible to transform the conditions that make and remake human history. Specifically in the context of school life, capital produces new human productive and intellectual capacities in alienated form. Critical pedagogy's basic project over the last several decades has been to adumbrate the problems and opportunities of political struggle through educational means as a means of challenging the alienation of intellectual capacity and human labor. It is incoherent to conceptualize critical pedagogy, as do many of its current exponents, without an enmeshment with the political and anti-capitalist struggle.

In its U.S. variants, the genesis of critical pedagogy can be traced to the work of Paulo Freire in Brazil, and John Dewey and the social reconstructionists writing in the post-depression years. Its leading exponents have cross-fertilized critical pedagogy with just about every transdisciplinary tradition imaginable, including theoretical forays into the Frankfurt School of critical theory, and the work of Richard Rorty, Jacques Lacan, Jacques Derrida, and Michel Foucault. Here the focus mainly has been on a critique of instrumental reason and the nature of governmentality in educational sites. An emphasis has been placed on the nonconceptual in which thinking is constructed as a performance of ethics, or as a post-truth pragmatics, or as an open-ended, nondeterminate process that resists totalizing tropological systems (hence the frequent condemnation of Marxism as an oppressive totalizing master narrative). Critical pedagogy's reach now extends to multicultural education, bilingual education, and fields associated with language-learning and literacy (including media literacy). Clearly, critical pedagogy is checkered with tensions and conflicts and mired in contradictions and should in no way be seen as a unified discipline.

I do not wish to rehearse this decidedly potted history here because it will serve little purpose other than adding cumbersomely to its growing historical weight or rehashing what I assume most progressive educators already know or about which they at least have some working idea.

In the mid-1970s to mid-1980s the role of critical pedagogy was much more contestatory than in the decade of the 1990s with respect to dominant social and economic arrangements. Critical pedagogy has always had an underground rapport with the working class, a rapport that virtually disappeared post-1989. In contrast to its current incarnation, the veins of critical pedagogy were not in need of defrosting in the early 1980s but were pumped up with Marxist-inspired work coming from the Birmingham School of Contemporary Cultural Studies, as well as a re-engagement with the work of John Dewey, Paulo Freire, and the Frankfurt School. During that time, critique flowed generally unimpeded and was directed not simply at isolated relations of domination but at the totality of social relations (although stressing cultural Marxist strands and often overinflating them). That it was often conflated with liberation theology in Latin America and with anti-imperialist struggle worldwide accounts for its failure to be preconized in the cultural chambers of the ruling elite.

POSTMODERN THEORY AND THE DOMESTICATION OF CRITICAL PEDAGOGY

Authoritative as the term may sound, *critical pedagogy* has been extraordinarily misunderstood and misrepresented. Once considered by the faint-hearted guardians of the American dream as a term of opprobrium for its powerful challenge to the bedrock assumptions characterizing the so-called U.S. *meritocracy*, critical pedagogy has become so completely psychologized, so liberally humanized, so technologized, and so conceptually postmodernized, that its current relationship to broader liberation struggles seems severely attenuated if not fatally terminated. While its urgency was once unignorable, and its hard-bitten message had the pressure of absolute *fiat* behind it, critical pedagogy seemingly has collapsed into an ethical licentiousness and a complacent relativism that has displaced the struggle against capitalist exploitation with its emphasis on the multiplicity of interpersonal forms of oppression. The conceptual net known as critical pedagogy has been cast so wide and at times so cavalierly that it has come to be associated with anything dragged up out of the troubled and infested waters of educational practice, from classroom furniture organized in a "dialogue-friendly" circle to "feel-good" curricula designed to increase students' self-image. Its multicultural education equivalent can be linked to a politics of diversity that includes "respecting difference" through the celebration of "ethnic" holidays and themes such as "black history month" and "Cinco de Mayo." I am scarcely the first to observe that critical pedagogy has been badly undercut by practitioners who would mischaracterize its fundamental project. In fact, if the term *critical pedagogy* is refracted onto the stage of current educational debates, we have to judge it as having been largely domesticated in a manner that many of its early exponents, such as Brazil's Paulo Freire, so strongly feared.

In the United States, critical pedagogy has collapsed into left liberal attempts by progressive educators to remediate the educational enterprise. This has resulted in a long list of reform initiatives that include creating communities of learners in classrooms; bridging the gap between student culture and the culture of the school; engaging in cross-cultural understandings; integrating multicultural content and teaching across the curriculum; developing techniques for reducing racial prejudice and conflict resolution strategies; challenging Eurocentric teaching and learning as well as the ideological formations of European immigration history by which many White teachers judge African-American, Latino/a, and Asian students; challenging the meritocratic foundation of public policy that purportedly is politically neutral and racially colorblind; creating teacher-generated narratives as a way of analyzing teaching from a transformative perspective; improving academic achievement in culturally diverse schools; affirming and utilizing multiple perspectives and ways of teaching and learning; and de-reifying the curriculum and exposing metanarratives of exclusion. Most of these pedagogical initiatives are acting on the recommendations of the National Commission on Teaching and America's Future—a commission bent on challenging social class and ethnicity as primary determinants of student success. And for all their sincere attempts to create a social justice agenda by attacking asymmetries of power and privilege and dominant power arrangements in U.S. society, progressive teachers have, unwittingly operated under the assumption that these changes can be accomplished within the existing social universe of capital. Critical pedagogy has been taken out of the business of class analysis and has focussed instead on a postmodernist concern with a politics of difference and inclusion—a position that effectively substitutes truth for singular, subjective judgement and silences historical materialism as the unfolding of class struggle (Ebert, 2002).

In capturing the "commanding heights" of left educational criticism, postmodernist educators have focussed their analysis on the subject as consumer in contrast to the Marxian emphasis of the subject as producer and in doing so have emphasized the importance of a textual subversion of fixed identity, and a decentering of subjectivity. Too often this work collapses politics into poetics. Marxist educationalists maintain that neoliberal ideology as it applies to schooling is often given ballast by poststructuralist–postmodernist/deconstructive approaches to educational reform because many of these approaches refuse to challenge the rule of capital and the social relations of production at the basis of the capitalist state.

Insofar as postmodern educationalists do not address the fact that class exploitation creates the conditions of possibility for other antagonisms such as forms of racialization and sexism, postmodern educational criticism and neoliberalism can be considered to be two species of the same genus: capitalist schooling. They can be considered as two forms of one and the same social type. Both postmodern critique and neoliberalism serve as a justification for the value form of labor within capitalist society. Here postmodernists and neoliberals adopt the role of the sorcerer's apprentice who has been summoned to serve his master: capital.

My point here is that the debates over educational reform are far richer today when seen through the palimpsest of Marxist critique. Marxist critique serves as a counterpoint to the subversive acts of the proto-Foucauldians-and-Derrideans, who, garbed in theoretical attire of Ninja academics, relish in foot-sweeping the metaphysics propping up the "totalitarian certainties" of the Marxist problematic, dismembering "totalities" by inworming them and opening them up to multiple destinies other than those circumscribed by Marx. The point is not that the gallery-hoping titans and fierce deconstructors from the postmodern salons have not made some important contributions to a *fin-de-siècle* politics, or that they have not exerted some influence (albeit proleptically) in the arena of radical politics, but that, in the main, their efforts have helped to protect the bulwark of ruling class power by limiting the options of educational policy in order to perpetuate the hegemony of ruling class academics. Their herniated ideas have made for good theatre, but their words have often turned to ashes before leaving their mouths. They have not left educators much with which to advance a political line of march within a theoretical framework capable of developing an international strategy to oppose imperialism.

The above is unavoidably a sweeping synthesis of the limitations of a postmodernized critical pedagogy in the North American context. The main bone of contention that I have with the direction of increasingly postmodernized critical pedagogy over the last several decades is its studied attempt to leave the issue of sexism and racism (i.e., the politics of difference) unconnected to class struggle. Of course, this conveniently draws attention away from the crucially important ways in which women and people of color provide capitalism with its super-exploited labor pools—a phenomenon that is on the upswing all over the world. San Juan (2002) sees the continuing racialization of the American national identity occurring in novel ways as long as citizenship is based on citizenship and individual rights are needed to legitimate private property and to further capital accumulation. Capitalism *is* an overarching totality that is, unfortunately, becoming increasingly invisible in postmodernist narratives that eschew and reject such categories *tout court*. Postmodernist educators tend to ignore that capitalism is a ruthless "totalizing process which shapes our lives in every conceivable aspect" and that "even leaving aside the direct power wielded by capitalist wealth in the economy and in the political state" capitalism also subjects all "social life to the abstract requirements of the market, through the commodification of life in all its aspects." This makes a "mockery" out of all aspirations to "autonomy, freedom of choice, and democratic self-government" (Wood, 1995, pp. 262–263).

The voguish academic brigandism of educational postmodernists that gives primacy to incommensurability as the touchstone of analysis and explanation has diverted critical analysis from the global sweep of advanced capitalism and the imperialist exploitation of the world's laboring class. Their pedagogically distilled animosity toward Marxism is no secret. This is not the time to evaluate the jousts between Marxists and postmodernists for the spoils of the critical tradition (see Hill, McLaren, Cole, & Rikowski,

2002). Suffice it to say that what drives postmodern pedagogy is a pedagogy of desire over a pedagogy of need, where desire remains autonomous and linked to an imaginary object in a re-materialized psychic economy. Needs are erroneously seen as proceeding from desire.

Arguably the vast majority of educationalists who are committed to critical pedagogy and multicultural education propagate versions of it that identify with own their bourgeois class interests. One doesn't have to question the integrity or competence of these educators or dismiss their work as disingenuous—for the most part it is not—to conclude that their articulations of critical pedagogy and multicultural education have been accommodated to mainstream versions of liberal humanism and progressivism. While early exponents of critical pedagogy were denounced for their polemical excesses and radical political trajectories, a new generation of critical educators have since that time emerged who have largely adopted what could be described as a pluralist approach to social antagonisms. Their work celebrates the "end of history" and the critique of global capitalism is rarely, if ever, brought into the debate. These pedagogues primarily see capital as sometimes maleficent, sometimes beneficent, as something that, like a wild stallion, can eventually be tamed and made to serve humanity. Marxism is seen from this perspective as a failed experiment. They instruct that the teaching of Marx be put to rest since the persistence of capital appears to have rendered the old bearded devil obsolete. Apparently no one noticed—or cared to notice—that Marx had outwitted its Cyclopian capitalist foe by clinging to the underbelly of lost revolutionary dreams that have been herded out of the caves of the Eastern Bloc. After biding time for the last decade—a period that witnessed a particularly virulent example of capital's slash and burn policy—his ghost is reappearing in reinvigorated form in the West (at least among some members of the academic left) where Marx is now seen to have anticipated much about the manner in which the current world-historical crisis of capitalism would manifest itself.

A RENEWAL OF THE MARXIST PROBLEMATIC

My concern over the last decade has been to introduce Marxist scholarship into the field of critical pedagogy, since, as I argued earlier, it has been taken over by postmodernists who have been attempting to suture together in recent decades the ontological tear in the universe of ideas that was first created when history was split in two by the dialectical wave of Marx's pen in the *Communist Manifesto* and the subsequent development of the communist movement in the mid-1800s. My own Marxism is informed by the philosophy of Marxist-Humanism that posits, after Hegel, that forward movement emerges from the negation of obstacles. It is the negation of "what is" and a critique of the given that spurs development and creates the path to liberation. Absolute negativity occurs when negativity becomes self-directed and self-related to become the seedbed of the positive. According to *News and Letters*, a Marxist-Humanist publication,

> The key is the difference between the first and second negation—the two moments of the dialectic. The first negation is the negation of the given; it takes what appears positive, the immediate, and imbues it with negativity. The second negation, "the negation of the negation," turns the power of negativity upon the act of negation; it takes what appears negative and shows that it is the source of the truly positive. (*News & Letters* Committee, 2002)

Marxist humanists believe that the best ways to transcend the brutal and barbaric limits to human liberation set by capital are through practical movements centered on class struggle. But today, the clarion cry of class struggle is spurned by the bourgeois left as politically fanciful and reads to many as an advertisement for a B movie. The liberal left is less interested in class struggle than in making capitalism more "compassionate" to the needs of the poor. This only leads to the renaturalization of scarcity. What this approach exquisitely obfuscates is the way in which new capitalist efforts to divide and conquer the working class and to recompose class relations have employed xenophobic nationalism, racism, sexism, ableism, and homophobia. The key here is not for critical pedagogues to privilege class oppression over other forms of oppression but to see how capitalist relations of exploitation provide the ground from which other forms of oppression are produced and how postmodern educational theory often serves as a means of distracting attention from capital's global project of accumulation.

It is not my purpose here to develop an exegesis of Marxist-Humanism (one among dozens of identifiable schools of Marxist thought but the one most pertinent to my own work) but simply to draw attention to the ways in which the Marxist tradition has been woefully absent from critical pedagogy as it is engaged in the U.S. academy (i.e., in colleges of education or university departments of education)—an absence that has brought with it irreparable damage to the tradition of critical education. Unscrolling the present state of critical pedagogy and examining its depotentiated contents, processes, and formations puts progressive educators on notice in that few contemporary critical educators are either willing or able to ground their pedagogical imperatives in the concept of labor in general, and in Marx's labor theory of value in particular. This is certainly more the case in North American educational settings than it is in the United Kingdom, the latter context having had a much more serious and salutary engagement with the Marxist tradition in the social sciences and in adult education, one of its professional offshoots.

FAREWELL TO ALL THAT

These days, it is far from fashionable to be a radical educator. The political gambit of progressive educators these days appears to be silence in the face of chaos, with the hope that the worst will soon pass. There are not many direct heirs to the Marxist tradition among left educational scholars. To identify your politics as Marxist—especially in the slipstream of the recent terrorist attacks on September 11 and the bombastic odes to the military machine and the U.S. unilateral quest to create a New World Order that are now suffusing U.S. politics—is to invite derision and ridicule from many quarters, including many on the left. It is to open one's work to all species of dyspeptic criticism, from crude hectoring to sophisticated Philippics. Charges range from being a naive leftist, to being stuck in a time warp, to being hooked on an antediluvian patriarch, to giving in to cheap sentimentality or romantic utopianism. Marxists in the academy are accused with assuming an untenable political position that enables them to wear the mantle of the revolutionary without having to get their hands dirty in the day-to-day struggles of rank-and-file teachers who occupy the front lines in the schools of our major urban centers. Marxist analysis is also frequently derided as elitist in its supposed impenetrable esotericism, and if you happen to teach at a university your work can easily be dismissed as dysphoric ivory tower activism—even by other education scholars who also work in universities. Critics often make assumptions that you are guilty of being terminally removed from the lives of teachers and students until proven otherwise. Some of the criticism is productive and warranted but much of it is a desperate attempt to dismiss serious challenges to capitalism—to displace work that attempts to puncture the aura of inevitability surrounding global capitalism. Although some of the criticism is substantive—including a welcomed critique of the enciphered language of some academics and a challenge to radical educators to come up with concrete pedagogical possibilities—much of it is small-minded and petty. The beneficiaries of the current disunity among the educational left are the business-education partnerships and the privatization of schooling initiatives that are currently following in the wake of larger neoliberal strategies.

In this interregnum, in particular, where the entire social universe of capital is locked up in the commodity form, where capital's internal contradictions have created a global division of labor that appears astonishingly insurmountable, and where the ecological stakes for human survival have shifted in such seismic proportions, creating a vortex in which reactionary terrorism has unleashed its unholy cry, we lament the paucity of critical/pedagogical approaches to interrogating the vagaries of everyday life within capital's social universe.

In retrospect, progressive educators are often wont to ask: Were the 1960s the last opportunity for popular revolutionary insurgency on a grand scale to be successful? Did the political disarray of prodigious dimensions that followed in the wake of the rebuff of the post-1968 leftist intelligentsia by the European proletariat condemn the revolutionary project and the "productionist" meta-narrative of Marx to the dustbin of history? Have the postmodernist emendations of Marxist categories and the rejection—for the most part—of the Marxist project by the European and North American intelligentsia signaled the abandonment of hope in revolutionary social change? Can the schools of today build a new social order?

A nagging question has sprung to the surface of the debate over schooling and the new capitalist order: Can a renewed and revivified critical pedagogy distinctly wrought by an historical materialist approach to educational reform serve as a point of departure for a politics of resistance and counter-hegemonic struggle in the 21st century? And if we attempt to uncoil this question and take seriously its full implications, what can we learn from the legacy and struggle of revolutionary social movements? The fact that Marxist analysis has been discredited within the educational precincts of capitalist America does not defray the substance of these questions. On the surface, there are certain reasons to be optimistic. Critical pedagogy has, after all, joined anti-racist and gay, lesbian, transgender and feminist struggles in order to articulate a democratic social order built around the imperatives of diversity, tolerance, and equal access to material resources. But surely such a role, while commendable as far as it goes, has seen critical pedagogy severely compromise an earlier, more radical commitment to anti-imperialist struggle that we often associate with the anti-war movement of the 1960s and earlier revolutionary movements in Latin America.

What does the historical materialist approach often associated with an earlier generation of social critics offer educators who work in critical education? We raise this question at a time in which it is painfully evident that critical pedagogy and its political partner and congener, multicultural education, no longer serve as an adequate social or pedagogical platform from which to mount a vigorous challenge to the current social division of labor and its effects on the socially reproductive function of schooling in late capitalist society. In fact, critical pedagogy no longer enjoys its status as a herald for democracy, as a clarion call for revolutionary praxis, as a language of critique and possibility in the service of a radical democratic imaginary, which was its promise in the late 1970s and early 1980s. As I argue throughout the remainder of this chapter, part of this has to do with the lack of class analysis evinced in its work, but it also is related to the general retreat of the educational left in the United States over the last several decades.

CRITICAL PEDAGOGY: CONTEMPORARY CHALLENGES
FOR THE EDUCATIONAL LEFT

Critical pedagogy has had a tumultuous relationship with the dominant education community both in North America (McLaren, 1997) and the United
Kingdom (Allman, 1999, 2001) for the past 25 years. Clearly, on both sides
of the Atlantic, the educational community has been aprioristically antagonistic to Marxist critique, effectively undercutting the development of
Marxist criticism in education. Many of the current attempts to muster a
progressive educational agenda among education scholars in suffused with
an anti-communist bias. Only occasionally is the excessive rejectionism of
Marxism by postmodern educationalists accompanied by analysis; rarely is
it ever accomplished beyond the level of fiat. To borrow a commentary that
Barbara Foley (1998) directed at the post-Marxism of Laclau and Mouffe, "it
conflates politics with epistemology in an irrevocably linked chain of signi-
fiers: the authoritarian party equals class reductionism equals logocentricity;
totality equals totalitarianism" (¶8).

Our own practices—what Paula Allman (2001) christened "revolutionary critical pedagogy"—ups the radical ante for progressive education that,
for the most part over the last decade, has been left rudderless amidst an
undertow of domesticating currents. It ups this ante by pivoting around the
work of Karl Marx, Paulo Freire, and Antonio Gramsci and in doing so
brings some desperately needed theoretical ballast to the teetering critical
educational tradition. Such theoretical infrastructure is necessary, we argue,
for the construction of concrete pedagogical spaces—in schools, university
seminar rooms, cultural centres, unions, social movements, popular forums
for political activism, and so on—for the fostering and fomenting of revolutionary praxis.

Although it certainly remains the case that too many teachers take
refuge in a sanctuary of assertions devoid of critical reflection, it would be
wrong to admonish the educational activism of today as a form of pedagogical potvaliancy. Courageous attempts are being made in the struggle for
educational reform in both North America and the United Kingdom. In this
case, we need to be reminded that the lack of success of the educational left
is not so much the result of the conflicted sensibilities of critical educators,
as it is a testament to the preening success of Western Cold War efforts in
indigenising the cultural logic of capitalism, the fall of the Eastern Bloc nonprofit police states, and the degradation and disappearance of Marxist metanarratives in the national-popular agendas of decolonising countries. It can
also be traced to the effects of the labor movement tradition that keeps
labor-left educators struggling inside the labor/capital antagonism by supporting labor over capital, rather than attempting to transcend this divide

entirely through efforts to implode the social universe of capital out of which the labor/capital antagonism is constituted.

The critical pedagogy we are envisioning here operates from the premise that capital in its current organizational structure provides the context for working-class struggle. Our approach to understanding the relationship between capitalism and schooling and the struggle for socialism is premised on Marx's value theory of labor as developed by British Marxist educationalist, Glenn Rikowski, and others (see Cole, Hill, McLaren, & Rikowski, 2001). In developing further the concept of revolutionary critical pedagogy and its specific relationship to class struggle, it is necessary to focus on labor's value form. We follow the premise that value is the substance of capital. Value is not a thing. It is the dominant form that capitalism as a determinate social relation takes. Following Dinerstein and Neary (2001), capital can be conceived as "value in motion." Marx linked the production of value to the dual aspect of labor. Workers do not consume what they produce but work in order to consume what others have produced. Labor is thus riveted in both use value and exchange value (see also Allman, 1999, 2001; Rikowski, 2000a, 2001a, 2001d). Domination in this view is not so much by other people as by essentially abstract social structures that people constitute in their everyday social intercourse and sociopolitical relations. In the *Grundrisse,* Marx emphasized that "society does not consist of individuals; it expresses the sum of connections and relationships in which individuals find themselves . . . [Thus,] to be a slave or to be a citizen are social determinations" (cited in San Juan, 1996, p. 248). Labor, therefore, has a historically specific function as a social mediating activity.

Labor materializes itself both as commodified forms of human existence (labor power) and structures that constitute and enforce this process of generalized social mediation (such as money and the state) against the workers who indirectly constituted them. These determinate abstractions (abstract labor) also constitute both human capital and the class struggle against the exploitation of living labor and the capitalization of human subjectivity. This split within capital-labor itself is founded on the issue of whether labor produces value directly or labor-power. Following Dinerstein and Neary (2001), we adopt the premise that abstract labor is underwritten by value-in-motion, or the expansive logic of capital (referring to the increases in productivity required to maintain capitalist expansion). Abstract labor is a unique form of social totality that serves as the ground for its own social relation. It is socially average labor power that is the foundation of the abstract labor that forms value (Rikowski, 2001a). In the case of abstract labor, labor materializes itself twice—first as labor and second as "the apparently quasi-objective and independent structures that constitute and enforce this process of generalized social mediation: money (economics) and the state (politics) against the workers who constituted them" (Neary, forthcoming; see also Postone, 1996). This value relation—captured in the image of the capitalist juggernaut driving across the globe for the purpose of extracting surplus value (profit)—reflects how the abstract social dimension of labor formally arranges (through the imposition of socially necessary labor time) the concrete organization of work so that the maximum amount of human energy can be extracted as surplus value. Here, concrete labor (use value) is overwhelmed by abstract labor (value in motion) so that we have an apparently non-contradictory unity. That is to say, capital's abstract-social dimension dominates and subsumes the concrete material character of labor and so becomes the organizing principle of society—the social factory where labor serves as the constituent form of its own domination. This is the process of real subsumption where humanity's vital powers are mightily deformed. This helps to explain how workers become dominated by their own labor. Labor becomes the source of its own domination.

Following Marx, Rikowski noted that labor power—our capacity to labor—takes the form of human capital in capitalist society. It has reality only within the individual agent. Thus, labor power is a distinctly *human force*. The worker is the active subject of production. He or she is necessary for the creation of surplus value. Through living labor, the worker provides the skills, innovation, and cooperation on which capital relies to enhance surplus value and to ensure its reproduction. Thus, by its very nature, labor power cannot exist apart from the laborer.

Education and training are what Rikowski referred to as processes of labor-power production. They are, in Rikowski's view, subspecies of relative surplus-value production (the raising of worker productivity so that necessary labor is reduced) that leads to a relative increase in surplus labor time and hence surplus value. Human capital development is necessary for capitalist societies to reproduce themselves and to create more surplus value. The core of capitalism can thus be undressed by exploring the contradictory nature of the use value and exchange value of labor power.

Within the expansive scope of revolutionary critical pedagogy, the concept of labor is axiomatic for theorizing the school–society relationship and thus for developing radical pedagogical imperatives, strategies, and practices for overcoming the constitutive contradictions that such a coupling generates. The larger goal that revolutionary critical pedagogy stipulates for radical educationalists involves direct participation with the masses in the discovery and charting of a socialist reconstruction and alternative to capitalism. However, without a critical lexicon and interpretative framework that can unpack the labor/capital relationship in all of its capillary detail, critical pedagogy is doomed to remain trapped in domesticated currents and vulgarized formations. The process whereby labor power is transformed into human capital and concrete living labor is subsumed by abstract labor is one that eludes the interpretative capacity of rational communicative action and requires a dialectical understanding that only historical materialist critique can best provide. Historical materialism provides critical pedagogy with a theory of the material basis of social life rooted in historical social relations and assumes paramount importance in uncovering the structure of class conflict as well as unravelling the effects produced by the social division of labor. Today, labor power is capitalized and commodified and education plays a tragic role in these processes. According to Rikowski (2001a), education "links the chains that bind our souls to capital. It is one of the ropes comprising the ring for combat between labor and capital, a clash that powers contemporary history: 'the class struggle'" (p. 2). Schools therefore act as vital supports for, and developers of, the class relation, "the violent capital–labor relation that is at the core of capitalist society and development" (p. 19)

In so far as schooling is premised on generating the living commodity of labor power, on which the entire social universe of capital depends, it can become a foundation for human resistance. In other words, labor power can be incorporated only so far. Workers, as the sources of labor power, can engage in acts of refusing alienating work and delinking labor from capital's value form. As Dyer-Witheford (1999) argued: "Capital, a relation of general commodification predicated on the wage relation, needs labor. But labor does not need capital. Labor can dispense with the wage, and with capitalism, and find different ways to organize its own creative energies: it is potentially *autonomous*" (p. 68).

In so far as education and training socially produce power-power, this process can be resisted. As Dyer-Witheford noted: "In academia, as elsewhere, labor power is never completely controllable. To the degree that capital uses the university to harness general intellect, insisting its work force engage in lifelong learning as the price of employability, it runs the risk that people will teach and learn something other than what it intends" (p. 236). Critical educators push this "something other" to the extreme in their pedagogical praxis centered on a social justice, anti-capitalist agenda. The key to resistance, in our view, is to develop a critical pedagogy that will enable the working class to discover how the use value of their labor power is being exploited by capital but also how working-class initiative and power can destroy this type of determination and force a recomposition of class relations by directly confronting capital in all of its hydra-headed dimensions. Efforts can be made to break down capital's control of the creation of new labor power and to resist the endless subordination of life to work in the social factory of everyday life (Cleaver, 2000; see also Rikowski, 2001). Students and education workers can ask themselves, following Rikowski (2001): What is the maximum damage they can do to the rule of capital, to the dominance of capital's value form? Ultimately, the question we have to ask is: whether we, as radical educators, should help capital find its way out of crisis, or whether we should help students find their way out of capital.

The success of the former challenge will only buy further time for the capitalists to adapt both its victims and its critics, the success of the latter will determine the future of civilization, or whether or not we will have one.

The struggle among what Marx called our vital powers, our dispositions, our inner-selves and our objective outside, our human capacities and competencies and the social formations within which they are produced, *ensures* the production of a form of human agency that reflects the contradictions within capitalist social life. Yet these contradictions also provide openness regarding social being. They point toward the possibility of collectively resolving contradictions of everyday life through revolutionary/transformative praxis (Allman, 1999). Critical subjectivity operates out of practical, sensuous engagement within social formations that enable rather than constrain human capacities. Here, critical pedagogy reflects the multiplicity and creativity of human engagement itself: the identification of shared experiences and common interests; the unravelling of the threads that connect social process to individual experience; rendering transparent the concealed obviousness of daily life; the recognition of a shared social positionality; unhinging the door that separates practical engagement from theoretical reflection; the changing of the world by changing one's nature.

Our work in critical pedagogy constitutes in one sense the performative register for class struggle. Although it sets as its goal the decolonization of subjectivity, it also emphasizes the development of critical social agency while at the same time targeting the material basis of capitalist social relations and thus the conditions of possibility of racism, sexism, and other antagonisms. Critical educators seek to realize in their classrooms social values and to believe in their possibilities—consequently we argue that they need to go outside of the protected precincts of their classrooms and analyze and explore the workings of capital there. Critical revolutionary pedagogy sets as its goal the reclamation of public life under the relentless assault of the corporatization, privatization and businessification of the lifeworld (which includes the corporate–academic complex). It seeks to make the division of labor coincident with the free vocation of each individual and the association of free producers. At first blush, this may seem a paradisiacal notion in that it posits a radically eschatological and incomparably "other" endpoint for society as we know it. Yet this is not a blueprint but a contingent and manifestly concrete utopian vision that offers direction not only in unpicking the apparatus of bourgeois illusion but also in diversifying the theoretical itinerary of the critical educator so that new questions can be generated along with new perspectives in which to raise them. Here the emphasis not only is on denouncing the manifest injustices of neoliberal capitalism and serving as a counterforce to neoliberal ideological hegemony, but also on establishing the conditions for new social arrangements that transcend the false opposition between the market and the state.

In contrast to postmodern education, revolutionary pedagogy emphasizes the material dimensions of its own constitutive possibility and recog-
nizes knowledge as implicated within the social relations of production (i.e.,
the relations between labor and capital). I am using the term materialism here
not in its postmodernist sense as a resistance to conceptuality, a refusal of the
closure of meaning, or whatever excess cannot be subsumed within the sym-
bol or cannot be absorbed by tropes; rather, materialism is being used in the
context of material social relations, a structure of class conflict, and an effect
of the social division of labor (Ebert, 2002). Historical changes in the forces
of production have reached the point where the fundamental needs of people
can be met—but the existing social relations of production prevent this
because the logic of access to "need" is "profit" based on the value of people's labor for capital. Consequently, critical revolutionary pedagogy argues
that without a class analysis, critical pedagogy is impeded from effecting
praxiological changes (changes in social relations). Critical revolutionary
pedagogy begins with a three-pronged approach: First, students engage in a
pedagogy of demystification centering around a semiotics of recognition,
where dominant sign systems are recognized and denaturalized, where common sense is historicized, and where signification is understood as a political
practice that refracts rather than reflects reality, where cultural formations are
understood in relation to the larger social factory of the school and the global universe of capital. This is followed by a pedagogy of opposition, where
students engage in analyzing various political systems, ideologies, and histories, and eventually students begin to develop their own political positions.
Inspired by a sense of ever-imminent hope, students take up a pedagogy of
revolution, where deliberative practices for transforming the social universe
of capital are developed and put into practice. Revolutionary critical pedagogy supports a totalizing reflection upon the historical-practical constitution of the world, our ideological formation within it, and the reproduction
of everyday life practices. It is a pedagogy with an emancipatory intent.

Practicing revolutionary critical pedagogy is not the same as preaching
it. Revolutionary critical educators are not an apocalyptic group; they do
not belong to a predicant order bent on premonising the capitalist crisis to
come. Revolutionary critical pedagogy is not in the business of presaging as
much as it is preparatory; it is in the business of pre-revolutionizing: preparing students to consider life outside the social universe of capital—to
"glimpse humanity's possible future beyond the horizon of capitalism"
(Allman, 2001, p. 219). What would such a world be like? What type of labor
would be—should be—carried out? Thus, critical revolutionary pedagogy is
committed to a certain form of futurity, one that will see wage labor disappear along with class society itself.

But revolutionary critical pedagogy is not born in the crucible of the
imagination as much as it is given birth in its own practice. That is, revolu-

tionary critical education is decidedly more praxiological than prescored. The path is made by walking, as it were. Revolutionary educators need to challenge the notion implicit in mainstream education, that ideas related to citizenship have to travel through predestined contours of the mind, falling into step with the cadences of common sense. There is nothing common about common sense. Educational educators need to be more than the voice of autobiography, they need to create the context for dialogue with the Other so that the Other may assume the right to be heard.

The principles that help to shape and guide the development of our vital powers in the struggle for social justice via critical/revolutionary praxis have been discussed at length by Allman (2001). These include principles of mutual respect, humility, openness, trust and cooperation; a commitment to learn to "read the world" critically and expending the effort necessary to bring about social transformation; vigilance with regard to one's own process of self-transformation and adherence to the principles and aims of the group; adopting an "ethics of authenticity" as a guiding principle; internalizing social justice as passion; acquiring critical, creative, and hopeful thinking; transforming the self through transforming the social relations of learning and teaching; establishing democracy as a fundamental way of life; developing a critical curiosity; and deepening one's solidarity and commitment to self and social transformation and the project of humanization.

For those of us fashioning a distinctive socialist philosophy of praxis within North American context, it is clear that a transition to socialism will not be an easy struggle, given the global entrenchment of these aforementioned challenges. The overall task ahead is what Petras and Veltmeyer (2002) referred to, after Marx and Engels, as the creation of a dictatorship *of* the proletariat, not a dictatorship *over* the proletariat. It consists of managing the inherent contradiction between the internal socialist relations and the external participation in the capitalist marketplace. Meeting this challenge will require, among other things, a long list of initiatives, such as moving from a globalized imperial export strategy to an integrated domestic economy that entails reorienting the economy away from the reproduction of financial elites and replacing privatization with a socialization of the means of production. Joel Kovel (2002) made the point that the transition to socialism will require the creation of a "usufructuary of the earth." Essentially, this means restoring ecosystemic integrity across all of human participation—the family, the community, the nation, the international community. Kovel argued that use value must no longer be subordinated to exchange value but both must be harmonized with intrinsic value. The means of production (and it must be an ecocentric means of production) must be made accessible to all as assets are transferred to the direct producers (i.e., worker ownership and control). Clearly, eliminating the accumulation of surplus value as the motor of "civilization" and challenging the rule of capital by directing money toward the free enhancement of use values goes against the grain of the transnational ruling class.

If every new society carries its own negation within itself, then it makes sense for critical educators to develop a language of analysis that can help to identify the habits, ideas, and notions that help to shape and condition— either in a forward-or backward-looking way—the material and discursive forces of production. These habits, ideas, and notions—which stir as contradictions in the womb of subjectivity—are never static but always are in motion as possibilities given birth by history, that is, by class struggle. We need to develop a critical pedagogy, therefore, that can help students reconstruct the objective and subjective contexts of class struggle by examining the capitalist mode of production as a totality in relation to the aggregate of social relations that make up our distinctively human character—an examination that is centered on Marx's labor theory of value. This mandates teaching students to think dialectically, to think in terms of "internal relations," such as creating an internal relation between diversity and unity, and between our individuality and our collectivity (Allman, 2001). The idea here is not simply to play mediatively with ideas but to interrogate the social grammar of capitalist society inhibiting its refractory relations while struggling for a political recomposition of social subjects that want a different world; indeed, who seek a socialist alternative.

THE POLITICS OF ORGANIZATION

This brings us to an issue that has plagued the left for over a century: the politics of organization. Elbaum (2002) noted that organizations are crucial in the struggle for social justice. He wrote that "[w]ithout collective forms it is impossible to train cadre, debate theory and strategy, spread information and analysis, or engage fully with the urgent struggles of the day. Only through organizations can revolutionaries maximise their contribution to ongoing battles and position themselves to maximally influence events when new mass upheavals and opportunities arise" (p. 335). Yet at the same time, Elbaum warned that we must avoid what he calls "sectarian dead-ends" in our struggle for social justice. Reflecting on his experiences with the New Communist Movement of the 1970s, he explained that when a movement becomes a "self-contained world" that insists on group solidarity and discipline, this can often lead to the suppression of internal democracy. The rigid top–down party model is obviously a problem for Elbaum.

On the one hand, social activists need to engage with and be accountable to a large, active, anticapitalist social base; on the other hand, there are pressures to put one's revolutionary politics aside in order to make an immediate impact on public policy. There is the impulse to "retreat into a small but secure niche on the margins of politics and/or confine oneself to revolutionary propaganda" (p. 334). Elbaum cited Marx's dictum that periods of socialist sectarianism obtain when "the time is not yet ripe for an independent historical movement" (p. 334).

Problems inevitably arise when "purer-than-thou fidelity to old orthodoxies" are employed to maintain membership morale necessary for group cohesion and to compete with other groups. He reported that the healthiest periods of social movements appear to be when tight knit cadre groups and other forms are able to co-exist and interact, while at the same time considering themselves part of a common political trend. He wrote that "diversity of organizational forms (publishing collectives, research centers, cultural collectives, and broad organizing networks, in addition to local and national cadre formations) along with a dynamic interaction between them supplied (at least to a degree) some of the pressures for democracy and realism that in other situations flowed from a socialist-oriented working-class" (p. 335). It is important to avoid a uniform approach in all sectors, especially when disparities in consciousness and activity are manifold. Elbaum noted that Leninist centralized leadership worked in the short run but "lacked any substantial social base and were almost by definition hostile to all others on the left; they could never break out of the limits of a sect" (p. 335). The size of membership has a profound qualitative impact on strategies employed and organizational models adopted. Elbaum (2002) warned that attempts to build a small revolutionary party (a party in embryo) "blinded movement activists to Lenin's view that a revolutionary party must not only be an 'advanced' detachment but must also actually represent and be rooted in a substantial, socialist-leaning wing of the working class" (p. 335). Realistic and complex paths will need to be taken that will clearly be dependent on the state of the working-class movement itself.

It is axiomatic for the ongoing development of critical pedagogy that it be based on an alternative vision of human sociality, one that operates outside the social universe of capital, a vision that goes beyond the market, but also one that goes beyond the state. It must reject the false opposition between the market and the state. Massimo De Angelis (2002) wrote that "the historical challenge before us is that the question of alternatives . . . not be separated from the organizational forms that this movement gives itself" (p. 5). Given that we are faced globally with the emergent transnational capitalist class and the incursion of capital into the far reaches of the planet, critical educators need a philosophy of organization that sufficiently addresses the dilemma and the challenge of the global proletariat. In discussing alternative manifestations of anti-globalization struggles, De Angelis itemizes some promising characteristics as follows: the production of various counter-summits; Zapatista Encuentros; social practices that produce use values beyond economic calculation and the competitive relation with the other and inspired by practices of social and mutual solidarity; horizontally linked clusters outside vertical networks in which the market is protected and enforced; social cooperation through grassroots democracy, consensus, dialogue, and the recognition of the other; authority and social cooperation developed in fluid relations and self-constituted through interaction; and a new engagement with the other that transcends locality, job, social condition, gender, age, race, culture, sexual orientation, language, religion, and beliefs. All of these characteristics are to be secondary to the constitution of communal relations. He wrote:

> The global scene for us is the discovery of the "other", while the local scene is the discovery of the "us," and by discovering the "us," we change our relation to the "other." In a community, commonality is a creative process of discovery, not a presupposition. So we do both, but we do it having the community in mind, the community as a mode of engagement with the other. (p. 14)

But what about the national state? Should left educators support it or challenge it? According to Wood (2001), "the state is the point at which global capital is most vulnerable, both as a target of opposition in the dominant economies and as a lever of resistance elsewhere. It also means that now more than ever, much depends on the particular class forces embodied in the state, and that now more than ever, there is scope, as well as need, for class struggle" (p. 291). Gindin (2002) argued that the state is no longer a relevant site of struggle if by struggle we mean taking over the state and pushing it in another direction. But the state is still a relevant arena for contestation if our purpose is one of transforming the state. He wrote:

> Conventional wisdom has it that the national state, whether we like it or not, is no longer a relevant site of struggle. At one level, this is true. If our notion of the state is that of an institution that left governments can "capture" and push in a different direction, experience suggests this will contribute little to social justice. But if our goal is to transform the state into an instrument for popular mobilisation and the development of democratic capacities, to bring our economy under popular control and restructure our relationships to the world economy, then winning state power would manifest the worst nightmares of the corporate world. When we reject strategies based on winning through undercutting others and maintain our fight for dignity and justice nationally, we can inspire others abroad and create new spaces for their own struggles. (p. 11)

John Holloway's (2002) premise is similar to that of Gindin and one well worth considering by leftist educationalists (although it is a largely misguided approach, as I will explain later). He argued that we must theorist the world negatively as a "moment" of practice as part of the struggle to change the world. But this change cannot come about through transforming the state through the taking of power but rather must occur through the dissolution of power as a means of transforming the state. This is because the state reproduces within itself the separation of people from their own "doing." In our work as critical educators, Holloway's distinction between power-to do (potentia) and power-over (potestas) is instructive. Power-over is the negation of the social flow of doing. Power-to is a part of the "social flow of doing," the construction of a "we" and the practice of the mutual recognition of dignity. We need to create the conditions for the future "doing" of others through a power-to do. In the process, we must not transform power-to into power-over, because power-over only separates the "means of doing" from the actual "doing" which has reached its highest point in capitalism. In fact, those who exercise power-over separate the done from the doing of others and declare it to be theirs. The appropriation of the "done" of others is equivalent to the appropriation of "the means of doing", and allows the powerful to control the doing of others, which reaches its highest point in capitalism. The separation of doing from the doers reduces people to mere owners and nonowners, flattening out relations between people to relations between things. It converts doing into being. Whereas doing refers to both "we are" (the present) and "we are not" (the possibility of being something else) being refers only to "we are." To take away the "we are not" tears away possibility from social agency. In this case, possibility becomes mere utopian dreaming while time itself becomes irrefrangibley homogenized. Being locates the future as an extension of the present and makes the past into a preparation for the present. All doing becomes an extension of the way things are. The rule of power-over is the rule of "this is the way things are," which is the rule of identity. When we are separated from our own doing we create our own subordination. Power-to is not counter-power (which presupposes a symmetry with power) but anti-power. We need to avoid falling into identification, to an acceptance of what is.

Holloway reminded us that the separation of doing and done is not an accomplished fact but a process. Separation and alienation is a movement against its own negation, against anti-alienation. That which exists in the form of its negation—or anti-alienation (the mode of being denied)—really does exist, in spite of its negation. It is the negation of the process of denial. Capitalism, according to Holloway, is based on the denial of "power-to," of dignity, of humanity, but that does not mean power-to (counter-capitalism) does not exist. Asserting our power-to is simultaneously to assert our resistance against being dominated by others. This may take the form of open rebellion, of struggles to defend control over the labor process, or efforts to control the processes of health and education. Power-over depends on that which it negates. The history of domination is not only the struggle of the oppressed against their oppressors but also the struggle of the powerful to liberate themselves from their dependence on the powerless. But there is no way in which power-over can escape from being transformed into power-to because capital's flight from labor depends on labor (on its capacity to convert power-to into abstract value-producing labor) in the form of falling rates of profit.

Holloway's (2002a) work is an important advance in theorizing the nature of power but it remains highly problematic. Asking the revolutionary subject to forego revolutionary movements and their historical importance in class struggle worldwide in favor of becoming a Marxist phenomenologist is not exactly the most pragmatic way forward. Forms of power over are unavoidable and in some cases desirable, at least in the limited context of developing a revolutionary organization with some form of direct or representative democracy. I agree with Michael Löwy that direct democracy at the horizontal level of local assemblies works well for factories or universities or communities or barrios. Even though the state is admittedly part of the network of capitalist domination, beyond the local level, regional and national levels of representation are necessary, such as a body, network, or federation based on direct democracy or council democracy (Löwy, 2004). A revolutionary council democracy from below, combining direct and representative forms, needs to be struggled for, a new form of political power that can bring about the supercession of the capitalist system (Löwy, 2004).

Clearly, the revolutionary praxis driven by a Marxist-Humanist pedagogy, has faith in overcoming commodity fetishism through a dialectical approach to self and social transformation, an approach grounded in the self-emancipation of everyday class struggle.

Present-day left educationalists need to rethink the state as a terrain of contestation while at the same time reinventing class struggle as we have been doing in the streets of Seattle, Porto Alegre, Prague, and Genoa. We have to keep our belief that another world is possible. We need to do more than to break with capital or abscond from it; clearly, we need to challenge its rule of value. The key to resistance, in our view, is to develop a revolutionary critical pedagogy that will enable working-class groups to discover how the use-value of their labor power is being exploited by capital but also how working-class initiative and power can destroy this type of determination and force a recomposition of class relations by directly confronting capital in all of its multifaceted dimensions. This will require critical pedagogy not only to plot the oscillations of the labor/capital dialectic, but also to reconstruct the object context of class struggle to include school sites. Efforts also must be made to break down capital's creation of a new species of labor power through current attempts to corporatize and businessify the process of schooling and to resist the endless subordination of life in the social factory so many students call home (Cleaver, 2000; see also Rikowski, 2001b).

The myriad obstacles facing the progressive educational tradition in the United States—such as whether or not critical pedagogy can be revivified in this current historical juncture of neoliberal globalization—can be overcome—albeit haltingly rather than resoundingly. The recent advance of contemporary Marxist educational scholarship (Hill, 2001; Hill & Cole, 2001; Hill, McLaren, Cole, & Rikowski, 2002; McLaren & Farahmandpur, 2000; Rikowski, 2001c, 2001d), critical theory (Giroux, 1981, 1983; Kincheloe, 1998), and a rematerialized critical pedagogy (Fischman & McLaren, 2000; McLaren, 2000; McLaren & Farahmandpur, 2001a, 2001b)—although the offerings are still only modest glimmerings—in my view is sufficient enough to pose a necessary counterweight not only to neoliberal free market imperatives but also to post-Marxist solutions that most often advocate the creation of social movements grounded in identity politics or, as evident in recent anti-Marxist pedagogical polemics, a pedagogy grounded in uncertainty (Lather, 1998).

In the face of such a contemporary intensification of global capitalist relations and permanent structural crisis (rather than a shift in the nature of capital itself), we need to develop a critical pedagogy capable of engaging everyday life as lived in its midst. In other words, we need to face capital down. This means acknowledging global capital's structurally determined inability to share power with the oppressed, its implication in racist, sexist, and homophobic relations, its functional relationship to xenophobic nationalism, and its tendency toward empire. It means acknowledging the educational left's dependency on the very object of its negation: capital. It stipulates a concerted effort at developing a lateral, polycentric concept of anticapitalist alliances-in-diversity to slow down capitalism's metabolic movement—with the eventual aim of shutting it down completely. It means looking for an educational philosophy that is designed to resist the capitalization of subjectivity, a pedagogy that we have called revolutionary critical pedagogy.

Keening the death of Marxism will do little more than momentarily stir the ghost of the old bearded devil. It will do little to resurrect the best of the Marxist tradition so that it can be rethought within the contextual specificity neoliberal globalization. Novel ingressions toward rebuilding the educational left must be made concrete. It will not be easy, but neither will living under an increasingly militarized capitalist state where labor power is constantly put to the rack to carry out the will of capital. Although critical pedagogy may seem driven by lofty, high-rise aspirations that spike an otherwise desolate landscape of despair, where pock-marked dreams bob through the sewers of contemporary cosmopolitan life, they anchor our hope in the dreams of the present. Here the social revolution is not reborn in the foam of avant-garde antifoundationalism, which only stokes the forces of despair, but emerges from the everyday struggle to release us from the burdens of political détente and democratic disengagement. It is anchored, in other words, in class struggle.

REFERENCES

Ali, T. (2002). *The clash of fundamentalisms: Crusades, jihads and modernity.* London: Verso.

Allman, P. (1999). *Revolutionary social transformation: Democratic hopes, political possibilities and critical education.* Westport, CT: Bergin & Garvey.

Allman, P. (2001). *Critical education against global capitalism: Karl Marx and revolutionary critical education.* Westport, CT: Bergin & Garvey.

Cleaver, H. (2000). *Reading capital politically.* Edinburgh: AK Press.

Cole, M., & Hill, D. (1999). *Promoting equality in secondary schools.* London: Cassell.

Cole, M., Hill, D., McLaren, P., & Rikowski, G. (Eds.). (2001). *Red chalk: On schooling, capitalism & politics.* London: Tufnell Press.

Davies, S., & Guppy, N. (1997). Globalization and educational reforms in Anglo-American democracies. *Comparative Education Review, 41*(4), 435–459.

De Angelis, M. (2002, May). From movement to society. *The Commoner, 4.* Retrieved from http://www.commoner.org.uk/01-3groundzero.htm

Dinerstein, A., & Neary, M. (2001). Marx, labor and real subsumption, or how *No Logo* becomes *No To Capitalist Everything.* Unpublished paper.

Dyer-Witheford, N. (1999). *Cyber-Marx: Cycles and circuits of struggle in high-technology capitalism.* Urbana: University of Illinois Press.

Ebert, T. (2002). *University, class, and citizenship.* Unpublished manuscript.

Elbaum, M. (2002). *Revolution in the air: Sixties radicals turn to Lenin, Mao and Che.* New York: Verso.

Fischman, G., & McLaren, P. (2000). Schooling for democracy: Towards a critical utopianism. *Contemporary Society, 29*(1), 168–179.

Foley, B. (1998). Roads taken and not taken: Post-Marxism, antiracism, and anticommunism. *Cultural Logic, 1*(2). Retrieved from http://eserver.org/clogic/1-2/foley.html

Gindin, S. (2002, June). Social justice and globalization: Are they compatible? *Monthly Review, 54*(2), 1–11.

Giroux, H. A. (1981). *Ideology, culture & the process of schooling.* Philadelphia, PA: Temple University Press.

Giroux, H. (1983). *Theory and resistance in education: A pedagogy for the opposition.* South Hadley, MA: Bergin & Garvey.

Hill, D. (2001). State theory and the neo-liberal reconstruction of schooling and teacher education: A structuralist neo-Marxist critique of postmodernist, quasi-postmodernist, and culturalist neo-Marxist theory. *British Journal of Sociology of Education, 22*(1), 137–157.

Hill, D., & Cole, M. (2001). Social class. In D. Hill & M. Cole (Eds.), *Schooling and equality: Fact, concept and policy* (pp. 137-159). London: Kogan Page.

Hill, D., McLaren, P., Cole, M., & Rikowski, G. (2002). *Marxism against postmodernism in educational theory*. Lanham, MD: Lexington Books.

Hill, D., Sanders, M., & Hankin, T. (2001). Marxism, social class and postmodernism. In D. Hill, P. McLaren, & G. Rikowski (Eds.), *Marxism against postmodernism in educational theory*. Lanham, MD: Lexington Books.

Holloway, J. (2002). Twelve theses on changing the world without taking power. *The Commoner, 4*. Retrieved from http://www.commoner.org.uk/04holloway2.pdf

Kincheloe, J. (1998). *How do we tell the workers? The socioeconomic foundations of work and vocational education*. Boulder, CO: Westview Press.

Kovel, J. (2002). *The enemy of nature: The end of capitalism of the end of the world?* London: Zed Books.

Lather, P. (1998). Critical pedagogy and its complicities: A praxis of stuck places. *Educational Theory, 48*(4), 447-498.

Lenin, V. (1951). *Imperialism: The highest stage of capitalism*. Moscow: Foreign Language Publishing House.

Löwy, M. (2004). Just an answer to John Holloway. *New Politics, IX*(4, Winter), 142-143.

McLaren, P. (1997). *Revolutionary multiculturalism: Pedagogies of dissent for the new millennium*. Boulder, CO: Westview Press.

McLaren, P., & Farahmandpur, R. (2000). Reconsidering Marx in post-Marxist times: A requiem for postmodernism? *Educational Researcher, 29*(3), 25-33.

McLaren, P., & Farahmandpur, R. (2001a). Educational policy and the socialist imagination: Revolutionary citizenship as a pedagogy of resistance. *Educational Policy, 13*(3), 343-378.

McLaren, P., & Farahmandpur, R. (2001b). Teaching against globalization and the new imperialism: Toward a revolutionary pedagogy. *Journal of Teacher Education, 52*(2), 136-150.

McQuaig, L. (2001) *All you can eat: Greed, lust and the new capitalism*. Toronto: Penguin Books.

Neary, M. (forthcoming). Travels in Moishe Postone's social universe: A contribution to a critique of political cosmology. *Historical Materialism: Research in Critical Marxist Theory.*

News & Letters Committee. (2002). Confronting permanent war and terrorism. Why the anti-war movement needs a dialectical perspective. A Statement from the Resident Editorial Board of *News & Letters* (pamphlet).

Parenti, M. (2002). Global rollback after communism. *CovertAction Quarterly, 72*, 41-44.

Petras, J., & Veltmeyer, H. (2001). *Globalization unmasked: Imperialism in the 21st centry*. London: Zed Books.

Postone, M. (1996) *Time, labor, and social domination: A reinterpretation of Marx's critical theory*. Cambridge: Cambridge University Press.

Rikowski, G. (2001a, June). *After the manuscript broke off: Thoughts on Marx, social class and education*, Paper presented at the British Sociological Association Education Study Group, King's College, London.

Rikowski, G. (2001b). *The battle in Seattle: Its significance for education.* London: Tufnell Press.

Rikowski, G. (2001c). Fuel for the living fire: Power-power! In A. Dinerstein & M. Neary (Eds.), *The labor debate: An investigation into the theory and reality of capitalist work.* Aldershot: Ashgate.

Rikowski, G. (2001d, May). *The importance of being a radical educator in capitalism today.* Guest lecture in the Sociology of Education, The Gillian Rose Room, Department of Sociology, University of Warwick, Coventry.

Robinson, W. (2001). Social theory and globalization: The rise of a transnational state. *Theory and Society, 30,* 157–200.

San Juan, Jr., E. (1996). *Mediations: From a Filipino perspective.* Pasig City, Philippines: Anvil.

San Juan, Jr., E. (2002). *Racism and cultural studies: Critiques of multiculturalist ideology and the politics of difference.* Durham, NC: Duke University Press.

Wood, E. M. (1995). *Democracy against capitalism: Renewing historical materialism.* Cambridge: Cambridge University Press.

Wood, E. M. (2001). Contradictions: Only in capitalism. In L. Panitch & C. Leys (Eds.), *A world of contradictions, socialist register.* London: Merlin.

About the Authors

E. Wayne Ross is professor in the Department of Curriculum Studies at the University of British Columbia in Vancouver, Canada. He is the author of numerous publications on curriculum theory, politics of education, and critical pedagogy. His edited books include *Race, Ethnicity, and Education* (Praeger), *Defending Public Schools* (Praeger), *Teacher Personal Theorizing: Connecting Curriculum Practice, Theory, and Research* (SUNY Press), *The Social Studies Curriculum* (SUNY Press) and *Democratic Social Education* (RoutledgeFalmer), which he co-edited with David Hursh. He is also co-author, with Kevin D. Vinson, of *Image and Education: Teaching in the Face of the New Disciplinarity* (Peter Lang). He is a former day-care and secondary school teacher and a co-founder of The Rouge Forum, an organization of school workers, parents, and students seeking to transform education and society toward equity, democracy, and the freedom to live creative, connected lives.

Rich Gibson, associate professor at San Diego State University, is a former auto worker, elementary and secondary school teacher, organizer, and bargaining specialist for several unions. He is the cofounder of The Rouge Forum. His research, asking "what do people need to know, and how do they need to come to know it in order to live in solidarity?" serves that end.

CONTRIBUTORS

Richard A. Brosio is the author of *A Radical Democratic Critique of Capitalist Education* (Peter Lang, 1994) and *Philosophical Scaffolding for the Construction of Critical Democratic Education* (Peter Lang, 2000). For many years a professor of social foundations of education at Ball State University, Brosio currently teaches at the University of Wisconsin, Milwaukee.

Gilbert G. Gonzalez is professor of Chicano/Latino studies at the School of Social Sciences and Director of the Labor Studies Program at the University of California, Irvine. He is the author of *Chicano Education in the Era of Segregation* (Balch Institute, 1990); *Labor and Community: Mexican Citrus Picker Villages in a Southern California County, 1900-1950* (University of Illinois Press, 1994); and *Mexican Consuls and Labor Organizing: Imperial Politics in the American Southwest* (University of Texas Press, 1999).

Dave Hill is professor of education policy at University College Northampton, United Kingdom. Previously, he taught in schools and colleges in Brixton and in Tower Hamlets in inner-city London, and in Sussex. For 20 years he was a political and labor union leader. He writes from a democratic Marxist perspective, on issues of radical right policy and ideology; New Labour/ Third Way ideology and policy; radical left ideology and policy; social class, state theory and critiques of neoliberalism and of postmodernism. He is founder director of the Institute for Education Policy Studies, the independent radical left policy research and publishing unit founded in 1989. He is also founding editor/chief editor of *The Journal for Critical Education Policy Studies*. His most recent co-written book (with Peter McLaren, Mike Cole, and Glenn Rikowski) is *Red Chalk: On Schooling, Capitalism and Politics* (Institute for Education Policy Studies, 2001). His two most recent edited collections (with the same co-writers) are *Postmodernism in Educational Theory: Education and the Politics of Human Resistance* (Tufnell Press) and *Marxism Against Postmodernism in Educational Theory* (Lexington Books).

David W. Hursh is associate professor in the Warner Graduate School of Education at the University of Rochester. In the 1970s, he co-directed an alternative university, directed two private elementary schools (one of which he founded), and was a consultant on race and gender equity. He is the author of numerous students on democracy, neoliberalism, and education reform. He is co-editor, with E. Wayne Ross, of the book *Democratic Social Education: Social Studies for Social Change* (RoutledgeFalmer).

Les Levidow is a research fellow in the technology faculty at the Open University, where he has been studying mainly the safety regulation and innovation of genetically modified crops. He also has been managing editor of *Science as Culture* since its inception in 1987, and of its predecessor, the *Radical Science Journal*. He is co-editor of several books, including *Science, Technology and the Labour Process*; *Anti-Racist Science Teaching*; and *Cyborg Worlds: The Military Information Society* (Free Association Books, 1983, 1987, 1989).

Pauline Lipman is Professor of Policy Studies and Director of the Collaborative for Equity and Justice in Education in the College of Education, University of Illinois-Chicago. Her research focuses on race and class inequality in schools, globalization and neoliberal urban development, and the political economy and cultural politics of race of urban education. She is the author of *Race, Class, and Power in School Restructuring* (SUNY, 1998) and numerous articles on these topics. Her recent book, *High Stakes Education*; *Inequality, Globalization, and Urban School Reform* (Routledge, 2004) analyzes the relationship of educational policies to the restructuring of the labor force, globalization, and the politics of race in urban school districts. An advocate of activist scholarship, she is currently collaborating with Chicago community organizations fighting gentrification and for educational justice. She is a founder and active member of the Chicago-area *Teachers for Social Justice*. Before becoming an academic, Pauline was a full-time labor and community activist.

Peter McLaren is professor of education, in the Division of Urban Schooling, Graduate School of Education and Information Studies, University of California, Los Angeles. He worked for 6 years as a public school teacher in his native Toronto, Canada, where he also served as a journalist for the teachers' union, authoring a regular column, "Inner City Insight." After teaching for 1 year in the College of Education at Brock University, St. Catherines, Canada, McLaren moved to the United States, where he has worked since 1985. McLaren is author and editor of 35 books on the sociology of education, critical theory, and critical pedagogy, the most recent of which include *Red Seminars* (Hampton Press), *Teaching Against Global Capitalism and New Imperialism*, with Ramin Farahmandpur (Rowman & Littlefield), *Life in Schools* (4th ed.), and *Marxism Against Postmodernism in Educational Theory* (edited with Dave Hill, Mike Cole, and Glenn Rikowski). McLaren's works have been translated into 17 languages.

Glenn Rikowski is senior lecturer in educational studies in the School of Education at University College Northampton in the United Kingdom.

From 1999 to 2001, he was research fellow in lifelong learning in the Faculty of Education at the University of Central England, Birmingham. He was previously research fellow in the School of Education at the University of Birmingham. Prior to that, Rikowski taught in schools, vocational education colleges, and in the early 1980s, was a research and development officer for Coventry Local Education Authority. He has held visiting lectureships at the universities of Hertfordshire, London, and North London. He has been involved in research projects on working students, college finance, vocational education and training, youth labor markets, and Education Action Zones. He is currently researching the "businessification" of schools. Rikowski has written articles and conference papers on Marxian educational theory, labor power, lifelong learning, time and speed. He is the author of *The Battle in Seattle: Its Significance for Education* (Tufnell Press), and co-editor of *Marxism Against Postmodernism in Educational Theory* (Lexington Books).

Patrick Shannon is professor of education at Penn State University. He is the author of *Becoming Political Too*; *iSHOP, You Shop*; *Text, Lies and Videotape: Stories about Life; Literacy and Learning* and *Reading Poverty*. He is currently working on a book concerning the commercialization of classrooms from kindergarten to graduate school.

Kevin D. Vinson is associate professor of teaching and teacher education at the University of Arizona. His areas of specialization include social studies education, critical pedagogy, and educational theory. He is the co-author of *Image and Education: Teaching in the Face of the New Disciplinarity* (with E. Wayne Ross, published in 2003 by Peter Lang). His work has appeared in journals such as *Social Education, The Social Studies, Z Magazine*, and *Theory and Research in Social Education* as well as in several books, including *The Social Studies Curriculum* (edited by E. Wayne Ross), *Critical Issues in Social Studies Research for the 21st Century* (edited by William B. Stanley), and the *Encyclopedia of Educational Standards* (edited by Joe Kincheloe and Dan Weil). He has also presented his scholarship at meetings sponsored by the American Educational Research Association, the National Council for the Social Studies, and the Socialist Scholars Conference.

John F. Welsh is Professor of Education at the University of Louisville. He earned a Bachelor of Arts in Sociology in 1973 from Samford University, a Master of Arts in Sociology in 1975 from Emory University, and a PhD in Sociology from Oklahoma State University in 1978. Dr. Welsh has extensive experience in higher education, including both faculty and administrative responsibilities. He has published widely in social science and higher education research journals, including the *Journal of Higher Education, Race,*

Ethnicity and Education, Journal of Higher Education Policy and Management, Community College Journal of Research and Practice, Assessment and Evaluation in Higher Education, Campus-Wide Information Systems, Community College Enterprise, Trusteeship, Cultural Logic, Quality Assurance in Education, Connection: The New England Journal of Higher Education, Midwest Quarterly, Humanity and Society, Free Inquiry, and *Quarterly Journal of Ideology.* He has also published chapters in recent books on several topics including the future of public education and innovation in information technology in higher education.

Author Index

Subject Index

Lightning Source UK Ltd.
Milton Keynes UK
UKOW04f1331270915

259332UK00001B/29/P